Handbook for Rebels and Outlaws

Resisting Tyrants, Hangmen, and Priests

Mark L. Mirabello, Ph.D.
Professor of European History
Shawnee State University (USA)

Published by
Mandrake of Oxford
PO Box 250
OXFORD
OX1 1AP (UK)

ISBN 978-1-906958-00-8

Contents

Dedicated to Paul Joseph Mirabello, the "master of those who know."
This book is intended for historical reference only.

A special thanks to John Leo Kelley, a professor emeritus of history at Shawnee State University, Jennifer Reed, a graduate student at the University of Northern Kentucky, and Jennifer Sheroian, an independent scholar, for their comments and criticisms. I must also thank Regina Baranski Mirabello, Bradley Sheroian, Paula Sheroian, Stacey Sheroian, Ashley Sheroian, Donald Sheroian, Neil Reed, Jennifer Foster, Jill Gardner, Laura Munion, and Mogg Morgan.

At the time of writing, gold costs 5,900 dollars per pound, cocaine costs 61,000 dollars per pound, and pamidronic acid, an anti-cancer drug, costs 133,043 dollars per pound.

The price of the *ingredients* to make one pound of pamidronic acid is twenty-three dollars.

In today's world, what is a crime?

"*Everyone would work for everyone else; there would be no more war; and the whole world would be turned into one big jolly factory without an owner, and with playgrounds attached. . . . You say you want to make men brothers. What you really want is to make them ants.*"

Rex Warner. *The Professor*

"*After all, the United States fought one of the bloodiest civil conflicts in history little more than a century ago. We know that it can happen here because it has.*"

Roy Licklider. *Stopping the Killing: How Civil Wars End.*

"*I foresee that man will resign himself to new abominations, that soon only soldiers and bandits will be left.*"

Jorge Luis Borges. *The Garden of Forking Paths*

INTRODUCTION

This work—the *Handbook for Rebels and Outlaws*—is a book about freedom. Written for intellectual swashbucklers–men and women who are radicals in politics and infidels in religion–warriors who hammer the stake of fear into the heart of tyranny–this volume belongs in select book collections, between the *black magic* and the *pornography* texts.

Designed as a reference book for the enemies of all orthodoxies and despotisms, the *Handbook for Rebels and Outlaws* contains much information that is not beautiful. The reader must remember, however, that brutality is a fact in nature. When the autumn comes—observe the Chinese—no leaf is spared because of its beauty, and no flower is spared because of its fragrance.

The information detailed here has been excavated from diverse sources. I have quarried the writings of philosophers and fiends, saints and mass murderers, sages and madmen, beneficent societies and sinister conventicles, illuminated religions and blasphemous cults.

Why have I used evil sources? According to a traditional teaching—this one found among Kabbalahists—the wise man can learn from any source—even a thief. The thief is ever watchful, he takes every opportunity, and he does not despise the least gain.

Besides, as the Argentine Jorge Luis Borges pointed out, "In adultery, there is usually tenderness and self-sacrifice; in murder, courage; in profanation and blasphemy, a certain satanic splendor."

* * *

This work–it is important to emphasize– is *not* an instruction manual for criminals. Frankly, in the current age–an era of depravity that the Hindus call the "Age of Kali"—violating laws is unnecessary. In the proper "context," all crime is legal in our corrupt civilization.

Do you like to lie? Become a journalist. Do you like to slander the dead? Become a historian. Do you like to libel the species? Become a novelist.

Are you an authoritarian? Do you like to degrade, humiliate, and dominate others? Become a prison warden–or an elementary school teacher.

Are you a sadist? Are you excited by the agonized shrieks of helpless beings? If you like to torture animals to death, become a kosher butcher. If you like to torture people to death–to poison, burn and cut them with impunity— become an oncologist.

Do you enjoy doing evil and spreading terror? If killing strangers from behind with a knife, a garrote, or your naked hands arouses you, become a military commando. If mass murder is your interest–if exterminating thousands of people like germs and insects pleases you—become a combat pilot. Or–if you prefer to kill without danger to your own person–find employment in an abortion clinic. Over his career, one abortion pioneer in Canada personally killed more than thirty thousand unborn humans!

* * *

Finally, this clarification must be made: although the *Handbook for Rebels and Outlaws* is a book about freedom, in a real sense pure and unsullied "freedom" does not exist. In the words of one anarchist writer—Yves Fremion, the author of *Orgasms of History*–only "liberation" exists, and "liberation" has no final stage. It is a "process of ongoing amelioration."

But if the struggle is perpetual–if there will always be statute laws and moral codes, straitjackets and leg irons, priests and hangmen–what is the point of rebellion? And what is the point of outlawry?

"Victory," to cite Yves Fremion again, "comes in the form of the oppressors never feeling safe and secure and of tyrants living everywhere in a state of fear."

Besides, although they are always reviled and crucified in life, rebels and outlaws become cultural icons in death. Refusing to be slaves–refusing to toil and obey–these men and women–their short lives enriched by vengeance and loot—inspire our legends and shape our hopes.

MAXIMS OF THE REBEL AND THE OUTLAW

1. Understand that no one can give you freedom. Freedom is a treasure that must be stolen.

2. Do not believe anything until it has been officially denied.

3. Remember the words of Frederick the Great of Prussia: "he who defends everything defends nothing."

4. Remember Aleister Crowley's warnings: your friend can do more harm than a stranger and the greatest danger lies in your own habits.

5. Keep plans simple. Do not take unnecessary risks. Trust only what you control.

6. Follow the wisdom of Sun Tzu, and always provide the enemy with an escape route. When surrounded, even a rodent will fight ferociously.

7. Know that when you fight alone and on foot, you are the most difficult target to locate on the battlefield. Your intelligence makes you the stealthiest of all weapons.

8. If you must die fighting, have an audience.

9. Never forget that dupes believe, slaves fear, and rebels defy.

A-Z of Rebels and Outlaws

ACTION

Action is all-important. According to a Neo-Confucian maxim, "To know and not to act is not yet to know."

AFGHANISTAN

A harsh country populated by implacable warriors, Afghanistan has been called the "grave of empires."

The tribal code in Afghanistan is based on loyalty and revenge. The Pashtun teach their children to be aggressive, to lie to avoid punishment, and to fear only public humiliation.

In 1839 the British Empire invaded Afghanistan, ousted the leader, and installed a puppet government. The victory seemed complete, but small-scale fighting continued.

In 1842 Kabul rose up, and the British promised to withdraw, under a promise of safe passage.

Approximately 16,500 people–British Empire soldiers and camp followers–left the city. Ruthlessly harried during their retreat, only one person in the group, a British surgeon named William Brydon, would survive to reach the British fortress at Jalalabad.

In the twentieth century, the brave Afghans helped destroy the awesome Soviet Empire. Fighting a classic "guerrilla war of a thousand cuts" against the Soviet invaders, the Afghans ambushed convoys, mined roads, and destroyed bridges and railroads. They struck at night, in the rain, when the enemy was eating, or when the enemy had just finished marching. The Afghan guerrillas attacked aircraft on the ground, the power supply, dams, bridges, pipelines, isolated posts, convoys, and the enemy's ammunition and fuel.

AFLATOXIN

A lethal substance—allegedly used by illicit secret police forces—aflatoxin is found in fungus-infested wheat and peanut crops.

Aflatoxin causes swift death in high concentrations. In low doses, however, aflatoxin causes flu-like symptoms in the victim, who then develops cancer years later.

Since one-fourth of the people now alive in the industrialized world will die of cancer, the aflatoxin murder does not appear suspicious.

Oddly, although medical science cannot cure cancer, it knows how to cause the disease.

AFRICA

A great continent with the same surface area as the Moon, Africa is only fifteen miles from Europe.

It is said that diamonds, ivory, and women are the gifts of Africa.

For five centuries, the Europeans ravaged the "Slave Coast" and seized as many as twenty-four million people. About fifteen million survived the slave trade to toil in thralldom.

So many were taken away that the Africans believed that the Europeans were cannibals who ate blacks. Mungo Park, the Scottish explorer, referred to the "deeply rooted idea that the whites purchased Negroes for the purpose of devouring them, or of selling them to others, that they may be devoured hereafter." According to rumors, blood became wine, brain became cheese, skin became black shoe leather, and African bones were burned until they became the gray powder used in gunpowder.

AGENT PROVOCATEUR

Typically sent by the police, an agent provocateur is an undercover operative sent to infiltrate a political or religious group. The agent provocateur tries to incite the group to commit crimes that will discredit them or lead to jail sentences for members.

Whenever possible, the Russian secret police will try to penetrate a group with two agent provocateurs. Neither agent will know the identity of the other.

One notorious agent provocateur was George Gapon, a Russian Orthodox priest who led the 1905 "Bloody Sunday" march on the tsar's Winter Palace in which thousands were massacred. Ultimately, Gapon was exposed and killed by "revolutionaries."

AGHORI

Extreme rebels against convention, the Aghori, called the "fearless ones," are a group of Hindu anchorites who follow Shiva, the god of death and procreation.

Drawn to what Joseph Conrad called "the fascination of abomination," the "fearless ones" carry human skulls as begging bowls, they smear themselves with their own excrement, and they devour bits of charred human corpses at cremations. During the Sepoy Rebellion against the British, the Aghori followed the troops and ate the casualties.

With their extreme behavior, the "fearless ones" demonstrate that Shiva is all and everything. Nothing, they believe, is outside god. Nothing is horrible or terrible to someone who has overcome all illusions.

ALEXANDER THE GREAT (356-323 B.C.)

A celebrated conqueror–ultimately deified as a god–Alexander carved out an empire that stretched from the Adriatic Sea to the Indus River, from the Punjab to the Sudan.

In battles, Alexander earned twenty-two victories without a defeat. Because his victories were so overwhelming, his army lost fewer than seven hundred men to the sword.

ALIAS

An alias is a false identity.

Curiously, it is not against the law to use an alias as long as there is no criminal intent. For example, it is legal to use a stage name or pen name as long as the pseudonym is not used in a fraudulent scheme.

Also, when no sworn oath or signature is involved, it is legal to give incorrect information to others. Prudent people will open all electronic mail accounts under false names.

ALIAS (CREATION OF)

There are many ways to create a second identity.

One basic technique–used by people with foresight–is to take a vacation in the same locality every year. They use a false name–make friendships–establish a reputation–and they are free to assume their "holiday" identity in an emergency.

To create a fake employment history, list companies on your *curriculum vitae* that are defunct. Make certain that the companies existed in the time to which you are referring.

Another technique used to create a second identity is the substitution method. Simply take the identity of a dead person, one who did not leave behind a family.

Or, assume the identity of someone who died as a child. Ideally, the child should have the same year of birth as you and the same physical characteristics (race, eye color, and so forth).

Another method—one used only by outlaws—is to steal the identification papers of someone who resembles the outlaw. For this type of crime, a tourist on the street is a good target.

Of course, stolen documents should never be used in the country of origin. In other words, the outlaw should never travel to Canada on a stolen Canadian passport. He may, however, use the document to travel elsewhere, such as to Africa.

When creating an alias, never *purchase* false or forged identification documents. The type of person who forges documents for money will readily betray his customers to the police for a reward.

ALIAS, OUTLAWS AND

In the interests of prudence, a resourceful outlaw will establish a second identity. If apprehended, he will try to serve his prison term under the false identity, thereby keeping his true identity unblemished.

Minority groups who are harassed by society—such as the so-called "gypsies" (the people who speak the Romany language)—often have children delivered under aliases. The gypsies will also have a telephone under one alias, an apartment under a second alias, and an automobile under a third.

ALIBI

An alibi is "a claim or a piece of evidence that one was elsewhere when an alleged act took place."

The best alibi is always a simple one.

As crime writer Colin Wilson noted, no one can remember what they were doing on May 9 of last year. He pointed out that an "airtight alibi" always makes the police suspicious.

AMBUSH

An ambush is a surprise attack from a concealed position on a moving or a temporarily halted target. The most obvious ambush site is a spatially restricted area that slows traffic, a so-called "choke point."

John Kennedy, the slain American president, was killed at a "choke point."

Traditionally, Asiatic warriors have been the masters of the ambush. In the American-Vietnamese War, the Viet Cong guerrillas sometimes hid for ten days before launching an ambush.

In a classic Maoist ambush, a powerful intruder is allowed to enter the position and is then attacked at close range from every direction at once.

The enemy cannot call in air or artillery support without hitting his own people. By the time the enemy establishes his bearings, he is facing only rearguard operatives.

AMIN, IDI (1925-2003)

An African tyrant, who called himself "His Excellency President for Life," "Lord of All the Beasts of the Earth and Fishes of the Sea," and "Conqueror of the British Empire in Africa in General and Uganda in Particular," Idi Amin terrorized Uganda, the "pearl of Africa," between 1971 and 1979.

Amin was ridiculed by some, but was feared by all.

A master of propaganda, Idi Amin had himself photographed in a sedan chair borne by four underweight Englishmen. A fifth white man–a Swede–carried a sunshade for the dictator.

ANARCHISM

In narrow terms, anarchism is the rejection of the state. In broad terms, anarchism is the rejection of coercion and domination in all forms, including that of the priests and the plutocrats.

The anarchist is a man in revolt. He abominates all forms of authoritarianism, and he is the enemy of parasitism, exploitation, and oppression. The anarchist frees himself from all that is sacred and carries out a vast program of desecration.

The classic anarchist embraces the convict and the outcast—the so-called subproletariat—and he uses bombs and commits assassinations.

The classic anarchist believes that the established order is based on crime and murder, so crime and murder are justified. In the words of one anarchist tract: "Our modern civilization is a Moloch temple reared upon the bodies of slaughtered slaves. Let the terrorists do what they will, they cannot equal the crimes of our masters."

The anarchists who flourished from 1880 to World War I were especially dedicated to the destruction of established governments, making way for a new order.

Anarchists killed a Russian tsar in 1881, a French president in 1894, an Italian king in 1900, and an American president in 1901. In addition to these leaders, police stations, churches, law courts, and establishment figures were also attacked.

One celebrated anarchist was Nestor Makhno. A Ukrainian active in the Russian civil war, Makhno destroyed prisons wherever he went. The banknotes printed on his behalf declared–on the notes–that no one would be prosecuted for counterfeiting them.

ANARCHISM, BOMBS AND

The bomb is fundamental to classical anarchism. The purpose of dynamite, the anarchists believe, is not to kill, but to make the deaf hear.

To the anarchists, bomb throwing represents the "aesthetics of terrorism." The victim is unimportant, they believe, as long as the gesture is "beautiful."

ANARCHISM, DEMOCRACY AND

Anarchists view democracy as a cunning swindle. Universal suffrage, they insist, is a mask that hides a really despotic state power based on the police, the banks, and the army.

Anarchists do not believe in emancipation by the ballot. Abstentionist, they believe that voting is an act of weakness—a form of complicity with a corrupt regime.

Anarchist Mikhail Bakunin claimed that universal suffrage is "the most refined manifestation of the political charlatanism of the state." It is, he wrote, the "surest means of making the masses co-operate in the building of their own prison."

According to Emma Goldman, "If voting changed anything, they would make it illegal."

ANASTASIA, ALBERT (1903-1957)

A Mafia leader and chief executioner of "Murder, Incorporated," Albert Anastasia avoided the electric chair five times. On every occasion, witnesses against him would disappear or "die."

Anastasia's most notorious murder involved Arnold Schuster, an ordinary salesman who contacted the police after recognizing a bank robber.

Although the press praised Schuster as a "hero" who was doing his civic duty, Anastasia had the man, who was a stranger to him, killed. Anastasia said that he hated "rats."

ANIMALS (HUMANS AND)

Man's relationship with animals has been a violent one. For more than 99 percent of all recognized human existence, man lived as a hunter, killing instead of growing.

Later, with the development of pastoralism and agriculture around ten thousand years ago, the animal world avenged itself on mankind. The domesticated herds of the farmers, it appears, spread diseases to humans. Flu, for example, came from pigs and leprosy came from the water buffalo.

Indeed, according to some historians, "all human infectious diseases have an animal origin."

In contrast, domesticated plants—at least so far—have taken no such revenge.

ANIMALS (RIGHTS OF)

Thomas Aquinas said that animals have no afterlife and no inherent rights. "Both their life and their death are subject to our use," claimed Aquinas.

And Albert Camus claimed that there was "not enough love in the world to squander it on anything but human beings."

Others disagree, however.

In a pamphlet entitled *To War for a Liberated Society*, the Animal Liberation Front called for the assassination of vivisectionists and hunters. Seeing animals as the helpless victims of predatory humans, the Animal Liberation Front has declared war on furriers, slaughterhouses, zoo keepers, and—above all—medical research laboratories.

ANTI-BIOGRAPHY

An anti-biography is a scurrilous work on a person's life. It is a species of non-violent, white-collar terrorism.

When Leon Trotsky, the communist leader, was murdered in Mexico with an ice ax, he was trying to complete an anti-biography about Joseph Stalin.

Trotsky had already written *Stalin's Crimes*, *The Real Situation in Russia*, and *The Stalinist School of Falsification*.

ANTI-CHRIST

The "man of sin," the Anti-Christ is the son of Satan and a harlot. Often described as the ultimate rebel, in reality he has a walk-on part in the Bible— a cameo role.

According to Revelation 17:3, world leaders will follow the man of sin and they will "give their power and authority to the beast."

According to the Bible, the "number of the beast" is *CHI XI STIGMA* or DCLXVI. In the oldest New Testament manuscript, however, the number is *CHI LOTA STIGMA* or DCXVI.

ARISTOCRACY

Aristocracy means "rule by the best" in Greek. According to Baron Giulio Evola, "superiority and power need to go hand in hand, as long as we remember that power is based on superiority and not vice versa ."

According to the author of *Might is Right*, "Aristocracies have always originated in War. Sham ones grow up (like mushrooms) in times of peace."

A pure aristocracy existed in the Aztec Empire. The Aztec aristocracy was not hereditary, but any Aztec male could become an aristocrat by manifesting skill and courage in war.

If an Aztec killed or captured four men, he joined the upper ranks of society and received a share of the tribute. He was eligible to join the jaguar knights (who wore jaguar skins in battle) or the eagle-knights (who wore eagle heads).

Interestingly, Aztec punishments were harsher on the upper class. If plebes became drunk in public, they were admonished and their heads were shaved. If nobles became drunk in public, they were executed.

ARMAGEDDON

In religious terms, "Armageddon" is a final battle at the end of the eon. In secular terms, "Armageddon" refers to a disaster that will destroy the world as we know it.

Pliny the Younger, while watching the eruption of Vesuvius, was not afraid because he thought "that all mankind were involved in the same calamity, and that I was perishing with the world itself."

Any number of cosmically trivial events could easily exterminate the human race. For example, a few dozen asteroids swing inside the orbit of the Earth and these asteroids could eventually collide with our planet.

ARMY OF THE DEAD

There are reports that Islamic radicals have recruited special suicide bombers, called an "Army of the Dead," who will launch a "Great March of Destruction" on the "infidels."

Allegedly, this Army of the Dead is composed of HIV-positive men and men with full-blown AIDS (Acquired Immune Deficiency Syndrome). By sacrificing their lives, the bombers believe they will purge themselves of sin.

ARSENIC

A lethal poison, arsenic causes vomiting, diarrhea, and a weak pulse. Arsenic was once so commonly used to kill relatives that it was called "inheritance powder." Arsenic was favored because it is tasteless and odorless.

In 1836, however, James Marsh developed the first chemical test to prove the presence of the poison. Science can now detect arsenic in even badly decomposed corpses.

ARSON

Arson is the criminal act of deliberately setting fire to property.

According to fire marshals, the telltale signs of arson are two or more separate fires, an especially fast-burning fire, or a strong odor of flammable liquids such as kerosene. Also, if investigators cannot find a credible source for a fire, they will suspect arson.

Arson is difficult to prove in court. By definition, most of the evidence is circumstantial.

ARSON (MURDER AND)

The firebombing of Tokyo by the United States, which annihilated 80,000 to 200,000 children, women, and men, is humanity's worst example of arson and murder. The U.S.A. Strategic Bombing Survey concluded that "probably more people lost their lives by fire in a six-hour period than at any time in the history of man."

The attack, which occurred on March 9-10, 1945, created a conflagration that lasted four days. More than sixteen square miles burned.

During the raid, some of the B-29 crewmen became sick from the stench of burning flesh.

According to some estimates, firebombing raids on Japan during World War II killed as many as three million people.

ARTICLE 58

An infamous law in the penal code of Soviet Russia, Aleksandr Solzhenitsyn pointed out that Article 58 was so encompassing that *anyone* could be charged with crimes against the state.

Curiously— in the Soviet "terror"—most arrests occurred because ordinary people were denouncing other ordinary people. By contacting the secret police, anyone could cause an enemy, a friend, a neighbor, a stranger, or a relative to disappear into the horrible gulag system.

According to one historian, "Strange as it may seem, in Stalinist Russia the decision about who would go to jail was left largely to the discretion of ordinary citizens. Because anyone could cause anyone else's arrest, Soviet terror acquired the awesomely random quality that rendered it so effective."

ASCETICISM

An ascetic is a self-disciplined person who avoids any sensory pleasures or luxuries. An ascetic has been defined as someone who kills the senses.

According to Vilfredo Pareto, "In our Western races three abstinence taboos have come down across the ages, and in order of increasing violence: abstinence from meat, abstinence from wine, abstinence from everything pertaining to sex."

Although William Morris called for the "utter extinction of all asceticism," seventy-two castrated men—eunuchs—are saints in the Roman Catholic Church.

And, on the subject of eunuchs, Jesus the Nazarene makes this statement in Matthew 19:12: "For there are eunuchs who have been so from birth, and there are eunuchs who have been made eunuchs by men, and there are eunuchs who have made themselves eunuchs for the sake of the kingdom of heaven. He who is able to receive this, let him receive it."

ASSASSINATION

When the powerful kill the powerless, it is an execution. When the weak slay the mighty, it is called an assassination.

When the weak kill their peers—it should be noted—it is simple murder.

In ancient Rome, when the citizen body was small and everyone knew everyone else, assassination was extremely rare. Later, during the Empire, when the Roman territories comprehended some three million square kilometers, the situation was different. Assassins killed nearly two-thirds of all Roman emperors.

Indeed, of the twenty emperors who ruled between A.D. 235 and A.D. 284, all but three were killed by assassins.

In modern history, the great period of assassination was from 1865 (Abraham Lincoln's death) to 1914 (Archduke Franz Ferdinand's death). In that period of forty-nine years, one head of a state or major minister was killed every eighteen months.

And, between 1893 and 1901, assassins dispatched a French president, a Spanish Prime Minister, an Empress from Austria-Hungary, an Italian king, and an American president.

According to Niccolo Machiavelli, the most dangerous assassin is the suicide attacker. Since he expects to die—and therefore is beyond all reprisals—he is the perfect killing machine.

ASSASSINATION, EFFECTIVENESS OF

The United States of America has been involved in approximately two hundred wars and military "incursions," but none of these has ever killed a president.

Assassins, however, have killed four presidents. Not without reason did Niccolo Machiavelli observe that a plot is more dangerous to political leaders than an "open war."

More often than not, however, assassination attempts are unsuccessful.

Queen Victoria of Britain survived seven assassination attempts on her life. The last attempt was by an aspiring poet.

Charles de Gaulle survived thirty-one documented assassination attempts without serious injury. In one spectacular attack—during a church service at Notre Dame Cathedral—assassins opened fire and two civilians were killed. Notoriously brave, De Gaulle did not flee or even duck under the pew during assault, but continued to face the altar and continued to sing *Te Deum*, a hymn to the Christian God.

But, although an assassination is difficult, it is possible. In 1984, after a failed attempt on the life of the British prime minister, the Irish Republican Army issued this statement: "Today we were unlucky, but remember we have to be lucky only once."

ASSASSINATION, METHODS OF

The Central Intelligence Agency of the United States produced a manual called "A Study of Assassination" in 1954. Written anonymously, the probable author was William "Rip" Robertson.

Written for operatives, the manual details the strengths and weaknesses of various assassination methods, from drugs and poisons (effective if the target is under "medical care"), knives (it recommends "severing" both the "jugular and cartotid blood vessels" or "the spinal cord in the cervical region"), improvised weapons such as a hammer or a length of rope (these are "efficient," "readily available," and "not incriminating" if the assassin is searched), bombs (they should be pre-positioned, because throwing a bomb is "sloppy and unreliable"), shotguns (fire from "just beyond arm's length" and aim at the solar plexis), submachine guns (effective "for indoor work when more than one subject is to be assassinated"), and handguns ("inefficient," but often used because a handgun is "easily concealed"). As for the rifle, this is the best weapon if the target must be killed at a distance. The manual recommends a hunting rifle, with a "telescopic sight" and an expanding bullet. The "firing point" should be established beforehand.

ASSASSINATION, MORALITY OF

In the modern world, assassination is a morally repugnant act. Indeed, it is a felony in America to publicly call for the assassination of a "public official."

In contrast, in ancient Athens, the world's first democracy, the assassination of a tyrant was a moral obligation.

The assembly declared that all Athenians must swear an oath–always before the annual festival of Dionysus–to kill–with their own hands–anyone who tries to subvert the democracy, anyone who holds office after the democracy is subverted, anyone who tries to make himself a despot, or anyone who helps a despot establish himself. The Athenians also swore to regard a slayer of a despot or a subverter of democracy as holy.

In the *Bhagavad-Gita* of India, Krishna justifies killing, as long as one does not kill under the influence of desire and anger.

ASSASSINATION, SECRET

A secret assassination is a concealed assassination. The killer uses deception to make the death appear to be one from natural causes or an accident.

Since real assassins normally seek fame and publicity, most "secret assassinations" are actually murders orchestrated by governments.

The C.I.A.'s how-to manual, entitled "A Study of Assassination," provides details on the secret assassination. The most effective technique, it claims, is a contrived accident. The text recommends "a fall of seventy-five feet or more on to a hard surface." "Elevator shafts, unscreened windows, and bridges" are recommended. The text adds that if the murderer makes an outcry–and pretends to be a "horrified witness"—no alibi or stealthy exit is required.

If the victim cannot swim, the text notes that falls into swiftly flowing rivers or seas are effective. The killer can guarantee the victim's death and create an alibi by diving in and pretending to arrange a rescue.

According to the C.I.A., accidents involving trains, subway cars, or automobiles are less reliable. Exact timing is required and there is the danger of unexpected observation.

Whatever the method used, the manual adds that—if the victim's personal habits make it feasible—preparing him with alcohol increases the chances of success.

ASSASSINATION, SECRET (COVER-UP OF)

According to "A Study of Assassination" by the C.I.A., a successful secret assassination must include an effective cover-up.

First, according to the manual, the secret assassin must plant subtle clues at the scene which are designed to mislead or frustrate the investigation.

Second, after the murder, the government responsible must denounce the act as deplorable. This will help cover its guilt.

Third, the government behind the deed must volunteer to aid in the investigation of the crime. By assisting in the investigation, the guilty government can decrease the chances of being "compromised."

Finally, throughout the operation–from beginning to end—"planning factors must include provisions for . . . plausible denial in the event of a compromise or failure."

ASSASSINATION, THREATS AND

In a study of eighty-three people who tried to kill a public official in a fifty-year period, the U.S.A. Secret Service found that not one had made a threat.

Clearly, threats are for amateurs. Effective operatives do not write letters to newspapers, make public threats, or send hate mail.

In the year of their respective deaths, Abraham Lincoln received eighty death threats in the mail and John F. Kennedy received eight hundred. But none of the threats came from their assassins.

ASSASSINS, MADMEN AS

According to one historian, Gilbert Burnet, the perfect assassin is deranged. If he is apprehended, society assumes he needs no motive, for no one ever tries to find a motive for a madman.

Even better, if he is caught and confesses, no one will believe him. And, if he indicts others, they can dismiss his accusations as the ravings of a lunatic.

ASSASSINS, ORDER OF

The Order of Assassins–known also as the Order of Devoted Masters of the Quiet Death—was organized by Hasan-bin-Sabbah, who was born in 1034 in Iran.

Hasan was one of the founders of asymmetric warfare. He discarded orthodox war–war, he believed, was wasteful–and he used assassination instead. Hasan's Order targeted leaders, either killing them or (more commonly) threatening them with death unless they complied.

According to one Assassin poem:

By one single warrior on foot a king may be stricken with terror,
though he own more than a hundred thousand horsemen.

The elite killers of Hasan's Order were masters of disguise, treachery, and murder. Sent against kings, religious leaders, and military commanders, the killers were deployed alone or in pairs. They infiltrated the enemy's palace—usually as service staff.

The assassins used the "Doctrine of Intelligent Dissimulation." That is to say, they pretended to be something they were not. Lying allowed them to move close to their targets.

The two assassins who killed Conrad of Montferrat—for example—let themselves be baptized as Christians. While praying, they were able to move close to Conrad and assassinate him.

Famous for their patience, members of the Order waited—sometimes for years—until the opportunity was right. Then they struck suddenly. Their favorite weapon was the poisoned dagger.

Always, members of the Order made no attempt to escape. Nor was any effort made to rescue them. They were effective because these pious assassins wanted to die in order to kill.

Little is known about the secrets of the Order. According to Christian accounts, the assassins had three grades of initiation. Interestingly, the teaching of each level negated anything that had been previously taught. The innermost secret–it was alleged–is that heaven and hell are the same, all actions are indifferent, and there is no good or evil.

The actual assassins–members who had attained the highest degree– were taught that there is no such thing as belief. All that matters is action.

"Nothing is true," taught Hasan, and "all is permitted."

ASSASSINS, PUNISHMENT OF

Not all assassins are treated equally.

Pal-dorje, who killed a king who persecuted Buddhism, is today honored in Tibet as a saint.

Aleksei Grigorevich Orlov, who assassinated tsar Peter III, was given an aristocratic title, estates, and 200,000 rubles by Catherine "the Great," the tsar's widow and successor.

Walter Audisio, whose *nom de guerre* was Colonel Valerio, killed Benito Mussolini and Clara Petacci, the mistress of Mussolini. For his action, Audisio was later elected to the Italian parliament.

In contrast, Bertholde, who assassinated Charles the Righteous in the church of St. Donat in Bruges in 1127, was crucified on the order of King Louis the Fat.

Francois Ravaillac, who assassinated King Henry IV of France in 1610, was brutally tortured to death, his family was exiled, and his surname was officially banned in France.

And after an *unsuccessful* July 1944 assassination attempt on Adolf Hitler, perhaps seven thousand individuals were arrested, and some two thousand death sentences were handed down by "People's Courts."

ASSAULT

According to modern law, raising a stick and threatening someone is assault. Raising a stick and striking someone is assault and battery (there is always assault with battery). Raising a stick to rob, rape, or commit some other felony is aggravated assault. (The intention to commit another crime makes the action worse.) Using a deadly weapon—such as a firearm, an ax, or an automobile—is also aggravated assault.

ASYMMETRIC WARFARE

Asymmetric warfare is warfare between forces that are markedly different from each other in size, technological sophistication, and goals.

One especially effective asymmetric attack occurred on September 11, 2001. Using simple tools (pepper spray and ninety-cent box cutters), nineteen hijackers allegedly seized four commercial aircraft and crashed them into the World Trade Towers and the Pentagon. Approximately three thousand Americans were killed.

Although the United States is a "superpower," and spent 396 billion dollars on defense in 2001, during the attacks the Muslim world noted that America's leaders "fled the White House like frightened mice."

The technique—using skyjacked planes as missiles—is a plot device in Thomas Clancy's novel, *Debt of Honor*, published in 1994.

ATHEISM

Atheism is the belief that god does not exist.

The dictator named Enver Hoxha outlawed religion in Albania in 1967, and Albania became the first and only officially atheist state in history. Churches and mosques were razed, and anyone apprehended with copies of the Koran, the Bible, or religious objects faced a long prison sentence.

According to Albert Camus, "The future is the only transcendent reality to men without god."

ATROCITIES, STATE USE OF

States often use atrocities as a matter of tactics. In December 1941, for example, the Nazis issued the "Armed Forces High Command." According to this order, ten civilians were to be shot for every soldier killed by the resistance.

Later, when the Russians reached German soil at the end of World War II, the Soviet propagandist Ilya Ehrenburg made this inflammatory declaration:

> *Kill! There is nothing that is innocent that is German. Neither in the living nor in the unborn. Follow the directive of Comrade Stalin and trample forever the fascist beast in his cave. Break by force the racial haughtiness of German women. Take them as your lawful prey! Kill, you brave advancing Red soldiers!*

ATTACK (INVISIBLE)

An invisible attack is one that is unnoticed by all. For example, if a biological weapon spreads cholera where the disease already exists—the attack would not be recognized.

AUTHOR

According to "Saint" Bonaventure, a thirteenth-century scholar, there are four ways to make a book:
1) Copy and change nothing. That is a scribe.

2) Copy the writings of others together, and change nothing. That is a compiler.

3) Copy the writings of others and add your own comments. That a commentator.

4) Copy the writings of others, but give your comments main place. That is an author.

AUTOPSY

An autopsy is an examination of a dead body to discover the cause of death. In some societies, all deaths are suspicious.

According to one medical historian, there are many popular fallacies regarding an autopsy. These fallacies include: 1) that embalming will not obscure autopsy findings (not true), 2) that poison is always detected at an autopsy (not true), and 3) the autopsy always yields the cause of death (not true).

BABEUF, FRANCOIS (1760-97)

Francois Noel Babeuf, who called himself "Gracchus Babeuf," was a proponent of radical egalitarianism and the violent enemy of economic injustice. According to Babeuf, the French Revolution, which had established only political equality, had not gone far enough.

Forming a secret society called the "Conspiracy of Equals," Babeuf advocated the abolition of private property. Only then, with the establishment of a pure democracy with egalitarian communism, he argued, could mankind eliminate the "revolting distinctions between rich and poor, great and small, masters and servants, rulers and ruled."

Betrayed by a police spy, Babeuf and thirty of his followers were executed for plotting against the government. His doctrines, known as Babouvism or Babeuvism, were kept alive by his co-conspirators and by secret revolutionary societies.

BAKUNIN, MIKHAIL (1814-1876)

A celebrated and dedicated anarchist, Mikhail Bakunin was the eldest son of a large Russian aristocratic family.

An apostle of freedom, Bakunin was the enemy of "all the tormentors, all the oppressors, and all the exploiters of humanity—priests, monarchs, statesmen, soldiers, public and private financiers, officials of all sorts, policemen, gendarmes, jailers, executioners, monopolists, economists, politicians of all shades, down to the smallest vendor of sweetmeats."

Bakunin's portrayal of history was eloquent and simple: "Following cannibalism came slavery, then came serfdom, then wage serfdom, which is to be followed by the terrible day of retribution, and later–much later–the era of fraternity."

In the area of politics, Bakunin believed that the state was evil, the incarnation of crime. "The smallest and most inoffensive state," he wrote, "is still criminal in its dreams."

BANDITS

A bandit is a rural outlaw.

To be successful, the bandit must "travel light, hit hard, and run fast." Also, wise bandits never rob their own territory.

Types of bandits include the social bandit, a Robin Hood figure who fights against landowners and priests on behalf of the downtrodden; the transport bandit, a category which includes pirates, train robbers, and aircraft hijackers; and the national bandit, who is involved in insurrection and rebellions, such as William Wallace of Scotland.

BANDITS, LEGENDS AND

As historian Eric Hobsbawm pointed out, the bandit in legends becomes a noble figure who is celebrated, feared, and admired.

The "noble" bandit's career also is characterized by the following:

1. He begins not as a criminal, but as a victim of injustice. Pancho Villa, for example, avenged a sister raped by a landowner.
2. The noble bandit robs from the rich and gives to the poor.
3. He kills only in self-defense, or to exact just revenge.
4. He is the people's champion, the man who rights wrongs.
5. He is virtually invisible and invulnerable to the "authorities."
6. In the end, the legendary bandit is destroyed by treachery. Jesse James, for example, was betrayed by Robert Ford, and Billy "the Kid" was destroyed by Patrick Garret.

BANKS, EMBEZZLEMENT FROM

Before the computer age, there were an estimated two hundred ways to embezzle money from a bank without immediate exposure. Now, the ways are too numerous to count.

BANKS, POWER OF

The Bank of England, founded by William Peterson in 1694, was the first privately owned institution to issue the currency of a nation.

According to Ezra Pound, that event marked the beginning of the rule by bankers and the end of the rule by governments. Pound referred to the period as the "Age of Usury."

Lord Josiah Stamp, a former director of the Bank of England, made this comment: "The modern banking system manufactures money out of nothing. The process is perhaps the most astounding piece of sleight of hand that was ever invented."

BARBARIANS

According to some thinkers, barbarism is normal. Civilization—bright, shiny, and fragile—is an unnatural intrusion.

Robert E. Howard, the American writer who invented the "sword and sorcery" genre in fiction before he committed suicide at the age of thirty, has a character make this declaration in "Beyond the Black River": "Barbarism is the natural state of mankind. Civilization is unnatural. It is a whim of circumstance. And barbarism must always triumph."

The medieval Scandinavians were a classic barbarian culture. A warlike race with an inclination to poetry, they lived for the friendship of men and the love of women, for battle and plunder and glory.

BARBARIANS, VALUES OF

To barbarians, life is a glimpse of beauty, a flash of joy, and the sharing of fellowship. The barbarian lives to destroy monsters, slaughter tyrants, and breed sons.

To their enemies, however, barbarians are animals in the shape of men. Savages, they kill, burn, and rape.

BAR KOCHBA, SIMON (died A.D. 135)

A failed rebel and Jewish freedom fighter, Simon Bar Kokhba was the leader of revolt against Rome between A.D. 132 and A.D. 135.

The revolt was sparked when Hadrian, the Roman emperor, decreed that a temple to Jupiter should be built on the ruins of Solomon's temple. In another edict, Hadrian prohibited circumcision, which the Romans viewed as a form of child cruelty.

Although Bar Kochba and his men fought heroically (according to legend, men wanting to join Bar Kokhba's army had to cut off a finger), the

Romans crushed the rebellion and killed Bar Kochba. On the ruins of Jerusalem, Hadrian built a model city, "Colonia Aelia Capitolina," where a temple dedicated to Jupiter was constructed. Jews were forbidden to enter the city.

Although the Jewish Talmud denounces Bar Kochba, during his life he was recognized as the messiah by Rabbi Akiba ben Joseph, who claimed that Bar Kochba was the "Star of Jacob" predicted in Numbers 24:17.

BARRIERS

Barriers exist in many forms. They may be constructed from steel, concrete, or phobias that exist only in the mind.

The most common barriers are walls. Typically, walls are structures that protect the rich. They are also used to imprison the poor.

BARRIERS, PENETRATION OF

Climbing a fence or a wall silhouettes an intruder, and this can be dangerous. If the wall must be climbed, keep your body low and parallel to the top.

If it is possible, go under the fence by digging. The earth should be pushed to the other side so that the hole can be filled after passage.

If the barrier contains high-technology sensors—devices that detect sound, heat, vibrations, the presence of metal, and so forth—the intruder must be especially careful.

Know that the weakness of high-technology barriers is their sensitivity. Sensors can be triggered by small animals, leaves in wind, and even snowflakes.

To penetrate high-technology barriers, cause false alarms. Eventually, the guards will become complacent and will stop reacting.

If possible, cross in bad weather. The ideal is a wet, stormy night with no Moon.

BATTLE, ETHICS OF

In war, laws are suspended, lies are legitimate, and even murder is moral.

BATTLEFIELDS

A battlefield is "field of death," a region of "desolation and woe" where slaughter occurs.

Battlefields, of course, are universal. Even the Christian heaven—with its rebel angels—had a war. In the words of Revelation XII:7: "And there was war in heaven: Michael and his angels fought against the dragon."

Against modern weapons, the best defense is extreme dispersion and entrenchment, and this has caused battlefields to assume an eerie, empty look.

BATTLEFIELDS, URBAN

The nature of modern cities–Baghdad is two thousand square miles of brick, glass, steel, and asphalt–means that urban combat is distinctive.

In cities, combat occurs in confined spaces–places where small numbers are able to fight numerically superior opponents.

The strife is three dimensional, and lethal fire can come from every direction. Moreover, the effect of explosions is compounded by the enclosed spaces.

Also, the physical cover is multidimensional. Walls, roofs, basements, sewers, and utility passages provide cover or a refuge.

Remember, however, that although walls and buildings are good concealment, they do not provide good protection. Modern walls—one brick thick—are easily penetrated by high-velocity rounds. A .50-caliber machine gun will penetrate sixteen inches of dry sand (the penetration power is even greater through wet sand), ten inches of concrete, or two inches of steel plate.

In urban combat, avoid being seen. Present as small a silhouette as possible.

Stay low, and do not stay up longer than three to five seconds so the enemy cannot make a "fix." Minimize movement and have nothing that rattles.

Always select your next position of cover before making a move. Always move quickly.

Stay parallel to flat surfaces. Roll over a wall. Use multiple-layered structures for cover.

When peering around a corner, do so close to ground. The enemy does not expect a human head at street level.

Where it is possible, break holes through the walls of adjoining buildings to create passages.

BATTLEFIELDS (URBAN), TECHNOLOGY AND

Urban features restrict the mobility, the communications, the intelligence, and the firepower of organized armies. In particular, walls and other obstructions reflect, absorb, and block communication signals, and hinder radios, sensors, and other technology devices.

For asymmetric warfare against high-technology opponents, urban terrain is highly desirable.

BATTLES, DURATION OF

In ancient Greece, battles lasted a day, and the actual killing required about an hour.

The modern world is different. The battle of Verdun, one of the worst of the twentieth century, lasted from February to November in 1916.

BAUDELAIRE, CHARLES (1821-1867)

A poet and a rebel, celebrated for *The Flowers of Evil*, Charles Baudelaire died insane, paralyzed, and speechless at the age of forty-six. The combined effects of syphilis, alcohol, hashish, and opium killed him.

A decadent, a man who reveled in the atmosphere of "brothels, opium dens, and morgues," Baudelaire was attracted to "pallor and thinness" in women. Thinness, he believed, was "more obscene" than plumpness.

BEAUTY

Francis Galton, who spoke of a "beauty map," classified people as "attractive," "indifferent," or "repellent."

But what is beauty?

One French writer made this observation: "What is a pretty girl? Nothing more than a mixture of carbon, hydrogen, oxygen, and nitrogen, with a little phosphorous and some other ingredients, all of which is destined promptly to disintegrate."

BEY, HAKIM (born 1945)

A rebel author, Hakim Bey (the pseudonym of Peter Lamborn Wilson) is best known as the developer of TAZ, the concept of the "Temporary Autonomous Zone."

Hakim Bey's writings contain these declarations:
* "Shamans not priests, bards not lords, hunters not police."
* "No free person will die for another's aggrandizement."
* "Never seek power—only release it."

* "Don't picket–vandalize. Don't protest–deface"
* "Paganism has not yet invented laws–only virtues."
* "Banks transmute imagination into feces and debt."
* "Nietzsche says somewhere that the free spirit will not agitate for the rules to be dropped or even reformed, since it is only by breaking the rules that he realizes his will to power."

BIBLE

A collection of iron-age texts, the Bible is sacred to Christianity. The sixty-six books of the Bible supposedly had forty-two different authors and were written over a period of 750 years. In the Bible, 2930 different characters appear.

Revered by millions, the oddest part of the Bible is the Old Testament. The latter, which the anti-Semitic Ezra Pound called "the record of a barbaric tribe, full of evil," describes the doings of inspired "prophets" and anointed "kings."

The most important part of the Old Testament—the Torah or Pentateuch—tells the story of a god who has neither a home nor a people. He chooses a people who have neither a home nor a god.

The god of the Torah seems obsessive about matters of diet and hygiene. The god of the Torah forbids tattooing, wearing clothing woven from two kinds of material, and eating lobster. He allows slavery, animal sacrifice, and genocide.

The New Testament is the part of the Bible used by Christians only. Significantly, the name of the Mosaic God—YHWH, rendered variably as Yahweh or Jehovah—never appears in the New Testament.

The New Testament focuses on the life and actions of Jesus, the alleged messiah. There are fifty-one Old Testament prophecies about the messiah, but they are not found in the Gospel of Mark, the oldest gospel.

The prophecies are found in the Gospel of Matthew, but some allege the prophecies were collected and the Gospel of Matthew was written around them.

Curiously, Jesus himself misquoted the Bible. According to Luke 24:46, Jesus made this declaration: "Thus it is written, that the Christ should suffer, and rise from the dead the third day."

In reality, there is no such scriptural statement on the messiah's resurrection on the third day in the Old Testament.

BIBLE, DESTRUCTION OF

According to Porphyry, writing in *Against the Christians,* "All the things attributed to Moses were really written eleven hundred years later by Ezra and his contemporaries."

Chapter fourteen of 2 Esdras details tells how the Bible was destroyed and rewritten. Apparently, Nebuchadnezzar burned the Jewish scriptures in 586 B.C. Over a century later, however, a "burning bush" instructed Ezra to restore the sacred texts.

Employing five scribes, Ezra dictated the holy books over a period of forty days and nights. Ninety-four books were dictated. Of these, twenty-four were scriptural and seventy were reserved for the wise.

The book the Protestants call 2 Esdras is known as 4 Esdras by the Roman Catholics and 3 Esdras by Russian orthodoxy and *Izra Sutu'el* by the Ethiopian Church. It was considered scriptural by the early church fathers, such as Origen, Jerome, and St Ambrose.

BIBLE, SOME CURIOUS OPINIONS ON

According to Rabbi Judah ben Ezekiel, who lived in the third century of the "current era," "he who would order his entire life according to strict and literal interpretation of Scripture is a fool."

According to Pope Clement VIII, who died in 1605, "The Bible published in vulgar tongues ought not to be read or retained. Perhaps it had been better for the church if no scriptures had been written."

According to Robert Ingersoll, a militant nineteenth-century atheist, "If a man would follow today, the teachings of the Old Testament, he would be a criminal. If he would strictly follow the teachings of the New, he would be insane."

BIN LADEN, OSAMA (born 1957)

Osama bin Laden, an Islamic vigilante, is a twenty-first century outlaw hero. Reviled by the Christian West and adored by the Muslim East, Osama bin Laden has a life that is strangely epic in stature. Born wealthy, he freely embraces hardship and danger.

In the tradition of the outlaw hero, bin Laden defies authority and eludes capture. With his colleague, Ayman al-Zawahiri, he avenges the humiliated.

Knowing that the ultimate measure of any warrior is the size of his opponent, Osama bin Laden has won glory in the Muslim world by attacking the mightiest empire in history.

Bin Laden appears to be the master of asymmetric warfare. Mobile and protean, he knows how to trade space for time, he understands the disproportionate effect of attacks on several targets at once, and he uses propaganda to confuse and paralyze his opponents.

BLACK AGENCY

A "Black Agency" is a government office or department that is so secret its existence is denied by state.

"BLACK-BAG OPERATIONS"

A "black-bag operation" is an illegal government operation conducted in secret. A "black-bag operation" may be anything from burglary to bribery, from kidnapping to murder.

In the United States, the most common "black-bag operation" is an illegal break-in. The operative secretly enters a residence or place of business to copy records, steal papers, sabotage machinery, install listening devices, or plant illegal contraband, such as drugs or firearms.

One standard procedure is to plant contraband and start a fire. The firemen who arrive to fight the flames must report any contraband they encounter. The owner will then be charged with the possession of contraband and arson.

BLACKMAIL

Blackmail is the extortion of money by threats of public disclosure, censure, or exposure to ridicule.

A relatively new crime, a law against "threatening to publish with intent to extort money" was not passed until 1893 in the United Kingdom.

Blackmail laws were developed to protect the rich from the poor. Obviously, no one blackmails the poor. If someone has scandalous information on the poor that is newsworthy, he sells it directly to the press.

Usually, when a blackmailed person reports the blackmail to the police, he is not prosecuted even though he committed the crime he is being blackmailed for. But this is convention—not law. (The exception is treason.)

BLACK OPERATIONS (MILITARY)

A "black" military operation is a covert operation not attributable to the government carrying it out.

In these "black operations," volunteers are used. Since the operatives cannot reveal any information to wives, girlfriends, parents, or friends, only men who have no interest in fame or recognition are selected.

In black operations, all men and machines that are lost are not reported.

During the 1950's and 1960's, for example, at least 138 Americans were lost on aerial spying missions over the Union of Soviet Socialist Republics. The United States covered up the losses and lied to the relatives of the missing men. In the interests of "national security," alternative explanations were given to the families, such as their son had died in an "accident."

BLANQUI, LOUIS AUGUSTE (1805-81)

Louis-Auguste Blanqui was an activist and an insurgent. The "dictatorship of the proletariat" was a phrase he coined.

Blanqui believed that political equality without economic equality was a sham, so he advocated an uncompromising form of communism.

Organized into small revolutionary cells, Blanqui's followers swore this oath: "In the name of the Republic, I swear eternal hatred of all kings, aristocrats, and oppressors of humanity."

Blanqui led several unsuccessful plots and insurrections, including an abortive rising that began on May 12, 1839.

A brave rebel, Blanqui spent half of his adult life in prison.

BLASPHEMY

Blasphemy has been defined as irreverent talk about god or sacred things. According to Aleister Crowley, the notorious occultist, blasphemy is the quickest way to attract god's attention. According to the pious, blasphemy means irreverent slanders and sacrilegious lies.

The ancient Romans had no penalty for verbal attacks on the gods. The gods, they believed, could defend themselves.

In contrast, the Bible–in Leviticus 24:16—states that anyone blaspheming the name of God—Jew or Gentile—should be put to death.

As recently as 1868, G. J. Holyoake received "six months imprisonment with hard labor" for stating in a lecture in London that "there is no such a thing as a God."

Of all modern works, perhaps the most blasphemous is *Last Days of Christ the Vampire* by J. G. Eccarius. Noting that Jesus was seen outside the tomb after his death–and noting that Jesus taught that drinking blood leads to eternal life (see the Gospel of John, chapter 6)—the book argues that Jesus is one of the "undead."

BLOOD

Called the essence of life–and the seat of the soul—blood is the most significant of all fluids.

In spite of its importance, the average adult has only a gallon and a half of blood.

Historically, many cultures—such as the Gauls, the Carthaginians, and the Sioux—would drink the blood of their enemies.

According to the Bible (in Hebrews 9:22), "without the shedding of blood there is no forgiveness of sins."

BODYGUARDS

A bodyguard is a type of mercenary. He is paid to protect another individual from murder or assassination.

The ideal bodyguard is an expert marksman. He is also a trained paramedic who can provide emergency first aid if his client is wounded.

BODYGUARDS, HISTORY OF

In ancient Greece, any leader who needed bodyguards or who traveled with weapons or who was afraid to mingle with the people was considered a tyrant. When this was made clear to Philip of Macedon–the conqueror of the Greeks–he disarmed, eliminated his bodyguard, and went to the public marketplace. He was assassinated, but Philip WAS a tyrant.

Today, flak-jacketed presidents, surrounded by their armed mercenaries, routinely parade the regalia of tyrants in public, and the population does not object to security checkpoints, crowd barriers, and intrusive frisking.

Indeed, as the *Illuminatus Trilogy* observes, "The people reason–or are manipulated into reasoning–that the entire population must have its freedom restricted in order to protect the leaders."

BONAPARTE, NAPOLEON (1769-1821)

A tyrant, in thirteen years Napoleon Bonaparte went from artillery captain to Emperor. Friedrich Nietzsche called him a synthesis of the "inhuman and superhuman." Carl von Clausewitz called Napoleon "the God of War."

In the course of his career, Napoleon invented the modern coup d'etat, imprisoned two popes (Pius VI and Pius VII), placed an iron crown on his own brow with his own hand, and caused the deaths of millions.

When Napoleon invaded Egypt, he took two hundred scholars with his army.

BONAPARTISM

Bonapartism is government by a "populist" tyrant who claims to personify the will of the people. Claiming unlimited authority on their behalf, the Bonapartist leader uses the "plebiscite" to invest his rule with a veneer of legality.

A Bonapartist leader, such as Adolf Hitler, simultaneously tyrannizes and worships the people. He is, to use Otto Weininger's phrase, both "a pimp and a whore."

BONDS

When being tied up, expand your chest. This will loosen bonds.

Since all handcuffs are the same, a professional outlaw keeps a key hidden in his clothing. Or, he has a handcuff key built into the tongue of his belt buckle.

Interestingly, Harry Houdini, the celebrated escape artist, secreted a wire to open locks under a specially crafted dental bridge.

BOOBY TRAPS

A pre-positioned weapon, a booby trap is an object containing a concealed hazard that kills or injures on contact.

Booby traps range from an explosive devices (up to and including nuclear weapons) to punji sticks, which are simply spikes or stakes, often smeared with a "septic poison" such as excrement.

Booby traps and land mines are effective because they demoralize and hurt the enemy without risk. In the American-Vietnamese War—in the period 1965 through 1970—such weapons caused half of all American deaths.

One authority listed these rules of booby traps:

1. The booby trap should be camouflaged as much as possible.

2. Place the booby traps in clusters, so the enemy will set off at least one.

3. Position "dummy traps" to lull the enemy into complacency.

4. Place the booby traps on obstacles so that when obstacles are moved, the traps are detonated.

5. Booby trap weapons, food, and supplies.

Booby traps are sometimes deployed with great imagination. To kill Americans, the Viet Cong booby trapped beer cans and pornography. They also booby trapped radios, flashlights, books, children's toys (such as stuffed animals), candy boxes, and food tins.

In the Malayan Emergency, the British forces allegedly contaminated communist stockpiles of rice with bamboo hairs. Bamboo hairs are fine and almost invisible. When ingested they become embedded in stomach (because of their fish-hook shape) and cause a chronic inflammation that is practically incurable.

Less cleverly, the Americans manufactured and used anti-personnel mines made to resemble dog feces.

BOOTH, JOHN WILKES (1838-1865)

A noted assassin, John Wilkes Booth shot Abraham Lincoln to avenge the defeat of the Confederacy in the Civil War.

Booth, a so-called Copperhead or pro-South Northerner, was an actor by profession. He shot Lincoln in a theater on Good Friday, April 14, 1865, during a performance of the play *Our American Cousin.* Using a .44-caliber weapon made by Henry Deringer, Booth fired during a moment in the play (Act III, Scene II of a performance) when the audience laughed.

Booth shot Lincoln at the base of the head. The bullet entered behind the left ear, passed through the brain, and stopped behind the right eye .

Leaping to the stage, Booth shouted these words: *"Sic Semper Tyrannis"* and "the South is avenged."

After making a daring escape from the city of Washington, Booth was allegedly shot to death in a burning barn by Sergeant Boston Corbett. The latter, a religious fanatic who castrated himself, was later placed in a mental institution, but he escaped and vanished.

A final note: there were four people seated in Lincoln's accursed box that fateful evening, and everyone present would become a victim of murder or madness.

Major Rathbone, who was with Lincoln in the box, fought Booth and was stabbed. Rathbone later married the woman that he had escorted that night (Clara Harris), but Rathbone ultimately went insane, killed her, and died in an asylum. Mary Lincoln, Lincoln's wife, also would become a victim of madness. She died in 1882.

BORGIA, CESAR (1475-1507)

An infamous tyrant, Cesar Borgia was the son of a cardinal (the future Pope Alexander VI) and a courtesan. A lover of fine art—he was a patron of Leonardo and Raphael—Cesar Borgia had his enemies strangled, stabbed, or hacked to pieces. A master of poisons, Borgia knew which substances killed quickly, and which poisons killed slowly.

This tyrant, who was Niccolo Machiavelli's ideal prince, used cruelty and murder as tools. Lusting after uncorrupted innocence, in one captured town he had forty of its prettiest virgins sent to him to deflower.

A master politician—completely without scruple—Caesar Borgia used Remirro de Orco, a cruel and capable man, to bring peace and order to Rome. Orco, using brutalities, made Rome orderly, but Borgia knew that the policies had aroused hatred. So "in order to purge the minds of the people and to win them over completely," Borgia had Orco cut in half and displayed the mutilated corpse in public.

Ambushed in Spain in 1507 at the age of thirty-one, Cesar Borgia died bravely. He received twenty-three wounds on his body.

Borgia's tombstone reads: "Here, in a scant piece of earth, lies he whom all the world feared."

BOUNTY

A bounty is a reward paid for killing or capturing someone.

After the governor of Louisiana put a price of five thousand dollars on the head of the pirate named Jean Lafitte, Lafitte responded by offering fifty thousand dollars for the head of the governor.

BOYCOTT

A pacifist weapon—a form of civil disobedience—a non-violent punishment or protest—a boycott is an organized refusal to have commercial or social dealings with a person, organization, or country. Charles Stewart Parnell—an Irish leader—recommended it for all disputes.

Boycotting was first used in Ireland, and it was first applied to a man named Captain Boycott. No one would have any social or commercial contact with the target.

BRAINWASHING

Brainwashing, a form of mind control, is the technique of transforming the opponent rather than eliminating him. It is also called "thought reform,""behavior modification," and "conditioned reflex therapy."

In the Soviet Union, brainwashing involved the following: 1) deprive the victim of sleep, 2) destroy time by keeping the victim in a windowless room with bright lights constantly burning, 3) bombard the victim with high-pitched sounds, 4) beat him and –oddly–tickle him, 5) force him to spend time in solitary confinement in a sweat box or in a padded cell, 6) force him to stand for days in feces or in ice, 7) infest him with rats and lice, 8) starve him, 9) make threats alternated with promises, humiliations, and intimidation to induce confusion, 10) increase uncertainty by keeping the sentence and the punishment indefinite, 11) threaten the victim's loved ones and family members, and 12) bombard the victim with lies and the endless repetition of slogans by radio or from fellow prisoners (those who are on the road to change).

If the noise of the slogan is constant, this will create anxiety in the mind of the prisoner. Once he starts to think "perhaps I could be wrong," his brainwashing will be successful.

BRAINWASHING, OF MASSES

Adolf Hitler said that the endless repetition of slogans is the way to train masses. The masses, he said, are like parrots.

Thought modification also makes use of philanthropy (so that people will think well of the controllers), psychology (to control how people think), and history (to indoctrinate people with patriotic lies).

According to Robert Anton Wilson, "Any brainwashing system . . . can be successfully resisted by those who understand the techniques being used. Programming, imprinting, and conditioning whole populations can only work where there is total secrecy about what is being done."

BRIBERY

A bribe is an inducement designed to dishonestly persuade someone to act in your favor.

According to Georges Sorel, "no important undertaking is carried through without bribery," and bribes are indeed a force in history.

Note that in Hindu lore the gods protect their interests by corrupting their opponents. Remember that.

BRIBES, OUTLAWS AND

Among the *Cosa Nostra*, outlaws traditionally wear a diamond ring on one of their little fingers. This provides a bribe that is always accessible.

In poor and corrupt societies, the police expect "gratuities" and "gifts." Do not be too generous, however. If you give too much, the police will assume you must be guilty of a serious crime.

BRIBES, VIOLENCE AND

The most effective bribes include a threat of violence.

The Russian *Mafiya*, for example, will offer someone "silver or lead." Their meaning, of course, is accept the bribe or die.

Sometimes, however, the gift/threat combination does not work. To silence Savonarola, Pope Alexander VI first offered a cardinal's hat. When Savonarola refused to cooperate, the pope had him arrested and burned.

BRIBES, TYPES OF

Generally speaking, there are four types of bribes:
1. Ordinary bribery: significant payments made to officials with decision-making powers to convince them to do their jobs IMPROPERLY.
2. Grease: "facilitating" payments made to minor officials to encourage them to do their jobs PROPERLY.
3. Protection money: payments made to powerful people to avoid harm from them.
4. Political contributions: payments made to politicians and political parties in return for influence, favors, or special treatment. The most common type of bribery, it is legal in most modern states.

BRITISH EMPIRE

An extreme form of imperialism, between 1815 and 1865 the British Empire expanded at an average annual pace of 100,000 square miles.

Nakedly aggressive, during Victoria's reign alone the British Empire fought seventy-two separate military campaigns, often using "native" troops to kill "natives."

Of all the empire's wars, the vilest was the First Opium War. Fought against China, Britain forced China to accept British opium!

At various times, the Mahdi's forces, the Afghans, and the Zulus all humbled British power, but by 1921, the British Empire covered one-quarter of the world's land area (the Empire was 14.3 million square miles) and held one-quarter of the world's population.

BROEDERBOND

The Afrikaner Broederbond, a nationalist secret society, grew up among Afrikaners after their defeat in the Boer War in 1902.

Founded in 1918, after the "Century of Wrong," a 1964 study found it had 6,768 members in 473 local divisions. Membership was restricted to white, Afrikaans -speaking males, who were Protestants over the age of twenty-five. Freemasons were not permitted in the group.

In the initiation ceremony, the new member pledged not to divulge his membership or that of others. He promised not to disclose anything about the Bond's discussions, decisions, or activities. He also pledged to serve the Afrikaner nation.

In 1948 the Broederbond helped elevate a white-supremacy move-ment—the Nationalist Party–to a position of power.

BRUTUS, MARCUS JUNIUS (85-42 B.C.)

A noted assassin, Marcus Junius Brutus was called"the noblest Roman of them all" by William Shakespeare.

In 44 B.C., Brutus led a conspiracy to kill Julius Caesar, a warlord and a demagogue. More than fifty senators were involved in the plot, and more than twenty senators participated in the actual attack.

The assassins stabbed Caesar twenty-three times, with Brutus stabbing the tyrant in the groin.

Initially, the senate offered an amnesty to the killers, but a funeral ora-tion by Mark Anthony inflamed Rome. All the chief conspirators would be hunted down and killed.

As for Caesar, he was deified by the senate.

BUDDHA (circa 563–circa 483 B.C.)

A successful rebel, the Buddha–whose birth name was Siddhartha Gautama–was born into a royal family. He left the luxuries of court, his beautiful wife, and all earthly ambitions to find wisdom.

As the Buddha, Siddhartha Gautama taught that all existence is char-acterized by suffering, that suffering is caused by desire, and that eliminat-ing desire ends suffering.

The Buddha–like the Christ–believed that health, strength, beauty, culture, learning, and wealth are vanities.

Oddly, in Hinduism, the Buddha appears as the ninth avatar of Vishnu. According to the Hindus, too many people were becoming enlightened, so

Vishnu appeared as the Buddha to mislead millions into abandoning the Vedas.

BUG

A bug is a concealed surveillance device. In today's world, an advanced bug is almost impossible to find.

As long ago as 1952, the U.S.S.R. developed a bug that had no battery and no circuits. It was a hollow metal device with a "tail" like a tuning fork. The human voice made the device vibrate—the Soviets bounced microwaves off the vibrating tail—and then converted the reflection back to sound waves.

Until a British expert determined how the device worked, the Americans were completely mystified.

BUNKER REGIMES

A "bunker regime" is a repressive and corrupt regime—one divorced from the aspirations and needs of the society it dominates.

In Haiti, for example, the leaders traditionally treat citizenry the way lions treat gazelles. While Haiti's political leaders plunder the nation without regard for the people, a plutocratic elite of some two thousand individuals dominates commerce and industry.

BUREAUCRACY

Franz Kafka referred to the "slime" of bureaucracy.

According to John Stuart Mill, "The disease which afflicts bureaucratic governments, and which they usually die of, is routine. They perish by the immutability of their maxims."

BURGLARY

A burglary is a stealthy form of theft. The thief enters a location secretly and tries to exit without being observed.

The skilled burglar will carry no documents or identification papers, but he will carry a significant amount of cash. The cash can be used to pay a bribe, post bail, or hire an attorney.

The professional burglar will conduct his operation on a dark, warm night, when people leave windows open. He knows that the first few hours of sleep are the soundest.

The professional will break in and then wait at least 30 minutes. If he has triggered a silent alarm, it is easier to explain his presence outside rather than inside the house.

He will wear synthetic gloves (genuine leather leaves pore marks like fingerprints). Once in the house, he will take the telephone off the hook. He will also open the front and back doors so that he will have two escape routes.

BURTON, MARY (flourished 1741)

A reviled informant, Mary Burton was a key figure in the "Great Negro Plot."

In 1741, a white indentured servant named Mary Burton, described in the court records as a "spinster, aged about sixteen years," claimed that she had information on an alleged plot by slaves to burn New York City.

Hysteria gripped New York. Ultimately, thirteen blacks were burned alive, eighteen were hanged, and one committed suicide in jail. Four whites (two men and two women) were hanged as accomplices.

Mary Burton received a hundred-pound reward and freedom from her indenture. She also received a note from the New York council thanking her "for the great service she has done." She took the money and note and disappeared from New York and from history.

BURTON, RICHARD (1821-1890)

Sir Richard Burton, an extraordinary product of the British Empire, was an adventurer, a student of erotica, and a spy. His exploits took him across Asia, Africa, and the Middle East.

A "Faustian" hero, Burton risked his life to complete a pilgrimage to Mecca. ("Infidels" in Mecca were executed.) To disguise himself, Burton mastered the language (he was proficient in twenty-five languages and could become fluent in two to three months), darkened his skin with walnut juice and henna, and was careful to have himself circumcised in the "Muslim" (not the "Jewish") fashion.

Interestingly, Sir Richard Burton's wife, a product of the Victorian era, drew up a rather unusual code of conduct for herself. She pledged to hide her husband's faults from the world, to never criticize him, to never answer when he criticized her, and to never ask for anything. She also pledged to let him find in her what men think can be found only in mistresses.

BUSHIDO

Bushido–the way of the warrior–is the knightly code of honor of Japan. The seven values of the code are justice, courage, generosity, politeness, honesty, honor, and loyalty. Famously, the Code of Bushido does not allow for surrender.

Bushido is not like European chivalry. Bushido allows a disreputable act if it gains a desired end.

Bushido was originally the code of the samurai class–an elite class. In 1899, however, Dr. Imazo Nitole wrote an influential work in which he applied the concept of samurai ethics (previously reserved for an elite) to all the social classes of Japan.

Yukio Mishima, the Japanese writer, created the Shield Society, a group of one hundred young men who were dedicated to the revival of Bushido.

CACHE

A prudent person will have a supply dump or cache, containing perhaps a weapon, some money, and an "emergency knapsack."

The knapsack (a second one should be kept in your home) should contain a miniature flashlight (with extra batteries), a small compass, a map, waterproof matches or a disposable lighter, dry lint (lint lights and burns easily), a large knife, large plastic trash bags (for emergency shelter and camouflage), a "space blanket" made of aluminum or mylar, a metallic container (to cook, collect water, and signal), women's nylon stockings (these are multipurpose, and they can be used to catch fish, filter water, scrub surfaces, and store things), two quarts of water (note that water weighs about sixty pounds per square foot), dried, high-energy food, money, and soft earplugs (to sleep in a battle zone).

By the time you need an emergency cache, it is too late to start one. Plan now, before it is too late.

CALAMITIES, OPPORTUNITIES FROM

Calamities—properly exploited—can be sources of wealth. Interestingly, in the Chinese language the word for "crisis" is represented by two pictographs. One is defined as "danger" and the other means "opportunity."

Natural disasters, for example, are excellent times for looting. And, during war and civil unrest, fortunes can be made from the black market.

And, when there is a complete breakdown of law and order (such as in a civil war), a member of the subproletariat (someone drawn from the criminal/prisoner class) can thrive. Without the artificial constraints imposed by the police and the military, he may kill men who had once humiliated him, possess women who had once rejected him, and seize wealth that had once been beyond his reach.

Indeed, because members of the subproletariat have little education and no "legal" earning power, they really have no stake in social stability. Since they possess no skills marketable in normal times, for them the end of chaos means the end of "good times."

CAMORRA

An organized crime group, the Camorra emerged in Italy in the nineteenth century. The Camorra seems to have started in the crowded jails of the city of Naples.

Similar to the Sicilian Mafia, men in the Camorra are obliged to help friends, avenge injuries, and keep secrets.

The Camorra has a solemn initiation ceremony that involves a dagger, a pistol, and a glass of poison.

CAMOUFLAGE

Camouflage is a form of passive defense. Camouflage employs disguise to protect someone or something.

In effect, anything can be camouflaged. Smut, for example, can be given respectability by disguising it as science (the research of Alfred Kinsey) or art (*The Image of my Sister—her Anus Red—with Bloody Shit* by Salvador Dali).

Blasphemy can be disguised as philosophy (*The Anti-Christ* of Friedrich Nietzsche) or literature (*The Last Temptation of Christ* by Nikos Kazantzakis).

For seditious books—including terrorist tracts and bomb-making manuals—a good cover is a novel. Nathaniel Pierce disguised his blueprint for a white revolution as a work of fiction, the *Turner Diaries*, written under the pseudonym of Andrew MacDonald. And Edward Abbey disguised his plan for ecoterrorism as a novel, *The Monkey Wrench Gang*.

Censuring fiction is odious in a free society, and novels will be the last medium to be suppressed.

CANADA

Geographically, Canada is the world's second-largest country.

The U.S.A. has tried to conquer Canada twice, once during the Revolutionary War and once during the War of 1812. Both attempts were abject failures.

CANNIBALISM

The ultimate transgression, cannibalism is the act of an animal eating its own kind.

Older than modern humans, there is evidence of Neanderthal brain being eaten (apparently by other Neanderthals) in 100,000 B.C.

Anthropologists identify four types of cannibalism: survival cannibalism (famine), ritual cannibalism (religion), gourmet cannibalism (food), and atrocity cannibalism (war).

Pacific islanders—in the nineteenth century—said that human flesh is sweeter than pork. (The heart, the thighs, and the arms above the elbows are the most desirable portions.) Baby flesh, they claimed, tastes like fish, because the flesh is very soft.

One Frenchman, who shared a cannibal feast with them, claimed that testicles have the taste and texture of marshmallows.

CAPITALISM

Capitalism is an economic system in which a country's trade and industry are controlled by private owners for profit, rather than by the state. In its purist form, capitalism is an extreme example of asocial individualism.

Usury and greed–vices that were classified as sins in early Christianity– are the basis of capitalism. Capitalism–in contrast to early Christianity– also denied the holiness of poverty.

Capitalism follows these rules: 1) As much as possible, privatize profits and socialize costs. 2) Pay "African" wages and charge "European" prices. 3) Destroy all competitors because, as arch-capitalist John D. Rockefeller noted, "Competition is a sin."

According to Karl Marx, a critic of capitalism, capitalism was a source of great progress and great misery.

Although capitalism is often viewed as modern, Joseph Schumpeter argued that capitalism may be the last senile stage of feudalism.

Indeed, capitalism, because it is decentralized, can be viewed as a feudal economy, whereas "a command economy"—such as the economy of Stalinist Russia—represents absolutism.

CARBONARI

The Carbonari—the so-called Charcoal Burners—were a revolutionary secret society. According to tradition, the earliest lodges were established between 1802 and 1810 (in Capua) by French officers hostile to Napoleon Bonaparte.

The Carbonari's initiation ceremony involved a blindfold, a fire, a cross, and an ax. With his hand on the ax, the blindfolded initiate swore "upon this steel, the avenging instrument of the perjured," to "keep the secret of Carbonism," and never to "write, engrave, or paint anything concerning it, without having obtained written permission."

CASANOVA, GIACOMO (1725-1798)

A sexual rebel, Giacomo Casanova was also a necromancer, swindler, swashbuckler, and author.

A fabled lover, Casanova lost his virginity at age eleven. He claimed 150 women, including two nuns, and he said that he had deflowered thirty-one virgins. Guilty of incest, Casanova made this statement: "I have never been able to understand how a father could tenderly love his charming daughter without having slept with her at least once."

Curiously, since excess leads to ennui, Casanova eventually suffered from impotence. He was probably celibate during his last thirteen years of life, when he served as a librarian in Bohemia.

Always, we increase sterility by increasing promiscuity.

CASUALTIES, PSYCHIATRIC

"Combat stress," formerly called "shell shock," is a form of psychiatric collapse.

In World War II, 23 percent of all allied medical evacuations were psychiatric. In especially serious cases, men had to be led by the hand like children, or they defecated uncontrollably whenever they heard a loud noise. .

R.L. Swank and W.E. Marchand, in a famous study published in 1946, estimated that after sixty days of *continuous* combat 98 percent of all soldiers will be psychiatric casualties. Swank and Marchand discovered that the 2 percent who did not break down were predisposed "aggressive psychopathic personalities."

Curiously, the Nazi regime refused to recognize "combat stress." The Nazis court-marshaled and executed fifteen thousand German soldiers for suffering psychiatric disorders.

CAT'S-PAW

A cat's-paw is a surrogate used by clandestine organizations, from secret societies to terror groups. To find and deploy a cat's paw, take these actions:

1) Read the letters published in the editorial pages of newspapers, study radical Internet sites, and attend public demonstrations to find a zealot who supports your cause. Be careful not to be seen by the zealot.

2) Next, send the zealot an anonymous parcel containing a *large* amount of untraceable currency and this message: "We have been watching you. If you wish to serve our cause, go to _____. If you do not want to serve our cause, keep the money and do nothing. We will never again contact you."

3) At the site named in the first letter, hide a *large* amount of untraceable currency and directions detailing the mission. Above all, the you must have patience. A dozen wasted contacts may be made before one cat's-paw is recruited.

CELL, ORGANIZATION OF

A method of organization for terrorists, guerrillas, bandits, secret societies, and conspiracies, cells are compact "action groups."

For a criminal or terrorist organization–hunted by the immense power of the state–the cellular structure is probably the only way to survive.

The Irish Republican Army—the Irish terrorist group—originally saw itself as an army. It had a hierarchical structure with a chain of command. It had rules, handbooks, court-marshals, and orders.

But hierarchical structures, as the IRA quickly discovered, are vulnerable to infiltration and betrayal. And so, to protect itself from informants and the confessions of captured members, the IRA, like all modern terror organizations, had to resort to the cellular structure of organization.

The cellular structure is designed to protect the entire organization from penetration. If one cell is destroyed, the whole organization is not compromised.

The individual cell consists of between five and eight members. Fewer than five, personalities become too dominant. When the cell has more than eight members, it tends to split into factions.

Ideally, the leader of a cell recruits his own subagents. They are people he knows and trusts through family or friendship.

The subagents have no knowledge of the existence of other cells or their members. The subagents have no link to rest of the organization except through their cell leader.

Curiously, subagents may be unaware of the true affiliation of organization for which they work. One American, who was a subagent in a cell spying on the United States for the U.S.S.R., actually thought that he was spying on the U.S.A. for Israeli intelligence!

Members of the cell operate on "a need to know basis." If a subagent of a cell has an order to destroy a bridge, for example, he may not know that his action is actually a cover for a bank robbery that will be conducted by other operatives.

In the best cells, subagents never meet. Information is passed within the cell via a courier (called a cut-out) whom cell members never actually see. The courier leaves and collects messages at a prearranged location, a so-called "dead letter box" or "dead drop."

Communications between the leaders of different cells are also indirect. (Every level is protected by cut-outs.) Couriers deliver instructions or materials between dead letter boxes or between members operating under assumed identities.

Tactically, not all cells have the same functions. Some, of course, are operational cells that plan and execute actions.

Other cells conduct intelligence. They spy and gather information on targets.

Still other cells are support groups. They forge documents and keep safe houses. They will know nothing about the identities and activities of the operatives they assist.

Finally, there will be an overt propaganda cell that stays within the law. It writes and distributes literature, disinformation, and propaganda to inspire supporters and paralyze opponents.

CENSORSHIP

A crime against freedom, censorship seems inescapable in human history. According to historian Morton Smith, for example, someone excised material from the Gospel of Mark. In its present form, Mark 10:46, from which material was obviously deleted, reads as follows:"They reached Jericho; and as he left Jericho."

Elsewhere in the Bible, in the Acts of the Apostles (19: 17-19), the first book burning in the name of Jesus is described.

In the modern era, even in the so-called democracies, books are not safe. In 1956, for example, the federal government of the United States seized all of Wilhelm Reich's books and burned them. This "holocaust of books," which took place in New York City, destroyed six tons of Reich literature.

Reich himself, a one-time associate of Sigmund Freud, was sentenced to federal prison and died there in 1957.

Oddly, labeled a "communist Jew" by the Nazis, Reich had come to the United States in 1939 to escape persecution.

CHANCE

As Aleister Crowley pointed out, no one is "strong enough to have no interest," so no one can be completely impartial. "Therefore," according to Crowley, "the best king would be Pure Chance."

Crowley believed that "it is Pure Chance that rules the Universe; therefore, and only therefore, life is good."

CHEATING

According to Lysander, the classical Greek leader, one cheats children with dice–and men with promises.

CHILDREN, ATTITUDE TOWARD

The modern idea of child–a special class of people requiring special forms of nurturing and protection–who are different from adults–is a recent invention.

Classical civilization viewed children simply as imperfect adults, incapable of war or reproduction. Considered intrinsically uninteresting, it is significant that no surviving classical Greek statue depicts a child.

It was only in the late nineteenth century that the idea that children were emotionally priceless treasures developed. The same era developed the cult of motherhood and the family.

It was in the late nineteenth century, moreover, that children became "economically worthless." Children had once provided one-third to one-half of the family's income, but "child labor" laws ended the practice.

Ironically, at the time children became "emotionally priceless" they became "economically worthless."

CHILDREN, CHARACTER OF

The Japanese say a person's character is determined by the age of three.

CHILDREN, PUNISHMENT OF

In many civilizations, the discipline of children is harsh. According to the Bible–in Proverbs 23:13—"Do not withhold discipline from a child; if you beat him with a rod, he will not die."

Plato–in *Protagoras*–claimed that disobedient children should be corrected with "threats and blows, like a piece of wood."

Among the Aztecs, wayward children were ferociously chastised: they were beaten with sticks, scratched with thorns, or forced to inhale the acrid fumes of burning chili peppers.

In nineteenth-century Europe, fathers touched their children only to discipline and mothers touched their children only to groom. In that period, a father who did not "spank" was considered bad, and a mother who hugged and kissed her child was viewed as a potential sexual deviant.

In the twentieth century, however, discipline started to disappear in Western civilization. The Nazis (!) abolished corporal punishment in their schools, starting a trend. Later, the spanking of children by parents was outlawed in Sweden (1979), Finland (1983), Denmark (1985), Norway (1987), and Austria (1989).

CHILDREN (PUNISHMENT OF), MERITS OF

Regarding children, what is best, discipline or indulgence?

The Indians of the Great Plains were indulgent and affectionate parents, and they never inflicted pain on their offspring. (Indeed, these Indians thought that peace with the whites was impossible because white people–who struck their children–must be crazy!)

The children raised by the Plains Indians were happy and free-spirited, but their culture never advanced beyond a primitive level.

The Aztecs–in contrast–were ferocious disciplinarians, and their children were subjected to blows, lacerations, and other severities. The Aztec children developed into grim and sullen adults, but they produced an advanced and sophisticated civilization.

CHILDREN, RIGHTS OF

The Declaration of the Rights of man–a product of the French Revolution—abolished the duty of filial obedience to fathers.

Note, however, that in the next century and a half, although fathers lost rights, children did not gain them. Control went to teachers, doctors, courts, social workers.

CHILDREN, SALE OF

A bastard child could be purchased in the nineteenth century for ten dollars. By 1920, however, people were paying one thousand dollars for a child.

Miss Georgia Tann of Memphis was the first woman in the world to become a millionaire running an adoption agency.

CHILDREN, TREATMENT OF

In the United Kingdom, the Royal Society for the Prevention of Cruelty to Children was established in 1884. This was sixty years *after* the British had established the Royal Society for the Prevention of Cruelty to Animals!

In modern America, parents kill at least six hundred children each year. Most murders are by mothers.

If a father does kill his child, it almost always his son. In America, fathers rarely kill a daughter—or a baby.

CHIMPANZEE

One of the higher primates, chimpanzees share 98.4 percent of their DNA with humans.

Native only to Africa, African tradition maintains that chimpanzees are the product of a human mating with an animal. Scientists, however, claim that chimpanzees and humans evolved from a common ancestor.

Today—in our human-dominated world—chimpanzees are hunted (for food) and enslaved (for experimentation). For the latter function, young chimpanzees are especially prized.

The African chimpanzee population declined from 2,000,000 to about 150,000 during the twentieth century.

CHRISTIANITY

A quasi-monotheistic religion, and a "Hellenized form of Judaism," Christianity is one of the most successful ideologies in history.

Admirers claim that Christianity is a pure religion of love and peace. Dedicated to "the Christ," it glorifies poverty, chastity, nonresistance, humility, and obedience.

According to critics, such as Helena Blavatsky, the theosophical leader, "The church can claim but one invention as thoroughly original with her— namely, the doctrine of eternal damnation, and one custom, that of anathema." Everything else was copied from paganism.

Regarding damnation, St. Thomas Aquinas, the author of the *Summa Theologica*, "the saints" in heaven "are permitted to see the punishment of the damned in hell" so that they "may enjoy their beatitude and the Grace of God more abundantly."

CITIES, DANGER OF

An interesting place in time of peace, a city is a perilous place in a crisis.

Not only do cities provide "target-rich environments" for terrorists and enemy armies, but modern cities are difficult to evacuate. One scholar estimated (at the end of the twentieth century) that using all the highways—and moving one thousand vehicles per lane per hour—it would require twenty-eight hours to move all the inhabitants out of Denver, Colorado.

As for New York City, it was estimated (in 1960) that 1.5 million people lived or worked above the sixth floor. Such an arrangement would increase evacuation time.

In contrast, ancient cities were safer and more compact. Ancient Troy, for example, was five acres in size.

CITIES, DEFENSE OF

In World War II, the Germans were quite skilled in urban defense.

The Germans placed their military well inside the city (so they could not be shelled or inspected easily). They used an irregular line of defense to allow for flanking fire. They canalized attackers into "kill zones." They set up in the maze of ruins (destroyed buildings are safer for snipers than standing buildings, which may collapse on the snipers). They created passages by hacking through the walls of adjoining buildings. Every window was broken or open, and shooters were placed in the center of a room to conceal their positions.

Interestingly, during World War I and World War II, the Swiss, if attacked, planned to abandon all the cities and retire into the mountains to fight.

CIVIL DISOBEDIENCE

A form of passive resistance used by protesters and non-violent rebels, civil disobedience is non-cooperation with the state. To effect change or send a message, practitioners refuse to vote, they decline military service, and they do not pay taxes.

The principles of civil disobedience were first articulated by Etienne de La Boetie, the author of *The Discourse of Voluntary Servitude*, which was originally circulated in manuscript form until it was published in 1576.

Later, Henry David Thoreau, Benjamin Tucker, Mahatma Gandhi, and Martin Luther King endorsed the practice.

CIVILIZATION

Civilization has been defined as an advanced stage of human development.

Historian Lewis Mumford, however, pointed out that even insect communities have the attributes of civilization, such as a strict division of labor, a specialized military caste, the technique of collective destruction (accompanied by mutilation and murder), the institution of slavery, and (in certain communities) the domestication of plants and animals. Insect communities also have a monarch–a tyrant called a queen.

Also, note that the human sacrifices of the Aztecs, the bonfires of the Inquisition, and the "death camps" of the Nazis were all the creations of highly civilized societies

CIVIL WAR

A civil war is a war between the citizens of the same country. According to Alexis de Tocqueville, "All those who seek to destroy the liberties of a democratic nation ought to know that war is the surest and shortest means to accomplish it."

The area now called the United States has experienced two major civil wars. The first–a successful secession–started in 1776 when thirteen colonies revolted from the British Empire.

The second—one of the most infamous civil wars in history—occurred between 1861 and 1865. Known as the "War Between the States," it began when the north invaded the south to deny the south the rights the colonies had jointly won in 1783. Ultimately, the "War Between the States" caused more than 620,000 battle-related deaths (in a population of thirty-one million). It destroyed nearly 40 percent of America's economy.

The "War Between the States" did end the institution of slavery in America, but there was one death for every seven slaves freed.

COMFORTABLE MURDER

The "comfortable murder," according to Albert Camus, is a deed committed only by the intellectual. Ensconced in his study, the intellectual incites others to make bloody sacrifices to the "god of history."

An example of the "comfortable" murderer is Johann Most. Although Most never shed blood, he pioneered the concept of the letter bomb and he wrote the first how-to manual for terrorists, *The Science of Revolutionary Warfare.*

COMMERCE

Archaic peoples understand that in a truly fair trade, goods of equal value are exchanged. To make a profit, they believe, someone must steal.

COMMUNICATIONS (CLANDESTINE)

The Sicilian Mafia has a maxim: "If you can say it, do not write it. If you can grunt it, do not say it."

Many clandestine operatives have a "Keltic distrust of the written word." On the other hand, transmission by way of mouth causes distortion, so Che Guevera recommended the use of ciphers or codes.

There are many methods of encrypting information, including the following:

1) Two operatives agree to use a certain text, such as the first edition of *Dorian Gray* by Oscar Wilde. In the message, the first word could be "13-18-4," which means the word will be found on page thirteen, line eighteen, word four in the Wilde text. If the operatives can keep the edition and book they are using secret, this method is secure.

2) In the message a simple cipher may be used, in which symbols (such as %, *, +) represent single letters or digits.

3) In the message, all consonants are represented by the previous LETTER in the alphabet, and all vowels are represented by the following vowel in series "A-E-I-O-U. With this technique, the name "Jesus" is IAROR.

4) A short message can be hidden as a "barn code" in an ordinary letter. Here, a three-page letter is written on some innocuous business, but every fifteenth word in the letter is actually the message.

5) An ordinary letter is sent, but a secret message is written on the page using "invisible ink." During World War II, British agents made invisible ink from one part alum mixed with one hundred parts water. The message became visible when a hot iron was passed over the sheet of paper bearing the message.

COMMUNICATIONS (CLANDESTINE), CONVEYANCE OF

In secure communications, there is never any direct contact between the sender and the receiver. Ideally, the sender does not even know the identity of the receiver and vice versa.

There are time-tested ways for agents and operatives to communicate information. These include the following:

1) A "cut out" is a person who carries messages back and forth between two people who cannot meet. The cut out may be "witting" (he is aware of his function) or "unwitting" (he is unaware of his function). An example of an unwitting cutout is a commercial courier who is hired to deliver a package containing a message.

2) A "live drop" is someone who accepts messages and holds them until they can be safely collected by another person. The messages may be in written form or they may be transmitted orally to the "live drop" who memorizes them.

3) A "dead drop" is a predetermined hiding place where operatives leave messages. The messages are later collected by another.

   A dead drop may be stationary (inside the hollow of a tree) or mobile (inside the spare tire of a car).

   Soviet agents often used soft-drink cans. They were rigged to explode or spill acid if they were not opened correctly.

   In today's world, a dead drop may be an e-mail account. An operative accesses the account, writes a message, but does not send it. A second operative, who also has the password, accesses the account, reads the draft message, and then deletes it. (Since the message never traveled over the Internet, it cannot be intercepted.)

   When a message is left at a dead drop which is a physical location, a sign or indicator is also left (a rock is moved, a chalk mark is made, and so forth). That way, from a distance the receiver knows a message is available and will not have to waste time (or unnecessarily arouse suspicion) by constantly checking the site.

   The advantage of the dead drop is that it allows no direct contact between the sender and receiver. Indeed, the sender and receiver need not know the identity of the other.

   The great disadvantage of the dead drop is that the message (for a time) is out of the control of the organization. The message may be copied, altered, stolen, or destroyed without the organization's knowledge.

COMMUNICATION (CLANDESTINE), PRISON AND

Prisons go to great lengths to control communication. In Alcatraz—the fiendish twentieth-century American prison—prisoners were never allowed to receive original copies of their mail. Only letters transcribed by the "authorities" were permitted.

Within the prison itself, inmates in solitary confinement use the "Knuckle Voice." Invented in Russia by a nihilist doctor, prisoners tap out messages based on the so-called "Siberian Square."

	1	2	3	4	5	6
1	A	B	C	D	E	
2	F	G	H	I	J	
3	K	L	M	N	O	
4	P	Q	R	S	T	
5	U	V	W	X	Y	Z

A is one-space-one (or two short taps)
B is one-space-two (or one short tap followed by two short taps)
J is two-taps-space—then five tap
Y is five taps-space—then five taps

In a North Vietnamese prisoner-of-war camp, an American pilot who was forced to utter enemy propaganda on film cleverly used his eyelids to say "torture" in Morse code.

In West German prisons, imprisoned members of the Baader-Meinhof gang communicated with one another through their lawyers.

COMMUNICATIONS (CLANDESTINE), RICE PAPER AND

If clandestine communications must be written, use tiny sheets of rice paper. The sheets are easily hidden and in an emergency they can be safely swallowed.

CONCEALMENT

Concealment is the act of hiding.

As Edgar Allan Poe noted in "The Purloined Letter," the best way to hide a secret is to place it in plain sight. As a disguise, add calculated misdirection to prevent proper appreciation by the onlooker.

CONCENTRATION CAMP

A concentration camp—typically an unhealthful facility with insufficient rations and brutal discipline—is a detention center for the victims of a regime. Detainees are incarcerated without a trial or any formal legal process.

The British Empire erected the first modern concentration camps during the Second Anglo-Boer War (1899-1902). In an attempt to deny Boer "freedom fighters" food and supplies, the British forces detained Boer women, Boer children, and Africans and sent them to thirty-one camps scattered around South Africa. Thousands perished.

The most infamous concentration camps in history were established by the Nazis in 1933. By 1941, some of the Nazi camps were extermination centers engaged in industrialized mass murder.

Aldous Huxley—with perceptive and frightening foresight—predicted the "painless concentration camp" of the future. According to Huxley, entire societies will belong. The liberties of the people will be taken away, but they will rather enjoy it. In fact—thanks to propaganda, brainwashing, and pharmaceutical drugs—they will love their slavery.

CONFESSION

To confess is to acknowledge guilt.

In traditional Japan, the principle was "no punishment without confession." This principle often led to "vigorous interrogation," a euphemism for torture.

CONFESSIONS, DANGER OF

According to Jim Hogshire, the author of *You Are Going to Prison*, when interrogated by the state, admit nothing. Even if the police film you committing the crime, deny everything.

Never confess. A confession will not help you in court—it will not make you feel better. It will, however, send you to prison or the gallows.

If you make a confession, notes Hogshire, the case is closed and the police have won.

CONFESSIONS, FALSE

Moral masochists—people with self-punitive tendencies—may confess to crimes they did not commit.

Gruesome crimes in particular produce false confessions. The "neurotic" makes a confession because he craves attention, and he wants the spotlight of revulsion and contempt.

With the murder of Elizabeth Short—the fabled "Black Dahlia"—police recorded thirty-eight written confessions from thirty-eight different people. Dozens and dozens were also telephoned in, and eventually the police stopped counting.

Interestingly, a man cannot incriminate himself in Jewish legal tradition. A confession without evidence cannot convict.

CONGO

A vast country in equatorial Africa, the Congo is soaked with human blood.

In 1890, before the Belgians arrived in force, it is estimated that the Congo had twenty to forty million people. By 1914, through forced labor and atrocities, the African population of the Congo had been reduced to 8,500,000.

Novelist Joseph Conrad, writing on the Congo, made this memorable statement: "We are accustomed to look upon the shackled form of the conquered monster, but there—there you could look at a thing monstrous and free."

CONSCRIPTION, MILITARY

A form of involuntary servitude—introduced by France in 1793— conscription is compulsory military service. In Japan, which introduced conscription in 1873, the people called it the "blood tax."

The first American draft was introduced in April 1862 in the Confederacy. The draft was unpopular and hurt the rebel cause.

When the United States drafted men during World War I, critics claimed that conscription violated the constitutional amendment that outlawed involuntary servitude. Although the draft is obviously a form of forced military labor, the argument was rejected by the Supreme Court on grounds of expediency.

During World War II the United States drafted ten million men. The draftees were 63 percent of all those who "served."

CONSPIRACY

Nesta Webster defined a conspiracy as a "combination of people, working in secret, for an evil or unlawful purpose."

According to historian George Fetherling, a conspiracy by its very nature is a committee. A conspiracy is therefore less efficient than an individual, it is prone to leave evidence behind, and it is relatively easy to infiltrate.

CONSPIRACY, ADAM SMITH ON

According to economist Adam Smith, "Men of the same profession never gather together except to conspire against the general public."

CONSPIRACY, DANGER OF

The most common danger in a conspiracy is betrayal. Every fellow conspirator, according to Niccolo Machiavelli, is a potential informant:

> *For anyone who conspires cannot be alone, nor can he find companions except from among those whom he believes to be dissatisfied; and as soon as you have revealed your intention to one malcontent, you give him the means to make himself content, since he can have everything he desires by uncovering the plot; so much is this so that, seeing a sure gain on the one hand and one doubtful and full of danger on the other, if he is to maintain faith with you he has to be either an unusually good friend or a completely determined enemy of the prince.*

Not surprisingly, Niccolo Machiavelli made this observation: "There have been many conspiracies, but history has shown that few have succeeded."

CONSPIRACY, FIRST GOAL OF

According to A. Ralph Epperson, the author of *The Unseen Hand: An Introduction to the Conspiratorial View of History*, the first task of a conspiracy is to convince people that the conspiracy itself does not exist.

CONSPIRACY, GEORGE ORWELL'S *1984* AND

In *1984*—the classic novel of George Orwell—the conspiracy of the "Brotherhood" is described. A kind of scarecrow, the Brotherhood is used by the totalitarian state to awe and terrify the people and to justify the state's atrocities against human rights.

The "Brotherhood" is reputedly led by Emmanuel Goldstein, a reviled heretic. Said to have been once a high-ranking party officer, Goldstein engaged in counterrevolutionary activities, was condemned to death, but then mysteriously escaped. He is said to be somewhere in hiding—still plotting conspiracies—and the government blames all sabotage, all heresies, and all deviations on him.

Orwell added these significant words: "It was impossible, in spite of the endless arrests and confessions and executions, to be sure that the Brotherhood was not simply a myth."

CONSPIRACY, THE LAW AND

Legally, conspirators are two or more people who agree to commit a crime. (Accomplices are "helpers," whereas conspirators are "principals.") Conspirators, rather curiously, can be guilty even if crime they agree on never occurs.

In most jurisdictions, however, individuals are not guilty of conspiracy unless one conspirator commits an "overt act." (An act that in some way moves the conspiracy or puts it into motion.) Talking about robbing a bank with another is not a conspiracy in most jurisdictions, but if one individual checks to see when the bank is open, an overt act has been committed. (Oddly, an overt act may be a legal act. What is important is that it in some way it helps the conspiracy.)

Note that the overt act may be trivial: writing a letter, making a telephone call, attending a meeting, and so forth.

Since the facts of a conspiracy are rarely written down, to prove a conspiracy the government uses circumstantial evidence. The government asks the jury to infer from the defendant's behavior.

Perversely, a conspiracy is considered a separate crime, so an individual can be convicted of conspiracy to rob a bank AND robbing a bank.

Also, a conspirator can be convicted of crimes committed by co-conspirators. In most jurisdictions, conspirators are responsible for crimes committed by any other conspirators, so long as these crimes fall within scope of conspiracy. In other words, although conspirators may plan to participate in one crime, they may end up being indicted for a number of felonies.

Curiously, although conspiracy is a well-entrenched concept in "Western" law, it is not an offense in Islamic law. Islamic law—the *sharia*—does not punish the planning of a crime, but only the crime itself. In Islam, the *intention* to commit a crime is not a crime.

CONSPIRACY OF ONE

The perfect crime should involve one person only. With more than one, secrecy may be compromised.

Note that even the Sicilian Mafia—with the code of *omerta*—the ring of silence has been broken. And even the twelve apostles had one informant, the man named Judas.

In *Philosophy in the Bedroom*, the Marquis de Sade issued this warning: "Never let your secret go out of your mouth, my dear, and always act alone: nothing is more dangerous than an accomplice: let us always beware of even those whom we think most closely attached to us."

"One must," wrote Niccolo Machiavelli, "either have no confederates, or dispatch them as soon as one had made use of them."

CONSPIRACY THEORY

In standard history–the orthodox version of history narrated by established historians– the fabled "Humpty Dumpty had a great fall." In conspiracy theory–the version of history narrated by unconventional writers– "Humpty Dumpty was pushed."

In a classic article, journalist Charles Paul Freund (*Washington Post*) summarized the world view of the conspiratorial mind:

> *Let us say that everything you know is not only wrong—it is a carefully wrought lie. Let us say that your mind is filled with falsehoods—about yourself, about history, about the world around you—planted there by powerful forces so as to lull you into complacency. Your freedom is thus an illusion. You are in fact a pawn in a plot, and your role is that of a compliant dupe—if you are lucky. If and when it serves the interests of others, your role will change: Your life will be disrupted, you could go penniless and hungry; you might have to die.*
>
> *Nor is there anything you can do about this. Oh, if you happen to get a whiff of the truth you can try to warn people, to undermine the plotters by exposing them. But in fact you are up against too much. They are too powerful, too far-flung, too invisible, too clever. Like others before you, you will fail.*

CONSPIRATORS

According to Giuseppe Mazzini, "There is no more sacred thing in the world than the duty of a conspirator who becomes an avenger of humanity and the apostle of permanent natural laws."

According to Serge Moscovici, "Other centuries have only dabbled in conspiracy like amateurs. It is our century which has established conspiracy as a system of thought and a method of action."

CONSPIRATORS, RECRUITING OF

On the subject of recruiting conspirators for a criminal enterprise such as murder, Niccolo Machiavelli said that men should be recruited who have committed the crime in the past. Without experience, he argued, a man is unreliable. Thus, killing should be done by people who have already killed:

> *For it is impossible for any man, even though he be strong-minded, and used to the sight of death and to the handling of deadly weapons, not to be perturbed at such a moment. Hence men should be chosen who have had experience in such deeds, and one should entrust them to no one else, brave as he may be*

thought to be. For when it comes to doing big things of which a man has no previous experience, no one can say for certain what will happen.

CONSTITUTION OF THE UNITED STATES OF AMERICA

The Constitution of the United States of America is the oldest functioning constitution on Earth. Its admirers maintain it is the most perfect legal document ever devised.

Indeed, patriotic Americans view the Constitution as a sacred text. Lawyers and judges–like Talmudic scholars pouring over "Holy Writ" – now argue over the framer's real meanings. The "founding fathers" are treated as apostles or prophets.

Detractors, however, are less enthusiastic. They note that Patrick Henry, the revolutionary-era leader, said of the Constitution: "I look upon that paper as the most fatal plan that could possibly be conceived to enslave a free people."

Detractors also note that the "founding fathers" were in reality a group of slaveholders, slave traders, successful speculators, and smugglers. A typical member of this group–men who dressed in satin pants, powdered wigs, and makeup–was Benjamin Franklin. Franklin, who owned slaves for thirty years, arrived every morning at the Constitutional Convention in a sedan chair carried by "convicts."

Detractors also note that the Constitution was the product of a "conspiracy." All sessions of the Constitutional Convention were secret and few Americans knew what happened or what was said until 1840.

Also, no special elections were held to select the delegates to the Convention. The delegates were simply appointed by state legislatures.

After the Constitution had been written, Rhode Island–unlike all other states–submitted the document directly to the people for a vote. More than 90 percent of the voters rejected it.

Whatever its merits, America's Constitution, like the Bible, is often misread. Note the following points of clarification:

1. The Constitution establishes a republic, not a democracy. The word "democracy," which actually means "rule by the poor," does not appear in the text. The Constitution provided for senators to be elected by state legislatures (that was changed by the Seventeenth Amendment), a president to be elected by electors chosen by state legislatures, and an unelected Supreme Court.

2. There is no RIGHT to vote in America. (A right, such as trial by jury, is something that cannot, hypothetically speaking, be taken away.) In the U.S.A., people in prison are usually not allowed to vote.

3. Slavery is still "constitutional" in the United States. Contrary to popular belief, the Thirteenth Amendment did not abolish *all* slavery—only slavery imposed without *due process*. According to the Thirteenth Amendment, "Neither slavery nor involuntary servitude, *except as punishment for crime whereof the party shall have been duly convicted*, shall exist within the United States."

   Presently, individuals serving life sentences in prison (by the start of the twenty-first century, 120,000 Americans were serving life sentences) are enduring a legal form of slavery. Like the helots of ancient Sparta, they may not be bought or sold, but they have no control over their own bodies, they have no claim to the fruits of their labor, and their utterances and their writings are restricted.

4. Judicial Review—the power of the courts to declare an act of Congress unconstitutional—is not found in the Constitution. The power was first usurped by the Supreme Court in 1803, in the decision *Marbury versus Madison*. The privilege is still claimed.

Oddly, in its present form, the Supreme Court—composed of nine black-robed individuals who serve life terms—is the real sovereign in the United States. Not only do they decree what the Constitution means, the Supreme Court decided the presidential election in A.D. 2000!

Does the Supreme Court use its awesome power wisely? In the mid-1850's the Supreme Court ruled that slaves are not human, in the late nineteenth century the court ruled that segregation is constitutional, in the mid-twentieth century the court ruled that concentration camps are constitutional, and in the 1970's the court ruled that killing unborn humans is a constitutional right.

CONTINGENCY PLAN

Always have contingency plans in case things go wrong.

Eammon De Valera, a leader of the 1916 Easter Rebellion in Dublin, avoided execution by the British only because De Valera held a U.S.A. passport. De Valera, a native-born Irishman, would ultimately become the president of a free Ireland.

Today, prudent American women make a journey to Canada to give birth. If America ever has a horrible war or a horrible dictator, her child can claim Canadian citizenship.

CONTRABAND

Contraband is material that is illegal to possess, sell, or transport. In the twenty-first century, contraband includes narcotic drugs, counterfeit money, and certain types of pornography. In previous eras, contraband included heretical texts, radical political tracts, and information on birth control.

In America the law prohibits the selling or promoting of contraband. Selling means exchanging the contraband for money. Promoting means giving or lending the contraband.

CONTRACT AGENTS

For especially illegal or immoral activities, states do not use the agents on their payrolls. Instead they hire mercenaries—skilled killers or burglars or forgers—who are euphemistically called "contract agents" or "stringers."

If the "contract agent" is killed, compromised, or captured, the state can deny all connection with him. This provides so-called "plausible deniability."

The oddest "contract agents" are official operatives who are "fired" or "retired" and are then hired as private "contract agents."

The most dangerous contract agents are "hired killers." Traditionally, to commit its murders the Soviet K.G.B. recruited assassins who believed in a cause. The American C.I.A., in contrast, traditionally recruited "obedient psychopaths" who killed for money and excitement.

One C.I.A. "asset" was Moses Maschkivitzan. Born of Jewish parents in Antwerp in 1910, Maschkivitzan was a stateless person with an extensive criminal record. He was paid an annual salary plus a larger amount for each murder. The latter was euphemistically referred to as "operational expenses."

It should be noted that any criminal working for a group like the C.I.A. would be virtually immune from prosecution if he committed other crimes.

CONVERSION

Conversion involves denouncing what was once adored. In some Muslim countries, conversion from Islam to another religion is a capital crime.

According to Eric Hoffer, the most fanatical believers make the most fanatical converts. Thus, if a communist fanatic becomes disillusioned with Marxism, he will probably become a fascist.

CORDAY, CHARLOTTE (1768-1793)

Charlotte Corday d'Armont, the pious daughter of a Norman nobleman, assassinated Jean Paul Marat, the French Revolutionary leader, on July 13, 1793. She confided to a friend that some higher being had ordered her to rid the world of the Anti-Christ.

A novice nun, Corday was planning to take her vows when the French Revolution closed the nunneries. Outraged by the assaults on her religion– and inspired by the example of Judith, the biblical assassin who saved the Jews by cutting off the head an Assyrian general—Corday concealed a six-inch butcher knife and a note to the French people in her white summer dress.

Walking two hundred miles to Paris, she gained an audience with Marat by claiming that she had evidence of a plot. As she drew near–allegedly to whisper the names of "traitors" in his ear–she plunged her weapon into his body, severing the aorta and penetrating a lung.

Humiliated at the "mockery" that was her trial, the mob ripped open her dress, exposing her breasts. In an attempt to discredit her, Revolutionaries examined her groin for evidence of sexual activity, but physicians discovered the twenty-five-year-old Corday was anatomically a virgin.

An icon of purity, Corday was executed on July 17, 1793. A fiercely chaste young woman, it was said that she faced death with "Roman firmness."

CORPORATIONS

The corporate charter, a grant of privileges extended by a state to a group of investors to serve a specific purpose, dates back at least to the sixteenth century.

One early corporation was the Dutch East India Company. By 1670 the Dutch East India Company was the richest company the world had ever seen, with fifty thousand employees and a fleet of two hundred ocean-going vessels.

Corporations have always been significant in American history. Not only were some American colonies settled by corporations, but in 1886 the United States Supreme Court ruled—in Santa Clara County vs. Southern Pacific Railroad—that a private corporation is a natural person under the

Constitution and is entitled to all the protections of the Bill of Rights! (In reality, of course, the Constitution does not mention corporations.)

According to Thomas Hartmann, a critical observer, "Corporations are non-living, non-breathing legal fictions. They feel no pain. They do not need clean water to drink, fresh air to breath, or healthful food to consume. They can live forever. They cannot be put in prison. They can change their identity or appearance in a day, change their citizenship in an hour, rip off parts of themselves and create entirely new entities. Some have compared corporations with robots, in that they are human creations that can outlive individual humans performing their assigned tasks forever."

Curiously, although "libertarians" proclaim that central economic planning does not work, successful corporations maintain more control over their product networks than the central planners of Moscow ever achieved over the Soviet economy. Central management buys, sells, dismantles, or closes component units as it chooses.

CORPSE, ABUSE OF

The abuse of the dead is common in history.

Sometimes the mutilation is simply an act of sadistic pleasure. Andrew Jackson, the American president, made this statement: "I have on all occasions preserved the scalps of my killed."

Usually, however, the abuse is designed to convey a message.

During the Protestant Reformation, for example, Swiss Roman Catholics quartered the dead body of Huldrych Zwingli, a Protestant leader, and burned it on a pyre of feces.

In 1824, after a British force led by Sir Charles Macarthy was defeated by ten thousand Asante warriors, the Asante chief had Macarthy's skull fashioned into a drinking cup. The skull was sawn off just below the eyebrow.

In 1828, after William Corder was hanged in England for the crime of murdering his pregnant girlfriend, the "authorities" removed his skin, tanned it like cowhide, and used it to bind a book telling the story of his crime. The book, *The Trial and Memoirs of William Corder*, can still be seen in Bury St. Edmund's Museum.

In 1891, in Rawlins, Wyoming, Dr. John E. Osborne, a future governor of Wyoming, participated in the lynching of George Parrott. Osborne skinned Parrott and made a medical bag, razor straps, and a pair of lady's shoes. Osborne also fashioned a tobacco pouch from Parrott's scrotum.

During World War II, Ilsa Koch, the wife of the commandant of Buchenwald concentration camp, made a lampshade from human skin.

And during the "Cold War," when Imre Nagy, the Hungarian leader, was executed by Soviet interests, his remains were buried in an unmarked grave with the corpses of zoo animals.

CORPUS DELECTI

Legally, no case can be tried without the "*corpus delicti*" or the "body of evidence." Of course, an actual human body is not needed.

Edward Ball was convicted in Ireland in 1936 of matricide, even though his mother's body was never located.

The evidence against Ball–the *corpus delicti* –included a bloodstained hatchet, some bloodstained clothing, and a bloodstained carpet.

In a curious case in Australia, the police recovered a human arm. A debate followed, but the court finally ruled that finding an arm does not prove a murder occurred because a person can live without an arm.

COSA NOSTRA

The *Cosa Nostra*, which means "This Thing of Ours," is the American branch of the Mafia.

Described in 1963 by an informant named Joseph Valachi, the *Cosa Nostra* is heavily involved in gambling and labor unions.

The Mafia has never prospered under dictatorships—the "mob" was suppressed by Mussolini and ousted from Cuba by Castro—but it thrives in the relative freedom of America.

The Mafia knows that the best climate for extortion is "capitalism," while the weakest system of law is under "democracy."

Like its parent—the Sicilian Mafia—the *Cosa Nostra* adheres to certain values, including contempt for so-called "constituted authority" (the politicians and the police), the need for the individual to protect himself and his family at all costs, a sense of honor and pride, an absolute solidarity toward supporters and friends, and gratitude toward anyone who has helped the "family."

COSSACKS

Cossacks (or Kazaks) were outlaws, adventurers, and guerrillas. They arose in the fifteenth century in response to Poland's domination of the Ukraine.

The name "Cossack" means "freeman," "nomad," or "adventurer." Most Cossacks were fugitives from servitude. Instead of bondage in Poland,

Lithuania, and Russia, they preferred to take their chances on the lawless areas of the steppe.

The Cossacks were fiercely egalitarian—lordless and propertyless—and they lived in freedom in free-ranging warrior bands.

Among the Cossacks, matters of general policy were discussed and voted on by the "host." Even the lowest Cossack had the right to speak and to vote.

The Cossack leader was called a *hetman* or headman. After his election, the Cossacks always pelted the new *hetman* with mud. This demonstrated that he was the servant of the host.

COSTA RICA

A beautiful land, Costa Rica is the only country in the area not invaded by the U.S.A.

It has no army (the military was disbanded in 1948) and only a small police force.

Costa Rica has no extradition treaty with the United States, and the country is a sanctuary of choice for American fugitives.

COUNTERFEITING

In the nineteenth century, at one time over one-third of the U.S.A. notes in circulation were fakes.

Perhaps the most skillful counterfeiter was the notorious "Jim the Penman." A master artist, he made top-grade notes by drawing them with a fine camel's hair brush.

COUNTERFEITING, ORGANIZED CRIME AND

Organized crime was once heavily involved in counterfeiting. Exploiting the fact that all American currency is the same size, the Mafia bleached one-dollar bills and printed hundred-dollar bills on the distinctive "cotton and linen"paper that the U.S.A. treasury uses.

Today, however, counterfeiting is considered a crime for amateurs. The mob knows that counterfeiting is not worth the risk. It is easier to forge and pass a thousand-dollar check than to counterfeit and pass ten hundred-dollar bills. Also, in the U.S.A. check forgery is a state crime and counterfeiting is a federal offense.

COUP D'ETAT

A coup d'etat, which is also called a *putsch*, is a political action by a small group using force of arms. On November 9, 1799, using reliable troops, Napoleon Bonaparte incapacitated France's political elite and staged the first modern coup d'etat.

To succeed, the coup plotters must conduct a surreptitious seizure of the nerve centers of the state. The coup operatives target key institutions, such as the presidential palace, the opposition party leaders, the headquarters of major labor unions, radio and television stations, newspaper offices, airports and crucial transportation links, and so forth.

To neutralize the population, the coup is carried out under false slogans. Usual promises include stopping corruption, restoring the Constitution, ending dictatorship, and so forth.

The classic elements in any coup are deception, surgically employed force, and sham legality.

Classic how-to manuals on the subject include *Technique du Coup d'etat* by Curzio Malaparte (1931) and *Coup d'etat: A Practical Handbook* by Edward Luttwak (1969).

COUP D'ETAT (EXAMPLES OF)

In the first fifty years of independence, Africa had eighty successful coups. Twenty-four African leaders were killed during the operations.

Bolivia, since its independence from Spain, has had more than two hundred coups.

In the United States, during the Great Depression, some plutocrats plotted to oust Franklin Delano Roosevelt and replace him with Marine Major General Smedley D. Butler, the winner of *two* "Medals of Honor." The plot failed because Butler exposed the conspiracy to Congress.

COUP D'ETAT (FAUX)

As defined by Ken Conor, a "faux coup d'etat" is a fake coup staged by an incumbent government to discredit the legitimate opposition. A faux coup may involve violence–including murder.

The faux coup will last only as long as it will take to arrest opposition politicians and their supporters and to plant incriminating "evidence" in their homes and offices.

Teodoro Obiang Nguema Mbasogo, a "president" of Equatorial Guinea, used the faux coup against his enemies on several occasions.

COURAGE

Courage has been defined as "strength in the face of pain or grief."

According to proverbial wisdom, courage is something a person can never totally own and never totally lose.

COVER, EFFECTIVE TYPES OF

A cover is a deception. A type of disguise, a cover conceals identity and function.

As a cover, an Islamic extremist in Al Qeda carries Christian paraphernalia, takes an unbeliever as a wife, never becomes involved in advocating good or denouncing evil, and never breaks any rules, including traffic laws.

To disguise an organization, operatives name it so that it appears to be doing the opposite of its real purpose. According to one conspiracy theorist, if the operatives are selling illegal drugs, they do it through an anti-drug agency. If they are running a Satanic ring, they do it through a Christian church.

COVER-UP

A cover-up is an attempt to camouflage the truth. Essential elements in a cover-up include brazen lying, discrediting witnesses, destroying evidence, and dreaming up a plausible cover story. The cover-up is especially effective if the people behind it control the information media.

CRIME

"Criminality," like "madness," in some respects does not exist. It is socially defined.

In ancient Sparta, citizens could be whipped for being too fat. In medieval Europe, putting semen "in the mouth" was condemned as the "worst evil." In the "Spice Islands" (now Malaysia and Indonesia), the Dutch colonial masters imposed the death penalty for anyone found growing, buying, stealing, or possessing (without authorization) nutmeg, cinnamon, or cloves. In Singapore today, importing or distributing chewing gum is a crime punishable by a fine or up to one year in prison.

In Marxist thought, the most serious crimes are the crimes of the powerful. In the law codes of capitalist societies, however, these are scarcely recognized. Serious crimes in the Marxist mind include exploitation of labor, destruction of the Earth for profit, defrauding consumers, "price gouging," "price fixing," malfeasance in public office, violating civil rights, and so forth.

In the Bible, Jacob (later called Israel) deceived his father, cheated his uncle, and robbed his brother, but he was blessed by Jehovah.

Whatever crime is, it is a significant force. According to Count Hermann Keyserling, "No radical change in the place of history is possible without crime."

And, according to Friedrich Nietzsche, "All progress is the result of successful crimes."

CRIME (CAUSE OF)

According to the Hindus, sin exists because man is made with hunger. Crime happens, according to the Hindus, because of a "design flaw."

And—indeed—by design man has to nourish himself by slaughtering other species. What if, like plants, he could nourish himself by purely chemical changes with his environment? If man lived by photosynthesis—instead of destruction and devouring—perhaps there would be no crime.

CRIME (CESAR LOMBROSO ON)

Cesar Lombroso, the founder of modern criminology, developed the theory of the "born criminal," popularly known as the "bad seed."

Lombroso argued that most criminality resulted from an inborn atavism in certain individuals which caused them to revert to an earlier phase of evolution. The criminal, Lombroso believed, is a throwback to our caveman forbears.

The Nazis used Lombroso's theory to stigmatize certain individuals as "hereditary criminals" and "degenerates."

CRIME, FUNCTION OF

The sociologist Emile Durkheim argued that crime is as normal as birth or death. Crime he claimed, actually benefited society, just as the challenge of survival benefited a species.

Durkheim thought that a crime-free society was probably impossible. And—since a crime-free society was too standardized—he thought that it was certainly undesirable.

CRIME (IMAGINARY)

An imaginary crime is an action stigmatized as illegal even though it is not unethical.

Imaginary crimes include smuggling (only governments view it as a crime), money laundering (here the mere act of spending or investing money from a crime becomes a *second* crime), and blackmail.

Regarding blackmail, it was first outlawed in Britain at the end of the nineteenth century. Since no one blackmails a poor person, the laws against blackmail are designed to protect the wealthy.

CRIME, PARABLE ON

Consider this riddle: two men meet to play a game. One has all kinds of advantages (in society, this is the rich man), and one has all kinds of disadvantages (in society, this is the poor man).

Should the latter follow the rules of the game and lose? (In real life, this is the honest poor man.) Or, should he break the rules and possibly win? (In real life, this is the criminal.)

In every organized society, the riddle in the parable applies.

CRIME (PERFECT)

When everyone is guilty, the crime is a perfect crime.

Colonel Daniel Parke, appointed a British colonial governor in 1706, normally resided in Antigua. Parke was greedy and possibly demented. He was hated by the settlers.

Outraged by Parke's behavior, armed Antiguans surrounded the governor's house and demanded that he leave the island. In the tumult which followed, the planters killed Parke, and they killed or wounded most of the seventy soldiers guarding him.

No one was ever punished for the rebellion or the murders. When the British crown investigated the crime, no Antiguan would testify, and the new governor could not punish the entire colony.

CRIMES, UNSOLVED

Many crimes remain unsolved.

In 1930, for example, someone murdered Judge Joseph Crater of New York, who had many enemies. Although federal and state investigators conducted a massive investigation, the body was never discovered and the case was never solved.

In 1973, someone stole 398 pounds of heroin and cocaine (with a street value of more than seventy-three million dollars) from the heavily guarded warehouse of the New York police. This case also remains unsolved.

CROSSBOW

Noiseless, powerful, and accurate, the ultimate pre-industrial weapon is the crossbow.

The steel crossbow—its shaft tipped with poisonous white hellebore—was a favorite Renaissance weapon.

Modern tests indicate that steel crossbows have a range of 460 yards. At 60 yards the bolt will penetrate three-fourths of an inch of plank.

Although the conventional longbow requires years of practice, the crossbow is learned quickly.

CROWD, BEHAVIOR OF

Gustav Le Bon, the French sociologist who influenced both Mussolini and Hitler, wrote that "Crowds are everywhere distinguished by feminine characteristics."

According to Le Bon, "Crowds exhibit a docile respect for force, and are but slightly impressed by kindness, which for them is scarcely more than a form of weakness. Their sympathies have never been bestowed on easy-going masters, but on tyrants who vigorously oppress them. It is to these latter that they always erect their greatest statues. It is true that they willingly trample on the despot whom they have stripped of his power, but this is because, having lost his strength, he has resumed his place among the weak, who are to be despised and not feared."

According to military studies, group behavior tends to less retrained than individual behavior. Predictably, atrocities are rarely committed by unobserved individuals.

CROWLEY, ALEISTER (1875-1947)

An author, occultist, mountain climber, drug user, and satyr, Aleister Crowley has been called the "Avatar" of the Anti-Christ.

Crowley taught that the era of the tyrant gods—the gods who demand abjection and obedience—had come to an end. The new era, he declared, was in the power of the "Lord of Freedom."

Crowley declared, in a private letter, "I want blasphemy, murder, rape, revolution, anything, bad or good, but strong."

A rebel by nature, Crowley made this declaration: "The dead dog floats with the stream; in puritan France the best women are harlots; in vicious England the best women are virgins."

CUI BONO

Cui Bono is Italian for "who benefits." According to the reasoning of conspiracy theorists, the French revolution enfranchised the Jews, so Jews caused it. The "Russian *Mafiya*" gained the most from the dismantling of the Soviet Union, so organized crime was behind Boris Yeltsin and his anti-Soviet machinations.

CYNICS

The Cynics, an ancient Greek philosophical movement, have been called the first anarchists.

The Cynics thought that men should strive for complete autonomy, for autarky (*autarkeia*). Virtue, they believed, is the highest good–and glory and wealth should be shunned.

The Cynics believed that imitating the beasts is the shortest way to godliness. Diogenes, the most celebrated Cynic, actually defecated and masturbated in public.

D'ANNUNZIO, GABRIELE (1863-1938)

Gabriele D'Annunzio—who viewed himself as a poet and a warrior—part Dante and part Caesar—was a writer and a "man of action."

D'Annunzio was a decadent, a poet, a novelist, a dramatist, an artist, a musician, an aesthete, a womanizer, a genius, and a cad.

An eccentric, the one-eyed D'Annunzio served guests wine from the skull of a virgin he had allegedly driven to suicide.

When he was in his fifties, D'Annunzio involved himself in World War I and participated in torpedo-boat raids on the Austrians. He also flew a biplane over the Alps to drop propaganda leaflets.

After the war, D'Annunzio decided to capture the city of Fiume and give it to Italy. After a necromantic ceremony with his mistress in Venice, on September 12, 1919 D'Annunzio seized Fiume with one thousand legionnaires.

During the fifteen months that he held Fiume, artists, Bohemians, adventurers, and anarchists flocked to the city, and D'Annunzio's gave his followers the main attributes that would later characterize fascism, such as the straight-arm salute, the black-shirted men with daggers, the harangues from the balcony, the rituals and the songs, and the humiliation of opponents by forcing them to drink castor oil.

DAVYDOV, DENIS (1784-1839)

A freedom fighter and a poet, Denis Davydov was one of Russia's leading partisans during the French 1812 invasion of Russia. He became a national hero.

Davydov wrote the "Essay on the Theory of Partisan Warfare." He emphasized the need for surprise, mobility, and flexibility. Partisans, he said, should never take part in set battles. They should have no fixed bases.

According to Davydov, partisans are best employed in attacks against the enemy's supply lines and lines of communication. They should capture couriers for information.

Davydov's partisan creed was "*ubit-da-vit*": "Kill and escape."

DEATH

A meaningful death is important. As one cynic pointed out, who would remember Jesus if had died of old age or food poisoning?

History is filled with creative deaths, including Cleopatra, who killed herself with two small, poisonous snakes, and Count Jan Potocki, a wealthy Polish aristocrat, adventurer, linguist, and writer, who committed suicide with a silver bullet.

A mysterious end can also be effective. Romulus, the founder of Rome, allegedly disappeared during a thunderstorm.

And Ambrose Bierce, an America author, disappeared in 1913 when he went to Mexico, presumably to report on the civil war there. According to one observer, "this sensational disappearance has done as much to keep his name alive as his writing ever did."

DEATH, CONQUEST OF

It is possible, according to many traditions, to be stronger than death.

If you want to maintain your present personality, during death you must keep your presence of mind. The technique is detailed in the Tibetan *Book of the Dead* and in the Egyptian *Book of the Dead*.

DEATH, ENCOUNTERS WITH

Although humans can be strangely resilient creatures—on January 26, 1972, a Yugoslav DC-9 exploded, and a twenty-three-year-old stewardess named Vesna Vulovic fell 33,000 feet in the tail section and survived —death may come in innumerable forms.

On August 13, 1984, for example, John Edward Blue—a thirty-eight-year-old Massachusetts man—drowned during his baptism.

And there is at least one reported death from transporting "dry ice" (frozen carbon dioxide) in an enclosed car.

Carbon dioxide is nontoxic at low levels (exhaled breath is 4-5 percent carbon dioxide), but at concentrations of 30 percent or more it can be lethal. It causes unconsciousness in one or two minutes—and death in five minutes—without much evidence of stress.

When the "dry ice" melted in the closed automobile, the driver quietly passed out and died..

DEATH, ERIC HOFFER ON

According to Eric Hoffer, "Dying and killing seem easy when they are part of a ritual, ceremonial, dramatic performance, or a game."

DEATH, HORRIFIC EFFECTS OF

Decay begins at time of death and proceeds outward from the intestines and other centers of bacteria in body.

Decay proceeds rapidly at temperatures of 50-80 degrees Fahrenheit, but it slows or stops at roughly freezing temperatures.

Generally speaking, the drier the conditions, the slower the decay.

Also, when there is no oxygen, as when a body is underwater, decay will hardly proceed at all.

Sand and peat bogs can preserve a body for centuries, but a body buried in light soil, close to the surface in a hot area like Florida, can be a skeleton in two months.

DEATH, PROPER TIME OF

Because of the uniformity which prevails in all that has been and all that will be, a man who is forty years old has experienced the gamut of human experience, including love, hate, beauty, ugliness, and fear, and is deprived of nothing by death. Marcus Aurelius, the Roman emperor and philosopher, said that.

DEBS, EUGENE (1855-1926)

A non-violent rebel, Eugene Debs was a candidate for the office of president of the United States six times. As the Socialist Party candidate he received 6 percent of the popular vote in 1912.

Debs opposed the entry of the United States into World War I. For his stand, Debs was sentenced to ten years in prison and had his citizenship revoked.

He ran for the presidency from the Atlanta Penitentiary in 1920. Although behind bars, Debs received 3.5 percent of the vote.

His sentence was commuted by Warren Harding, but he was disenfranchised for life.

DECEPTION

To deceive is to deliberately mislead another into believing something false.

According to master theorist Sun Tzu, "All warfare is based on deception."

According to Niccolo Machiavelli, "Although in all other affairs it is hateful to use fraud, in the operations of war it is praiseworthy and glorious."

According to Francesco Guicciardini, "deception is very useful, whereas your frankness tends to profit others rather than you."

DECEPTION, FUNCTION OF

Deception aims at leading the enemy into a predictable course of action or inaction which can be exploited.

Note that it is not useful to simply feed the enemy deliberately confusing information—or to keep the enemy ignorant of all information.

An enemy with ambiguous information or no information at all is likely to react in an unpredictable manner which you may be unable to exploit.

DECEPTION (SELF-DECEPTION)

Self-deception is common.

Aristotle said that those who commonly deceive themselves are easily deceived by others.

DECEPTION, SUN TZU ON

According to Sun Tzu, "All warfare is based on deception. Therefore, when capable, feign incapacity; when active, inactivity. When near, make it appear that you are far away; when far away, that you are near. Offer the enemy a bait to lure him; feign disorder and strike him. When he concentrates, prepare against him; where he is strong, avoid him. Anger his general and confuse him. Pretend inferiority and encourage his arrogance. Keep him under a strain and wear him down. When he is united, divide him. Attack where he is unprepared; sally out when he does not expect you."

DECEPTION, TECHNIQUES OF

There are several classic techniques of deception:

1. *The Lure.* Give the enemy what he thinks is a sudden opportunity. In reality, the apparent "opportunity" is actually a trap.

   In Indochina, the French dropped sacks of rice. They then bombed the Vietnamese guerrillas who tried to collect the rice.

2. *The Classic Lie.* On June 3, 1967, the Israeli minister of defense said that Israel would not strike her enemies first. On June 5, 1967, Israel attacked first.

3. *The Double Bluff.* In the "double bluff," reveal the truth to the enemy— and gamble that he will not believe it. The "double bluff" is effective against an enemy who *expects* deception. This technique is dangerous, so it is used mainly in poker.

4. *The Unintentional Mistake.* Convince the enemy that valuable information has come into his hands through a security problem or negligence. In World War II, the allies planted false invasion plans on a corpse in an incident referred to as "the man who never was."

5. *The Technique of Acclimatization by Slow Change.* This technique is based on the fact that evolutionary change is less noticeable than revolutionary change. It is well known that a toad dropped into boiling water will jump out. A toad placed in room-temperature water will stay in the water until death, however, if the temperature is SLOWLY raised. It is interesting that when the U.S.A. introduced the modern income tax in 1914, the annual income tax per capita was twenty-eight cents! Rates have been raised slowly—without incident—ever since.

6. *Fabricate a Pattern, albeit a Bogus One.* In this deception, repeat something to lull an opponent into a false sense of security. Before the cross-Suez attack in 1973, the Egyptian army had "war gamed" the assault over forty times before the eyes of the Israelis. Usually, however, only two feints are necessary. Typically, the enemy will react to the first feint, and often to the second as well, but he will hesitate to react to a third. Make the third effort the actual attack

DEFEAT

Between June and December 1941, two-thirds of the U.S.S.R.'s pre-war military strength was destroyed by Adolf Hitler's forces. In that period, the U.S.S.R. lost four million soldiers (including two million prisoners-of-war), fourteen thousand aircraft, twenty thousand guns, and seventeen thousand tanks.

But, on December 6, 1941, the U.S.S.R. counter-attacked. Ultimately, the U.S.S.R. won the war.

Curiously, when Russia was devastated in World War I, its government collapsed. When Russia was devastated even more catastrophically in World War II (in 1941-1945 the U.S.S.R. lost more people and more territory than the losses that brought down the tsar), the Russian state triumphed.

Clearly, defeat is a state of mind. In war, defeat depends on people accepting the political mythology of defeat.

DEMOCRACY

Democracy, a word which is perverted today, actually means rule by the "common" or "poor" people. Most states which claim to be democracies are actually oligarchies ruled by a small and rich elite.

Real democracies are possible, but only in restricted circumstances.

First, the democracy must be small. In Plato's *Republic*, the philosopher limited the number of citizens to 5,040, the largest number that one orator could address. As Lewis Mumford pointed out, the Greeks did not trust power to anyone out of their sight.

Second, all elections must be by lottery so that all citizens have an equal chance to hold office. This was the practice in ancient Athens.

Third, the citizens must be economically independent. In ancient Greece—a fiercely proud society—no citizen would demean himself by being the employee of another citizen.

DEMOCRACY (ANCIENT ATHENS)

Herodotus, the classical Greek historian, described Athenian democracy with these words: "All offices are assigned by lot, all officials are subject to investigation, and all policies are debated in public." (Note there were no "official secrets" in the first democracy.)

And, added Herodotus, Athenian democracy had "equality before the law" for all citizens.

DEMOCRACY, DEATH OF

According to Alexander Fraser Tyler, a British contemporary of George Washington, "A democracy cannot exist as a permanent form of government. It can exist only until the voters discover they can vote themselves largesse (defined as a liberal gift) out of the public treasury. From that moment on, the majority always votes for the candidate promising the most benefits from the public treasury, with the result that democracy always collapses over loose fiscal policy, always to be followed by a dictatorship."

According to John Adams, a former American president, "Remember, democracy never lasts long. It soon wastes, exhausts, and murders itself. There never was a democracy yet that did not commit suicide."

DEMOCRACY, MINORITIES AND

Minorities are impotent in real democracies. By the nature of things, when a minority votes it is automatically outvoted.

To secure change in a democracy, a minority must use persuasion or violence.

The United States, where the rich rule, is actually an oligarchy *disguised* as a quasi-democracy.

DEMOCRACY, WAR AND

General George C. Marshall said that a democracy cannot fight a seven-year war. This suggests that a democracy that attempts to do so runs the risk of ceasing to be one.

Aleksandr Solzhenitsyn, the Russian novelist, noted that "in the twentieth century Western democracy has not won any major war by itself." In World War II, for example, the Western democracies needed the assistance of the totalitarian state of Joseph Stalin.

DENIABILITY, PLAUSIBLE

When states conduct clandestine or covert actions (the so-called "black operations"), they want to keep their involvement secret at all costs. To accomplish this goal, they camouflage the operation with "believable lies." The lies—a form of disinformation—provide "plausible deniability."

According to William Guy Carr, the author of *Pawns in the Game*, "the more we study the methods employed by the Secret Powers behind international affairs, the more obvious it is to see that they make private assassinations look like accidents or suicides," and they make "sabotage look like carelessness, errors of judgment, and unintentional blunders committed due to excusable circumstances."

DEPRAVITY

To be depraved is to be corrupt.

According to Friedrich Nietzsche, "I call an animal, a species, and an individual depraved when it loses its instincts, when it chooses, when it prefers what is harmful to it."

Interestingly, as Juvenal noted, no person becomes depraved instantly. Corruption is a process—a gradual process.

DE SADE, MARQUIS (1740-1814)

A literary rebel and a Byronic hero, the author of *Justine, Juliette, Philosophy in the Bedroom, 120 Days of Sodom,* and other infamous works, the Marquis de Sade believed that "the most perfect being is the one whose activity causes the most change."

Although the Marquis de Sade dedicated his imagination to life, liberty, and the pursuit of beauty, he spent twenty-seven of his seventy-four years in prisons and asylums. Enduring loathsome conditions—rats and mice scurried over him when he tried to sleep—de Sade nevertheless managed to write his works, including one (*The 120 Days of Sodom*) on a single roll of paper twelve meters long.

According to de Sade, "'Tis false as well to say there is pleasure in affording pleasure to others; that is to serve them."

DESERT

The desert is a place of sterile wastes and noxious animals. There are more than fifty deserts in the world, including the Sahara in Africa (three million square miles) and the Mojave in North America (fifteen thousand square miles).

The "Empty Quarter," 250,000 square miles in size (one-fourth the area of Saudi Arabia), is the largest area of continuous sand in the world.

In the eyes of farmers, the desert is an obstacle. In the eyes of Bedouins, the desert is a highway. In the eyes of bandits, the desert is a sanctuary.

In Muslim tradition, Allah made the desert so that there will always be a place where a man can find freedom.

According to Aleister Crowley, the universe itself is a desert, and stars are thorns in the waste. "Now and again Travelers cross the desert; they come from the Great Sea, and to the Great Sea they go."

DESERTION

An imaginary crime, desertion is (according to the state) the act of "illegally" running away from military service.

Desertion was more widespread in the American Civil War than in any war in modern history. As the conflict drew to a close—in the spring of 1865—two-thirds of the men in the confederate army were "absent from the ranks." (Officially, 160,198 men were "present for duty" and 198,494 were "absent.")

The classic handbook for military deserters is *Sickness Saves You*. Written by J.T. McCurdy of Cambridge, under the pen name William Benefactor, M.D., the pamphlet gives the symptoms of difficult-to-diagnose maladies. The work describes symptoms that—when faked—will release the soldier from combat for one day, one week, or forever.

Written in German and dropped on German troops by the British, the guide was so good it was translated into English and dropped on English troops by the Germans.

Later, *Sickness Saves You* circulated as an underground classic for people interested in committing health-insurance fraud.

DESSALINES, JEAN-JACQUES (1758-1806)

A rebel *and* a tyrant, Jean-Jacques Dessalines was born a slave in the brutal French colony of Saint-Domingue. Ultimately the emperor of Haiti, he is now worshiped as a god (or *loa*) in the Voodoo pantheon.

Dessalines is remembered for ordering the massacre of all the whites in Haiti. He made Haiti a black nation and prohibited whites from ever owning land there.

On October 17, 1806, Jean-Jacques Dessalines was ambushed and murdered by his own people. Shot, stabbed, stripped, and mutilated, by the time his body had been dragged to Port-au-Prince (a two-mile journey), his corpse had been hacked into shapeless scraps of flesh.

Although he is now worshiped, in his 1805 Constitution Dessalines prohibited the religion of Voodoo.

DESTRUCTION

To destroy is to completely ruin or spoil.

As Hannah Arendt pointed out, destruction is the only "labor" left that can be done by simple implements without the help of machines. Machines, however, destroy more efficiently.

DESTRUCTION, AS AN AESTHETIC ACT

One branch of art–that of sculpture–is based on the notion that the act of destruction is itself a creative act. The sculptor, with his tools, destroys a block of marble, but he produces something higher–a work of art.

Curiously, Karl Heinz Stockhausen, a German musical composer, said that the September 11, 2001 attack on the World Trade Towers was the greatest work of art of all time.

DEVIL

Devils are outlaw gods.

In the New Testament—in II Corinthians, 4:4—the devil is called "the god of this world" and "the god of this age."

The Fourth Lateran Council—a Christian ecclesiastical assembly which met in 1215—asserted that the devil does exist and Christians must believe in his existence.

According to the theologians, encounters with the devil are always frightening. To escape dying from horror at the sight—or to escape catalepsy or idiocy—one must be already mad.

In Dante's *Divine Comedy*, Lucifer is six-winged and 1,720 feet tall.

DEVIL'S ISLAND

An infamous penal colony, Devil's Island is eight miles north-east of French Guiana. One square mile in size, Devil's Island is infested with alligators and flesh-hungry red ants and is surrounded by shark-infested waters.

The first prisoners sent to Devil's Island—lepers who were convicts—arrived in 1852. Physically healthy prisoners were first sent in 1895.

Prisoners on the island were kept in a wooden stockade. They knew they would never return home to France.

Rene Belbenoit and some comrades hollowed out a tree trunk and escaped from Devil's Island on Mach 2, 1935. Afloat for two weeks, they made the 700-mile journey to Trinidad.

Devil's Island was closed in 1938.

DHANU (1970?-1991)

A suicide assassin, a member of the lethal Black Tigers of Sri Lanka, the young and beautiful Dhanu killed Rajiv Gandhi, a former prime minister of India.

Wearing a denim girdle packed with explosives and steel pellets, Dhanu placed a sandalwood garland on Gandhi's neck, knelt at his feet, looked up, smiled, and exploded, killing over a dozen people.

Dhanu's technique was apparently taken from *The Negotiator,* a novel by Frederick Forsyth.

DIARIES AND NOTEBOOKS

In modern law a person cannot be forced to testify against himself. If he writes his private thoughts in a diary or a notebook, however, his entries may be used against him by the courts.

Shrewdly, Niccolo Machiavelli issued this advice: "And against writing anything down everybody should be on his guard as against a rock, for nothing is more likely to convict you than your own handwriting."

During the Nazi era, people were afraid to keep diaries. The diary-keeping Anne Frank, a young Jewish girl in Nazi-occupied Holland, was not behaving prudently.

DICTATORSHIP

Dictatorship is the rule of the many by the one.

Executive Order number 11490—signed by Richard Nixon in October of 1969—allows the president of the United States to assume dictatorial powers after declaring a national emergency.

Although dictatorship is the most powerful form of government, in one respect it is the most vulnerable of all forms of government. When power is concentrated in the hands of one person, destroying him may cause a revolution.

DIETROLOGIA

Dietrologia is the Italian science of seeking the hidden motives behind an act.

DILLINGER, JOHN (1902-1934)

A celebrated robber, John Dillinger's real career in crime began in May 1933, when he was freed after enduring nine years in prison. His career ended in July 1934, when he was apparently gunned down by the Federal Bureau of Investigation. In that brief period he robbed banks, broke into police armories, escaped prison twice, and survived six gun battles.

According to Dillinger, "We only robbed from the banks what the banks robbed from the people."

Today, the F.B.I. headquarters displays the gun John Dillinger allegedly was carrying when he was killed in Chicago.

According to Jay Robert Nash, however, the gun's serial number indicates that it was delivered five months *after* Dillinger's death. In other words, Dillinger was probably unarmed when he was killed.

DISCARD

A "discard" is an agent betrayed by his own intelligence service to protect a more valuable source of information (an asset). The discard may experience torture, prison, execution—or all the above.

DISCORDIANISM

A bogus religion, Kerry Thornley (a friend of Lee Harvey Oswald) and Gregory Hill established Discordianism in 1958.

Discordianism worships Eris, the Greek goddess chaos and confusion. In effect, Discordianism teaches that god is a crazy woman.

The movement's "holy book," a little "bible" called *Principia Discordia*, has become an underground classic.

DISCREDITING SOURCES

If discrediting the facts is not possible, discredit the source. This trick is used in Bible.

The only eyewitnesses to the alleged Easter resurrection of the Christ, the men in the "watch" assigned by Pontius Pilate to guard the tomb of Jesus (Matthew 27: 62-66), publicly declared that the resurrection was faked. In the words of the guards: "His disciples came by night, and stole him away while we slept." (Matthew 28:13).

How does the Gospel of Matthew counter the testimony of the guards? The gospel simply asserts that the "chief priests"--who were the enemies of Jesus—"gave a large sum of money unto the soldiers" (Matthew 28:11-15).

According to the author of *The Unseen Hand*, "Never try to refute the accusations, but always destroy the accuser."

DISGUISE (TECHNIQUES OF)

Sarah Emma Edmonds, a Civil War spy, stained her head, face, hands, and feet black with silver nitrate. She was able to pass herself off as a slave to spy on the Confederacy.

In contrast, John Dillinger, the legendary bank robber, spent a fortune on plastic surgery. He had his cheeks and eyebrows changed, and he had his finger ends shaved off to alter his fingerprints. He was not pleased with results, however, because plastic surgery can alter appearance, but it cannot change an individual's look completely.

In general, the best techniques are simple:

1) Hollowed-out nostril inserts made of cork or plastic can change the shape of the nose. This was a trick used by Willie Sutton, the bank robber.

2) Dye your hair and change the length. Do not, however, use false beards or mustaches. They appear fake and attract attention.

3) Make your skin darker with commercial tanning lotions, or canthaxanthin, a coloring agent taken orally. Use makeup and creams designed for black women to darken your skin.

   Skin may be made lighter with bleach (a harsh method), peroxide (either medicinal peroxide or the stronger hair-bleach peroxide), or lemon juice (this produces a mild effect). Skin may also be lightened with makeup made for white women.

4) Wear spectacles. Never, however, wear mirrored sunglasses, since they attract attention.

5) With clothing, use drab colors. The clothing should have no wording or symbols, since witnesses remember such things.

   Michael Collins, the Irish Freedom Fighter, dressed in a gray suit, a collared shirt, and a necktie to avoid arrest. He knew that security services are not suspicious about well-dressed individuals.

6) Remember, you can never be too careful. During World War II, British spies in occupied Europe had local labels sewn into their clothing and had all traces of "British dentistry" removed from their mouths.

DISGUST

Disgust is a strong revulsion or profound indignation.

A type of learned behavior, disgust only appears in humans above the age of four.

DISINFORMATION

Disinformation, a kind of propaganda, involves the perversion of truth. The function of disinformation is to discredit or mislead the enemy.

Some noted examples of disinformation include:

1) During the *First* World War, Phyllis Campbell, a British nurse, wrote *Back to the Front*, a work of Allied disinformation that circulated widely. Describing German atrocities against women and children, Campbell claimed that she saw a young woman—with her breasts cut off—holding her dead baby. Campbell also described hearing accounts of Germans crucifying nuns, chopping the hands and feet off children, and burning people alive.

2) In 1941, *My Sister and I: The Diary of a Dutch Boy Refugee* by Dirk Van Der Heide, became a bestseller in the United States. The book details the "true" story of the escape of a twelve-year-old Dutch boy and his nine-year-old sister. In moving but simple prose, it tells of ruthless Germans and helpful British soldiers. The book, however, was a fake. Written by a middle-aged editor at Harcourt Brace named Stanley Preston Young, it was commissioned by British intelligence to help lure the United States into the war.

3) On April 26, 1987, during the Cold War, an article appeared in the *Moscow News*. In a clever effort to discredit the Americans, the article claimed that Acquired Immune Deficiency Syndrome, the disease known as AIDS, was created by scientists in Fort Detrick, Maryland.

DOCTRINE

A doctrine is a set of beliefs held by a religion, a political movement, or some other group.

According to Eric Hoffer, "If a doctrine is not unintelligible, it has to be vague; and if neither unintelligible nor vague, it has to be unverifiable."

DOCUMENTS, DESTRUCTION OF

To effectively destroy documents, place them in an electric blender with water. Modern shredding machines are not reliable, and shredded papers can be reassembled.

When the Iranians seized the American embassy in Tehran in 1979, the Iranians used carpet weavers to painstakingly reconstruct the documents shredded by the C.I.A..

DODSON, BETTY (born 1929)

A sexual rebel, Betty Dodson suggested that the entire population of the Earth should masturbate simultaneously at midnight GMT on December 31, 1999.

She called the initiative, "An Orgasm for World Peace." Although advocating masturbation seems humorous, it is not. There are twenty-five known types of harmful sexually transmitted diseases. They are caused by viruses, bacteria, parasites, mites, and fungi. By some estimates, one in four Americans will contract a venereal disease.

DOE, SAMUEL (1950-1990)

A petty despot in the African state of Liberia, the illiterate Sergeant Samuel Doe (who later promoted himself to Field Marshall) seized power in 1980 when he and nine others scaled the wall of the executive mansion at night. The group overpowered the guards, cut the telephone wires, and murdered Tolbert, the Liberian "president." They disemboweled Tolbert, gouged out one eye with a bayonet, and shot him three times in the head.

After being publicly displayed for two days, Tolbert's body was buried in a mass grave. Twenty-seven other government officials—executed on television after being summarily tried—were tossed into the same hole.

In 1990 it was Doe's time to die. He was killed by Prince Johnson, a rebel leader, who had Doe tortured to death on videotape. Doe's ears were cut off, his eyes were gouged out, his genitals were cut off, and his tongue was cut off to silence his screams. Finally, Doe was shot to death.

Doe's body was paraded around the capital city of Monrovia in a wheelbarrow. The video tape of his death was copied and sold in Africa.

Liberia—the setting for these atrocities—was founded in the 1820's by freed African slaves. The country did not experience a coup d'etat for the first 130 years of its existence.

DOGS, COMBAT WITH

If a dog attacks, throw a stone at the beast. A dog, which lacks intelligence, will bite the stone that strikes him and not the man who threw it.

If the stone fails, know that a dog will go for an arm or a leg. If you wrap your jacket around your arm, a dog will bite that and hang on tenaciously.

Be careful, however. Guard dogs are trained to attack the throat or the groin.

Also, remember that rabies is transmitted through saliva. It is not necessary to be bitten.

The dog's skeletal system gives him a form of armor plating, but his soft spots are his abdomen, the area under his chin, and the region above his breast bone.

If grappling with a dog, fall on the animal and break its leg joint.

DOLE

Invented by the ancient Romans, the dole is public charity. Normally, it is paid to pacify the poor.

Regarding charity, the Marquis de Sade made this observation: "Would you have no flies in your bed chamber? Do not spread around sugar to attract them into it. You wish to have no poor in France? Distribute no alms."

DOOMSDAY SYSTEM

It was revealed in 1996 that Russia has installed an automatic doomsday system. The system would deploy Russia's nuclear weapons even if Russia's leadership were destroyed.

DOUBLE AGENT

A double agent is an operative who works for two intelligence organizations, but is loyal to one. A double agent is also called a counterspy.

DOUBLETHINK

The term "Doublethink," which was coined by George Orwell, refers to the ability of humans to hold two contradictory beliefs in the mind simultaneously and to accept both of them.

Modern scientists, for example, insist that the universe must contain other intelligent life—but they ridicule anyone who claims to encounter such life.

DOUGLASS, FREDERICK (1818-1895)

Born a mulatto slave, Frederick Douglass broke the law, lied to the authorities, and created false identities. He died a free man.

DRUGS, MOOD-ALTERING

Humans have been using mood-altering drugs since 30,000 B.C. All natural narcotics and hallucinogens known to modern man were known to primitive man.

Distilled alcohol, developed by Arab alchemists, was the first synthetic drug.

DRUGS, RELIGION AND

Drugs seem to play some role in religion.

According to Kerry Thonley, "Every thousand years some shepherd inhales smoke from a burning bush and has a vision or eats moldy rye bread in a cave sees God."

According to the Bible, "angels" gave Ezekiel in the Old Testament and John in the New Testament "scrolls" to eat. Sweet to the taste and bitter to the stomach, these "scrolls," which may have been drugs, induced visions.

DUDS

A dud is a thing that fails to work properly.

Up to 20 percent of bombs, grenades, rockets, and mortar shells are duds. And all weapons—especially complex ones—may malfunction.

The "duds" of regular armies often become a source of armaments for guerrillas. With bombs, every 500-pound dud has enough explosives to make five car bombs.

DUEL

A duel is a prearranged contest with lethal weapons between two people to settle a point of honor.

In the seventeenth century, three hundred and fifty French nobles died EACH year in duels. Count Montmorency Bouteville, from one of grandest French families, fought twenty-two duels by the time he was twenty-eight years of age. He fought his first duel at the age of fifteen.

Interestingly, deciding war by the single combat of champions apparently was an established institution in ancient Sumeria.

DUPES, USE OF

A dupe is a victim of deception.

An unwilling dupe is someone who does not realize he is being used. For example, a commercial delivery man is paid to deliver a sealed package that is actually a bomb. The American Central Intelligence Agency refers to such people as "useful idiots."

A willing dupe is someone who agrees to work for an organization—a government or a sub-national group—and does not realize he is a "disposable asset." When he is no longer useful to his "handlers," he will be discarded, killed, exposed, or "compromised."

Typically, the best "disposable assets" are emotionally unstable people who are drawn to violence and appear to be mentally ill. Their instability, their interest in bloodshed, and their apparent madness will "discredit the operatives if they ever go public and tell their tale."

Interestingly, Soviet intelligence understood that terrorists should be "exploited" rather than "controlled."

DUVALIER, FRANCOIS "PAPA DOC" (1907-71)

A successful tyrant, a dictator in a "kleptocracy," Francois Duvalier ruled Haiti from 1957 to 1971.

Called "Papa Doc" by the Haitians, Duvalier perfected the arts of terror and bribery. His secret police had unlimited power to extort, torture, and kill. They were called the "Tontons Macoutes," which means "bogeymen."

Although trained as a physician, Duvalier practiced voodoo. He belonged to a secret society of sorcerers called the *Secte Rouge*.

Interestingly, Duvalier changed the national flag of Haiti, using the colors red and black. In Voodoo, red and black symbolized blood and night.

On November 22, 1962, "Papa Doc" issued a death hex on John F. Kennedy, who had tried to undermine Duvalier. Exactly one year later—on November 22, 1963—Kennedy was killed.

For divination purposes, in his office Duvalier kept the shrunken head of an enemy. Duvalier claimed that he could predict the future by addressing this severed human head, which had belonged to Blucher Philogenes.

After his death, Duvalier became *Loa Os 22*, a god in the Voodoo pantheon.

DZERSHINSKY, FELIX (1877-1926)

A master of spy-craft and a wicked genius, Felix Dzershinsky was a Polish aristocrat and a dedicated communist. Vladimir Lenin entrusted the establishment of the intelligence service and the secret police to Dzerzhinsky, leading to the formation of the so-called Cheka in December 1917.

Dzershinsky recruited men personally loyal to him. The men were often brutal and semi-educated.

Dzerzhinsky divided the service into two sections: Counter-Espionage and Secret Operations. Disloyal or incompetent agents were killed.

Citizens who fell into the hands of the Cheka were tortured and killed without trial.

In one of his most ingenious and sinister operations, Felix Dzerzhinsky created the "Trust," which appeared to be an anti-communist organization. In reality, its function was to lure enemies of the "revolution" to their deaths.

EASTER ISLAND

Easter Island, in the Pacific Ocean, is the most isolated inhabited place on Earth. It is 2,500 miles from the next populated area.

In the nineteenth century, slave traders raided Easter Island and its king was put to work in the South American guano mines.

The island is best known for its enigmatic stone statues and its strange hieroglyphic writing.

ECOTERRORISM

Ecoterrorism supports violence against man and his works in the interest of the planet. Ecoterrorists believe that the salvation of Earth depends on the destruction of civilization, which they believe is an odious system.

Because the Biblical god gives man dominion over nature in the first chapter of Genesis, many ecoterrorists are hostile to Judaism and Christianity. They tend to support paganism, which reveres—even worships—nature.

For the ecoterrorist, the Industrial Revolution in the eighteenth century was a turning point toward the abyss. The new technology—with its perverted science—gave humans a special ability to abuse and squander the resources of nature.

According to ecoterrorists, modern humans–multiplying out of control–plundering, poisoning, and polluting the planet–will eventually degrade the Earth into a crowded slum.

ECOTERRORISM, HUMAN POPULATION AND

According to the "Deep Ecology" Movement, the human population would be sustainable at 100 million individuals. With extreme birth control, this number could be achieved within a century.

Interestingly, before the development of agriculture, the population of the Earth probably did not exceed five or ten million people.

EDEN, GARDEN OF

According to Judaism, Christianity, and Islam, the place called Eden, described in the second chapter of the Book of Genesis, was a paradise. It was lost to man because of the "sin" of disobedience.

In the eyes of anarchists, however, the fabled Garden of Eden was a "slave pen" disguised as a paradise. Jehovah was the tyrant, Adam and Eve were his slaves, and the serpent was the outlaw and the rebel.

EGYPT

Ancient Egypt, a unified kingdom by 3100 B.C., was protected by the desert, the Mediterranean Sea, the Red Sea, and the cataracts on the Nile, and it was not invaded until 1674 B.C., when the Hyksos attacked from Asia.

In other words, ancient Egypt was at peace for fifteen centuries, almost as long as Europe has been Christian! It was with that peace that the Egyptians built a great civilization.

ELECTIONS, SUBVERSION OF

When subverting or "rigging" an election, do not create extra "fake" votes. When a "corpse" casts a vote, this can be traced.

The safest way to rig an election is to "spoil" ballots so that they are disqualified. (After the voter marks the ballot, for example, the subverter marks them a second time, so it appears the voter has voted for two people for the same office). In the Gore-Bush election in 2000, an estimated four to six *million* ballots across the nation were not counted because they were allegedly "spoiled."

In so-called "third world" countries, rigging an election is often amateurish. In the 1916 Cuban presidential election, both sides padded their votes. There were 500,000 eligible voters in Cuba, but 800,000 votes were cast.

In 1928, Charles King, the incumbent president of Liberia, defeated challenger Thomas Faulkner by 600,000 votes in the presidential election. There were only 15,000 registered voters in Liberia.

Not without reason did Octave Mirbeau refer to the "good voter" as an "unspeakable imbecile" and a "poor dupe."

ELOQUENCE

Eloquence is persuasive speaking or writing. Properly crafted, eloquence can be intoxicating–even bewitching.

Henri, Comte de La Rochejacquelein, a leader of the Vendean rebels against the French Revolutionaries, issued these famous words: "Let us find the enemy. If I retreat, kill me; when I advance, follow me. If I am killed, avenge me."

Sir Ernest Shackleton, the noted polar explorer, placed this recruiting advertisement in a London newspaper and received an overwhelming number of inquiries:

Men wanted for hazardous journey. Small wages, bitter cold, long months of complete darkness, constant danger, safe return doubtful. Honor and recognition in case of success.

And in France, the bank robbers who had spent two months in the summer of 1976 digging a tunnel, left this brief and eloquent note in the empty vault: "Without weapons, without hate, and without violence."

What are the rules of eloquence? According to Vilfredo Pareto, "to influence people thought has to be transformed into feeling."

It is also important, of course, to refrain from publicly denouncing "fashionable delusions."

EMPIRES, DESTRUCTION OF

To destroy an empire, start a World War. World War I destroyed the Russian empire of the tsars, the German empire of the kaisers, the Austrian-Hungarian empire, and the Ottoman empire.

World War II, which destroyed the Japanese and Italian empires immediately, would ultimately begin the economic, political, and moral collapse of the British, French, and Dutch empires.

When a universal state emerges—such as the Roman Empire, the Ottoman Empire, or the British Empire—it becomes blinded by what historian Arnold Toynbee called "the mirage of human immortality." Thus, in 1897 the British thought that their empire would endure forever.

ENTRAPMENT

Entrapment is "the act of officers or agents of the government inducing a person to commit a crime not contemplated by him, for the purpose of instituting a criminal procedure against him."

Technically, entrapment is illegal, but an entrapment defense is difficult–especially when the defendant has a criminal record.

In the United States in the 1980's, postal inspectors continued to publish a pedophile contact magazine, even though the publisher had died. The federal agents used the magazine as an entrapment ploy.

EQUALITY

All people are equal, according to Thomas Hobbes, the English philosopher, because "the weakest has strength to kill the strongest, either by secret machination or by confederacy with others that are in the same danger with himself."

Lee Harvey Oswald, the nondescript man who killed a president of the United States with a seventeen-dollar rifle purchased from a pawnbroker, confirmed the theory of Hobbes.

EQUALITY, DEMANDS FOR

According to Vilfredo Pareto, "The demands for equality are always demands for special privileges."

EROTICISM

Purity arouses some and lubricity arouses others.

According to Vilfredo Pareto, "as regards stimulating physical passion the chaste may be as effective as the obscene and vice versa. It all depends on individuals. Some people are sensuously susceptible to talk and writing of the chaste variety, others rather to indecent literature."

EVIDENCE, EYEWITNESS TESTIMONY AS

An eyewitness is a kind of unpaid informant. They are commonly used in modern trials, even though eyewitnesses are notoriously unreliable.

In one famous case from the twentieth century, five witnesses positively identified Bertram Campbell as a bank forger. Fortunately, the real forger, Alexander Thiel, later confessed. Campbell, after an eight-year ordeal, received a pardon and 115,000 dollars for "wrongful conviction." Eighty-two days after receiving the award, he died.

Interestingly, ancient Mosaic law—as defined by the Torah—required the testimony of at least *two* witnesses to convict an individual of a capital crime. According to Mosaic reasoning, the testimony of one witness was canceled out by the testimony of the defendant.

EVIDENCE (PHYSICAL)

Physical evidence–thanks to modern science–is a useful police tool. In legitimate states, physical evidence from the crime is matched with a suspect. In corrupt regimes, physical evidence is *planted* to convict innocent people.

A pioneer in the legitimate use of physical evidence was Edmond Locard, the founder of the Institute of Criminalistics. In 1910 Locard articulated the iron law of forensics: "Every contact leaves a trace."

Forensics is possible because people constantly exchange bits of themselves with their surroundings. The trace-evidence specialist studies hairs, fibers, pollen, paint, soil, and glass to determine who was present at a crime scene. The ballistics expert looks at tools and weapons. The biologist analyzes blood, saliva, and semen to tie perpetrators to victims or locations.

Physical evidence has been used to solve innumerable crimes. The "acid bath murderer" was convicted because the acid failed to dissolve the dentures of one of his victims. Theodore Bundy, a killer of young women, was convicted by a bite mark he left on a naked body. Richard Ramirez, the "Night Stalker," was convicted by a fingerprint. Another murderer was convicted because he left the imprint of his buttocks on a toilet seat in the victim's home. Clifford Irving, a forger, was convicted by a voice print. One extortionist was convicted because he left saliva residue on the blackmail letter. William Jefferson Davis Clinton, an erstwhile president, was impeached because of a sperm stain on a young woman's clothing. Rapists have been convicted by the pubic hairs they leave behind. And Wayne Williams, a murder of twenty-eight young men, was convicted by carpet fibers.

Several features of forensic science include the following:

1) Since each gun leaves distinctive markings on the bullets it fires and leaves residues on the person who fired it, experts can determine a great deal if they have a gun, a bullet, or a suspect accused of firing a gun.

2) Semen can be removed by laundering, but sperm cannot. Unless a rapist has had a vasectomy, his clothing and that of his victim will show evidence of the deed regardless of the hasty cleaning he may have done.

3) Teeth marks on food or on a body can be matched with a suspect.

4) Shoes are made in a variety of patterns, and the prints they leave at the crime scene identify the "make and model" of the shoe. (Intelligent outlaws always wear common shoes.)

If the shoe is NOT new, the print cast may reveal patterns of wear dictated by the owner's gait, a characteristic unique to each individual.

If the footprints are clear, they can indicate if the "perpetrator" was walking, running, limping, or carrying a weight.

5) Trace particulates—such as dust, soil, mud, or pollen on a suspect's shoes, clothing, or vehicle—can be compared with samples from the crime scene.

6) Tools used by the criminal to pry open doors or perform other labor will leave distinctive markings at the crime scene. The patterns are visible with a microscope.

If the outlaw does not destroy his tools, the tools can convict him.

7) Bombs always leave clues. With time bombs, part of the clock will usually survive. With parcel bombs, the police have used the stamps,

fragments of wrapping paper, or the postmark to convict. Grenades leave chemical traces that can be traced to manufacturers.

8) Most famously of all, each individual has a unique set of fingerprints. (Even the prints of identical twins are different.) These may be observed at the crime scene and matched with a suspect.

Although identifying fingerprints is not an exact science–matching prints that are partial or smudged is more of an art–they have been used in American police work since 1910.

Prints are held by paper of all kinds, live plants, copper pipes, coins, painted surfaces, shells left inside a revolver, and so forth. They have been taken even from the *inside* of surgical gloves left at a crime scene.

Police CANNOT find prints on bricks, rocks, most cloth, and most dusty surfaces.

How long do prints last? On a hard surface—in cold, dry weather—a print may disappear almost instantly. On some surfaces—in warm, humid weather—the same print may last for weeks. On absorbent surfaces—like unglazed paper—a print may last for centuries. Today, we can still see the prints left by scribes on ancient Egyptian papyri.

EVIDENCE (PHYSICAL), FALSIFICATION OF

Some outlaws try to sterilize a site–they attempt to remove all traces of their presence–but that is nearly impossible.

Since it is nearly impossible to leave no evidence, some outlaws leave false leads:

1) In 1941 in Kansas City, Missouri, a twenty-three-year-old woman was killed by a person who came in through her first-floor bedroom window. To mislead police, the killer planted dozens of phony clues at the scene. He left a shirt and trousers from a prominent business man (the killer had retrieved them from a trash receptacle). The killer also left knives (from a restaurant), bullets and stained gloves not connected with the crime, 30 matchboxes with telephone numbers, and more than fifty cigarette butts (some bearing lipstick stains) from a public ashtray. After all the clues led to innocent men, the police gave up. No motive was ever established and no suspect was ever arraigned.

2) In 1991 in France, the police found a woman who had been stabbed to death. On the wall by her body, the words *"Omar m'a tuer"* ("Omar killed me") were written with her blood. A young Moroccan gardener named Omar was arrested and prosecuted, but he was innocent. The real murderer had written the message to trick the police.

3) In many cases, organized crime has planted an innocent person's fingerprints at a crime scene. Using a photocopy machine that has had its "heating element" removed, the Mafia makes a copy of the "patsy's" prints. The toner dust (which will not be bonded to the paper) is then collected and is placed at the crime scene.

EVIDENCE (PHYSICAL), LIMITATION OF

Alone, physical evidence is useless. The police need to link it with a suspect.

At the time of writing, only criminals and soldiers have their fingerprints and DNA on record with governments. If an ordinary citizen commits a random crime, against someone he does not know, in a place he had never previously visited, the police will never find him no matter how many fingerprints and DNA samples he leaves.

In the future, however, governments will try to register every man, woman, and child.

EVIL

According to Charles Baudelaire, evil is natural: "We do evil without effort, naturally; good is always the product of art."

According to the Marquis de Sade, if a man casts his lot wholeheartedly with evil, to that man nothing evil can ever happen.

EVIL (GOOD AND)

According to Thomas Aquinas, we usually do evil by seeking good in the wrong way.

EVIL, FACES OF

History shows that some humans can indulge in pure evil. A few examples:

Joseph Briggen (1850-1903) killed homeless men in California to feed his award-winning pigs.

Joseph Ball (1894-1938) killed as many as twenty girlfriends. If a girlfriend became pregnant, it was his practice to feed her to the five pet alligators he kept in a concrete swimming pool.

Jack Gilbert Graham (1932-1957) blew up a civilian airliner and murdered his mother and forty-three other people in 1955. Graham, who had hidden dynamite in his mother's suitcase, purchased flight insurance on his mother and was hoping to collect.

Mary Bell (born 1957), an eleven-year-old girl with big blue eyes and a cute, heart-shaped face, killed two boys, both three-years-old.

Gary Heidnik (1943-1999), a financial wizard who made a fortune on the stock market, began kidnapping and raping women in 1986. Of the six he chained up in his basement, two died of abuse. He forced his captives to eat the flesh of the dead women mixed with dog food.

In 1990, in Warren, Michigan, someone skinned and beheaded a fifteen-year-old girl named Stephanie Dubay.

Gerard Schaefer (1946-1995), who was a serial killer and an author (he wrote *Killer Fiction*), wrote these words in a personal letter: "One whore drowned in her own vomit while watching me disembowel her girlfriend. Does that count as a valid kill? Did the pregnant ones count as two kills? It gets confusing."

EVIL, PSYCHOPATHS AND

In terms of evil, the people capable of the worst crimes are the psychopaths. According to some observers, one out of every one thousand people is a psychopath.

Psychopaths possess a great sense of self-entitlement. Grossly self-centered, they cannot comprehend being thwarted in any of their desires. They demand self-satisfaction, regardless of the cost to others.

Cold-blooded in the extreme, psychopaths cannot feel any emotion deeply. Other people are objects to be exploited for profit or pleasure.

Psychopaths are fully aware of how much suffering they inflict, but they do not care—they cannot care. Because they can feel neither guilt nor remorse, psychopaths are calm during the commission of crimes.

Curiously, psychopaths are often highly intelligent and charming. Skillful manipulators—compulsively deceitful—they make deceptively effective politicians, businessmen, and religious leaders

Psychopaths are rarely apprehended unless their criminal behavior is acute. If they are apprehended, they are incapable of learning from punishment. They are also incapable of learning from experience.

Psychologists estimate that only 10 percent of all psychopaths are ever *charged* with any crime.

EVOLA, GIULIO (1898-1974)

Baron Julius Evola, who was born in Rome to an aristocratic family of Sicilian origin, was an extremist writer.

Evola glorified hierarchy. "Where there is equality," he wrote, "there cannot be freedom."

Evola believed that modern forms of pseudo-equality are symptoms of decadence. He claimed that plebeians could not be powerful in a society dominated by real kings and real aristocrats; likewise, women could not be powerful in a society dominated by real men.

Evola was critical of what he called "the virus of democracy." Democracy, he argued, believes in the "fundamental equality of anything that appears to be human."

Interestingly, Evola claimed that modern man falsifies history. Modern man views himself as superior, but in fact he is "decrepit, defeated, and crepuscular."

EXECUTION

An execution is a government-sanctioned murder. A form of "political necrophilia"–a consecrated and licensed sacrifice–an execution is useful to the "state" and gratifying to "society."

According to the *Encyclopedia of Capital Punishment*, there have been twenty thousand judicial executions in the United States since the establishment of Jamestown. Four hundred of the victims were women, including twenty-seven who were executed for witchcraft.

Even the Pilgrims on the Mayflower hanged one of their own! His name was John Billington.

According to Aleister Crowley, "every man is a condemned criminal, only he does not know the date of his execution."

EXECUTION, ESCAPE FROM

Although escaping an execution is difficult, it is possible. In 1983, for example, six men escaped from the "death row" of Mecklenburg Correctional Center in Virginia.

Other escapes from death row include:

1) Abraham Abulafia, who was condemned to be burned at the stake by Pope Nicholas III for claiming to be the messiah, was saved when the pope died three days later.

2) The English Duke of Norfolk, who was scheduled to be executed in the morning, was saved when King Henry VIII died in his sleep.

3) Corporal Moula, a French army soldier who was scheduled to be shot in May 1917 for mutiny, escaped when German artillery shells struck

his firing squad. Moula escaped in the confusion, and he eventually found safety in South America.

4) Thomas O'Connor, who was condemned to be hanged in 1921 for killing a Chicago policeman, escaped from death row days before the scheduled execution. Using a guard's gun, O'Connor reached the prison yard, and he and another inmate climbed over the 20-foot wall by standing on the shoulders of other prisoners. O'Connor was never recaptured.

5) The most spectacular escape of all, however, was the case of Raoul Sarteret, a convicted murderer.

Sarteret was in a dungeon—on the island of Martinique—awaiting execution for murder. At 7:50 A.M., on May 8, 1902, the 4,430-foot volcano of Pelee exploded, with a blast that was heard three thousand miles away. In three minutes Saint-Pierre (Martinique's largest city) was obliterated. An estimated thirty thousand people perished (the largest number of casualties for a volcanic eruption in the twentieth century), but one person survived in the city. It was Sarteret.

Although permanently blinded by the explosion, Sarteret was still alive when rescuers found him four days later. Pardoned by the French, who were awed by his remarkable survival, Sarteret became a Christian missionary.

EXECUTION, METHODS OF

The methods of execution devised by humans are countless in number. To kill, the state has used the rope, the ax, and the bullet. It has also used poison gas, electricity, and lethal injections, as well as fire (Sweden burned its last woman—for child murder—in 1839) and even the foot of a pachyderm (in Asia, condemned criminals sometimes had their heads crushed by an elephant).

On May 30, 1817, after witnessing an execution in Venice, Lord Byron wrote:

The day before I left Rome I saw there three robbers guillotined—the ceremony—including the masqued priests—the half-naked executioners—the bandaged criminals—the black Christ and his banner—the scaffold—the soldiery —the slow procession—and the quick rattle and heavy fall of the axe—the splash of blood—and the ghastliness of the exposed heads—is altogether more impressive than the vulgar and ungentlemanly dirty "new drop" and dog-like agony of infliction upon the English sufferers of the English sentence.

In the Nazi state, where the broadaxe was used, the headsman dressed in formal evening attire, but wore a mask.

EXECUTIONER

A type of mercenary, an executioner is a hired killer. Like policemen and soldiers, the state allows the executioner to commit certain murders with impunity.

The most famous executioners came from the Sanson family of France. Between 1635 and 1889 the Sansons produced six generations of executioners, including Charles Henri Sanson, who executed Marie Antoinette in front of 250,000 spectators.

In American history, the most famous executioner later served as a president of the United States. Known as the "Buffalo Hangman," Grover Cleveland personally hanged several prisoners when he was the sheriff of Erie County.

In modern America, the executioner's identity is kept secret. When lawyers for the American Civil Liberties Union tried to learn the names and qualifications of hangmen in Washington state, the court ruled against them.

EXTORTION

According to governments, extortion is the "unlawful" taking of anything of value by force, threat, or under the cover of authority. According to anarchists, extortion is the taking of *anything* of value by force, threat, or under the cover of authority.

EXTREMISTS

Intellectual outlaws, extremists are people who hold radical ideological views. They are typically found on frontiers and margins.

According to one intellectual historian, "One way of looking at extremists is as random mutations who, if their mutative traits are adaptive, may thrive and usher in social change."

FABIAN TACTICS

Named after a brilliant Roman tactician, Quintus Fabius Maximus, the term "Fabian tactics" refers to the technique of employing cautious delaying actions to wear out an enemy.

Quintus Fabius Maximus, who lived in the third century before Christ, used rearguard actions and scorched-earth tactics against the army of Hannibal.

FAILED STATE

When all government collapses or disappears in an area, a failed state is produced.

At one time, the authority of "the state" reached every area of the planet. Hakim Bey made this observation:

> The last bit of Earth unclaimed by any nation-state was eaten up in 1899. Ours is the first century without terra incognita, without a frontier. Nationality is the highest principle of world government—not one speck of rock can be left open, not one remote valley, not even the Moon and planets. This is the apotheosis of "territorial gangsterism." Not one square inch of Earth goes unpoliced or untaxed . . . in theory.

By the end of the twentieth century, however, certain areas, such as in Africa, were becoming state-free zones. Utterly lawless, they were developing a new form of feudalism, where warlords and bandits rule.

FAITH

Faith means complete trust or confidence. In metaphysical terms, faith is a strong belief in a religion or a philosophy.

Faith can be a fire that inspires millions to act. Faith can also be a poison that "paralyzes the mind."

FAITH, CHARLES DARWIN AND

Curiously, Charles Darwin, the father of natural selection or what came to be known as evolutionary theory, was so disillusioned by the habits of an especially ruthless wasp that he lost his religious faith.

The eggs of the wasp are embedded in a living caterpillar. When the eggs hatch, the larvae eat their way out through the flesh of their host.

"I cannot persuade myself," Darwin wrote, "that a beneficent and omnipotent God would have designed the Ichneumonidae with the express intention of their feeding within the living bodies of Caterpillars."

FALSE-FLAG OPERATIONS

False-flag operations are deceptive attacks or atrocities that are disguised so that others will be blamed.

In the Lavon Affair in 1954, Israeli operatives bombed American and British cultural targets in Egypt in an attempt to discredit the Egypt's dictator.

In cold-war Italy, American-trained right-wing terrorists staged attacks that appeared to be left-wing operations. These attacks were designed to discredit the "left." Moreover, the attacks—which terrorized the public—encouraged the people to surrender their rights to the state in return for security.

FAME

According to the philosopher Heraclitus, "The best of men see only one thing worth having: undying fame. They prefer fame to wealth. The majority of men graze like cattle."

A piece of you—your fame—may outlive you. Even as a piece of you—your skeleton—may last millions of years.

Defined in abstract terms, fame is a kind of power.

According to the ancient Egyptian text popularly known as the *Book of the Dead*, fame conquers death itself and keeps a man's soul alive. The importance of preserving one's memory is discussed in chapter ninety and chapter twenty-five of the text.

In West African cultures, an ancestor is not dead until he is no longer remembered by the living.

Africans respect all ancestors, but the ones that are esteemed are the great warriors and the exceptionally wise and virtuous. No-account people—commonplace people—are not revered after death. They rest in peaceful oblivion.

FAME, CRIMINALS AND

To be revered is beautiful—to be blessed in life, lamented at death, and admired by posterity—but it is not always possible.

Committing a great crime, however, can make a person famous—or at least infamous. He can acquire what Albert Camus called the "immortality of Cain."

A Greek man named Herostratus burned the temple of Artemis in Ephesus in 356 B.C. to make his name immortal. The temple was one of the "Seven Wonders of the Ancient World."

FAMINE

Famine is an extreme scarcity of food.

In Chinese history, there were more than 1,800 famines in the period between 100 B.C. and A.D. 1910.

In the British Isles, between A.D. 10 and 1850, there were more than two hundred famines, some local, some widespread.

In the twentieth century, between 1921 and 1922 there was a famine in the Ukraine, one of the world's most fertile areas, and another famine in the same location between 1930 and 1933. In the latter famine, perhaps five million died.

Although there are hundreds of thousands of edible plants, humans eat about six hundred.

Obviously the "obscenity of famine" is unnecessary.

FANATICS

According to Voltaire, there are two types of fanatics: those who want to pray and die, and those who want to reign and massacre.

J.B.S. Haldane counted fanaticism among the four really important inventions made between 3,000 B.C. and A.D. 1400. It was, he noted, a Judaic-Christian invention.

A typical fanatic was Benedict Carpzoz II, a sixteenth-century lawgiver of Saxony. He read the Bible fifty-three times and burned twenty thousand witches.

FANATICS, WORLD VIEW OF

In terms of world view, the fanatic sees three types of people: idealized heroes, demonized enemies, and people of no consequence.

FARBER, NISAN (1886-1904)

The first known suicide bomber, Nisan Farber, was a radical anarchist. Of Jewish heritage, the eighteen-year-old killed himself in an attack on a police station with a homemade bomb. Farber became a celebrated martyr among anarchists.

FASCISM

A modern ideology of domination, fascism was inaugurated in March of 1919 when the *Fasci de Combattimento* formed in Italy. Its leader was Benito Mussolini.

Enemies see fascism as a form of political Satanism. The fascists themselves define fascism as government of the people by the leader.

Denouncing the concepts of "Liberty, Equality, Fraternity"—the principles of the French Revolution—the fascist principles are "Believe, Obey, and Fight."

The most extreme form of fascism was the National Socialist movement in Germany. Believing in the creation of a superman elite, the extermination of those demonized as "lesser" beings, and the establishment of a "new world order," Nazism directly and indirectly caused the deaths of millions.

Significantly, both Hitler and Mussolini came to power through democracy. In the words of historian Max Ascoli, "Once political freedom is eliminated, the instruments of democracy can be so used to multiply the power of the tyrannical state. This constitutes the essence of fascism, that is democracy without freedom."

FATE

Fate refers to the inevitable outcome of a person's life.

Africans believe that fate COULD be subverted—changed—with the help of the "divine trickster." The trickster—in Africa—is often the youngest child of a deity.

Hindus believe in fate, but they believe that humans create this fate by exercising their free will, which produces "karmic" effects.

FEAR

Aristotle said that it is noble to fear dishonor, so the great man fears.

During World War II, it was estimated that in combat 50 percent of American soldiers vomited, urinated, or defecated from fear.

Interestingly, animals in the wild are afraid of nearly everything.

FEIGNED RETREAT

The feigned retreat is a common tactic, especially in steppe warfare. When an enemy becomes disordered in his pursuit, he is ambushed with hidden forces.

FENIAN BROTHERHOOD

Named after mythical heroic warriors, the Fenian Brotherhood was an Irish radical group that was established in Dublin in 1858. A secret society, members were bound by oath to secrecy and loyalty.

The Fenian Brotherhood's goal was the establishment of an Irish republic. The group ultimately became the Irish Republican Brotherhood and the Irish Republican Army.

FEUDALISM

A form of political organization, Joseph de Maistre, Charles de Montesquieu, and Julius Evola believed that the feudal regime was the most perfect system of rule that has ever existed on the Earth.

In "feudalism from above," political power is seen as a personal property right, and not as a public function. A king grants it to someone, as in a conquered territory.

In "feudalism from below," a local strong man holds court, collects taxes, and imposes order, just because he is strong enough to do so.

FIRE

Called the most powerful of all purificatory agents, fire is deadly and destructive.

Between 1870 and 1906, four American cities—Chicago, Boston, Baltimore, and San Francisco—burned to the ground.

During World War II, the British discovered that, in strategic bombing, fire is more effective than explosives.

FOOL, PLAYING THE

Brutus (under Tarquinius Superbus), Claudius (under Caligula) and Nikita Khrushchev (under Stalin) pretended to be fools to survive.

Claudius, for example, was lame and stuttered. By acting moronic, he was able to survive Caligula's rein of terror.

In George Orwell's dystopian novel *1984,* what one needs to survive in the fictional Oceania is "discretion, aloofness, a sort of saving stupidity."

FOOLS, FREEDOM OF EXPRESSION OF

In most historical epochs, only the fool—or jester—had freedom of speech. Scholars, critics, rebels, and nonconformists could be tortured or executed for expressing opinions, but usually not the fool. Often, he was able to heckle the worst of tyrants.

In all societies, the clown enjoys a special privilege. Learn from this.

FORCE, SUN TZU ON

Sun Tzu, in his *Art of War,* emphasized the economic use of force. He argued that deception and surprise could achieve success without fighting at all.

"To fight and conquer in all your battles is not supreme excellence; supreme excellence consists in breaking the enemy's resistance without fighting."

FORGERY

To forge is to produce a fraudulent copy of a document, a work of art, a signature, or something else of value.

If an item exists or had once existed, it can be forged; if not, it is said to be faked. A fraud is whatever improper use is made of what has been faked or forged.

To age a document, rub it with steel wool to create "wear."

FORT, CHARLES (1874-1932)

An intellectual rebel who rejected the fetish of modern science, Charles Fort published *The Book of the Damned* in 1919.

"Science," Fort argued, can not explain reality. Scientific "laws" are simply statistical approximations.

FRAGGING

Fragging, a kind of mutiny, was a term coined during the American-Vietnamese War. "Fragging" refers to the fragmentation grenades that American soldiers used to kill overzealous officers and non-commissioned officers.

There were officially 209 reported fragging incidents in Vietnam, but the actual number was much higher. Indeed, one historian estimated that 20 percent of the American officers killed in Vietnam were killed by their own men.

Fragging is not a new phenomenon. In an atmosphere of violence where life is cheap, military leaders have always been at risk.

FRANCIA, JOSE GASPAR RODIGUEZ DE (1766-1840)

Dr. Jose Gaspar Rodriguez de Francia, called "The Supreme One," was a successful tyrant. He ruled Paraguay with savagery, genius, and madness. Utterly frugal, he returned his unused salary to the treasury.

Francia established a Paraguayan secret police force, closed the country's borders, stopped all foreign trade, and abolished higher education.

Curiously, "The Supreme One" ordered the mixture of the races. He declared that whites could not marry whites, and miscegenation became the law.

Every marriage was subject to the tyrant's approval. When his sister married without his consent, "The Supreme One" had his sister, her husband, and the priest who married them shot.

When "The Supreme One" died in 1840, his furniture was burnt and his corpse was fed to wild reptiles.

Oddly, his brand of absolute power was admired in nineteenth-century Europe. Modern Paraguayans admire him, and they say his regime was a time of no debt and no crime.

FREDERICK II (1194-1250)

A blasphemer and a Holy Roman Emperor, Frederick's domain included Sicily. He spoke nine languages, kept a harem, and allegedly wrote *De Tribus Impostoribus* or "About the Three Impostors." The book dealt with Moses, Jesus, and Muhammad.

Although excommunicated by the Church, Frederick II led a crusade. He successfully freed Jerusalem through negotiation.

FREE LOVE

Free love is complete licentiousness.

According to Aldous Huxley, "As political and economic freedom diminishes, sexual freedom tends compensatingly to increase." Promiscuity, he argued, helps reconcile people to their "servitude."

In the Soviet Union–during the fanaticism of the early revolution–the town of Vladimir implemented a "Free Love" decree. Ordering the "socialization of women," "every young girl" from "the age of eighteen" became "state property." According to the decree, all babies born were the "property of the revolution."

FREEDOM

To be free is to be unrestricted.

According to Etienne de la Boetie, the author *The Discourse of Voluntary Servitude*, "some men never become tamed under subjection." Indeed, he added, "even if liberty had entirely perished from the Earth"–even if the very concept of freedom had become eradicated from the mind of humanity, "such men would invent it."

FREEDOM, HATRED OF SLAVES FOR

According to Aleksandr Radishchev, "It appears that the spirit of freedom is so dried up in slaves that they not only have no desire to end their sufferings, but cannot bear to see others free."

FREEDOM, LOSS OF

Traditionally, there are three ways to lose freedom. Freedom is lost as a consequence of warfare, enslavement, or transgression of legal or social rules.

Although the loss of freedom usually involves brute force, trickery is also effective. An Indian chief was enslaved because one of Christopher Columbus's men persuaded the chief that polished steel manacles were the regalia of sovereignty.

FREEDOM, MODERN WORLD AND

Modern humans are not free. Instead, we are like tethered dogs: as long as we keep our heads close to the stake, we do not feel the leash.

Modern humans—the products of decadence—prefer comfort to freedom.

FREEDOM OF EXPRESSION

During World War I, Rose Pastor Stokes, a prominent American peace activist, was convicted in a federal court and given a ten-year sentence for writing in a letter: "I am for the people and the government is for the profiteers."

In the last half of the twentieth century, the state of Israel deported virtually the entire faculty of one Islamic university.

In most modern societies, "freedom of expression" is allegedly "guaranteed," but governments still control what the people can "see" or "hear."

FREEMASONRY

A "secret society that exists in broad daylight," Freemasonry, which played a role in the American and French Revolutions, has been called "the oldest and most powerful secret society on Earth."

Freemasons never ask anyone to join the movement. People must approach them.

The Roman Catholic church has officially condemned Freemasonry. Indeed, eight popes have condemned the Freemasons on four hundred different occasions.

FUGITIVE

A fugitive, a victim of legal persecution, is a man or a woman on the run. An outcast, he is perhaps the most abused of all humans. Those who betray or kill him are rewarded, while those who help him are punished.

Although his situation is difficult, the fugitive may survive. When World War II ended, for example, almost eight thousand Jews emerged from the rubble of Nazi Berlin. Most had escaped the Gestapo and the war by maintaining a low profile.

In some countries–in some circumstances–the fugitive may find confederates who will assist him. In Italy, according to Luigi Barzini, "The people's dislike of legal persecution and their kind hearts make them indiscriminately help all victims of the authorities: they feel irresistibly drawn to bandits, fugitives from justice, escaped convicts, as well as political refugees."

In most countries, however, the people eagerly betray the fugitive.

FUGITIVE (DOGS AND)

To evade dogs, know their abilities and shortcomings.

Dogs see in monochrome. They have difficulty seeing over long distances, but they see movement. Their hearing and smell are acute.

These conditions help dogs track their prey: dense grass, wet ground, high humidity, light wind, rain or fog, still water (like a marsh), and a person's excess perspiration.

These things hinder a dog's scent: bad weather (high winds, snow, ice, or heavy rain), dry and dusty areas, sparse vegetation, hard surfaces (like roads, rock, or sand), and areas contaminated with chemicals (like oil, synthetic fertilizers in a field, and so forth).

To evade a dog, rub a heavy, obnoxious scent (such as ammonia or turpentine) on the soles of your shoes. Also, go in and out of streams and running water to create a false trail. Carry tacks, and throw them on the trail in short grass. If the tacks are dipped in nicotine, the dog that steps on them will be disabled in minutes.

FUGITIVE, LONG-TERM STATUS OF

How long must the fugitive remain on the run?

In the case of major police organizations—such as the F.B.I. in America—the manhunt lasts only as long as the fugitive is newsworthy.

Remember, however, that there is no statute of limitations on major crimes. Leonard T. Fristoe, who received a life sentence in 1920 for killing two deputy sheriffs, served three years and escaped. He was ultimately caught, at age seventy-seven, after being a fugitive for forty-six years.

Also remember that most fugitives are not caught in a massive manhunt. They break minor laws and their fingerprints give them away during a routine arrest. So do not violate traffic laws, do not loiter, and do not carry guns, bomb manuals, or identification papers giving you different aliases.

Carry cash at all times so that you can post bail and escape before you are identified. One man arrested for a traffic violation could not post bail, and it cost him his life. Three days later, while still in jail, he was identified as a "terrorist," and he was ultimately executed.

For money, do not steal. An ideal job for a fugitive is a low-salary, manual-labor position, such as a dishwasher. Restaurants have difficulty hiring, so they do not ask questions.

Also, the dishwasher job keeps you out of the public eye, and you can eat for free.

FUGITIVE (RULES FOR)

Wherever he is, if a man is on the run, time is on his side. If a prisoner escapes and he covers five miles an hour, after one hour he could be anywhere in a circle with a radius of five miles, or area of seventy-eight square miles. If he covers ten miles in two hours, he could be anywhere in an area of 314 square miles.

If you are a fugitive, you must avoid your family, friends, and lovers. In standard police work, they will watch your home and interrogate your acquaintances.

The police will also try to track you—the fugitive—through your interests. For at least two years, you must not indulge in hobbies, favorite pastimes, or preferred activities.

As a fugitive, you must avoid *all* technology, especially computers, bank and credit-card machines, telephones, and cellular telephones. (Activated cellular telephones reveal location, and the Israelis have killed at least six Palestinian leaders by "locking in" on cellular phone signals.)

If—in an emergency—you must steal an automobile, you should steal one from a factory parking lot. The car will not be immediately missed.

Normally, however, the fugitive must avoid major roads and populated areas. If people see you, do not appear furtive. Be bold.

Avoid dwellings, open ground, and roads. If following a highway, walk on a parallel course one hundred to two hundred yards to the side. Use cover, such as hedges and trees. Cross open ground at the narrowest point. Do not cover grasslands during the day. Wrap your boots in cloth to make your prints appear old and blurred.

The safest way to move through mountains is to follow the biggest rivers. Contour hills at a point two-thirds up the slope. Always, avoid leaving tracks at the bottom of a hill and avoid being silhouetted at the top.

To cross foreign frontiers, use bleak, rugged, and uninhabited regions of wilderness. Mountains, swamps, desert, jungle, tundra, and heavy bush are geographical back doors to an otherwise well-defended country. The easiest way to enter America, for example, is via the Canadian tundra.

Of course, when moving through a wilderness you must plan for environmental stress, such as cold or heat, dryness or wetness.

In cold temperatures, layer your clothing. The layering system transfers perspiration away from the body.

Always keep your head and extremities covered. Up to 40 percent of body heat may be lost through the head.

When it is colder, travel at night. Sleep during warmer day. Never lie on the bare ground, but use brush or grass if necessary. Lying on the ground will cause you to lose body heat.

In desert areas, wear light-colored, loose-fitting clothing. Understand that being naked in the desert kills a person faster than lack of water.

Wrap cloth around your shoes to keep out the sand. Sand can be abrasive on the feet.

In deserts, travel at night. In desert areas, the temperature range in one day can be 86 degrees Fahrenheit.

In hot, humid areas, wear loose clothing. Understand that mosquitoes—carriers of malaria and other illnesses—usually do not venture above 1200 meters.

Whatever the terrain, plan to use some time for sleep. Remember that a man can live without food longer than he can live without sleep.

A sleeping man is defenseless, so an overnight stop should offer concealment from the ground or the air. The spot selected should have a single approach route. It should have an escape lane if the "hide" is discovered.

If there is no opportunity for ordinary sleep, army research shows that a twenty to thirty-minute nap, with a similar period for waking up, can counter the effects of sleep deprivation. Elite units train for it.

If you have time to construct an evasion shelter, it should be small, survivable (offering adequate protection against cold and so forth), secluded, irregular in shape, low in height, and should blend into the surroundings.

FUTURISM

A philosophical and artistic movement, Futurism represents a total rejection of the past, including the "dead" world of libraries, museums, and academies.

Futurism glorifies the technology of the machine age, and it celebrates speed, noise, and the growth of cities. It glorifies destruction, war, violence, and all that is dynamic in the modern world.

In literature, Futurist writing is lean and muscular. It contains no adjectives or adverbs.

Filippo Tommaso Marinetti, who founded the Futurist movement in 1909 with his *Manifesto of Futurism*, was an early member of Mussolini's party and supported the Salo Republic.

GAME, THE MOST DANGEROUS

Hunting humans is "the most dangerous game." The phrase is from a 1924 story (by Richard Connell) about a Russian count named Zaroff. A big-game hunter who has slain innumerable animals, Zaroff decides to stalk the ultimate prey. He buys an island, stocks it with castaways and shipwreck survivors, and hunts them.

Oddly, a killer named Robert Hansen actually played "the most dangerous game." The murderer of seventeen women in Alaska, he released his victims naked into the wilderness—gave them a head start—and then stalked them with a rifle. Hansen was given life in prison in 1984.

GEMSTONE

A false-flag operation, Gemstone was the codename for the operation against Richard Nixon's enemies and rivals.

The operation employed many "illicit" tricks, including planting fake protesters with bizarre quirks among anti-Nixon demonstrators. The planted operatives made the protesters appear to be violent and freakish.

GENGHIS KHAN (1162-1227)

Genghis Khan, the son of a raped woman, was a successful Mongol warlord. By some estimates, Genghis Khan and his diabolic hordes were responsible for twenty million deaths. At the time, that was 10 percent of the world's population.

Before Genghis Khan, the Mongols had been a collection of nomadic tribes who only formed occasional alliances. Thanks to Ghenghis Khan, the Mongols would become the most successful conquerors in history. In two centuries, they subdued and plundered everything from Eastern Europe to China, from northern Russia to Thailand.

GENIUS

A genius is an exceptionally talented or creative person. Like a hysteric, a genius puts ideas together in unconventional patterns.

The masses—who simply eat, breed, and die— typically do not recognize a genius. When Goethe's collected works were published in 1790, only six hundred copies were sold.

GENOCIDE

The term genocide, which was coined by Raphael Lemkin in 1944, refers to the extermination of racial and national groups. It was first used to describe the efficient, industrialized murders of Jews by the Nazis.

Genocide, however, has occurred on numerous occasions in history. Typically, a certain group is declared to be sub-moral, sub-rational, and sub-human, and then they are exterminated.

In the Old Testament, Jehovah or Yahweh orders genocide in Deuteronomy 7: 2: "And when the Lord thy God shall deliver them before thee; thou shalt smite them, and utterly destroy them; thou shalt make no covenant with them, nor shew mercy unto them."

GIFT, AS A WEAPON

A gift makes an effective stealth weapon. With the Trojan Horse, the ancient Greeks used a gift to destroy the city of Troy.

In colonial America, the British gave smallpox-infected blankets to the Indians.

In the Soviet Union, Pavel Sudoplatov, a sinister intelligence genius, assassinated a Ukrainian dissent with a poisoned box of chocolates.

According to Adolf Hitler, the gift of tobacco was the red man's revenge on the white man for giving him alcohol.

GILLESPIE, PATRICK (1948-1990)

A "forced" or unwilling suicide bomber, Patrick Gillespie worked in a British military base in Ulster as a cook. On October 23,1990, Irish gunmen invaded his house and seized his wife and children.

By threatening his family, the gunmen forced Gillespie to drive into a British army checkpoint strapped into a car with 1600 pounds of high explosive. Gillespie and five British soldiers were killed.

GLORY

Glory is renown won by achievement.

According to Eric Hoffer, "Glory is largely a theatrical concept. There is no striving for glory without a vivid awareness of an audience."

GODS

A god is a masterful being.

The gods, argued Epicurus, probably exist, and they must dwell outside our world and must, by their very nature, have no interest or concern for human beings. It is obviously a folly to try to attract the attention of such superior entities.

According to the Hindus, however, any contact with a god is beneficial, even if the contact is hate.

GODS, PLOTINUS AND

When Plotinus, a philosopher from the third century, was asked to attend the public worship of the gods, he made this reply: "It is for them to come to me."

GODS, REBELS AND

According to Albert Camus, the rebel "does not suppress God; he merely talks to him as an equal."

The Greek word *isotheos* means "god-equal." The term is used in the *Iliad* for heroes like Menelaus.

GOVERNMENT

A government—the ruling power in a state—claims the authority to command, to seize property, to kill, and to destroy. Because the government holds the keys to the armories and the prisons, it can enforce its commands.

According to the ancient Greeks, there are three types of governments: the government by one, the government by the few, and the government by the many.

According to the anarchists, government is organized crime.

According to Friedrich Nietzsche, the state is "the coldest of all cold monsters." Nietzsche said that whatever the state says is a lie and whatever it owns is stolen.

GOVERNMENTS, EXTREME FORM OF

In their most extreme form, governments control life: every act is either prohibited or mandatory.

Some day, in the infamous "brave new world" of the future, humans will be designed and controlled, from the uterus to the grave.

GOVERNMENTS, VULNERABILITY OF

According to innumerable observers, from Etienne de La Boetie to Jose Ortega y Gasset, rule is always based on public opinion. Governments have power only because people *choose* to obey.

And, as Jose Ortega y Gasset noted, even the man who attempts to rule with troops depends on their opinion and the opinion which the rest of the inhabitants have of the soldiers.

In eastern and central Europe in 1989, European dictatorships, with their secret police forces, gulags, and large standing armies, collapsed easily when public opinion rejected them.

Jean Baudrillard, commenting on the demise of European communism, made this observation: "The spectacle of those regimes imploding with such ease ought to make Western governments—or what is left of them—tremble, for they have barely any more existence than the Eastern ones."

GRADUALISM

Tyrants know that gradualism is an effective method to enslave and impoverish.

Even a coward will react if he is "mugged" or "put in irons"—but he will quietly surrender his money and freedom in small increments.

In 1914, the per capita income tax in the United States was twenty-eight cents *per year*. With great success—and no resistance—it has been slowly increased ever since.

GRAY-AREA PHENOMENON

"Gray-Area Phenomenon" refers to areas of a country where control has shifted from "de jure" governments to so-called criminal gangs.

In such areas, the police and military refuse to enter except to make massive, ineffectual raids. After such forays, they quickly leave.

According to one historian, urban crime may develop into a "low-intensity conflict" by coalescing along racial, religious, social, and political lines. If that occurs, the existing distinction between war and crime disappears.

GRIMALDI, FRANCOIS (died 1309)

A master of deception, Francois Grimaldi was known as "the Cunning."

On the night of January 8, 1297, Francois Grimaldi and a group of soldiers disguised themselves as Franciscan friars. With weapons concealed under their robes, they entered a fortress that controlled an ancient port town. Once inside, they drew their swords and quickly subdued the place.

The Grimaldi family still controls the principality that their ancestor seized in the thirteenth century. Known as Monaco, it is among the smallest and richest countries on Earth.

GUERRILLA WAR

The term "guerrilla" is derived from the Spanish word for "little war." A form of asymmetric combat, guerrilla warfare is waged without fronts, heavy weapons, or lines of communication.

Instead, lightly armed guerrillas launch attacks to disrupt and intimidate. They use the terrain to hide from the enemy: rural guerrillas use the mountains, swamps, and forests, and urban guerrillas use densely populated cities, where the crowds themselves provide cover.

One early guerrilla campaign was the Hasmonean Revolt, which was fought against the Seleucid monarch, between 168 B.C. and 164 B.C. Another was the Bar Kokhba Revolt, which was fought against the Romans from A.D. 132 to A.D. 135.

In its modern form, guerrilla warfare first appeared in the framework of the Napoleonic wars in Spain, southern Italy, and Russia.

Historically, Latin America has been the ultimate guerrilla continent. Latin America has experienced only a handful of regular wars, but guerrilla wars have been common.

GUERRILLA WAR, EFFECTIVENESS OF

Thomas Edward Lawrence, famous as "Lawrence of Arabia," believed that a successful guerrilla insurgency could be accomplished with the active support of only 2 percent of the population, provided 98 percent sympathized with or acquiesced to the struggle.

In the twentieth century, all great powers met frustration and humiliation at the hands of guerrillas: the British in Ireland, the Germans in the Balkans, the Japanese in China, the French in Algeria, the U.S.A. in Vietnam, and the U.S.S.R. in Afghanistan.

Thanks in part to guerrilla warfare, European colonial empires, which required centuries to construct, collapsed in the thirty years following World War II.

In the case of French Algeria, the colony had 10,000,000 people in an area the size of Western Europe, and that number included 1,000,000 European settlers. France sent in 450,000 troops at one point, or one soldier for every 23 inhabitants. (France also deployed 150,000 Muslim auxiliaries!) France became a nuclear power during the war, but she still lost in 1962.

Guerrilla insurgency has its best chance of success against an occupying power. There have been successes against indigenous regimes—such as against Batista's Cuba or against Somoza's Nicaragua—but these are rarer.

GUERRILLA WAR, FIGHTING AGAINST

To regular armies, a guerrilla war is an endless war with invisible enemies and no ground gains, just a constant flow of troops in and out of the combat theater.

Obviously, it is difficult for regular armies to defeat guerrillas. In the American-Vietnamese War, for example, American troops conducted military sweeps over every inch of South Vietnam, often hundreds of times! Yet, the United States lost the war.

In the standard counter-guerrilla campaign, the army creates a barrier around the guerrilla area, they remove or destroy anything that could provide logistical support to the guerrilla (including the inhabitants), they divide the area into small sections, and they use "flying columns" to clear each section one by one.

Thus, to defeat the Boer guerrillas in the Second Anglo-Boer War, the British Empire erected more than 8,000 blockhouses (manned by 66,000 troops) and 6,400 kilometers of barbed wire. To drive the enemy back on these defenses, the British deployed a massive mobile force (one armed man on a horse every ten meters over an eighty-kilometer front). To deprive the guerrillas of support and supply, the British created a wasteland by destroying farms and crops, seizing all the livestock, and forcing the civilian population into filthy and disease-ridden concentration camps. (Approximately 116,000 Boer civilians were confined inside forty camps, where 28,000 women, children and old people died. The British also forced 120,000 blacks into 66 camps, where 16,000 to 20,000 perished.)

Curiously, the mighty British Empire (which covered one-fourth of the globe and contained more than 400 million people) deployed an army of 460,000 men to fight a Boer population in the Orange Free State and Transvaal which numbered only 405,000 men, women, and children!

Russian counter-insurgency techniques, although more brutal, have been similar. The Russians, who are known for their "massive application of force," used the following tactics against guerrillas in Chechnya: 1) the Russians deployed a large number of troops, 2) they isolated the guerrilla area from the outside world, 3) they gained control over the central cities first, and then extended their domination outward from them, 4) they built forts or strongholds (to restrict the guerrillas' movements to smaller and smaller areas), 5) they destroyed settlements, livestock, crops, and orchards to deny supplies to the guerrillas, and 6) they conducted mass deportations of civilians, the assassination of insurgent leaders, and "exemplary massacres."

In fighting Chinese guerrillas during World War II, the Japanese imperial forces introduced the savage policy of the "Three-Alls" in 1941. Directed less against the guerrillas—and more against the population that supported them—the Japanese would surround a given area—and kill everything—people, animals, crops, and even the trees.

In contrast, the more adroit Portuguese Empire successfully waged three anti-guerrilla wars, 5,000 miles from home, for thirteen years, in 800,000 square miles of territory. The Portuguese used a subdued, low-tempo, affordable, long-term, low-technology, and limited-casualty approach. Highly successful, the Portuguese forces suffered only 4,027 combat deaths, of which 23 percent were African volunteers and the rest were Portuguese.

The Portuguese used wide ranging, deep-penetration patrols, which were Spartan and low-profile. Small groups of thirty men, brought into the bush by helicopters or vehicles, conducted their missions on foot or on horseback, carrying everything with them.

The Portuguese always traveled cross-country, avoiding roads because of mines. Their patrols were able to penetrate rugged terrain, and kill guerrillas, disrupt the insurgent's food supply, call in air strikes, and make contact with population.

Like the French in Algeria and the British in Kenya, the Portuguese recruited African troops to fight Africans in a "divide and conquer" tactic. But, unlike the French or the British, the Portuguese fully integrated their units and paid the Africans the *same* pay as the Europeans. (Portugal did not have a single example of rebellion or mass desertion by "native troops," as happened in French Algeria.)

When the Portuguese captured guerrillas, the captives were not tortured. Information extracted with torture, the Portuguese believed, was suspect, and they knew that torture had undermined the French in Algeria. The Portuguese found it more useful to greet prisoners politely, offer coffee, and talk!

And–to win the "hearts and minds" of the civilians in the war zone– the Portuguese used social initiatives. They invested in infrastructure, and built schools, hospitals, and roads during the war.

GUERRILLA WAR, RURAL FORM OF

The classic form of guerrilla war is asymmetric warfare focused on the countryside.

Ernesto "Che" Guevara said that guerrilla war should have a rural *foco* or "focus." Fidel Castro agreed, and insisted that the city was the graveyard of revolutions. And, according to Mao Tse-tung, "wars are won by encircling the towns by the countryside."

Traditionally, from the Maccabeans to the Mau Mau, guerrillas locate in sparsely populated, geographically "remote," and typographically "difficult" areas, such as mountains, forests, swamps, and wastelands.

The best terrain is that which hampers the movements of regular forces and enables guerrillas to hide. With such terrain, a few determined men can defeat an army, even one with atomic weapons and tanks.

In the American-Vietnamese War, guerrillas used the wild terrain effectively. Virtually unchallenged in most of the country, they were molested only by aircraft or helicopter-borne forces.

The American troops spent most of their time in the relative safety of urban areas. When they left the cities—in helicopters or on roads in armored cars or tanks—they were ambushed.

Indeed, the American army usually encountered the enemy only when guerrillas were ambushing them.

The American-Vietnamese War demonstrated how towns could become prisons—rather than bases of operation—for an invading army.

GUERRILLA WAR, TECHNIQUES OF

A technique of "harassment and attrition," guerrilla warfare is neither offensive nor defensive–it is "evasive." According to Ernesto "Che" Guevara, the guerrilla is the master of "secretiveness," "treachery," and "surprise."

Guerrillas operate in small groups so that one reverse cannot be decisive. For protection, they disguise themselves as civilians.

Unheroic by definition–scorning all "romantic and sporting conceptions of war"—guerrillas attack weakness only. They ambush small units or patrols, or soft targets, such as hospital trains. After every attack, the guerrillas rapidly disperse.

Guerrilla attacks, according to *The War of the Flea*, a standard text on the subject, have four functions: 1) to demonstrate the impotence of enemy, 2) to steal weapons, ammunition, and supplies, 3) to inflict casualties, and 4) to force the enemy to overextend his lines so that his communications can be disrupted and small units can be destroyed, one at a time, by "locally superior" forces.

Guerrillas, as Mao Tse-tung pointed out, are masters of maneuver warfare: "The enemy advances, we retreat; the enemy camps, we harass; the enemy tires, we attack; the enemy retreats, we pursue."

Because mobility is crucial to their survival, guerrillas travel with few supplies and light weapons only. Friedrich Wilhelm Rustow, a Prussian military theorist, said that "irregulars" should carry no more than twenty-four pounds. When guerrillas carry too much, mobility and stealth are reduced. Also, fatigue affects alertness.

Guerrillas hold no territory, and they have no objectives that must be held. As a result, the army fighting guerrillas has nothing substantial to attack.

"To gain territory is no cause for joy," wrote Mao Tse-tung. "To lose territory is no cause for sorrow. The only crucial thing is to destroy the enemy. Always use surprise, always be secret."

When attacked by the French, the Viet Minh dispersed and withdrew. They reassembled at a predetermined point that was a twelve hours' march away. If the French attacked again, the guerrillas repeated the maneuver. As a result, the French as a rule conquered only empty spaces.

Eventually the French would be far from home and short on supplies, so they had to return to their bases. As they were returning, they were harassed by guerrillas.

The object of the guerrilla is not to win battles, but to avoid defeat. Against a great power, declares *The War of the Flea*, the "guerrilla's mere survival is a political victory."

The guerrilla strives not to end the war, but to prolong it. According to Wojciech Chrzanowski, a nineteenth-century Polish rebel, time is always on the side of the guerrilla.

The goal of the guerrilla is not to conquer, but to "create an intolerable situation" for the occupying power or the tyrant.

In the EOKA struggle against the British in Cyprus, for example, EOKA never tried to win a military victory, but by harassing, confusing, and exasperating the British the EOKA made the occupation unacceptable to the British government.

Led by George Grivas, who took command in 1954, EOKA used a cellular structure to resist counter-intelligence. Although at the height of the struggle EOKA had no more than 350 rural guerrillas (in cells of 5-15 men) and 200 urban operatives (in cells of 4-5 people), the guerrillas tied up thousands of troops. The reason, of course, is that it requires many men to guard a bridge or a power plant—it requires only one man to destroy these things.

In a classic asymmetric campaign, the EOKA launched raids on armories for weapons, killed collaborators to "blind" the enemy, and used arson, sabotage, street murder, booby traps, and bombings. EOKA's attacks were so widespread that they even planted an explosive device under the British governor's bed.

EOKA also had a "passive wing" of supporters who used "non-violent" measures, such as demonstrations, riots, boycotts, and strikes. The passive wing also conducted an effective propaganda campaign, and they mobilized support for the struggle by highlighting British atrocities.

Whatever techniques the guerrilla uses, he must never establish a pattern. Always, he must do the unexpected. In the legendary words of Sun Tzu, "The enemy must not know where I intend to give battle. For if he does not know I intend to give battle, he must prepare in a great many places . . . . And when he prepares everywhere, he will be weak everywhere."

GUERRILLA WAR (URBAN)

Urban guerrilla warfare, a kind of "lightning war" against modern society, is asymmetric warfare focused on the cities. According to Carlos Marighella, the author of the *Minimanual of the Urban Guerrilla*, modern urban guerrilla warfare started in 1968 in Brazil.

Since modern technology can identify and target the rural guerrilla, urban environments are now becoming more attractive to insurgents, who can use the concentrated population in cities for concealment.

In the opinion of some, urban guerrilla warfare is indistinguishable from terrorism.

GUERRILLA WAR (URBAN), FIGHTING AGAINST

To fight urban guerrillas, the modern state suspends the rule of law and decency.

In 1972, the Uruguayan military ordered a state of internal war, which would last thirty days. Forty thousand troops systematically searched Montevideo, using state-of-siege powers to seize ten thousand people. The Uruguayan military dismantled and eliminated the Tupamaro organization– and destroyed the country's democracy in the process.

In another example of state terrorism against terrorism, the French conducted the so-called "Battle of Algiers" from January through September in 1957.

The French broke the rebels with constant patrolling, house-to-house searches, and checkpoints. The whole city was divided into sectors, subsectors, blocks, and buildings. Each designated area had an informant—or a collaborator—to report suspicious behavior.

Normal legal limitations on detention were set aside, and the French arrested 24,000 people in Algiers. At least three thousand of these would "disappear" in detention.

After an initial screening (aided by informants), suspects were interrogated. The French routinely used "special measures" (a euphemism for torture), which included electric shocks to nipples and genitals, the crushing of limbs and organs in vices, and the forced pumping of air or liquid into bodies.

The information extracted helped locate terror cells and hideouts, and targeted raids followed.

With their extra-legal terrorism, the French completely broke the rebels in Algiers, but the French would lose the war. On July 3, 1962, France recognized Algerian independence.

GUERRILLA WAR (URBAN), TECHNIQUES OF

For the guerrilla, an urban center offers innumerable targets, anonymity, and an audience.

A city provides physical cover (three-dimensional urban terrain) and political cover (the rules of warfare are more stringent with civilians present). The infrastructure of a city means that logistical supplies—such as food and medicine—are not a problem.

Unlike the rural guerrilla, the urban guerrilla's successes are immediately visible. His victories cannot be hidden by censorship.

The tactics of the urban guerrilla are simple: he assassinates, he places pre-positioned bombs and booby traps, and he avoids all pitched battles. He has no fixed urban base to maintain or defend.

He should remain anonymous–living in the city and holding a job. Invisible, he strikes "targets of opportunity," and then blends back into the population.

The urban guerrilla does attempt to actually inflict military defeat on the regular army. That would be "foolish adventurism." The urban guerrilla simply tries to demoralize the enemy and raise the stakes of governing.

A classic (albeit unsuccessful) urban guerrilla campaign was mounted by the Tupamaros of Uruguay, who conducted operations largely in the city of Montevideo. The Tupamaros lived at home, and they met only to plan or to conduct operations. They did not live on donations or requisitions, but held jobs or subsisted—ironically—on state welfare payments.

GUEVARA, ERNESTO "CHE" (1928-1967)

A classic theorist of guerrilla warfare, Ernesto "Che" Guevara was born in an aristocratic family in Argentina. Guevara completed medical studies but never practiced professionally.

"Che" Guevara said that a nucleus of fifty armed men is sufficient to initiate an insurrection. When the group exceeds fifty, it should split and part should go elsewhere to spread the revolt. (Guerrillas spread their message like "missionaries.")

"Che" Guevera believed that to survive a new guerrilla force needs "constant mobility, constant vigilance, constant mistrust."

GUILT BY ASSOCIATION

Tyrants punish not only their victims, but also the victim's relatives, friends, associates, and neighbors. Tyrants assume "guilt by association."

A classic example of the practice occurred in the case of Ching Ch'ing, who was killed in 1402 while attempting to assassinate the emperor of China. Not only was Ching Ch'ing's corpse skinned, stuffed with straw, and mounted at the palace entrance, but all his relatives (by blood or marriage) were murdered along with all the people in his village.

During the Soviet era, Joseph Stalin made whole families disappear. Horrifically, even the memory of their existence was eradicated.

GULAG

The Gulag was the Soviet slave-labor system created by Vladimir Lenin and developed by Joseph Stalin. It was based on the internal exile to Siberia used by the tsars.

The gulags, which were supervised by ruthless guards, were euphemistically called "Corrective Labor Camps." When an inmate was worked or starved to death, it was referred to as a "dry execution."

At one camp in the gulag system—one involved in mining—it is estimated that there were one thousand dead for every ton of gold extracted.

GYNECOCRACY

Gynecocracy is rule by the women.

Feminists claim that gynecocracy will bring about a golden age.

In contrast, Aristotle, a misogynist, claimed that a state like Sparta fell in part because Sparta failed to control its women.

HATE

Hate is a strong aversion to someone or something. Often denied, it is a fundamental human emotion and a factor in history.

According to Eric Hoffer, hate is a unifying force. "We do not look for allies when we love," wrote Hoffer, "but we always look for allies when we hate."

Curiously, it is a truism that people must hate those whom they wrong.

HEADHUNTING

Headhunting is performed to acquire power, to prove a kill, or to procure a souvenir. Usually perceived as a "species of villainy," in some cultures it is a sacred act.

As late as 1912, the Montenegrins in Europe cut off the heads of enemies and wore them on belts. And, after the Battle of Guadalcanal in

World War II, some American marines began to take Japanese skulls as trophies.

Perhaps the most famous (and fearsome) headhunters are the Jivaros in South America, who make "shrunken heads." Also called the Shuar, they live in the dense forest covering the eastern slopes of the Andes in Ecuador and Peru.

The Jivaros, who believe that the soul is in the head, make shrunken heads to thwart the hostile power of a slain enemy's spirit. Altogether, the head shrinking and the religious ceremony involved requires two years.

To fabricate their "fetish," the Jivaros make a cut at the back of the head from the apex down, and they slowly peel off the skin. The most difficult part is skinning the face.

After immersing the skin in boiling water, the trophy is eventually dried and reduced in size by using hot stones and hot sand. Repeated many times, the head is ultimately reduced to one-fourth its original dimensions (about the size of an orange). Throughout the process, the headshrinker is careful to mold the features.

Contrary to popular belief, most headhunters are not cannibals.

HERO

At the time of writing, when—to cite Baron Giulio Evola—"the heroic ideal has now been lowered to the figure of the policeman," the word hero has lost all meaning.

In earlier times, however, the concept was well understood. The "indomitable" hero was a man—confident in his strength—who put himself above the rules. An implacable figure—beyond good and evil—he vanquished tyrants and monsters.

In archaic Greece, the hero was defined in virile terms. This was a culture that glorified piracy because the pirate used force and needed courage.

In the words of historian Lewis Mumford, archaic Greek heroes were "quick to pick a quarrel, zealous at hunting, skilled in violence and theft, audacious at piracy," and had an aristocratic contempt for "work" and "trade."

In this passage from the *Iliad*–which relates Hector's prayer to the gods– the heroic spirit of a bygone age is captured: "Grant that this my son may become as I am, most distinguished among the Trojans as strong and valiant, and that he may rule by might in Ilion. . . . May he bring back spoils stained with the blood of men he has slain, and may his mother's heart rejoice."

Interestingly, in Aztec lore, the "House of the Sun" is reserved for heroes. In Viking lore, Valhalla is reserved for the heroic dead.

HINDUISM

An ancient religion—its origins lost in time—Hinduism may be the planet's oldest living tradition.

Hinduism is from India, a complex land where even today 325 languages are spoken and twenty-five written scripts are used.

The enemies of Hinduism—mainly the adherents of the Abrahamic faiths—dismiss Hinduism as a false or heathen tradition. Curiously, William Wilberforce called Hinduism "one grand abomination" and a "dark and bloody superstition" whose gods are "absolute monsters of lust, injustice, wickedness and cruelty."

One interesting tradition of Hinduism involves Hiranyakashipu, the demon tyrant.

As an "Asura" and the king of the Rakshasas, Hiranyakashipu practiced austerities and gained immense powers.

Declaring himself the lord of the universe, Hiranyakashipu began a reign of absolute terror, dominating even the gods themselves. A jealous tyrant, Hiranyakashipu ordered all beings to worship him alone.

When his son, Prahalad, disobeyed and worshiped Vishnu, Hiranyakashipu tried to kill his son. The latter, however, was saved by an avatar of the god Vishnu, who appeared as Narasimha, the man-lion, and killed the demon tyrant.

HINDUISM, FREEDOM AND

According to the Hindus, we are not born free. We must liberate ourselves through discipline.

HISTORY

History, the study of past events, is the record of disasters, massacres, revolts, swindles, strikes, and wars.

Of immense significance, George Orwell made this famous observation: "Who controls the past controls the future; who controls the present controls the past."

Oddly, remembered history is often distorted history. Great Britain, for example, declared war on Germany in both world wars—the Germans did not attack them—yet few remember that.

Also, how many Englishmen know that England's government business was conducted in French after the Norman conquest? King Edward III, who reigned two and one-half centuries after the conquest, was the first king who spoke more than a few words of English.

HISTORY (BELIEFS AND)

As a force in history, beliefs are more important than facts.

It matters not that archaeology cannot prove the existence of King David or King Solomon. What matters is that millions believe that the kings existed.

HISTORY, FALSIFICATION OF

The falsification of history is common.

In 213 B.C.—in the Qin dynasty in China—Shi Huang Di tried to erase the past and start anew. He ordered all books burned (except the practical ones in agriculture, divination, and medicine), and scholars who disobeyed were executed.

Another tyrant—Abdul Aziz, an Ottoman sultan who reigned between 1861 and 1876—also tried to rewrite history. His government expunged from the history books all references to Turkish military defeats, the French Revolution, and Christianity.

In "free" societies, the perversion of history is more subtle. American children are taught, for example, that the Pilgrims of Plymouth colony came to America for religious freedom. In reality, the Pilgrims did not have a minister for their first nine years in America; half the people on the Mayflower were indentured servants (temporary slaves) to the other half; and, one of the men on the *Mayflower*, John Billington, would ultimately be hanged by the Pilgrims for murder.

In American national mythology, the people of Plymouth colony are also remembered for having a kindly "thanksgiving feast" with native Americans. The reality was grimmer. To terrify the aboriginal people, the Pilgrims of Plymouth colony exhibited on a stake for twenty years the severed head of a tribal leader.

HISTORY, GEORGE ORWELL ON

"Historical engineering," or "designing the facts of history to serve state policy," is one of the most important themes in *1984*, Orwell's dystopian novel. Orwell noted that "past events" have "no objective existence, but survive only in written records and in human memories. The past is whatever the records and the memories agree upon."

And further:

It struck him as curious that you could create dead men but not living ones. Comrade Ogilvy, who had never existed in the present, now existed in the past, and when once the act of forgery was forgotten, he would exist just as authentically, and upon the same evidence, as Charlemagne or Julius Caesar.

According to Orwell, once the "past was erased, the erasure was forgotten, the lie became truth."

Orwell instinctively understood that history is one of mankind's most powerful fictions.

HISTORY, MIKHAIL BAKUNIN ON

According to Mikail Bakunin, we must study history "in order to establish what we have been and what we must no longer be."

HITLER, ADOLF (1889–1945)

A self-made tyrant and a murderer of Jews, Adolf Hitler killed himself on Walpurgis Night—the "Night of the Witches"—April 30, 1945.

According to his enemies, Hitler was pure evil. According to Gabriele D'Annunzio, Hitler was a "ferocious clown."

According to George Lincoln Rockwell , the leader of the American Neo-Nazis, the Fuehrerbunker in Berlin where Hitler made his final stand was "the Alamo of the White race."

Politically and militarily, Hitler's initial successes were impressive. Without firing a shot, his Germany took Austria, Czechoslovakia, and part of Lithuania. Then, unleashing his war machine, Hitler and his legions conquered Poland in three weeks, Denmark in four hours, Norway in two months, the Netherlands in five days, Belgium in eighteen days, France in thirty-five days, Yugoslavia in twelve days, and Greece in eighteen days.

Finally checked outside of Moscow in 1941, Hitler would lead Germany to defeat and devastation. Germans would perish on the sands of the Sahara, drown in the dark waters of the Atlantic, freeze on the vast steppe lands of Russia, and burn in the bombed-out ruins of their own cities.

Tragically, the greatest number of German casualties were in the last two years of the war. In other words, three million German soldiers died *after* defeat had become inevitable.

HONEY

Honey (produced by bees as a food) is the best natural source of energy for man. On long expeditions, the Masai warriors of Africa expeditions would take no other food.

According to legend, the young Zeus was fed on milk and honey.

HONEY TRAP

A "honey trap" is a sexual entrapment operation. Specifically, it uses sexual desire to compromise a targeted victim.

Samson, the biblical hero, was a victim of a "honey trap." His downfall involved lust and betrayal by Delilah.

In modern times, the Israelis used a French prostitute to blackmail an Iraqi nuclear scientist to reveal the secrets of the Osirak nuclear complex in Baghdad.

In today's especially corrupt world, if the target is a heterosexual male who is not ashamed to fornicate with women, an unusual variation is used. The man finds himself the center of attention of a strikingly beautiful female. He becomes drunk—they go to a hotel room—and there he is drugged. Operatives replace the woman with a young boy, and the target is photographed in compromising postures.

In still another version of the "honey trap," East Germans used attractive men to seduce lonely West German secretaries who worked with sensitive documents and personnel.

HOSTAGE

A hostage is a person seized or held in order to induce others to comply with a demand or condition.

Hostage-taking has been used as an asymmetric weapon of war. In Nicaragua, on December 27, 1974, a band of ten men and three women from the Sandinista National Liberation Front invaded the home of a wealthy Managua businessman during a dinner party and seized a number of hostages, including a brother-in-law of the dictator, the foreign minister, and a number of diplomats. The hostages were held until Anastasio

Somoza (the dictator) agreed to pay a large ransom, release fourteen political prisoners, publish a Sandinista communique, and allow the Sandinista band to be flown safely out of the country. The action electrified the nation, and cheering crowds applauded the terrorists as they passed through the streets to the airport.

On August 22, 1978, twenty-five men, this time disguised in the National Guard uniforms of the Nicaragua security service, took the Congress of the country hostage! Once again, the dictatorship agreed to pay a ransom, release sixty political prisoners, publish Sandinista propaganda, and grant a safe passage out of the country.

On July 17, 1979, Somoza fled Nicaragua. Eventually—in 1980—he was killed in South America. In an unusual assassination, his armored limousine was destroyed by a bazooka.

"HOSTAGE" BANK HEIST

The "hostage bank heist" was a robbery technique developed by Joseph Dougherty and Terry Connor.

Dougherty and Connor would go to a bank employee's home at night and seize everyone there. Early the following morning, the robbers would force the employee to go to the bank and open the vault.

HOUSE, ASSAULT ON

In particular, commandos and hunter-killer teams like to clear houses and buildings from the top down. Moving down gives them greater speed, and it is easier to deploy weapons. As every commando knows, grenades thrown upstairs may bounce back.

To enter a structure, commandos like to plant "shaped charges" and blow a hole through a ceiling or a wall. The explosion will come without warning.

To enter a room, commandos are taught never to use the door handle. Instead, the commandos will shoot off the lock and kick open the door.

The first thing into the room will be one or two hand grenades. The commandos will pull the pins—hold the grenades for two seconds—and then throw them. The delay prevents the enemy from picking up the grenades and throwing them back.

If the room has walls made of thin plaster, fragments can go through and kill the attackers. To protect themselves—or if they are rescuing hostages—the commandos may use the same tactics with stun grenades.

HOUSE, DEFENSE OF

No house can be defended indefinitely. It is possible, however, to stop a brief assault.

To defend a house, place wire mesh over the windows to deflect grenades, molotov cocktails, and tear-gas canisters.

Remove all shrubbery, trees, and exterior obstacles. To provide protection inside the house, fill chests of drawers with sand. Place fire extinguishers, buckets of water, and wet blankets near each shooting adult.

Cut "gun points"—or "kill holes"—just above the crawl space or basement lines.

The best secret hiding place in a house is a shelter hidden by a basement wall. The shelter should extend under the yard—not under the house. This will allow you to escape if the house burns or collapses.

Remember, in 1993 the Branch Davidians in Waco, Texas built their bunker *under* their compound, and the children located there were crushed and incinerated during the law-enforcement assault.

HOUSE, OPERATIONAL

An operational house is a house used for so-called "illegal" activities.

An ideal operational house should be owned, so there is no inquisitive landlord. It should have easy access, and all approaches must be visible from inside and outside the house.

The house should have almost no furniture. That will make it easier to see if something has been moved or planted.

Occupants should maintain friendly but distant relations with all neighbors. Lifestyles of the occupants should mirror their declared "cover" professions: doctors may leave at night, for example, and salesmen are away for long periods.

Parties can be used to mask meetings. Parties also accustom neighbors to the appearance of strangers.

If possible, no compromising material is kept at the site. If there is an accidental fire, firemen will report any contraband that they encounter.

The Irish Republican Army ordered members not to keep arms on their persons or in any place associated with them. All weapons were secreted in a central location. To insure the caches were secure, the Irish Republican Army used women and teenagers to watch the weapons.

HOUSE, SAFE

A safe house is a secret hideout, unknown to the adversary, where an operative or a fugitive can find sanctuary when the situation is perilous.

Al- Qaeda, the Islamic terror group, locates safe houses in new residential developments, where the neighbors do not know one another. To make escapes easier, they prefer ground-floor accommodations. They also like houses that allow entry and exit unobtrusively by a number of different routes.

The Russian secret police like safe houses in densely populated urban areas with a transient population. Furnished rooms in university towns are considered ideal.

Unlike an operational house, a safe house is never used for overtly illegal purposes. No weapons or compromising materials are kept at the site.

The safe house must appear normal. Blinds and curtains should be open during the day.

The house should have simple furnishings. That makes it easy to see if something has been moved or changed, or a surveillance device has been planted.

The safe house is staffed by one or more support agents—sympathetic to the cause—who in all other respects lead a normal life. They have occupations and they maintain friendly (but distant) relations with the neighbors.

The safe-house keeper should use signals, such as chalk marks on a post, to indicate if the safe house is occupied, empty, secure, or compromised.

When a fugitive stays in a safe house, he uses the cover story that he is a friend or relative.

To remain effective, the safe house should be moved periodically.

HRYNIEWIECKI, IGNACY (1855 or 1856-1881)

A Polish revolutionary and the assassin of Tsar Alexander II of Russia, Ignacy Hryniecki was called Ignaty Grinevitsky in Russian.

On March 13, 1881, during a military parade, Hryniewiecki threw a nitroglycerin bomb enclosed in a glass ball. Several were killed, including the tsar and the assassin himself.

HUBRIS

Hubris is excessive pride or self-confidence.

Hubris comes in many forms. In the ancient world, Domitian, the Roman emperor, wanted to be recognized as *dominus et deus* ("lord and god").

In the modern world, when the first atomic bomb was tested in the Manhattan Project, some of the scientists involved believed that the device might set off a universal chain reaction that would ignite the nitrogen in the Earth's atmosphere and incinerate the planet.

In spite of the theoretical risk, the scientists deployed the weapon!

HUMANITY, INDIFFERENCE OF

Humans are often indifferent to the suffering of others. In 1964, for example, thirty-eight people in a New York suburb watched for an hour and a half out of apartment windows as a terrified young woman, Kitty Genovese, was slowly murdered in the courtyard below. The murderer, who was a necrophile, completed the crime by raping Genovese after she was dead. No one helped, no one raised a voice, and no one called the police.

HUMANS

Naked, alone, and helpless, we emerge into the world. In the words of St. Odon of Cluny, "We are born between feces and urine."

But what is a human?

The ancient Greeks believed that gods differed from man only in being immortal. So if a man becomes immortal, he becomes a god.

The Tibetans believe that man originated from a male ape having sexual intercourse with a female demon.

In the Koran, Allah makes man from dust, drops of semen, and congealed blood.

Giovanni Pico della Mirandola, the Renaissance humanist, said that man is higher than the angels. The nature of angels is fixed, but man can change.

Some modern occultists believe that man is a product of interstellar miscegenation. We are hybrids, with one parent from the stars.

According to science, mankind is a freak occurrence in a boundless, cold, and dark void. The first life, say the evolutionists, was spontaneously generated in a primordial slime, and those germs ultimately developed into a bloodthirsty vertebrate called man.

HUMANS, TAMING OF

With domesticated animals, as a rule, the size of the brain becomes relatively smaller as specimens are produced that devote more energy to growth and less to activity. Placid and infantilized sheep, the most domesticated of herd animals, have none of the remarkable intelligence of wild sheep.

Likewise, modern humans–caged primates living in overcrowded cities–seem to lose their natural instincts.

Of course, we call the changes "compassion," "reasonableness," and "progress," but they are actually "enfeeblement," "stupidity," and "degeneration."

HUMANS, VULNERABILITY OF

Vassili Merkouloff, a Russian murderer, was obsessed with human vulnerability. Merkouloff, who tried to stop a thief from stealing sugar, was flabbergasted when he accidentally killed the man in the struggle.

Why, Merkouloff wondered, is a human such a fragile creature? Why are we designed so that any person can easily kill any other person at any time?

Thoughts of vulnerability tormented him. If he stood in a queue, Merkouloff knew that anyone who struck him with a blunt instrument on the temple—just below and behind the ear—could take his life.

And—as Merkouloff walked down the street—he knew that anyone who struck his throat—even with a moderate blow—could cause his death.

Ultimately, Merkouloff murdered three people before killing himself in prison. He used his chains to strangle himself.

HUNGER STRIKE

A hunger strike, also called also a "Death Fast," is a form of self-starvation.

Originally, fasting or self-starvation was used in traditional cultures in order to experience visions or dreams.

At the end of nineteenth century, however, activists developed the "hunger strike" as a political weapon. A form of defiance, the hunger strike is self-starvation as a public protest against situations viewed as illegal or unfair.

One noted hunger striker was Terence MacSwiney, the Lord Mayor of Cork and a member of parliament. Arrested and incarcerated by the British for his pro-Irish activities, MacSwiney died on October 24, 1920, on the seventy-fourth day of his fast. His death would inspire Mahatma Gandhi to use self-starvation as a political weapon.

During any prolonged fast, hunger-pangs normally subside after twenty-four hours.

HUNGER STRIKE (LENGTH OF)

Since a healthy, well-nourished man has about 141,000 calories stored in his fat tissue and 24,000 calories stored in his muscle mass, he can live for sixty days without food.

An obese man can survive even longer. In 1965, a twenty-seven-year-old man who weighed 465 pounds fasted for 382 days! Surviving on water and vitamin pills, he lost 276 pounds.

HUNTING AND GATHERING

It is estimated that hunting and food gathering can sustain about ten people per square mile.

Great Britain, which today is home to fifty-seven million people, probably sustained five thousand to ten thousand people in the Mesolithic Era, the period before agriculture.

Tasmania, an island one-third the size of Britain, supported two thousand to three thousand native hunter-gatherers when the Europeans arrived in 1800.

Interestingly, historians believe that humanity has spent more than 99 percent of its existence in the hunting-and-gathering mode. Indeed, as one primitivist noted, if one were to survey the entire expanse of human history, one would see "a very long and stable period of small-scale hunting and gathering was followed by an apparently instantaneous efflorescence of technology. . . leading rapidly to extinction. Stratigraphically, the origin of agriculture and thermonuclear destruction will appear essentially simultaneous."

IDEOLOGY

An ideology is a set of beliefs. In extreme cases, an ideology may simply be an intricate network of fallacies that mutually support one other.

Beliefs—whether they are true or false—have power.

Thus, although the Roman Empire conquered Israel militarily (the Romans destroyed Jerusalem twice within a century of the death of Jesus), yet today, as Friedrich Nietzsche pointed out, men bow down to a Jew (Jesus) in Rome. An idea conquered!

An ideology can be defeated, however. Manichaeism was virtually extinguished from the face of the Earth, and Buddhism and Christianity have been essentially displaced from the areas of their births (India and Palestine respectively).

ILLUMINATI

A fabled secret society, the Illuminati were established on May 1, 1776. Originally called the Order of Perfectibilists, the group was organized in Ingolstadt, Bavaria, the place where the fictional Frankenstein created his monster.

The founder of the Illuminati was Adam Weishaupt, a law professor at Ingolstadt University. He used the code name "Spartacus," in honor of the famous rebel slave.

Educated by the Roman Catholic Jesuits, Weishaupt was accepted into Freemasonry in 1774. He would recruit the Illumanti from the Freemasons. The Illuminati members took an oath vowing perpetual silence, unshakable loyalty, and submission to the order.

The Illuminati established the model of a secret society run by leaders who hide the true purposes from the general membership. Known as "double doctrine," the rank and file learn "anodyne" goals, while "unknown superiors" know the organization's true, and quite different, inner secrets.

According to their enemies, the alleged goal of the Illuminati is to destroy Christianity and all world governments. They will then unite everyone under one world government whose ruler is Lucifer.

Others allege that the Illuminati want a utopian "super state" and the abolition of private property, social authority, and nationality. They allegedly favor free love, universal brotherhood, peace, equality, and feminism. They are anti-king and anti-church.

According Robert Shea and Robert Anton Wilson, however, the Illuminati are "too sophisticated, ruthless, and decadent to want to take over the world." Instead, "it amuses them to play with the world."

ILLUMINATI, COMMUNICATIONS OF

To crack the code of Illuminati communications, according to David Icke, one must reverse everything said by the Illuminati. If they say that they believe something—they do not. If they say that they will not do something—they will.

Also, remember the words of the founder, Adam Weishaupt: "The great strength of our order lies in its concealment: let it never appear in its own name, but always covered by another name and another occupation."

IMMORTALITY

According to the Christian Bible, only the Judaic-Christian God lives forever. First Timothy (6:15-16) makes this declaration: "The King of kings, and Lord of lords; who only hath immortality."

In contrast, Hindu lore speaks of Markandeya, the celebrated boy who never dies. Markandeya is so old that he lived in the last universe, and now in this universe Hindus claim to occasionally see him.

According to the statisticians, however, if humans were immortal—if we were impervious to the effects of old age or sickness—we would live on average about six hundred years. Even if we remained forever young, accidents, disasters, crimes, and other misfortunes would kill us.

IMPERIALISM

Imperialism is a policy of extending power and influence through colonization, use of military force, or other means.

Essentially, there are three stages of imperialism. First, strangers arrive bearing gifts. Next, they build a fortress or a base. Finally, they conquer.

All imperialists—even from another planet—would follow the three steps.

IMPERIALISM, CAMOUFLAGE OF

According to Chalmers Johnson, in his *Sorrows of Empire*, the most effective imperialism is disguised. The imperial power pretends its exploitation of the weaker is in the weak's own best interest, or their fault, the result of forces beyond human control, the consequence of the spread of civilization, or in accordance with scientific laws—anything but the truth.

IMPERIALISM, HUMILIATIONS OF

The degradation of the weak is common in imperial history.

After a rebellion in Lesotho in 1879, Chief Moorosi was killed by the British and his body was paraded around the camp with a sword thrust into the rectum. The chief's head was sent to London to be exhibited.

After defeating the Ashanti in 1896, the British forced the Ashanti king and his mother to crawl to the seated British officers in order to surrender.

Of course, sometimes the victims strike back.

In the twentieth-century colonial wars in Kenya, the Africans staked a British settler on his back and wedged his mouth open. The entire village—including women and children—urinated into the British man's mouth until he died.

IMPERIALISM, PROTECTION FROM

Scotland—unlike England—was never subdued by the Romans. Scotland was protected by the poverty of the land and the ferocity of her tribes.

The people of the Pacific Island of Niue—a place also called "Savage Island"—had an especially effective defense against imperialism: they killed not only all strangers, but also any Niue native who left the island and returned. The custom of Savage Island, although brutal, protected the people from intruders *and* disease.

IMPERIALISM, UNIVERSALITY OF

Imperialism is universal. Indeed, even the Christians have a plot to take over the world. Armed with a sacred fetish—a book called the Bible—slogan-shouting missionaries want to conquer the whole planet for the Christ.

INDIANS (PLAINS)

Hunters and warriors, the Indians of the North American Plains were some of the most formidable fighters in the history of the planet.

Although few in number—the entire population of the Cheyenne nation, for example, numbered approximately 3,500 people in 1820—they defended their freedom with courage and tenacity.

The Indians of the Plains lived in hunting bands of fifty to one hundred people. Everyone was mounted, and the band could travel eighty miles in a day—or up to two hundred miles in an emergency. The bands would congregate in tribal units every one or two years for a religious festival, commonly called a Sun Dance.

Although they lacked iron and the wheel, the Indians of the Plains were a lethal military force.

At short range, an Indian warrior could shoot an arrow completely through a so-called buffalo (the North American bison). On a horse and at full speed, he could launch an arrow two hundred yards, and he could discharge three or more before the first arrow reached the target.

INDIANS (PLAINS), ANNIHILATION OF

The United States, which ironically refers to itself as the "land of the free and the home of the brave," systematically exterminated the Indians of the Plains, America's "freest" and "bravest" inhabitants.

How was it done?

The nomadic Indians of the Plains were fast and mobile and they had no farms or towns to defend. To destroy them, William Tecumseh Sherman—an exponent of "total war"—obliterated their way of life.

First, the American government encouraged tanning companies to slaughter the "buffalo" (the American bison), the animal upon which the Indians depended. The whites massacred twenty million buffalo between 1872 and 1882. Ultimately, only 1,200 animals survived.

Second, since Indian horses ate grass, the Indians had to camp in winter and were immobile. Therefore, beginning in the autumn and winter of 1874-75, Sherman launched huge winter campaigns. Columns of soldiers, carrying grain for their horses in wagons, looked for Indian camps and destroyed them. Surviving Indians were pursued across the plains and forced into reservations.

The Indians of the southern plains were destroyed first—then the Indians of the north. The imperialism was completed by 1881.

INEQUALITY

Tonga in the Pacific Ocean developed the most aggressively unequal society in history. In traditional Tonga, ordinary women were at the disposal of the male aristocracy and commoners were arbitrarily beaten or killed.

The commoners had no afterlife in the religion of Tonga, but the upper class enjoyed an afterlife of feasting.

INEQUALITY, MODERN "DEMOCRACIES" AND

In modern democracies, "societies that ostensibly proclaim equality for all individuals," relationships of "superiority and inferiority" are "changed in form," but are nevertheless retained. The words are from sociologist Vilfredo Pareto.

Where some are fabulously wealthy and others are obscenely poor, the inequities are inevitable.

INFORMANTS

An informant is someone who reveals compromising information on another. In contrast to the blackmailer, who extorts money on the promise that he will *not* inform, the informant is a mercenary who simply sells or barters information.

The psychologist Wilhelm Reich suggested that the informant and the assassin are similar types, psychologically. They steal status parasitically, taking it from the victims that they destroy.

There are two types of informants: 1) a so-called "snitch," who is someone who secretly passes information about his fellow citizens to the police, and 2) a "whistle-blower," someone who publicly passes information about the authorities to fellow citizens.

The snitch is usually rewarded, even when he lies. The whistle-blower is frequently punished, especially when he tells the truth.

The author of *The Outlaw's Bible* gives the five reasons that motivate an informant: 1) moral indignation (why should he get away with that?), 2) a sense of revenge, 3) the desire to eliminate a rival, 4) the desire for a reward, and 5) simple fear (the informant is afraid of the police or the people on whom he is "informing").

Whatever their motivations, informants are common in history. A snitch named Judas, for example, destroyed one god (Christ), and a "whistle-blower" named John Dean brought down one president (Richard Nixon).

INFORMANTS (EXPENDABILITY OF)

Although informants are useful to states, governments treat them as "disposable assets."

According to the Supreme Court of the United States, the police have no legal obligation to protect informants. The Court has also ruled that the government is not liable, in any way, when informants are killed or injured during police-sponsored undercover operations.

INFORMANTS, MAFIA AND

Organized crime reviles informants and commits atrocities against them.

Salvatore d'Amico of Italy, who became a "snitch" after his family had been murdered by the Mafia, told the "authorities" all that he knew.

Eleven years later, a dead d'Amico was found riddled with bullets. There was a cork in his mouth.

INFORMANTS, PUNISHMENT OF

In some traditions, the informant is ruthlessly punished.

In Chinese law, during the Han and Tang dynasties, if a son accused an innocent parent of a crime, the son was executed. If a son accused a guilty parent of a crime, the son received three years of penal servitude and one hundred blows from a heavy stick for betraying his parents.

Among Talmudic Jews, the rabbis speak of *din moser*. According to this obligation, pious Jews have a moral obligation to kill any Jew who intends to turn over another Jew to non-Jewish authorities.

INFORMANTS, RECOGNITION OF

How is an informant recognized? Or a spy?

Beware of people you meet in unusual circumstances who spontaneously want to be your friend. Become especially suspicious if they ask probing questions about you, and if they start boasting about their own secret or illegal actions.

Also, note that prostitutes are often informants, and they routinely cooperate with the police.

Oddly, many men feel comfortable revealing secrets to prostitutes.

INFORMANTS (STATE GLORIFICATION OF)

Modern states often idolize informants.

The Soviet propaganda machine, for example, made an informant, Pavlik Morozov, an official "hero" of young communists. Morozov was a thirteen-year-old boy who denounced his father to the Soviet secret police for the "offense" of hoarding grain. After the boy was killed for his action by his grandfather, the U.S.S.R. claimed that Morozov had been "martyred" and statues of him became commonplace.

In the twentieth century, the Union of Soviet Socialist Republics had mandatory "informant" decrees.

INFORMANTS (STATE USE OF)

Modern states routinely use informants.

In 1989–in the waning days of the East German communist regime– the secret police had 91,000 full-time employees and 300,000 informants. Approximately one in fifty East Germans had collaborated with it. The secret police had files on six million people (over a third of the population), and friends—even relatives—had been denouncing one another.

In Albania—under the dictatorship of Enver Hoxha—citizens were required to write out autobiographical reports every year. Citizens were also ordered to list relatives, neighbors, and work colleagues guilty of "subversion, treason, or propaganda."

INITIATION RITUALS, OUTLAW GROUPS AND

In outlaw groups, the initiation ritual requires new members to commit an atrocity that will make them odious to society.

The crime binds participants more closely to the outlaw group, forcing them to share a hateful secret that puts them beyond the pale of humanity. Outcasts–pariahs—they can never rejoin the ordinary collective.

In magical conventicles, initiates are required to commit brother-sister, father-daughter, or mother-son incest.

Among the traditional Navaho, to become a sorcerer the initiate must kill a close relative.

To join the Leopard Men of Africa, initiates must provide a daughter or niece for a cannibal-murder feast.

To qualify as a "soldier" in the Mafia (a full member), the individual must have killed at least one man. To complete the initiation, the soldier-to-be pierces his finger—rubs blood on the paper image of a saint—burns the image—takes the ashes in his hand—and swears this oath:

I swear to be loyal to my brothers, never to betray them, always to aid them, and if I fail may I burn and be turned to ashes like the ashes of this image.

According to reports, to join some American outlaw groups the initiates must commit murder and –in front of members of the chapter–they must have sexual intercourse with an underage girl, an elderly woman, and a corpse.

In some Latin American terror movements, recruits must kill a policeman or a soldier before they are fully accepted into the band.

In the Aryan Brotherhood (or Aryan Nation)–America's most dangerous prison organization–the rule is "blood in, blood out." Men become members by committing murder, and they may leave the group only with their own deaths.

The most famous outlaw initiation in history was described by Sallust, the Roman historian who left a written account of the "Catiline Conspiracy." These are Sallust's words:

There was a rumor current at the time that when Catiline, on the conclusion of his speech, called on the associates of his plot to swear an oath, he passed around bowls of human blood mixed with wine; and when all had tasted of it after invoking a curse upon themselves if they broke faith, in accordance with the usual practice at such solemn ceremonies, he revealed the details of his scheme. This he is said to have done in order that the consciousness of having jointly participated in such an abomination might make them more loyal to one another.

It should be added that in some states–such as modern America—the atrocity requirement would help exclude undercover policeman from an organization. But in especially heinous states—such as tsarist Russia—the secret police would readily commit murder, cannibalism, or other crimes to penetrate a targeted group.

INSANITY DEFENSE

Insanity is a concept in law. Medicine only speaks of "mental illness."

In English-speaking countries, a person is "not guilty by reason of insanity" if—at the time that he committed his crime—he was unable to distinguish between right and wrong. If it is determined that he could not make the distinction, he will be sent to a mental hospital instead of a prison.

Of course, the legal system rarely accepts an insanity verdict. In one case in Texas, a woman told a psychiatrist that the devil ordered her to murder her five children. The psychiatrist testified that she was *not* legally insane because she knew the devil was evil!

Technically, in the eyes of the law, psychotics are legally insane. Out of touch with reality—possessing bizarre beliefs—psychotics live in a nightmarish world of hallucinations, visions, and voices. Ed Gein, the model for Robert Bloch's *Psycho*, was a psychotic.

Psychopaths, in contrast, are mentally ill but legally sane. Although they are monsters—they are calm during crimes because they are incapable of feeling guilt or remorse—they are legally sane because they know the difference between right and wrong, and chose wrong. Theodore Bundy, the killer of women, was a psychopath.

INSURRECTION, URBAN

A rebellion by the masses in a city, an urban insurrection is normally bloody, destructive, and futile.

Radicals seized the center of Paris in 1871 and proclaimed an independent entity called the Paris Commune. The greatest urban uprising of nineteenth century, the Commune held out for two months against the forces of the French government.

Ultimately, however, the insurrection was defeated.

During World War I, Irish freedom fighters, seeking independence from British rule, launched the Easter Rebellion on Easter Monday, 1916, in Dublin. Two thousand men seized the Post Office, the railroad terminal, and the courts, and proclaimed Irish independence. The British stormed the rebel strongholds, killing insurgents and civilians, and crushed the uprising in six days.

Even more destructive was the Warsaw Uprising—against the Nazi occupation force—which began in August of 1944. The one major urban insurrection of World War II, it occurred in a city of 1.5 million people which covered fifty-four square miles. Lasting fifty-two days (at the start of the insurrection, only one in ten of Polish rebels had guns), there were 22,000 rebel casualties and 225,000 civilian deaths, with the Germans suffering 10,000 killed and 7,000 missing. The Germans also lost 270 tanks to elementary weapons such as molotov cocktails.

Why are urban insurrections almost always futile? According to Friedrich Engels, improvements in technology–and the broad roads and gridiron pattern of streets–have rendered street fighting and barricades obsolete. (In fact, Paris was intentionally given broad avenues in the nineteenth century to hinder street fighting.)

Engels said that urban insurrectionists could not win unless certain circumstances favored the rebels: 1) they had to be numerically superior, 2) they had to depend on attack (not passive barricade tactics), and 3) part of the army had to join them.

According to Engels, the third circumstance could happen only after a grave crisis, such as a split in the ruling class.

INTELLECTUALS

An intellectual is a person with a highly developed intellect. In most societies, academics are *not* intellectuals. Academics, especially in North America, tend to be memorizers and imitators.

The Russians refer to intellectuals as *beloruchki*. The word means "white hands" and describes men who never need to work.

Aldous Huxley said that an intellectual is a person who had discovered something more interesting than sexuality.

According to the philosopher Aristotle, the highest point of intellectual development is "about the fiftieth year of life."

INTERROGATION, BEHAVIOR UNDER

Under interrogation, outlaws and rebels deny everything and admit nothing.

The Irish Republican Army teaches its operatives to avoid looking at the eyes of the interrogator. Avoiding eye contact makes the person being questioned more resistant.

Of course, sometimes nothing will work. Remember the infamous Nazi directive: "The subject is to be questioned until he confesses."

When interrogators abuse their power–and exercise sadism toward prisoners–the sexual organs are usually targeted.

INTERROGATION, VICTOR SERGE ON

Victor Serge, the Russian anarchist, had these suggestions for individuals under interrogation by the "police":

1) "As a matter of principle, say nothing. Explaining yourself is dangerous; you are in the hands of professionals able to get something out of your every word."
2) Remember that "lying is extremely dangerous: it is difficult to construct a story without its defects being too obvious."
3) "Do not try to be cleverer than they are." The power relationship is too unequal for that.
4) Do not let yourself be "disconcerted" by the "classic" claim: "We know everything." That "barefaced trick" is used by all police forces and examining magistrates whenever they have someone under arrest.
5) "Do not believe a word of another classic ploy: 'We know everything because your comrade has talked.'" Remember, "with a few carefully selected clues the enemy is capable of feigning a profound knowledge of things."
6) Stay calm. Do not show surprise. Say nothing.
7) "Remember that the enemy is capable of everything."
8) Finally, remember that a "confession" will destroy you, but "a hermetically sealed defense," built on "silence" and firm "denials," can only help.

ISLAM, RELIGION OF

According to some individuals, Islam is the one true faith. It was given to man by Muhammad, the "seal of the prophets," who saw the archangel Gabriel on "the night of power."

According to its critics, Islam is a Jewish heresy, copied from the older monotheistic faith.

To become a Muslim, a person must recite a famous phrase three times in the presence of a Muslim witness. ("There is no god but Allah, and Muhammad is his prophet."). Once taken, the step can NEVER be revoked. The penalty for apostasy in Islam is death.

When a man becomes a Muslim, he is promised eternal orgasmic bliss in paradise. He will become thirty years of age in heaven and he will enjoy seventy-two modest virgins "with swelling breasts." The women will never age—their virginity will be constantly renewed—and the saved man's libido will be inexhaustible.

ISLAMIC MILITANCY

Islam divides the world into two regions: the House of Submission (the area under the Koran) and the House of War (the area not conquered by Islam).

Islamic militants fight the "Four Heads of the Monster." The first head is "the Jew," "the eternal schemer against Allah." The second head is symbolized by the Christian Cross, which represents the aggressions of the Crusaders (which have never ended). The third head is atheism. The fourth Head is secularism, the antithesis of *Shari'a* Law or Allah's law.

The militants believe, however, that the enemy is everywhere. In the Muslim world itself the enemy is in the form of corrupt governments and diseased culture.

ISOLATION, IMPOSSIBILITY OF

Horrified by World War I, a Frenchman searched the globe for an area where he could live in peace and freedom. He chose an isolated island which had once served as a coal station. According to his reasoning, the place would fall into obscurity with the development of diesel-powered boats and ships.

The name of the island was Guadalcanal. It would become one of the bloodiest battlefields of World War II.

JAMES III (1451-1488)

James III, a king of Scotland, was killed, at the age of thirty-seven, in a church. The assassin, disguised as a priest, heard the king's confession and then eviscerated him.

JEHOVAH

Called Yahweh by the scholars, Jehovah is a totalitarian god described in an iron-age text called the Bible. He last spoke directly with mankind when he addressed Job in the form of a whirlwind.

According to Jewish tradition, Jehovah is vast in size. The *Shiur Komah*, written in the second century of the current era, says that Jehovah is 236 "ten thousand thousands" parasangs high. Since a parasang is 3.6 feet, Jehovah is approximately 8,496,000,000 feet tall, or approximately 1,609,080 miles.

According to the Christians, Jehovah is a violent god of force and majesty–all-powerful, all-knowing, and all-good. An omnipotent disciplinarian, he rewards the "faithful" with eternal bliss and he damns all reprobates to the green fires of an eternal hell.

According to the Gnostics, an early Christian heresy, Jehovah is not the true god, but a demiurge. Sadistic and perverse, he is vindictive, jealous, and evil. This world, inaugurated in blood and crime, is the work of Jehovah.

According to Thomas Jefferson, Jehovah is the tyrant god, a "being of terrific character—cruel, vindictive, capricious, and unjust."

Interestingly, Jehovah preferred the blood sacrifice of Abel to the bloodless offering of Cain.

JESUS, SON OF MARY

The flogged and crucified god, "the late Jesus Christ of Biblical fame" was a murdered rebel. A nonconformist, he taught his followers to "resist not evil."

Although blood is taboo to all Jews, Jesus (according to the Gospel of John, Chapter 6) made this promise: "He who eats my flesh and drinks my blood has eternal life."

Who–exactly–was Jesus?

According to "orthodox" Christianity, Jesus was a Judaic avatar, the messiah who was truly god and truly man, the second person of a "blessed trinity." In an act of supreme generosity, he suffered a horrible death to save ungrateful mortals.

According to Islam, Jesus was a great prophet, but he was a man. This statement is written in the Koran (sura 5): "They misbelieve who say, 'verily God is the third of three. . . .' The Messiah, the son of Mary, is only a prophet."

According to Hermann Samuel Reimarus , an eighteenth-century skeptic, Jesus was nothing more than a failed revolutionary whose body was secretly removed by his disciples.

According to the Talmud (*Gittin 57a*), written by people persecuted by the Christians, Jesus was a false prophet who is now in hell "boiling in hot feces."

JESUS, DEATH OF

In the eyes of most, Jesus is a dead and resurrected god, like Osiris, Tammuz, Adonis, and Dionysus. But some people—including more than one billion Muslims—believe that Jesus did not die on the cross.

The Koran of Islam, in sura 4, makes this declaration: "Yet they slew him not, and they crucified him not, but they had only his likeness."

Oddly, an Islamic legend maintains that Jesus lived to an advanced age, and died in the east. According to this same tradition, his body is buried in a tomb in Srinagar, the capital of Kashmir.

In some so-called Gnostic texts–written by Christian heretics–the notion that Jesus was not crucified is also asserted. In the Second Treatise of the Great Seth, Jesus speaks these curious words: "It was another . . . who drank the gall and the vinegar; it was not I. They struck me with the reed; it was another, Simon, who bore the cross on his shoulder. It was another upon whom they placed the crown of thorns. But I was rejoicing in the height over . . . their error . . . . And I was laughing at their ignorance."

JOAN OF ARC (1412-1431)

A celebrated virgin—renowned for her courage and her beauty—Joan of Arc led French troops into battle during the Hundred Years' War.

Clad in white armor, she shed no blood herself, but she carried the battle standard and inspired the men. In her army, she forbade looting, blasphemy, gambling, and prostitutes.

Captured by the English, Joan was stripped naked and was burned alive at the age of nineteen. Her heart and intestines were ripped from her body and burned separately.

A contemporary, the Duke d'Alencon, expressed this opinion: "I looked at her breasts, which were beautiful."

Today, Joan is honored as a saint by the Roman Catholic church. The Catholics do not classify her as a "martyr" because she was murdered on the order of a legally constituted church court.

JUDAISM

An ancient religion, eldest of the three great Abrahamic faiths, Judaism is (with Manichaeism and Witchcraft) one of the most persecuted religions in history.

At various times, Jews have been the victims of massacres and pogroms, murders and expulsions. Jews were expelled from England in 1290, from France in 1306, from Austria in 1420, from Spain in 1492, from Florence in 1495, from Portugal in 1496-7, from Naples in 1541, and from Milan in 1597.

According to the devotees and admirers of Judaism, Jews are all the descendants of one man, a fabled Bedouin from Mesopotamia called Abraham.

As the presumed descendants of Abraham, Jews believe that they belong to a chosen family. They are encouraged by the biblical promise made by Jehovah (in Isaiah, chapter 60): "The nation and kingdom that will not serve you shall perish; those nations shall be utterly laid waste."

Yet, this same Jehovah made this declaration (in Leviticus, 25:55): "The descendants of Israel are my slaves."

JUDAS (died A.D. 29-33)

A reviled traitor, the apostle known as Judas Iscariot betrayed Jesus the Galilean "with a kiss." The poet Dante Alighieri condemned Judas to the lowest circle of hell.

In the twentieth century, however, the communists in the Soviet Union erected a statue of Judas Iscariat at Svishka, near Kazan, in 1923.

JURY NULLIFICATION

Jury nullification—a safeguard against bad laws and biased judges—is important in some legal systems, including the United States. According to this principle, the jury in a trial has the right and duty not only to judge the *facts* of the case, but also the *law* itself.

In other words, although the government may pass laws against narcotics, abortion, vigilante activities, and so forth, juries are under no obligation to convict individuals who violate those laws.

During the Prohibition Era of American history—when most citizens were better informed—50 percent of the individuals who appeared to be guilty of "bootlegging" charges were released by juries. The juries simply refused to enforce a law that they despised.

Today, in an effort to thwart jury nullification, some American judges perversely instruct juries to judge only the facts of a case. According to common law, however, this instruction can be ignored.

In Switzerland, it is interesting to note, the jurors are informed in all important criminal cases that they may judge both the facts and the law.

JURY TRIAL

The Sixth Amendment to the American Constitution guarantees the right to a jury trial.

With a jury trial, the defense has to convince only one juror that the defendant is innocent. That produces a "hung jury," which means the state has to try the accused a second time or release him.

JUSTICE (SUBVERSION OF)

Dante Alighieri referred to "the horrid art of justice." And—in all times and in all civilizations—justice has been subverted by some.

The methods of perverting justice are obvious in totalitarian systems: charges are invented, evidence is fabricated, and "confessions" are extorted with the application of torture.

Orwell, in *1984,* described the process:

It was always at night—the arrests invariably happened at night. The sudden jerk out of sleep, the rough hand shaking your shoulder, the lights glaring in your eyes, the ring of hard faces round the bed. In the vast majority of cases there was no trial, no report of the arrest. People simply disappeared, always during the night. Your name was removed from the registers, every record of everything you had ever done was wiped out, your one-time existence was denied and then forgotten.

In so-called democracies—and quasi-totalitarian regimes—the techniques are more subtle.

In the U.S.A., for example, the justice system ensnares people with innumerable tricks, all of which are legal. For example, after a thief stole fifty thousand dollars from a bank, Charles Johnson and his gang robbed the bank robber. Curiously, Johnson and his men were prosecuted for "receiving stolen property."

Standard snares in the laws of America include the following:

1) *The Felony Murder Law.* If a killing occurs during the commission of a felony, the criminal is guilty of murder in the first degree even if *he* did not kill anyone. Thus, if two men rob a bank, and a policeman kills one

of the robbers, the surviving robber is guilty of murder because a death occurred during the felony!

2) *Mistake of Law.* In the United States, not knowing the law is not a valid defense. The offender will be convicted of a crime even if he genuinely thought that the act was legal.

3) *Criminal Solicitation.* Simply to request, command, or encourage someone to commit a crime or to attempt to commit a crime is itself a crime.

4) *Multiplying Charges.* Prosecutors never charge the accused with *one* crime— they will file as many counts and charges as they can, hoping to win at least one conviction. Thus, a five-minute robbery of a retail store can become a confinement charge (for each person in the store), several counts of displaying a deadly weapon not in self-defense, one count of armed robbery, one count of carrying a concealed weapon, one count of possessing an unrestricted firearm, one count of fleeing the scene of a crime, one resisting arrest charge, and so forth.

In 1975, after a simple wrestling match between Native Americans and white teenagers ended in the theft of a white boy's cowboy boots, the F.B.I. (in an attempt to neutralize the American Indian Movement) initially accused a nineteen-year-old Jimmy Eagle of kidnapping (a capital crime!), aggravated assault, and aggravated robbery.

5) *Aggravating Circumstances.* So-called "aggravating circumstances" are used by the legal system to "enhance" the punishment. Aggravating circumstances are "dangerousness" (a gun is used by the criminal), "heinousness" (the crime is exceptionally cruel), and "repetitive nature" (the criminal keeps committing the same crime).

6) *Accomplices.* In the U.S.A., few states make any distinction between the perpetrators of a crime and criminal accomplices. All can be punished equally.

Legally, an accomplice is anyone who helps another commit a crime. Even if the accomplice does not participate in the actual commission of the offense, his previous assistance makes him just as guilty.

In 1955, for example, California executed an accomplice named Barbara Graham. Three others had robbed and murdered a widow, but Graham was executed for merely helping them gain entry into the widow's home.

7) *Accessory after the Fact.* Anyone who knows that a felon has committed a crime–and helps that felon avoid arrest or trial–is an accessory after the fact. Accessories are usually punished less than accomplices or principals.

To be an accessory after the fact, you must provide help after the crime is legally finished. (Legally, a crime is finished when the perpetrator reaches a place of temporary or permanent safety.) If the crime is not legally finished, you become an accomplice.

8) *The High Cost of Vindication.* In many jurisdictions, such as the United States, if the accused person is found innocent by a court of law, he is *not* compensated for his legal fees, and the arrest remains on his record, even though he may have been maliciously and falsely accused.

JUSTICE, VIGILANTE

A vigilante is a member of a self-appointed group of people who undertake law enforcement in their community without the sanction of the "state power."

Supporters refer to vigilante justice as "people's justice." Detractors refer to vigilantes as a "lynch mob."

Among the Germans, vigilante justice was traditionally imposed by the notorious Vehmic Tribunals. Allegedly established before the sixteenth century in Westphalia, the Vehm was a secret and powerful body that imposed justice (with a rope and a tree) in chaotic times.

KAMIKAZE

The classic state-sponsored suicide attackers were the Japanese kamikazes of World War II. The kamikazes were named after the "Divine Wind," the 1281 typhoon that destroyed the Mongol invasion fleet.

When interrogated after the war, Lieutenant General Torashiro Kawabe revealed the rationale behind the attacks. He declared to the Americans: "We believed that our spiritual convictions and moral strength could balance your material and scientific advantages."

Before an attack, a kamikaze operative conducted a special ritual. He donned a white scarf decorated with the "Rising Sun," he wrapped his waist with a belt of one thousand stitches (made by one thousand women making one stitch each), he consumed a traditional last meal (rice, beans, fish, and *sake*), and he composed and recited a death poem (a tradition once practiced by samurai knights committing *seppuku*).

According to Japanese estimates, 4,615 kamikaze fighters died in action. Euphemistically referred to as "special attack forces," the kamikazes were ordered to die only if they could kill. If the odds were too great and there was no chance of success, it was not dishonorable for the kamikazes to turn back. According to orders, they were not to squander their lives on a futile attack.

To evade radar, the kamikaze pilot came in fast and low. If possible, he attacked ships from landward (the shore echoes cluttered enemy radar). By dropping chaff—aluminum foil strips—he further obscured himself.

When the kamikaze spotted a ship, he gained altitude and made his attack dive with guns blazing. In night attacks, he would "ride down" the streams of tracer fire emitted from the target.

Diving at high speed—ideally at a 55-degree angle—the kamikaze was difficult to stop. A ship's anti-aircraft guns had no more than twenty seconds to destroy a kamikaze when it came within range, and "total disintegration" was the only way to neutralize a suicide attacker.

The ultimate target was an aircraft carrier. The optimum hit on a carrier was on the flight deck, at the base of the island.

Fearing hysteria, the American government deliberately imposed a news embargo on the kamikaze attacks.

KIDNAPPING

Kidnapping, the act of abducting and holding someone captive for ransom, is a form of entrepreneurial terrorism. Kidnapping is an old tradition in Greece, Sicily, and Corsica.

It was not until 1874, however, that professional criminals attempted to kidnap a victim for ransom in the U.S.A. In earlier times there was little contact between the rich and poor—the rich lived in stately houses and the poor languished in slums—so there had been little opportunity to seize a victim.

KIDNAPPING (POLITICAL)

Some terror groups organize political kidnappings for revolutionary ends (to help the struggle) or "entrepreneurial ends" (to raise money).

In Italy in 1978, for example, the Red Brigades kidnapped Aldo Moro, a former prime minister, on his way to the parliament. Moro's five bodyguards were killed during the abduction.

The Red Brigades detained Moro for fifty-five days, tried him before a "people's court," and ultimately executed him. Moro was shot eleven times.

KILLERS, NATURAL

Psychologists suggest that 3-4 percent of men, and 1 percent of women, are "natural killers." These "natural killers" are people who kill easily and without the powerful feeling of sacrilege that most humans feel.

Natural killers make effective soldiers and typically they account for a significant portion of the enemy dead.

KILLING

Historically, the ruling elite claims there are three types of killing: 1) murder (what the common people do), 2) punitive execution (what the state does), and 3) sacrifice (what the priests do).

KILLING, TRAINING AND

Anyone can be trained to kill.

In the American-Vietnamese War, there were *reports* that men in the "special forces" toughened themselves by killing harmless domestic animals.

KINGS

A king is a kind of political tyrant. Like all tyrants, he uses some of his subjects to enslave the rest.

According to Etienne de La Boetie, although tyrants "may ascend their thrones by differing routes, the manner of their ruling remains more or less the same. The people's elected leaders treat the people like a bull to be tamed; its leaders through conquest, like a prey with which they are entitled to do as they please; and those who rule by right of succession, like a troupe of slaves whose nature is to belong to them."

KLEPTOCRACY

Kleptocracy is a government in which a leader controls most economic activity for a portion of the profits. Typically, a kleptocracy is "a carnival of nepotism and graft."

Kleptocrats are often found in impoverished countries. In such places, public office is one of the few remaining ways for an ambitious man to become rich.

A classic kleptocrat was Francois "Papa Doc" Duvalier, who ruled and plundered the island nation of Haiti. Under Duvalier, tax revenues—extorted from the people—were not used for national development, education, or public health. Instead, taxes were squandered on the army, the police (including the dreaded *Ton Ton Macoutes*), and on propaganda. Duvalier simply used taxes to help him keep power.

Note that Aristotle argued that "it is in the interests of a tyrant to make his subjects poor." Since impoverished people are preoccupied with "daily tasks," they "have no time for plotting" rebellions or revolutions.

KNIFE

A lethal weapon, a three-inch knife can reach any vital organ in the body.

If confronted by a knife attacker, do not ignore his other hand. He may be holding crushed pepper, or he may punch, then stab.

During World War II bayonet charges, the Japanese bandaged pressure points on their bodies so that they could fight on longer if an artery were cut.

KNIGHTS OF THE APOCALYPSE

The Knights of the Apocalypse–a secret society which is only rumored to exist–is an outlaw group. Composed of fiercely pious Roman Catholics, the group was allegedly established in 1693.

Members of the group are assassins. Their mission is to save mankind. Whenever the Anti-Christ is born, they hunt Satan's child and murder him in the cradle. Allegedly, they have killed several children already.

KU KLUX KLAN

Called America's "most persistent terrorist organization," the Ku Klux Klan was established in 1865 by six confederate veterans in Pulaski, Tennessee.

The original Klan was an underground resistance movement to restore white supremacy. Members had to swear an oath of secrecy about Klan activities and the identities of other Klansmen.

Nathan Bedford Forrest, a confederate cavalry leader, was elected "Grand Wizard" of the Klan in 1867. The phrase "Invisible Empire," which referred to the territories where the Klan existed, was coined at the same time.

The original Klan was dormant for a time, but in 1905 Thomas Dixon, Jr. published a novel called *The Clansman : An Historical Romance of the Ku Klux Klan*. Dixon's novel depicted the Klan as an order of chivalry devoted to saving "the South."

The novel inspired D.W. Griffith's film, *The Birth of a Nation*, and the film and book led to the revival of the Klan in 1915.

President Woodrow Wilson, after viewing the film, claimed that the K.K.K. had saved civilization on the North American continent.

President Warren Harding, Wilson's successor, was initiated into the Klan in the Green Room of White House. Supreme Court Justice Hugo Black joined the Klan in the 1920's.

Also, a young Harry Truman paid a ten-dollar initiation fee to the Missouri K.K.K..

KU KLUX KLAN (MODERN)

At the end of the twentieth century, the Ku Klux Klan changed.

In 1983, Robert Miles, a Ku Klux Klan leader, claimed that the organization had to revert to its original form as a military underground operating in "enemy-controlled territory."

According to Miles, the Klan could no longer support the police or the American Constitution because hostile forces control both.

Also in 1983, Louis Beam, in his "Essays of a Klansman," said that for the third time in the history of the United States the government is the enemy of the people. The other two times, he claimed, were 1776 and 1861.

Beam said that resistance should come from decentralized cadres, like the Minutemen in 1776 and the original Klan. He claimed that 1776 was not a popular uprising—it was an "unpopular rebellion of a politically radical minority."

KURI, KONCA (died 1999)

A murdered martyr, Konca Kuri was a Turkish feminist. Kidnapped by Ilim—a Turkish Islamic Terror group—Ilim tortured her for thirty-five hours before she was killed.

The torture and murder were recorded on film.

LADY GODIVA (circa. 1040-1080)

A non-violent protester, Lady Godiva, the wife of the Earl of Mercia, became famous for her naked ride on a white horse through Coventry. With the unnamed naked man in the Gospel of Mark (14:51), she is the most fabled nudist in history.

The story was first told by a thirteenth century chronicler named Roger of Wendover. He claimed that she had made her ride in 1057 to protest the high taxes imposed by her husband, the Earl of Mercia.

Regarding nakedness, Leonardo da Vinci made the curious statement: "The act of coition and the members employed are so ugly that but for the beauty of the faces, the adornments of their parents, and the frantic urge, Nature would lose the human race."

LAMM, HERMAN "THE BARON" (1880-1930)

Herman "the Baron" Lamm was a German immigrant to America who perfected the "science" of bank robbing.

The "Lamm Technique," which was copied by John Dillinger and is still used today, treats the bank robbery as a military operation. Each gang member is given a specific objective, the time frame to complete it, and so forth.

The Lamm technique involves three steps: 1) "case" or "reconnoiter" the bank, 2) practice the robbery on a "mock up" of the bank, and 3) practice the "getaway" on the streets in all types of weather.

Above all, the "Lamm Technique" emphasizes two points: 1) treat the escape as important as the "heist" and 2) the robbers must always leave the scene at a prearranged time, no matter how much (or how little) loot they had collected.

The latter point is especially important. According to Lamm, robbers tend to be "drawn" into the crime and tarry too long.

LARGESSE

Largesse is generosity with money or gifts.

In the medieval period of European history, an honored knight did not hoard, save, or invest. He plundered and extorted ransoms in order to spend freely, to give away, to demonstrate his generosity, his largesse.

In traditional societies, generosity has this rule: the receiver becomes a debtor and now owes a gift.

LAST WORDS

The final words of any endeavor should be significant. According to the Theravada tradition, these were the last words the Buddha spoke: "Doubt everything. Find your own light!"

For a book, perhaps the most celebrated last words were written by Vladimir Nabokov: "And this is the only immortality you and I may share, my Lolita."

LAUGHTER

The expression of amusement or derision, laughter is caused by a sudden feeling of superiority.

In *The Republic*, book III, Plato condemns laughter, forbids it among the guardians, and says the gods should not be represented laughing.

LAW

The law refers to a system of rules.

Always–in every era and civilization–the function of law is to keep those who hold power, in power.

According to Henry David Thoreau, "The man for whom the law exists–the man of forms, the conservative–is a tame man."

According to Solon, the ancient Greek lawgiver, "To the strong all laws are cobwebs."

LAWRENCE, THOMAS EDWARD (1888-1935)

Thomas E. Lawrence, famous as "Lawrence of Arabia," was a modern "knight errant" and a successful guerrilla commander who led an Arab revolt against the Turks.

A curious character–Lawrence was a homosexual masochist–he survived combat only to be killed in a motorcycle accident.

LEADER

There are many types of leaders.

The commander of a conventional army is a master of slaves. His authority is supported by firing squads, leg irons, and prisons.

The guerrilla or terrorist leader, in contrast, is a leader of free men. They follow him only because they *chose* to follow him.

What qualities must a guerrilla or terror leader possess? In the Arab world, the leader most loved by his people is the leader most feared by his enemies.

He who intimidates enemies makes a splendid guerrilla or terror leader.

LEADERLESS RESISTANCE

Leaderless resistance is a form of "acephalous" organization for outlaw movements. Popularized in 1983 by Louis Beam, a "white supremacist," leaderless resistance is an extreme form of decentralized organization.

Where tyranny is especially dangerous—where surveillance is omnipresent—or where informants are effective—leaderless resistance is the only way for terrorists, guerrillas, bandits, secret societies, and conspiracies to survive.

Leaderless resistance involves one-person cells or small "action groups" of three to five members. Joined only by an ideology, each one-person cell or small action group remains completely autonomous. The cells never report to a central headquarters or single leader for direction or instruction. According to Beam, a movement without a visible head is difficult to detect. If detected, it is difficult to immobilize.

Moreover, since there is no explicit communication between cells, members of one cell have little or no information on the membership of other cells. If one cell is destroyed, the other cells will continue to function.

The Animal Liberation Front—a radical vegetarian and anti-vivisectionist movement—employs the leaderless resistance principle. The published manual of the movement states that there is no formal membership—no command structure—and people become members by taking part in actions, not by paying money or completing paper forms.

Despite the obvious advantages, leaderless resistance movements are often unstable. And—if actions are infrequent or unsuccessful—the formation of new cells may be retarded.

Leaderless resistance groups are also vulnerable to "false-flag operations," which may be conducted by the authorities to discredit them.

LEADERLESS RESISTENCE, PROPAGANDA AND

To disseminate the message, a leaderless resistance organization will typically possess an overt propaganda arm. This will consist of an author or an inspirational figure.

The propaganda operative never violates the law and he never manages or executes operations. He simply provides ideas for the struggle and spreads the ideology.

LENIN, VLADIMIR (1870-1924)

A successful rebel and revolutionary, Vladimir Lenin became the father of the Union of Soviet Socialist Republics.

Oddly, Lenin spent more of his life in the West than in Russia.

LEOPARD, SOCIETY OF THE

Centered in west Africa, in Sierra Leone, the Society of the Leopard is an ancient secret society of men who hunt humans.

To join the Society of the Leopard, initiates must provide a young girl for sacrifice. The victim, who has to be the initiate's own sister or daughter, is murdered with a claw knife.

Members of the society always kill at night, wearing leopard skins over the body and pronged, claw-like weapons with double-edged blades over the hands. The leopard is their totem, and they practice rites involving cannibalism and blood drinking to gain magic power.

When not hunting, the Leopard Society members live an otherwise normal existence. Like the Thuggee of India, they are sworn to secrecy.

On August 5, 1895, the British executed three Leopard men for murdering travelers. One of the Leopard men had been a Christian Sunday School teacher.

LETTOW-VORBECK, GENERAL PAUL EMIL VON(1870-1964)

A celebrated guerrilla leader, General Paul Emil von Lettow-Vorbeck was in charge of the German East African forces during World War I. Starting with a small force (in 1914 he commanded 156 Europeans, 1,168 native soldiers, and 3,000 native carriers), Lettow-Vorbeck used asymmetric warfare to tie up 250,000 British and British Colonial troops for the duration of the war. Only the defeat of Germany in Europe stopped him.

Interestingly, Lettow-Vorbeck learned in action. After some skirmishes that proved costly, he divided his army into small units, some as small as ten men, and sent them on special missions.

Lettow-Vorbeck gave his men standing orders that acquiring ammunition from the enemy was their primary function. They were ordered to have more bullets at the end of every battle than at the start!

Cut off from outside supplies, everything his army needed had to be produced under primitive conditions: shoes, shirts, quinine—even ersatz gasoline. The general's own shoes were made out of deerskin.

LEVIN, VLADIMIR (born 1971)

A twenty-four-year-old Russian graduate student, Vladimir Levin committed the first computer bank "heist" in history. (Stanley Rifkin had to physically enter the bank to steal codes and commit his crime.) Using a refurbished laptop and modem, Levin transferred ten million dollars from Citibank to accounts opened by accomplices in the United States, Israel, Finland, Sweden, Germany, the Netherlands, and Switzerland.

LIBERTATIA

Libertatia, also known as Libertalia, was a pirate state allegedly formed under the leadership of Captain Mission. Located on St. Mary, an island near Madagascar, Libertatia reputedly lasted about twenty-five years, ending in the early eighteenth century.

Although Libertatia had an economy based on rape and plunder, each pirate had an equal vote and Libertatia may have been the first democracy.

Libertatia is described in a book called *A General History of the Most Notorious Pirates* by one Captain Johnson. It is unclear to what extent the book is fact, fiction, or a mixture of both.

LINCOLN, ABRAHAM (1809-1865)

A successful tyrant, with Otto von Bismarck and Vladimir Lenin, Lincoln created the modern centralized state.

During his period in office, Lincoln worked to emasculate the states and exalt federal power. (World War II would complete the process.) Using the Civil War as a pretext, Lincoln introduced America to the income tax, forced conscription, and trials before military tribunals without juries or lawyers. Lincoln even deported one of his critics in Congress, Clement L. Vallandigham of Ohio, and imprisoned most of the members of the Maryland state legislature.

Although remembered in "sanitized" history as a great emancipator, the loutish and ill-bred Lincoln was in fact a racist. These words were spoken by Lincoln: "I will say, then, that I am not, nor ever have been, in favor of bringing about in any way, the social and political equality of the white and black races.... I am as much as any other man in favor of having the superior position assigned to the white race."

And Lincoln also made this declaration: "Negro equality! Fudge! How long, in the government of a God, great enough to make and maintain this Universe, shall there continue knave to vend, and fools to gulp, so low a piece of demagoguism as this?"

LISKOW, ALFRED (died 1941)

A murdered informant, Alfred Liskow was the first casualty of "Operation Barbarosa" in World War II.

A communist sympathizer in the Nazi army, Liskow deserted on June 21, 1941 to warn the Russians that the Nazis were planning to attack. He was not believed, and the naive Liskow was shot immediately on Stalin's orders.

The Nazis assaulted the Soviet Union on June 22–on the summer solstice.

LLOPART, FRANCISCO (1915-1960)

An anarchist guerrilla, Francisco Llopart raided Catalonia from France after World War II. As a matter of policy, whenever possible he moved toward the police in a fight, simply because it unnerved them.

Llopart robbed banks not simply for money, but (as a matador fights bulls) to show courage.

LONG, HUEY PIERCE (1893-1935)

A murdered demagogue, Huey Long was a politician from Louisiana. In 1934—in the depth of the "Great Depression—Long organized the "Share-Our-Wealth Society," which promised to redistribute wealth.

Long promised that every American would be guaranteed an income (2,500 dollars in 1934 moneys) and a homestead (up to 5,000 dollars in value). He said that the capitalist system would continue, but no American would be allowed to own more than five million dollars.

Long announced–in August 1935–that he would challenge Franklin Delano Roosevelt for the presidency. In September, Long was murdered under suspicious circumstances.

The alleged assassin–a successful young physician named Dr. Carl Weiss–was shot sixty-one times by Long's security people.

LOOKOUTS

A lookout is a person stationed to keep watch. They are used by outlaws and the police.

An effective lookout must always disguise his activity. He must appear to be doing something innocuous, such as waiting for a bus or talking on a telephone.

LOPEZ, FRANCISCO SOLANO (1826-1870)

A churlish tyrant, the grotesquely ugly and obese Francisco Solano Lopez was the president of Paraguay between 1862 and 1870. He spent most of his rule fighting a disastrous war against Argentina, Brazil, and Uruguay.

During the six-year war, Paraguay went from 1.4 million people to 29,000 adult males, 106,000 women, and 86,000 children. Paraguay's adult male population was reduced by 90 percent.

Near the end of his life—when his crushing military defeat showed he could not be a "Napoleon"—Lopez had himself declared a "saint." When twenty-three bishops objected, he had them shot.

When his seventy-year-old mother confessed he was illegitimate, Lopez had her publicly flogged and ordered her execution.

On the positive side, Francisco Solano Lopez died in battle against his country's enemies. Few modern leaders have done the same.

LOPEZ, RIGOBERTO (1930-56)

A successful assassin, Rigoberto Lopez killed Anastasio Somoza, a Nicaraguan dictator, in 1956. Lopez himself was killed by Somoza's bodyguard.

Showing foresight, Lopez bought an insurance policy before the attack. He made his mother the beneficiary.

LOVE

What is love?

According to Plato, love is the effect of beauty on the beholder.

According to Aristotle, love is proportionate to superiority, and whoever is superior must receive more affection than he gives.

According to the Marquis de Sade, "To love and enjoy are two very different things: the proof whereof is that one loves every day without enjoying, and even more often one enjoys without loving."

According to Arthur Schopenhauer, love does not exist to make us happy, but to deceive us under the cover of happiness, and to compel us to perform actions profitable to the human race, but suicidal to the individual.

According to modernists, no one can love a master or a slave.

LOYALTY

Loyalty refers to a strong feeling of support or allegiance.

Adam Mickiewicz, the Polish poet, commented that extreme loyalty is "commendable for a dog, but an offense for a human being."

LUCHENI, LUIGI (1873-1910)

An Italian assassin, Luigi Lucheni killed Elizabeth, the Austrian-Hungarian empress, in 1898. Lucheni used a stiletto he had fashioned from a second-hand screwdriver costing ten pence.

To prepare for his mission—to make certain his aim was perfect—Lucheni carefully studied human anatomy.

When he at last attacked, Lucheni penetrated his victim's heart so quickly—and the wound he made was so small–that the empress did not realize she had been stabbed. There was no sign of blood until her clothes were removed.

Thinking her pain was from shock, the empress continued her journey. She died before the end of the day.

LUDDITES

Established in 1811, the Luddites were a secret society (with oaths and passwords) dedicated to destroying the machines of the industrial age that were causing human unemployment.

The Luddite attackers operated at night, wore masks, and used hand tools to smash the machinery destroying jobs. The group took its name from a semi-mythical worker in Leicester who destroyed machinery.

In 1812, the British government introduced the death penalty for breaking machines. Note that the governing class valued a machine over a human life!

LYING

A lie is an intentionally false statement. According to Francesco Guicciardini, "Always deny what you do not want to be known, and always affirm what you want to be believed."

According to police interrogators, these are the classic signs that the subject is lying: 1) a hesitation or pause before answering, 2) a break in eye contact when answering, 3) staring at the walls or floor, 4) a constant repetition of the question before answering, 5) a hand placed over the mouth while answering, and 6) constant fidgeting.

Look for the signs to ascertain if another is lying; avoid the signs if you are lying.

When telling a lie, remember that a "lie of commission" (a completely fabricated story) is less effective then a "lie of omission" (a distortion of the truth by the selective deletion of details).

Also, remember that a plausible story is no more than thirty words in length. Anything else appears to be a fabricated story.

When dealing with the police or other representatives of a government, the general rule is you should withhold information but never lie to them. Remember, "forgetting" is not a crime.

LYING, AMERICAN LAW AND

In the United States, any person uttering one false word to a federal agent—even in casual street conversation—faces five years in prison and a large fine. The law is so comprehensive that a person can be prosecuted for making the false statement to an *undercover* federal agent.

Perversely, the ethics course at the F.B.I. Academy teaches that federal agents have an unlimited right to *deceive* a suspect.

LYING, NICCOLO MACHIAVELLI ON

According to Niccolo Machiavelli, never tell a lie unless you know the truth.

LYING, THE STATE AND

The modern state has mastered the technique of perverting language.

Note these examples from the state lexicon: *they* use violence, *we* use force; *they* plot, *we* plan; *they* conspire, *we* cooperate; *they* form a criminal syndicate, *we* form a coalition; *they* seize hostages, *we* arrest; *they* bribe, *we* plea bargain; *they* murder, *we* execute; *they* extort, *we* tax.

In George Orwell's *1984*, in the fictional state of Oceania, the "Ministry of Peace" concerns itself with war, the "Ministry of Truth" concerns itself with lies, and the "Ministry of Love" concerns itself with torture.

LYNCHING

An act of vigilante "justice"—allegedly named after Captain Lynch of eighteenth century Virginia—lynching is an act of murder *not* sanctioned by so-called established authority.

Americans in particular love to join a posse or a mob to assault "subversives." On June 27, 1844, for example, the thirty-nine-year-old Mormon prophet (Joseph Smith) was lynched in Carthage, Illinois.

Between 1882 and 1951 in the United States, mobs lynched 1,293 whites and 3,437 blacks. When the victims were black, they were often chained to a stake, flayed alive, soaked in kerosene, and burned.

In one especially heinous lynching on February 22, 1898, F.B. Baker was murdered in Lake City, South Carolina for simply accepting the office of postmaster. Baker was a black man.

MACHIAVELLI, NICCOLO (1469-1527)

A Florentine political philosopher and playwright, Niccolo Machiavelli is best known as the author of *The Prince*, an amoral political treatise which articulates the advantages of cruelty and deception.

Cesar Borgia, a ruler indifferent to moral restraints, was Machiavelli's ideal.

MAFIA

The Mafia is a violent conspiratorial group. The word "Mafia" was first mentioned in 1862, in *The Mafia in the Vicarage*, a play by Giuseppe Rizzuto. The play describes a clandestine criminal society with secret symbols, gestures, and ceremonies.

A form of organized crime, the Mafia corrupts public officials, infiltrates legitimate businesses, and makes profits on gambling, loan sharking, money laundering, murder, racketeering, extortion, counterfeiting, prostitution, the trade in human organs, and drug trafficking.

In contrast to terrorist groups, which view the state and its institutions as external enemies which must be destroyed, the Mafia penetrates and attempts to influence the very institutions that are supposed to be fighting it.

Although there are many "Mafias" in Italy—such as the 'Ndrangheta and the Camorra—the classic Mafia originated in Sicily. The heartland of the Sicilian Mafia is the triangle formed by the cities of Palermo, Trapani, and Agrigento.

Some believe that the Mafia was originally formed to fight the *potere occulto*, the hidden power that is rife in the world. Other conspiracy theorists believe that governments control the Mafia to have authority in the criminal world.

MAFIA (RUSSIAN)

One of the most powerful organized criminal groups in history, the Russian *Mafiya* is known for its violence and its resilience.

Since the Russian Mafia originated in the paranoid environment of the Soviet Union—in the face of Soviet surveillance, betrayals, and depredations—the Russian Mafia developed an organization based on cells and spies.

The leader of a Russian Mafia gang is a boss called a *Pakhan*. He controls four cells through his second in command, who is called a Brigadier.

The cells are made up of men who deal in drugs, prostitution, bribery, and so forth. Members of the cells do not know the members of the other cells, although they all report to the *Pakhan*.

Always, the *Pakhan* has spies to monitor the Brigadier.

Since the Russian Mafia was strong enough to survive the state security apparatus of a Marxist dictatorship, "open societies" under the "rule of law" are virtually powerless to stop the Russian mob.

MAFIOCRACY

Mafiocracy means rule by the mob. Post-imperial China was a classic Mafiocracy.

MAIL, READING OF

Postal mail is safer than electronic mail. All postal mail cannot be checked (except in dictatorships), but all electronic mail can be monitored for code words.

To read an intercepted letter, spray it with freon. This will make the envelope transparent for thirty seconds. When the freon evaporates, it leaves no visible traces.

MAIL, THEFT OF

Every day, 100,000 residential mailboxes are burglarized in the United States.

This is the standard technique: the thief goes door to door—with advertising fliers—and empties the boxes.

MANCHURIAN CANDIDATE

The term "Manchurian Candidate" refers to a "mind-controlled" assassin. The phrase comes from a novel by Richard Condon.

In Condon's book, "Raymond Shaw" is captured by the Chinese in the Korean War and is "brainwashed." He is sent back to the U.S.A. and appears normal. He has no memory of his capture.

Unknown to Shaw, he has been hypnotically programmed to assassinate a presidential candidate. After the killing, he is to lose all memory of the action and appear insane.

Curiously, between 1953 and 1973 the C.I.A. had a secret program ("MK-Ultra") that

researched mind control. Allegedly, one of the goals of the program was to create hypnotized assassins who were unaware of what they were and what their mission was. When they were exposed to certain words, signs, or other "triggers," they were supposed to kill.

MAO TSE-TUNG (1893-1976)

Mao Tse-tung was successively a librarian, a guerrilla leader, a revolutionary, and a dictator. He believed that "political power is obtained through the barrel of a gun."

Some see Mao, the "red emperor," as a monster who caused the deaths of millions. Others see him as the indispensable leader who ended a century and half of humiliation and raised China to world-power status.

Although Mao Tse-tung is renowned as a guerrilla theorist, he thought that guerrilla warfare alone could achieve only tactical gains. To achieve victory, he believed, a conventional army was needed.

MARAT, JEAN PAUL (1743-1793)

In one brief life, Jean Paul Marat began as a fearless rebel, became a pitiless tyrant, and ended as a slain martyr.

In his early years, Marat experienced poverty, misery, and persecution for the cause of "liberty." A radical journalist and an enemy of the king of France—forced to hide in cellars and sewers as a fugitive—Marat contracted a loathsome and apparently incurable skin disease.

When the revolution triumphed in France, Marat became the implacable enemy of all counter-revolutionaries. With George Jacques Danton and Maximilien Robespierre, Marat unleashed the Jacobin terror in the French republic.

Finally, at the height of his power, Marat was assassinated by Charlotte Corday, a former novice nun. Marat was killed while sitting in a medicinal tub, writing with a quill pen.

MAROONS

The Maroons were escaped slaves and their descendants. The term originally referred to domesticated animals that had reverted to the wild state.

In 1502 the first slave ship arrived in the New World–and it carried the first Maroon. One of the Africans on board managed to escape into the interior of Hispaniola.

By the early 1500's there were bands of runaways–Maroons—living in the inaccessible areas of Cuba and other places. The mosquito–the carrier of malaria and yellow fever–was the ally of Maroon freedom.

Eventually, there were significant Maroon communities in Brazil (Palmares in Brazil contained thousands of people), Haiti, Jamaica, and Suriname.

In Jamaica, the Maroons defied Great Britain, the superpower of the era. In 1739 the British signed a peace treaty with the Jamaican Maroons–recognizing their independence. (This was forty-four years before the Americans won their independence.)

Bryan Edwards, who wrote *Observations on the Disposition, Character, Manners, and Habits of Life, of the Maroon Negroes of the Island of Jamaica* in 1796, described the asymmetric or "skulking way of war" of the Maroons:

> *By this dastardly method of conducting war, they did infinite mischief to the whites, without much exposing their own persons to danger, for they always cautiously avoided fighting, except with a number so disproportionately inferior to themselves, as to afford them a pretty sure expectation of victory. They knew every secret avenue of the country, so that they could conceal themselves from pursuit, or shift their ravages from place to place, as circumstances required. Such were the many disadvantages under which the English had to deal with those desultory foes; who were not reducible by any regular plan of attack; who possessed no plunder to allure or reward the assailants; nor had anything to lose, except life, and a wild and savage freedom.*

Although modern writers glamorize the Maroons, their life was not easy. Before fugitives were allowed to join a Maroon community, they had to swear "holy allegiance" with a blood oath. Breaking the oath was punishable with death.

MARTYR

A martyr is a person killed because of his beliefs or ideology. The word martyr is derived from the Greek word meaning "witness."

In the eyes of some religions, martyrdom is a "short cut" to eternal bliss. St. Bernard of Clairvaux, referring to the Christian soldiers called crusaders, made this declaration: "If they kill, it is to the profit of Christ; if they die, it is to their own."

Martyrs often energize a movement or struggle. One Iranian revolutionary made this statement: "The more who die for our cause, the stronger we become."

According to Albert Camus, "Martyrs do not build Churches; they are the mortar, or the alibi. Then come the priests and the bigots."

MARTYR OPERATIONS

In the Muslim world, suicide attacks are called "Martyr Operations." In Islam, a martyr is someone who is killed in God's cause alone. If an individual gives his life in the name of an ethnic group, or national freedom, or some other secular cause, he is not a martyr.

Muslims believe that people conducting martyr operations will go to a higher place, a paradise of wine, honey, and amorous virgins. Because the martyrs are going to God, they dress nicely, shave, and perfume themselves before their attacks.

Jalal al Din al Suyuti, an Egyptian commentator who lived between 1445 and 1505, claimed that the martyrs will enjoy a permanent erection in paradise, and their penises will "never soften." They will have seventy-two deep-bosomed maidens—with dark eyes and appetizing pudenda—and these women will be always willing and always compliant.

According to Muslim custom, martyrs are buried with the blood still on their bodies.

MARXISM

Marxism is a radical movement founded by Friedrich Engels and Karl Marx.

In principle, Marxism supports economic as well as political equality. Utterly hostile to capitalism, Marxism claims that capitalism is a diabolical exploitative system in which the propertied classes literally rob the workers.

According to Marxism, there are only two classes: those who own capital and those who have nothing but their labor to sell. The relationship between the classes is exploitative, antagonistic, and highly unstable. This will lead to conflict, ending in the triumph of the workers or the ruin of the contending classes (the famous choice between socialism or barbarism).

According to Yves Fremion, "What is known today as 'Marxism' is in fact Leninism, a bastardized form of Jacobinism, and its chief theoretician was Stalin."

MASK

A cover for the face, the function of the mask is to disguise.

One celebrated group of robbers wore "president masks" to commit all their crimes, and this was not prudent. When the robbers were eventually apprehended, it was simple for the police to link the group to all their crimes.

Oddly, in most jurisdictions in America, the law prohibits wearing masks on any day except Hallow e'en.

MASOCHISM

Deriving pleasure from his own pain and humiliation, the masochist is someone who is strangely addicted to "the whip"–especially when it is commingled with "the kiss."

Masochism is named after Leopold von Sacher-Masoch, the Austrian novelist who described the experience. His most famous work, *Venus in Furs*, deals with a man who craves humiliation.

In his own life, Leopold von Sacher-Masoch was not a weakling. Decorated for bravery, he fought for Austria in war.

A non-smoker and a non-drinker, Sacher-Masoch was a university lecturer in history.

MASSACRE

A brutal slaughter of a large number of people, a massacre may be a matter of tactics, expedience, convenience, revenge, recreation, or an amoral disregard for human life.

Massacres are all too common among the human species.

In the thirteenth century, the Mongols needed only forty days to execute the entire population of Baghdad.

MASSES

The masses–also called the plebes–are the poor people. Condemned to a life of hard labor, they represent the great majority of the human race.

Perversely, in most societies the masses eagerly collaborate with their exploiters. From the ranks of the masses come the informants, the police, and the jailers that keep the tyrants in power.

MASTURBATION

A form of rebellion bordering on the ludicrous, masturbation is also called self-love, self-pleasuring, self-devotion, the secret indulgence, "lewdness with the hand," and the "solitary vice." The word masturbation is derived from *masturbare*, which means to ravish or defile with hand.

According to traditional Roman Catholic teaching, each indulgence in masturbation is a mortal sin that will damn the unrepentant soul. According to the theologians, the masturbator is committing debauchery if his fantasy focuses on a virgin, adultery if he focuses on a married woman, and sacrilege if he focuses on a nun. It is horrible sacrilege—said one nineteenth-century divine—if the masturbator fantasizes about the Virgin Mary.

A curious number of celebrated people were addicted to masturbation. Diogenes, the Greek philosopher of the Cynic school, masturbated in public. The poet Abu Nawas praised masturbation.

Nikolai Gogol, the Russian writer, was so afraid of women that his only sexual experience was "self-abuse."

George Bernard Shaw, the playwright, indulged in the "solitary vice" because he suffered from "coitophobia," a fear of sex. Shaw lost his virginity at age twenty-nine to an elderly widow. He was so shocked by the experience that he did not attempt intercourse again for fifteen years.

John Ruskin, the Victorian art critic and essayist, actually preferred masturbation. He married Effie Gray (he was twenty-nine and she was nineteen), and when the marriage was annulled six years later Queen Victoria's physician confirmed that Effie Gray was still a virgin. The couple had indulged only in masturbation.

Although masturbation has never been a crime under American law, nineteenth-century biologists were convinced that the "solitary vice" could cause sterility, insanity, or death.

Masturbation is still grounds for dismissal in some schools, including the United States Naval Academy.

MASTURBATION (WOMEN AND)

For women, masturbation in modern times is aided by two inventions: color photography and battery-powered motors.

William Masters and Virginia E. Johnson, the researchers in human sexuality, found that 100 percent of all women achieve orgasm with masturbation. On average, the act required only four minutes to complete.

The two researchers found that female orgasms involved three to five pleasurable contractions—to as many as ten to fifteen. The female orgasms were ten seconds in length to a minute or two.

Unexpectedly, Masters and Johnson also observed that women tended to experience more intense orgasms with masturbation than with intercourse.

Regarding technique, Masters and Johnson discovered that 84 percent of women use clitoral and labial stimulation, 20 percent use vaginal insertion (a hand, a mechanical vibrator, or a dildo), 2 percent use fantasy, and 10 percent use thigh pressure. They also noted that some women can experience orgasm through fantasy alone.

MATERIALISM

Materialism is the philosophy that nothing exists except matter and its movements and modifications. It is the belief that everything, including thought and emotion, can be explained by movements and changes in physical matter.

The philosophy of Lokayata, a product of ancient India, is materialistic and atheistic. Modern science is also materialistic.

MAU MAU

A classic African anti-imperial rebellion, the violence and the bloodshed of the Mau Mau rebellion occurred between 1952 and 1960.

The Mau Mau movement arose among the Kikuyu people. The situation in Kenya, in which forty thousand whites ruled over five million blacks, made it possible.

The Mau Mau oath, which involved anointing with goat's blood, was designed to be unclean. It was sworn at night—in secret—and the initiates were told to kill any opponent of the Mau Mau. Whoever killed a European would cut off the head, extract the eyeballs, and drink the liquid from them.

Since the Mau Mau had virtually no guns–they made homemade shotguns from metal pipes and door bolts—they rarely attacked security forces. Instead, they attacked civilians who collaborated with the British, using blades and axes to cut off genitals and limbs and to slit throats. The nature of the attacks allowed British propaganda to assert that the Mau Mau were atavistic savages.

To fight the Mau Mau, the British resorted to ingenuity (they used "witch doctors" to conduct "de-oathing rituals" for Mau Mau members) and utter savagery (the British killed or executed about twelve thousand Mau Mau operatives).

The British also moved thousands of Africans into concentration camps and fortified villages, where many died.

The Mau Mau, who seldom had over five hundred firearms, managed to kill only ninety-five whites (thirty-two were civilians) and about 2500 blacks (two hundred were civilians) in eight years of struggle.

Ultimately, however, the Mau Mau cause triumphed. Although the British declared victory
over the "terrorists" in 1960, Kenya became independent in 1963, Jomo Kenyatta became prime minister, and all the Mau Mau were pardoned.

MEDICI, GIULIANO DE' (1453-1478)

An assassination victim, Giuliano de' Medici, a Renaissance potentate, was killed in the Florentine Cathedral during High Mass. When the priest elevated the communion host–that was the prearranged signal–the assassins struck.

MEETINGS

Outlaws and rebels should avoid face-to-face meetings.

If such meetings must occur, however, use a site that is bland and normal. It should be accessible by two means of public transport, and it should be a place where people engaging in conversation does not appear suspicious.

If the two operatives do not know one another, each should have half of a torn dollar bill or other currency. Joining the halves provides verification.

MEGATERRORISM

Megaterrorism—or terrorism on a grand scale—is a form of terrorism that uses weapons of mass destruction.

Like all terrorism, megaterrorism can be curiously anonymous. The wrong entity may be blamed for the attack.

MEGATERRORISM, FICTION AND

Writer Jack London, in a 1907 short story entitled "The Enemy of All the World," pioneered the genre in fiction of "the evil genius who tries to blackmail countries or the whole planet."

MERCENARY

A mercenary is a professional soldier hired to serve in a foreign army.

Mercenaries have been known by many names. They have been called "soldiers of fortune," "wild geese," "contract soldiers," "freebooters," and "dogs of war." In medieval Europe, a mercenary was called a "free-lance."

Francesco Sforza, a fifteenth-century Italian warlord, was perhaps the most successful mercenary in history. He conquered Milan in 1450 and became its duke.

In the modern era, one effective mercenary was Bob Denard (born Gilbert Bourgeaud). On May 13, 1978 Bob Denard landed in the Comoros, an island nation in the Indian Ocean, with forty-six men in a trawler. The group went to the palace, killed the leader of the country, and seized power.

For the next eleven years, Denard effectively ruled the Comoros through a figurehead.

MERCENARIES (FRENCH FOREIGN LEGION)

Of modern mercenaries, the most famous belong to the French Foreign Legion. France created the fabled force in 1831.

Since World War II, barely a year has gone by without the legion seeing action somewhere. In a crisis, these well-trained and intrepid volunteers are the first troops deployed.

Thirty thousand legionnaires served in France's Vietnamese War, and half never returned home. At Dien Bien Phu in 1954, more than ten thousand legionnaires died.

Recruits to the French Foreign Legion must be aged between eighteen and forty. Thousands from all over the world apply, but only a minority pass the rigorous admission standards.

Men who are accepted into the French Foreign Legion sign a five-year contract. Completing the contract makes them eligible for French citizenship.

Legionnaires are expected to give up any allegiance to their homelands. Indeed, they may be asked to fight their former countryman.

The only way out of the contract is to desert. If a legionnaire deserts—and escapes French territory—he is free. If he is caught, however, he will be beaten (unofficially) and jailed. After his release from prison, he will be required to complete his contract.

MERCHANTS

A merchant is a person involved with commerce. An ancient vocation, some of the first merchants were traffickers in human slaves.

Many cultures despise merchants, the buyers and sellers of wares. Since retailers must be obsequious to their customers, the job is considered dishonorable.

In traditional China, merchants were officially classified at the bottom of the social scale. They were beneath both peasants and artisans.

In ancient Greece, Plato said that it is impossible to engage in commerce and be virtuous at the same time.

Islam, in contrast, has always shown enthusiasm for commerce. Muhammad himself had engaged in trade, and the Koran declares: "Merchants are the messengers of this world and God's trustees on Earth."

MESSALINA (circa A.D. 20-A.D. 48)

An infamous female, Valeria Messalina, a Roman empress, was the third wife of the emperor Claudius. The daughter of a cousin of Claudius, they married when she was fifteen and he was fifty.

A nymphomaniac, Messalina had sexual relations with gladiators, dancers, and anyone she fancied. She slept with the handsomest men of Rome and—for novelty—the ugliest. Those who refused were accused of treason and executed.

Reputedly, when Messalina challenged Scylla, a shameless prostitute, to a sexual competition, Scylla gave up at dawn after intercourse with twenty-five men, but Messalina continued well into the morning.

Messalina's end was violent. She plotted against her husband, and he ordered her to be executed with all the men with whom she had copulated. Her lovers numbered in the hundreds.

METESKY, GEORGE (1903-1994)

Called the "Mad Bomber," George Metesky was a disgruntled utility worker who had a sixteen-year career of terror. He planted approximately thirty explosive devices in New York City.

Metesky was difficult to apprehend because he used improvised explosive devices. Using plumbing pipe and propellant from shotgun shells, he made homemade pipe bombs.

"METHOD OF THE HUNDRED FLOWERS"

The "method of the hundred flowers" is a deception used in totalitarian states to lure dissent into the open so that it may be exterminated. The technique was used in Nazi Germany (in 1943) and in Marxist China.

First, there is a period of apparent liberalism. In this period, dissent, expressions of criticism, and deviations are tolerated, authorized, or even encouraged. Then, after all dissidents had spoken, the regime struck with a wave of repression and quickly liquidated its opponents.

MIND, CONTROL OF

The philosopher Bertrand Russell argued that any government that remained in charge of education for more than one generation would be able to control its people without arms or police.

Great Britain made primary education compulsory in 1870. France did so in 1882.

Winston Churchill remarked in 1943 that the empires of the future will be "empires of the mind." The emphasis will not be on the control of territory but on the control of thoughts and opinions.

According to the author of *Crown Against Concubine*, today the common man's mind is controlled by poisoning it with pornography, nihilism, and "lies" about democracy and equality.

MISHIMA, YUKIO (1925-1970)

A Japanese literary rebel, Yukio Mishima spoke of "tense, fragrant, youthful flesh." He also said that "true beauty is something that attacks, overpowers, robs, and finally destroys."

Mishima believed that we should meet death in state of beauty: "A powerful, tragic frame and sculptured muscles were indispensable in a romantically noble death. Any confrontation between weak, flabby flesh and death seemed to me absurdly inappropriate."

Mishima also claimed that the destruction of beauty is more beautiful than beauty itself.

To protest the post-war corruption of Japan by America, Mishima committed suicide on Japanese television in 1970. Using the traditional Japanese *seppuku* ritual of the warrior caste, Mishima plunged a dagger into the left side of his stomach, pulled the blade across horizontally, and then drew it upwards. To complete the ritual, an assistant stepped forward and decapitated Mishima.

MISSIROLI, MARIO (1886-1974)

Mario Missiroli, a political journalist during the time of fascism, managed to criticize Mussolini's regime with impunity.

How did he manage?

"Do not fret about the freedom of the press," declared Missiroli. "Freedom of the press, after all, is necessary only for bad writers."

In other words, a skillful writer can always convey seditious ideas cryptically.

MOB

Mob is slang for *mobile vulgus*, which means "the rabble on the move." It is composed of the masses, the people who "breed, consume, and infest."

When humans form a mob, they acquire animal characteristics, and they become a pack of wolves, a herd of cattle, or a flock of sheep.

Writing on the mob, the sociologist Gustav Le Bon made this observation: "Whoever can supply them with illusions is easily their master; whoever attempts to destroy their illusions is always their victim."

MOB, VIOLENCE AND

Insects are noticed only in crowds—or when they sting. Otherwise, we show them only indifference and contempt.

Poor people are the same. They are invisible when they are inoffensive, but when they gather in a crowd—or when they draw blood—they are impossible to ignore.

Totally unleashed, the mob is capable of atrocities. When a French Revolutionary mob murdered Princesse de Lamballe (the friend and alleged lover of Marie Antoinette), they cut off her breasts and vulva. The crowd laughed when one man put the vulva over his lips like a mustache.

During the Haitian slave revolt, a mob murdered the husband of Madame Sejourne before her eyes. They then cut Madame Sejourne open, ripped out her unborn baby, and threw it to the swine. Finally, the mob forced her husband's decapitated head into her wound and sewed the wound shut.

Later in Haiti, on July 28, 1915, an enraged mob literally tore President Vilbrun Guillaume Sam to pieces and paraded portions of his body around the capital.

And in America, in October of 1934, a mob tortured Claude Neal to death in Florida. Before lynching Neal, the mob cut off his penis and testicles and forced-fed them to Neal.

MOLE

A type of undercover operative, a mole is an agent sent to work within the ranks of an enemy in order to discover secrets.

Before invading Afghanistan in 1979, the U.S.S.R. first placed a Soviet operative in the presidential palace as a cook. The mole helped facilitate the invasion and the murder of President Amin of Afghanistan.

MOLOTOV COCKTAIL

The molotov cocktail, an improvised fire bomb, has been called the common man's street weapon. Deploying a molotov cocktail is a federal crime in the United States and it was a capital crime in White-controlled Rhodesia.

Although cheap, the weapon is effective. In their "Winter War," the Finns used them with great success against the tanks of the Soviet army.

In white-controlled Rhodesia, Africans made a simple molotov cocktail by pouring three parts kerosene and one part motor oil into a mason jar or some other breakable bottle. They sealed the bottle–wrapped it in waste cotton moistened with gasoline–ignited the cotton—and threw the weapon.

In other versions, the Africans used a mixture of gasoline and oil, thickened with pure soap, melted paraffin, moth balls, and/or pieces of styrofoam. A disposable lighter–or a firecracker–was attached to the bottle.

When it is used, the molotov cocktail is strictly a daylight weapon. Deploying it at night reveals the attacker's position.

MONEY

A medium of exchange–typically in the form of coins and banknotes–money can be anything of perceived value. During the Atlantic Slave trade, the slavers often bought their human cargo with cowrie shells.

The most bizarre money is "fiat money." Fiat money is government-issued money that is legal tender by law. Not based on gold or anything of value, it contains no promise of redemption. It is universal in "modern" economies.

Fiat money was observed by Marco Polo in China. Polo wrote that the emperor forced the people to accept pieces of paper with an official seal as legal money under pain of death. The emperor used this to pay his own debts.

Perhaps the only money that keeps its value is gold or silver. In the Roman Empire–at the time of Christ–an individual could buy a small farm for one hundred ounces of gold. One can still buy a small farm today with one hundred ounces of gold.

Quite rare, all the gold mined in recorded history–gathered in one place–would make a cube only eighteen yards on a side. The cube would weigh 91,000 tons.

MOON, STRATEGIC VALUE OF

The Moon, which has the approximate surface area of the continent of Africa, is the most strategic point in our solar system.

As Robert Heinlein noted, "The nation that controls the Moon will control the Earth." Missiles sent from the Moon to the Earth will come in at seven miles per second. At that speed, they do not have to be bombs. They simply have to be massive.

And firing from the Moon to the Earth requires less energy than firing from the Earth to the Moon. Not only is the Moon's escape velocity only 5,400 miles per hour, but its lack of atmosphere creates a resistance-free medium. (Compare the Saturn V rocket needed to lift the Apollo spacecraft to the Moon with the diminutive rocket used to lift the Lunar module from the Moon.)

Although one side of the Moon is always invisible to the Earth, in every twenty-four hour period all of the Earth is visible from the Moon, so any point on the surface of the Earth can be easily targeted.

But can an army on the Earth effectively counter-attack?

Since the Moon has no atmosphere, a nuclear blast there would not be efficient. (A blast is a wave of compression, which can be transmitted via the air or some other medium.) An explosion on the Moon would simply be a flash of light and (possibly) some radiation.

As a result, the Moon would be a perfect command post.

MORTOCRACY

A mortocracy is government by death. Very literally, the country is ruled by death squads.

MOST, JOHANN (1846–1906)

A theorist of terrorism, and the man credited with the development of the letter bomb, Johann Most published *The Science of Revolutionary Warfare* in 1884. The work was designed as a "handbook of instruction" on the "use and manufacture of nitroglycerin, dynamite, gun cotton, fumigating mercury, bombs, arson, poisons," and other weapons.

Most was not interested in mass action—the army and police would crush such attempts—instead he wanted terror. Most believed that modern science, if correctly used, favors the revolutionary terrorist.

Most believed that terrorists should act individually or in small groups. Bombs should be put in public places, such as churches, banks, police stations, and government offices.

Johann Most was one of the first to recognize the significance of the media. According to his concept, the "propaganda of the deed," the news is more important than the act itself.

Most understood that the media amplifies the effect of a terrorist act ("kill one to frighten a hundred"). He also knew that, with the media, violence becomes more important than just eliminating a victim.

MUHAMMAD (570-632)

A successful religious leader, Muhammad was the founder of Islam. To Muslims, he was sent by Allah and is the greatest of the prophets. They believe that he was the "paraclete" or "comforter" whose arrival Jesus predicted in the Gospel of John.

To Jews and Christians, Muhammad was a desert caravan merchant who created a hybrid religion based on elements from their faiths.

A classic example of what Niccolo Machiavelli called an "armed prophet," Muhammad participated in seventy-eight battles. Humiliated by his enemies early in his career as a prophet, he triumphed over adversity and died a leader.

Interestingly, Muhammad, even when a successful commander of men, lived in a simple cottage twelve feet square and eight feet high.

MURDER-FOR-HIRE

Hired killers are common in history. In the current era, perhaps the most infamous are the "contract killers" of the Mafia.

The killers—called "enforcers"—are at the disposal of the crime bosses. No one outside the Mafia can hire a contract killer from within the Mafia.

Prudently, the Mafia never uses its hired killers against law enforcement, journalists, or politicians. Killing such people is considered unnecessarily provocative.

Once a contract is issued, the killer, who is always from out of town, goes to the victim's city, kills the target, and then disappears, leaving the police with no suspects, no clues, and no motives. When a stranger kills a stranger, there is little or nothing on which to base an investigation.

Against their own kind, Mafia hit men traditionally prefer the knife, the garrote, and the bullet. When they assassinate, however, they prefer the bomb.

Their simplest bomb is made by placing shotgun shells in an automobile's exhaust pipe.

MURDER, MORALITY OF

Throughout history man has used various intellectual maneuvers to make murder a morally acceptable act.

In ancient Sparta, for example, each year the state declared war on the entire servile class, the people called helots. This act absolved in advance any Spartan who killed any helot for any reason.

In classical Rome, a citizen could legally kill any thief who came by night. Also, a citizen could legally kill–even in daylight–any armed robber.

In India, members of the Thuggee sect believed that all their murdered victims went straight to paradise. By serving Kali, the goddess of death, the Thuggee believed that they also went to paradise.

In modern states, soldiers are allowed to commit combat-sanctioned murder–as long as the victim is a designated belligerent.

In America and Europe, commandos are taught to kill silently from behind. They plunge the knife through the lower back into a kidney. The wound is so painful that it paralyzes the victim, who quickly and silently dies.

Commandos are taught that slitting a throat from behind is less effective. The victim can still make noise before he dies.

MURPHY'S LAW

The inherent tendency of things to go wrong is known in the British army as "Murphy's Law."

Karl Maria von Clausewitz, the Prussian military theorist, noted that "countless minor incidents"—the kind you can never really foresee—combine to lower the general level of performance."

During World War II, the U-120, a German submarine, was sunk by a defective toilet.

MUSSOLINI, BENITO (1883-1945)

A tyrant, Benito Mussolini was successively an elementary school teacher, a journalist, a sergeant in World War I, and a totalitarian dictator. Strangely, Thomas Edison—the renowned American inventor—called Mussolini the greatest "genius" of modern times.

Multi-lingual, Mussolini was an omnivorous reader who wrote novels and poetry and played the violin well. Friends called him "the professor."

Rising to power in Italy as the world's first fascist dictator, Mussolini was an effective demagogue. His linguistic style—which captivated millions— made frequent use of rhythmic and tonal variations, hyperbole, imagery, metaphor, and alliterative and onomatopoeic expressions chosen for their sound and evocative power.

Fantasizing about restoring the Roman Empire, Mussolini plunged into World War II on the side of Adolf Hitler. That alliance would lead to Italy's defeat and Mussolini's destruction.

Earlier—in 1933—Mussolini had made this observation about the Nazis: "I should be pleased, I suppose, that Hitler has carried out a Revolution on our lines. But they are Germans. So they will end up ruining our idea."

MUTILATION

The mutilation of defeated enemies is common.

Circa 1300 B.C., the Egyptian army returned with thirteen thousand severed penises cut from defeated Libyans.

In the ninth century after Christ, the Bulgars killed Nicephorus I, the emperor of Byzantine Empire, and made a gilded goblet from his skull.

In the nineteenth century, an army led by Muhammad Ahmad, who called himself the "Mahdi," defeated an Anglo-Egyptian army led by Pasha Hicks. The victorious Mahdi forces severed ten thousand Anglo-Egyptian penises and threw them into a well near El-Obeyd.

Until recent times, the Jivaro people of the Amazon shrank human heads to the size of oranges. They wore these heads of defeated enemies like medals.

MUTINY

A mutiny is an open rebellion against so-called authority—especially by soldiers or sailors against their officers.

Oddly, a mutiny is rare among troops in combat. Blaise de Montluc warned captains to keep a watchful eye on the rear, for it is there that mutinies originate.

Mutinies were especially serious during World War I. In the spring of 1917, half of all French divisions joined in a military strike. Similar breakdowns occurred in Italy and Russia later in the year, and in Germany in 1918.

There have been several famous mutinies in American history. In 1783, for example, unpaid soldiers invaded the Continental Congress headquarters in Philadelphia and forced the members to flee across the river to Princeton.

MYTH

To the masses, a myth is a widely held but false belief.

To the students of intellectual history, the primary function of myth is orientation. The myth, in effect, orders the world by providing a sacred reference point.

Without a myth a man's sufferings become purposelessness, his fears become unintelligible, and his death becomes meaningless.

The modern West is largely secular and materialistic, so its "myths" apply to the natural or profane world. In the West, there are four great modern myths or assumptions: 1) man's aim is happiness, 2) man is naturally good, 3) history develops in endless progress, and 4) everything is matter or energy.

NAKEDNESS

To be naked—to be without clothing—has many meanings.

To the ancient Egyptians, nakedness represented childhood and youth.

To the Aztecs, nakedness symbolized defeat and humiliation.

To modern Americans, nakedness represents eroticism.

NATION

The nation is an artificial collective.

One scholar argued that a nation is an "imagined community involving feelings of solidarity."

NATIONAL DIVIDEND

The National Dividend is a concept developed by C.H. Douglas, an engineer. It was revived by Ezra Pound, the poet and outlaw thinker.

According to the National Dividend concept, every citizen should be declared a shareholder in the nation, and should receive (by right) dividends on the Gross National Product. Properly administered, Douglas estimated that a citizen would receive five times the amount a typical welfare recipient receives.

Individual citizens would receive extra pay or bonuses for activities that increased the efficiency or productivity of the national economy.

'NDRANGHETA

An organized crime group in the Calabrian area of Italy, 'Ndrangheta means "bravery" or "courage" in the Greek dialect.

The 'Ndrangheta, which originated in the nineteenth century, is made up of about 140 families.

The group is best known for kidnapping, including the abduction of the sixteen-year-old heir of billionaire John Paul Getty III in the 1970's. The Getty family paid the ransom after receiving the boy's severed ear.

NECHAEV, SERGEI (1847-1882)

An implacable rebel, Sergei Nechaev was born in tsarist Russia. The son of a serf, Nechaev became involved in radical politics while a student in St Petersburg.

With Mikhail Bakunin, Nechaev wrote the *Catechism of a Revolutionist* in 1869. The influential work contains these famous words:

> The Revolutionist is a doomed man. He has no private interests, no affairs, sentiments, ties, property, not even a name of his own. His entire being is devoured by one purpose, one thought, one passion—the revolution. Heart and soul, not merely by word but by deed, he has severed every link with the social order and with the entire civilized world; with the laws, good manners, conventions, and morality of that world. He is its merciless enemy and continues to inhabit it with only one purpose—to destroy it.

Nechaev claimed to be a member of a secret organization of terrible power called the People's Retribution. When one of its members, I. I. Ivanov, questioned Nechaev's political ideas, Nechaev had him murdered.

Sentenced to twenty years of hard labor, Nechaev was found dead in his cell in 1882.

NEO-COLONIALISM

In contrast to traditional colonialism, which is a form of open control, neo-colonialism is control by other, more devious means.

Kwame Nkrumah, writing in 1965, made this point in *Neo-Colonialism: The Last Stage of Imperialism:*

> In place of colonialism as the main instrument of imperialism we have today neo-colonialism. The essence of neo-colonialism is that the state which is subject to it is, in theory, independent and has all the outward trappings of international sovereignty. In reality its economic system and thus its political policy is directed from the outside.

NEOFEUDALISM

Neofeudalism is a system in which an elite of technocrats, strategists, and corporate barons control the country, with the rest of the population effectively denied any meaningful decision-making role.

NIGHT FIGHTING

Firing weapons at night reveals the fighter's position. To remain hidden, fragmentation grenades and phosphorous grenades are better.

When fighting at night, avoid entering (or leaving) a room with a light source to your rear. You will present a silhouette in the darkness which will make you an excellent target.

Napoleon noted that the success of night attacks depended upon unpredictable circumstances, such as the barking of a dog.

NIGHT MOVEMENT

Whenever possible, avoid moving on hard ground at night. Hard ground produces an echo.

Soft ground—which produces little echo—is superior.

According to the Japanese ninja, the tread of a night fighter should be light and stealthy—almost furtive—and yet purposeful. It should be like the pace of a tiger that stalks a deer.

Wear no shiny objects—such as wrist watches—and wear nothing that rattles or makes noise.

NIGHT VISION

When deployed in darkness, remember that night vision, unlike day vision, uses the periphery of the retina to receive light. To examine an object at night, look slightly above, below, or to the side of it.

Remember that night vision can be degraded by a vitamin-A deficiency, by smoking tobacco, and by consuming alcohol.

NIGHT VISION (LIMITATIONS OF)

When moving at night, remember that darkness swallows colors, blurs shapes, and makes familiar things appear strange.

You can see when looking from darkness into light, but not when looking from light into darkness. A person in a lighted room cannot see you in the darkness, unless you let your shadow fall on his window.

Know also that guards using a spotlight develop a blind spot: they tend to see only what is in the spotlight.

NIHILISM

The term "nihilism," which was first used in the 1862 novel *Fathers and Sons* by Ivan Turgeniev, is the belief in nothing except reason and self-interest.

Nihilism is an anti-doctrine. The rejection of everything, Nihilism maintains that all values are useless and all morals are sterile.

NINJA

The ninja of Japan, practitioners of *ninjitsu* or the art of stealth or invisibility, were experts at disguise, spying, sabotage, assassination, and escape. They used exotic weapons and trickery.

Masters of camouflage, the ninja might appear as beggars, priests, or even women. They used reversible clothing—dark on one side, and light on the other.

Under water, they breathed through bamboo. In an open field, under a gray cloak, rolled into a ball, a ninja could stay motionless for hours disguised as a rock.

To escape after an attack, the ninja created smokescreens, including poisonous smokescreens.

They also took refuge in pre-dug holes in the earth.

The ninja were taught to dislocate joints, so they could squirm under fences and escape from ropes.

Commonly used as assassins, the ninja applied a variety of poisons to their blades, including human excrement. The excrement would not kill outright, but it would aggravate the wound, causing gangrene—even death.

Renowned for their patience, one ninja assassin concealed himself in a sewage pit in a lavatory. When the victim sat down, he was impaled.

NOBLE

The word "noble" means "well known."

In the Roman arena, even the vilest criminal became noble in Roman eyes if he showed courage. According to the Romans, a brave death offered a redemptive moment for a guilty man.

NUCLEUS FACTION

A Japanese terror organization, the Nucleus Faction is dedicated to overthrowing Japan's monarchy and its American-imposed Constitution.

Relying on homemade (but surprisingly sophisticated) incendiary bombs, flamethrowers, mortars, and rockets, the Nucleus Faction burned down a political building with a garage-manufactured flamethrower in 1984, and they fired homemade rockets at Tokyo's Imperial Palace in 1986.

NUMBERS

Numbers mean nothing.

The ferocious Mongols conquered the Chinese, even though the Chinese outnumbered the Mongols one hundred to one.

In 1917, there was one Russian Bolshevik for every 2,777 Russians. The Bolsheviks were able to seize power the same year.

In the Italian general election of 1919, the fascists received only 4,000 votes and not one of their candidates was elected. Three years later, there were only 30 fascist deputies (in a parliament with 535 seats), but on October 30, 1922 the king appointed Benito Mussolini the prime minister of Italy.

When the Vietnamese People's Army was established on December 22, 1944, they "were only thirty-four human beings equipped with rudimentary weapons." Ultimately, the Vietnamese People's Army would defeat France and the United States.

In December 1956, Fidel Castro left Mexico with an army of eighty-two. When he landed in Cuba, an ambush killed all but fifteen men. The survivors escaped into the mountains, and from that small beginning, Castro would conquer Cuba and its seven million people.

OCHLOCRACY

Ochlocracy is rule by the mob.

ODINISM

A rebel religion, Odinism is a neo-barbarian revolt against the modern world.

The antithesis of Christianity, Odinism glorifies the "hero" over the "saint." A "creed of iron," Odinism represents "strength over weakness, pride over humility, and knowledge over faith."

In the eyes of the Christians, however, Odinism is a pagan religion that perverts the beatitudes of their Christ. Odinists, say the Christians, are "whoring after strange gods."

The Odin Brotherhood, the oldest Odinist group, is a secret society that was organized in 1421.

OLIGARCHY

An oligarchy is a small group of people having control of a state.

According to conspiracy theorist David Icke, during the "Cold War" the Soviet Union was openly controlled by a few. The west, in contrast, was (and is) secretly controlled by a few.

According to Colonel L. Fletcher Prouty, the author of *The Secret Team*, about thirty or so C.I.A. agents, drug lords, multinational plutocrats, ideologues, and soldiers of fortune really run the government of the United States.

It is noteworthy that thirty to forty million Americans have college degrees—American universities award one million degrees each year—and thirty thousand individuals earn Ph.D.'s annually. Yet, the top government posts always go to the same select group of people.

OLIGARCHY, GEORGE ORWELL ON

According to George Orwell's *1984*, when everyone in a society is rich and educated, it becomes obvious that a privileged minority serves no purpose, so a hierarchy can exist only with poverty and ignorance.

Orwell noted, moreover, that hierarchies need wars. With constant war, he noted, "all power" to a "small caste" seems to be "the natural, unavoidable condition of survival."

OLIGARCHY, IRON LAW OF

Robert Michels formulated the "iron law of oligarchy." Stated simply, Michels argued that all forms of organization will eventually develop oligarchic tendencies, thus making democracy practically and theoretically impossible.

Indeed, although people in a primitive society live in a "consensual relationship" with others in the band, anthropologists estimate that an egalitarian order cannot be maintained when the group rises above four hundred or five hundred in number. With larger numbers, a chieftain organization emerges.

OMERTA

Omerta, pronounced "oh mair TAH," is a classic Sicilian concept. *Omerta* is the ruling principle of Mafia figures, men euphemistically called "the men of respect."

Omerta literally means manliness. *Omerta* obliges a man to be strong, to be potent, and to dominate.

More precisely, *omerta* means silence and self-restraint. If wronged, the "man of respect" will not show anger, he will not tell the police, and he will not act rashly. He will wait—for years if necessary—and avenge in the coldest way possible, often striking when he seems to be the victim's friend.

The chief of police who waged a brutal war on the Mafia during the fascist era made this comment: "The most salient and perplexing factor in the psychology of the typical Mafioso is his conviction that he is doing no wrong. As long as he obeys the rules of *omerta*—whether he extorts, steals, or even murders—he is, to himself, as well as his brethren, an honorable man."

OMNICIDE

Omnicide—the game of psychopaths—is the murder of all things. According to Medea (a character in a play by Seneca), "It is sweet to draw the world down with you when you are perishing."

One possible doomsday weapon is a biological agent with vectors that reach everyone in the world before the first symptoms present themselves.

OMNICIDE, DEFENSE AGAINST

To insure the survival of the human race, anthropologist Margaret Mead (in 1961) urged people to create an international shelter system that would be permanently occupied.

The shelter, she argued, should house on a rotating basis the most *productive* members of society (such as scholars), and it should also rotate through a sample of the most *reproductive* members of society (the recently married).

Since Mead's time, survivalists have proposed the establishment of extra-terrestrial space colonies or orbiting generation ships—just in case.

OPPRESSORS

There are two traditional oppressors of humanity: armed force and wealth.

When armed force dominates, it seizes all the wealth. Eventually, softened by luxury, the military elite collapses or is conquered.

When wealth dominates, it protects itself by buying armed force. Eventually, the police and soldiers realize they are stronger than their masters, and the rich are destroyed.

As Tacitus pointed out, "Nothing in human affairs is more unstable and precarious than power unsupported by its own strength."

ORDER OF THE SILENT BROTHERHOOD

The Order of the Silent Brotherhood—also called the *Bruders Schweigen*—was an American insurgent group. Rabidly anti-Semitic, they declared war on something they called the Zionist Occupation Government or ZOG.

Allegedly, ZOG is a secret government which controls federal and corporate America through marionettes or puppets.

The Order formed on the pagan holiday of Autumnal Equinox in 1983. Nine men were initiated in the beginning, but the Order grew to two dozen by July 1984. The leader was Robert Jay Matthews.

To conduct their insurgency, the Order practiced robbery, counterfeiting, and assassination over an eighteen-month period. Their most spectacular feats included the theft of 3.8 million dollars from an armored car and the murder of a prominent Jewish radio personality.

Ultimately, Robert Jay Matthew was burned to death during a confrontation with approximately two hundred federal police on Dec 8, 1984. In his last letter, Matthews wrote: "I have been a good soldier, a fearless warrior. I will die with honor and join my brothers in Valhalla."

OSWALD, LEE HARVEY (1939-1963)

The alleged assassin of John F. Kennedy, a Lothario and a president of the United States, Lee Harvey Oswald has been called a scapegoat, a dupe, a maverick, and a traitor.

If Oswald killed Kennedy, he committed the deed on November 22, 1963, a few weeks after Kennedy had sanctioned the murder of Ngo Dinh Diem, the "president" of South Vietnam. Diem was killed with his younger brother.

On November 24, 1963, Oswald himself was murdered on national television by Jack Ruby, who was also known as Jack Rubenstein. Significantly, "Jack Ruby" is a term used by pawn brokers to indicate a fake gemstone.

OUTLAW

Defined today as a fugitive from the law, originally the outlaw was the man outside the protection and the benefit of the law. No longer considered a man, he could be killed by anyone with impunity.

In A.D. 946, King Edmund I of England was killed while trying to subdue the outlaw named Liofa.

Those were purer times—when kings and outlaws met on more or less equal terms.

OUTLAWS, CASH AND

Prudent outlaws always carry cash. If arrested, they may quickly post bail and disappear. If the apprehended criminal is unarmed, bail is usually low.

Timothy McVeigh, after detonating an improvised vehicle bomb in Oklahoma City in 1995, fled with insufficient cash.

Originally pursued for traffic violations (excessive speed and no license plate), McVeigh was arrested when the policeman observed a loaded firearm. Unable to post bail, McVeigh was detained. Three days later he was identified as a "terrorist," and he was ultimately executed on June 11, 2001.

If McVeigh had carried cash—and had driven carefully—he could have survived.

OUTLAWS, FAME AND

Each era has its celebrated outlaws: the pirates in the seventeenth century, the highwaymen in the eighteenth century, the train robbers in the nineteenth century, the bank robbers in the twentieth century, the terrorists in the twenty-first century–and so forth.

PAIN

Pain is a form of suffering or distress.

Philosophers note that pleasure fertilizes and conceives, but pain brings forth.

In Russian culture, the notion that suffering regenerates is well-established.

PARANOIA

Paranoia is the assumption that there is a pattern—usually negative or hostile—in random events. Typical symptoms of paranoia, both individual and collective, are suspicion of others, concern with hidden motives, hostility, the inability to engage in self-criticism, and a poor sense of humor.

Paranoia has been defined as "an irrational fear." Curiously, there is no word in the English language for a "rational fear."

According to one fascinating and diabolical theory, "the psychological classification of paranoia" has been INVENTED by conspirators (the hidden powers that control the world) for the purpose of discrediting anyone who attempts to expose them.

Interestingly, Charles Manson, the cult-like leader of the "Manson Family," believed that "total paranoia is total awareness." It is also interesting that animals in the wild—which are free—are afraid of nearly everything—but domesticated animals—which are slaves—are not afraid.

PARASITE

A parasite is an organism that lives on or in another organism.

Since all humans were all once fetuses—living in the womb, and feeding off the blood of our mothers—we were all once parasitic vampires.

PARTIES, INSURRECTIONIST

In a democracy, insurrectionist parties are political organizations whose primary purpose is to destroy the system. Members strive to win elections, but their goal is to dismantle the democratic system itself, which they view as decadent, pernicious, or illegitimate.

After the National Socialist Party of Adolf Hitler failed in its attempt to seize power in 1923, for example, Adolf Hitler decided to use democracy to destroy democracy.

Noting that parliamentary membership gave National Socialist deputies immunity from arrest and free rail travel, Paul Joseph Goebbels, the propaganda minister, referred to winning elections as using "the arsenal of democracy."

PATRIOTISM

A patriot is someone who vigorously supports his country and is prepared to defend it.

Although patriotism is often viewed as a virtue, Mikhail Bakunin noted that patriotism—or loyalty to the collective—is found among ants, bees, and beavers.

Men are taught that dying for their country is an honor. Is this true? Do nations really remember their patriots? The answer varies from culture to culture, and from era to era.

On one extreme was the treatment of war dead in nineteenth-century Britain. At the beginning of the century the remains of dead soldiers—dug out of battlefields —were used as fertilizer.

On the other extreme are the traditional customs of Japan. In Japan, the war dead are literally honored as gods (*kami*).

Yasukuni—the shrine to Japanese war dead—was established in 1869. The spirits of those who died for Japan are enshrined there.

Shinto priests perform special rituals which transform the spirits into *kami* and guardian gods of the nation.

At present, 2.5 million spirits are enshrined there as gods. Some of the gods were executed as "war criminals" by the Americans after World War II.

PATSY

In criminal slang a "patsy" is a designated expendable, an innocent who receives the blame and becomes the scapegoat. After his arrest, Lee Harvey Oswald proclaimed: "I'm the patsy."

A patsy is a necessary component in any criminal conspiracy. The outraged public always demands a victim.

PEPPER SPRAY

A non-lethal weapon that incapacitates aggressors, pepper spray is easily manufactured.

Mix four ounces of ground cayenne pepper with sixteen ounces of SD alcohol. Boil mixture for thirty minutes. Six to eight ounces of fluid should remain. Strain the fluid through a cloth to remove solid matter.

Pour the mixture into a window-spray bottle. It is ready to deploy.

When spraying, aim for the eyes.

PERJURY

In the laws of Moses, lying is not a crime. Committing perjury, or lying under oath, is a serious offense, however.

According to chapter nineteen of the Book of Deuteronomy, anyone who commits false witness should suffer the same penalty that the man he accused would have suffered. Obviously, in capital crimes that penalty is death.

In today's world, however, there is a safe and legal way to commit perjury. According to modern laws, it is not a crime to forget.

The technique is commonly used by law enforcement. When testifying, they "forget" any detail that could help the defendant. The police testify that they cannot recall.

The technique is also used by political figures. When accused of illegalities, both Ronald Wilson Reagan and William Jefferson Davis Clinton claimed that they could not recall certain details. Again, they knew it is no crime to forget.

PERVERSION

A perversion is a species of abnormal or unacceptable behavior.

According to history and legend, no perversion seems universal. There are famous examples of adultery (Helen), bestiality (Leda and the swan), incest (Arthur and Morgana), rape (Lucretia), lust (Bathsheba), and sodomy (Oscar Wilde).

Among some traditional peoples, the fathers at one time claimed the virginity of their daughters before marriage. According to their logic, the fathers deserved the "first fruits" of the trees they had "planted."

In eighteenth-century England, the Earl of Sandwich specialized in seducing virgins because he enjoyed "the corruption of innocence, for its own sake."

In the Victorian era, Madame Mourez operated a prostitution ring which sold the virginity of young females. To silence the agonized shrieks of the deflowered little girls, Mourez used chloroform.

PETRUCCI, ALFONSO (circa 1490-1517)

A would-be assassin, Alfonso Cardinal Petrucci led a conspiracy in 1517 to kill Pope Leo X with a poison enema. The conspirators were betrayed by a servant.

Since executing a Christian cardinal was contrary to Vatican etiquette, the Church employed a Muslim to strangle Petrucci with a red silk noose.

The other cardinals involved were forced to pay huge fines.

PHINEAS PRIESTHOOD

An outlaw Christian organization, the Phineas Priesthood is a secret group of Christian assassins. Vigilantes, they enforce the biblical laws of the Judaic-Christian god by killing homosexuals, race mixers, and abortionists.

The group is named after "Phinehas," who appears in the Bible (Numbers, chapter 25). Phinehas was blessed by God for killing the members of a mixed marriage. (He killed a Jewish man and his gentile wife by impaling them through their genitalia.)

The movement is described in *The Vigilantes of Christendom: The Story of the Phineas Priesthood* by Richard Kelly Hoskins.

PHOSPHORUS

The thirteenth element to be discovered, phosphorus has been called the "devil's element." It has been used in fiendish weapons, including incendiary phosphorus bombs which ravage human flesh.

Although phosphorus has a strong taste and a powerful odor, it was once a favorite with poisoners because it is difficult to detect in autopsies. In one noted case, a woman was hanged after her husband noticed the eerie glow of phosphorus in his soup!

PIRACY, PIRATES

Piracy, a form of economic terrorism, is violent crime and extortion on the high seas.

Called a "nobler form of crime," the earliest and most notorious pirates were the ancient Greeks. Achilles and Ulysses were pirates.

In a more recent period—during the so-called "Golden Age of Piracy" from 1691-1724—the vast majority of pirates were Englishmen from Great Britain and America.

Curiously, pirate ships were traditionally organized on democratic principles. Pirate captains were usually elected, and they could be voted out of office. If a minority disagreed with the election results, they were free to split off and start their own crew.

Most pirates had served (and suffered) in the autocratic royal navy, so absolute power was anathema to them. So there was a quartermaster, also elected, who ran the ship *except* in battle.

The quartermaster was the one who divided up the plunder, with each crewman receiving one share, and the captain and the quartermaster receiving two shares each.

During actual combat—and only during actual combat—the captain exercised complete authority. At that time he could kill a crewman for not following orders.

PIRATES, INFAMOUS EXAMPLES OF

Jean-David Nau, known as Francois L'Olonnois, was the most notorious of the seventeenth-century Tortuga buccaneers, and he may have been the most depraved pirate in history.

On one occasion, to persuade captives to reveal the location of hidden treasure, Francois L'Olonnois cut out and ate the still-beating heart of one his prisoners.

Oddly, L'Olonnois was himself later cannibalized by Indians.

Another infamous pirate was Dick Chivers. Irritated by the reproaches of Captain Sawbridge, a captured merchant captain, Chivers had Sawbridge's lips sewn together. Sawbridge was then put on shore, where he died.

PLAGIARISM

According to the moralists, plagiarism is a form of intellectual theft. The malefactor hijacks the words or ideas of another.

The concept of plagiarism is an eighteenth-century invention. In earlier eras, the concept was unknown.

To the contrary, to invest their books with authority, ancient writers typically grafted entire passages from others into their writings.

As a result, in terms of concepts, ideas, and wording, readers can find most of the Old Testament in the New.

And—within the New Testament itself—the current Gospel of Mark is almost entirely duplicated in the Gospel of Matthew, with 606 of the 661 verses of Mark appearing word for word in Matthew. Also, 69 percent of the content of Luke is taken verbatim from Mark.

Regarding plagiarism, an excellent work is *The Road to Xanadu* by Professor John L. Lowes. Lowes examined a portion of Samuel Taylor Coleridge's "The Rime of the Ancient Mariner" and traced every idea and almost every phrase in it to something Coleridge can be shown to have read.

According to Lowes, there is a "strange but widely prevalent idea" that "the shaping spirit of imagination sits aloof, like God as he is commonly conceived, creating in some thaumaturgic fashion out of nothing its visionary world. That and only that is deemed to be originality—that, and not the imperial molding of old matter into imperishably new forms."

PLEASURE

Happiness involves peace of mind and the absence of pain. By nature, it is enduring. Pleasure, in contrast, involves transgression. By nature, it is fleeting.

In the words of Charles Baudelaire, "all pleasure is to be found in evil."

Honorable marriage is a source of happiness, and sinful adultery—with its secrecy and risk—is a source of pleasure.

PLEASURE (INCREASE OF)

There are two important ways to increase pleasure:

1) Since habit dulls intensity, change is pleasurable. Indeed, it has been argued that the only real aphrodisiac is change.
2) Suppressing desire increases the intensity of indulgence. Thwarting lust is like confining black powder in a cylinder. When the explosion eventually occurs, its power is magnified.

PLUTOCRACY

A plutocracy is government by the wealthy. Historically, the rich are the "drones and aesthetes" in a society, the people who only "sweat" when they "play."

A plutocracy organizes itself politically to perpetuate, for its own advantage, a regime of privilege and social injustice. In plutocracies, the parasitism of the rich is defended by state terror and force.

The United States, a civilization characterized by suffocating luxury, conspicuous expenditure, and extravagant waste, is a classic plutocracy. In all of its wars, the United States has allied itself with bankers, landlords, and investors.

In early America, the old families made their fortunes from smuggling, the slave trade, piracy, and opium trafficking. The great-grandfather of Millard Fillmore was tried for piracy. The Delano side of Franklin Delano Roosevelt's family made its money in the Chinese opium trade.

Among the extremely rich, fortunes can be obscenely large. In the nineteenth century, John Jacob Astor once held one-fifteenth of all the personal wealth in the U.S.A.

At the end of the twentieth century, the three richest men on Earth had a combined wealth greater than that of the people living in the poorest forty-eight countries. One man–Bill Gates –owned more than the poorest one hundred million Americans combined.

According to Oswald Spengler, when the economy wins the upper hand in a culture, it is a sure sign of decadence.

PLUTONIUM

A lethal element, plutonium, which was first discovered in 1940, has a silvery look and is radioactive. Since radioactive decay releases energy, a fairly large piece of plutonium will produce enough heat to boil water. Extremely heavy, plutonium's density is twice that of lead.

Plutonium is toxic when ingested or inhaled. With the botulinum toxin and ricin, plutonium is one of the most lethal substances known. Even one-millionth of a gram of plutonium (an invisible particle) is a carcinogenic dose.

In the last half of the twentieth century alone, the world has produced three million pounds of plutonium.

At the end of World War II, Nagasaki was destroyed by a plutonium bomb.

POLICE

The police—the talons of the state—are supposed to detect and prevent crime—and to maintain public order. In most societies, the police and the criminals are drawn from the same class—the lower class.

The first modern constabulary, the London Metropolitan Police, was established by the British in 1829. They were full-time and uniformed.

The establishment of a professional police force was initially resisted in America—the United States used private security and a traditional night-watch system manned by ordinary citizens—but the city of New Orleans established full-time police patrols in 1836. These early police were un-armed and did not wear uniforms.

In 1845 New York City created America's first armed police units, be-ginning with eight hundred men. Within a few years, most other major American cities had created police forces.

POLICE, CONSENT AND

The police never request permission to do what they have a legal right to do. They simply do it.

When the police ask for a citizen's consent—to search a vehicle or a home, for example—the citizen should refuse.

POLICE (SECRET)

Secret Police forces, euphemistically called the "security services," are the clandestine units of the modern state apparatus.

Officially, the secret police counter "illegal" organizations and engage in sabotage, subversion, and counter-espionage. They eavesdrop, bribe, smuggle weapons and contraband, kill, arm guerrillas, start insurgency groups, torture, trigger rebellions, and train rebels to kill. They also offi-cially deny all subversive activities.

An early form of a secret police force was the Council of Ten. A prod-uct of medieval Venice—a state based on violence and secrecy—the Coun-cil of Ten used private informants and secret assassinations to maintain control.

Formed in 1310 as a temporary response to a crisis, the Council of Ten quickly became a permanent body within the Republic. It had unlimited power—in secret police work and in espionage—until about 1454. At offi-cial meetings, the members of the Council of Ten covered their faces with masks, and most of the agents and spies they employed were Christian priests and Jewish tradesmen, who could enter many places without raising suspicions.

Another feared secret police organization was the Oprichnina, established by Ivan the Terrible. Called "the ones who serve," the agents wore black, and they hunted and destroyed the enemies of the tsar.

The Okhrana, the tsarist secret police which began under Alexander III, was the first modern secret police organization. A pioneer in infiltrating anti-government groups, planting agents provocateur, and abusing prisoners, it occasionally organized murders.

A list of other secret police forces includes the Gestapo of National Socialist Germany, the K.G.B. of Soviet Russia, MI-5 and MI-6 of the United Kingdom, and the Central Intelligence Agency of the United States. The last, established in 1947, is described as a global intelligence service and a covert action (paramilitary) force.

Special mention should also be made of the Eleventh Shock Regiment. Under the control of the Intelligence Community of France, the Eleventh Shock Regiment is used only for retaliation, including covert retaliation.

POLICE (SECRET), SUPERFLUOUSNESS OF

According to one French observer, writing in 1938, "The superfluousness of secret services is nothing new; they have always been haunted by the need to prove their usefulness and keep their jobs after the original task had been completed."

The same author added this interesting point: "It appears, for example, that there was not a single anti-government action under the reign of Louis Napoleon which had not been inspired by the police itself."

POLICE (SECRET), TACTICS OF

Secret police units have a number of classic "maneuvers" they employ against targets. Some of the most important include:

1. *The Agent Provocateur.* An agent provocateur is an operative who infiltrates an organization or group and attempts to sabotage it from within.

    An agent provocateur may persuade the members to do something illegal (to cause them legal problems), he may trick them into doing something unintelligent or stupid (to embarrass the group), or he may simply try to create internal unrest in the group in order to destroy it.

Essentially, an agent provocateur is active in betrayal and sabotage.

2. *Psychological Warfare from the Outside.* To discredit a group or an individual, the secret police will plant false media stories, publish bogus leaflets, create forged correspondence, make anonymous telephone calls, manipulate or browbeat the target's employers or friends, and spread false rumors accusing a target of being an informant or a police infiltrator.

   An extreme example of psychological war from the outside was the "Office T" in Soviet-dominated Poland. This office specialized in creating false documents, including false government documents!

3. *The Black-Bag Operation.* The "Black-Bag Operation" is an illegal break-in into a home or an office. The operation is conducted to find information, to install listening devices, or to plant incriminating evidence to discredit someone. If a "frame" is intended, the goal is to prosecute or blackmail the target.

4. *Harassment through the Legal System.* The secret police may use tax laws and other government regulations to harass. They may also use grand juries, subpoenas, and conspicuous surveillance to hound him.

5. *Extra-legal Harassment.* The secret police may manufacture evidence to incriminate their target. They may also hire perjurers (disguised as "informants") and paid liars (disguised as "expert witnesses").

6. *Establish False-Flag Operations.* The secret police may establish fake radical groups to discredit an enemy. The East German Ministry for State Security (the so-called *Stasi*), for example, had "double agents" posing as Neo-Nazis in West Germany. These bogus Neo-Nazis engaged in anti-Semitic activity and violence.

6. *The "Moonlight Extradition."* The "Moonlight extradition" is an extra-legal abduction, generally done in countries which have no extradition treaty with the country initiating the crime.

7. *Wet Work.* "Wet Work"—an extreme example of extralegal force—is a simple state-sanctioned murder. In American circles, the C.I.A. euphemistically calls it an "executive action."

Typically, an "executive action" is disguised as a suicide (they leave the victim's body on his dead lover's grave) or an accident (they push him out of a window or drown him).

POLITICAL PRISONERS

Political prisoners are the incarcerated enemies of a regime. Enduring bread, water, and darkness, political prisoners are usually depicted as criminals, terrorists, or traitors.

A list of famous political prisoners includes Jesus the Nazarene, Dante Alighieri, Mahatma Gandhi, and Nelson Mandela.

Modern states typically classify political prisoners as "terrorists." Terrorists are not recognized as belligerents in international law and states may treat them as criminals rather than as prisoners of war.

Ten members of the Provisional Irish Republican Army—prosecuted for fighting for Irish freedom—starved to death in 1981 while engaged in a "hunger strike" against the British regime that had imprisoned them. They were simply demanding "political prisoner" status, but the British refused.

POLITICS, GUIDES TO

According to Robert Shea and Robert Anton Wilson, there are two essential political guides: Edward N. Edward Luttwak's *Coup d'etat: A Practical Handbook* (this book describes how to take over a country) and Niccolo Machiavelli's *The Prince* (this book describes how to run a state).

POL POT (1924-1998)

A tyrant, Pol Pot ruled Cambodia for three years, eight months, and twenty days, in the period between 1975 and 1979. A former schoolteacher, Pol Pot was known as "Brother Number One."

Pol Pot and his "Khmer Rouge" movement wanted to create a pure communist state—purged of all feudal, bourgeois, and foreign elements—and they turned back the clock to "Year Zero."

Trying to establish an agrarian utopia, they emptied the cities, and they abolished money, private property, and religion. Everyone had to dress in black peasant garb. All people had to work.

Families were banned and parents and children were separated. Under Pol Pot, there was no freedom of speech or travel.

People who appeared bourgeois (intellectuals who spoke a second language—even people who wore spectacles) were targeted.

After Vietnam invaded and quickly defeated his forces, Pol Pot went into hiding. He continued as leader of a Khmer Rouge guerrilla group until his followers ousted him in 1997.

PONZI SCHEME

Carlo Ponzi, who lived between 1883 and 1949, developed the "Ponzi scheme," a financial fraud that is also known as "pyramid selling."

In a Ponzi scheme, there is no genuine investment to make funds grow. Early investors are simply paid with money from more-recent depositors. The scheme will work as long as new money keeps pouring in from investors.

In Ponzi's original scheme he attracted clients by promising a 50 percent return on money in forty-five days.

The largest Ponzi scheme in history is the social security plan of the United States, originally established by Franklin Delano Roosevelt.

POPE

To pious Roman Catholics, the pope is the "vicar of Christ," the successor of the Galilean fisherman and apostle named Peter, and the *servus servorum dei (*"the slave of the slaves of God"). A high priest, he is the absolute ruler of an independent state, 109 acres in size, located in Rome.

To his enemies, the pope is an ecclesiastical tyrant–adorned with gaudy jewels and skirted, female-like clothing—who has blackened the world with usurpations and crimes. His critics note that the pontifical throne, the so-called "chair of St. Peter," is actually decorated with the twelve labors of the pagan Hercules!

According to Malachi Martin, a papal historian, at least forty popes bribed their way into the papacy.

POPES, FAMOUS EXAMPLES OF

The best pope in the history of the Roman church was a pious hermit named Peter of Morrone (Pietro di Morrone), who was elected in 1294. Taking the name of Celestine V, after only a few months he abdicated the immense power, wealth, and material comfort of the papacy to pursue the austere and humble life of a holy man.

Sadly, Celestine was cast into a dungeon by his successor (Pope Boniface VIII), and the holy man died from starvation and neglect. Celestine is now recognized as a saint by the Roman church.

On the negative side, the "bad" popes are numerous. A few examples will illustrate this point. The dates of their reigns are provided:

Leo I (440-461) was the first pope who claimed the right to put heretics to death.

Stephen V (885-891) was the pope who declared: "The popes, like Jesus, are conceived by their mothers through the overshadowing of the Holy Ghost. All popes are a certain species of man-god. . . . All powers in heaven, as well as on Earth, are given to them."

John XII (955-963), who was infamous for his misrule and scandalous behavior, was murdered by the outraged husband of a woman he had seduced.

Benedict IX (1032-1044, 1045, 1047-1048) became the pope at the age of ten when his father, Count Alberic III, purchased the office for him. Benedict sold the papacy three times.

Gregory VII (1073-1085) was the pope who made this declaration: "The pope is the only person whose feet are to be kissed by all persons."

Pope Innocent IV (1243-1254) was the pope who established the Inquisition as a permanent institution. He issued *Ad Extirpanda*, a papal bull which authorized the use of torture.

Boniface VIII (1294-1303) was the pope who announced: "Therefore we declare, state, define and pronounce that it is altogether necessary to salvation for every human creature to be subject to the Roman pontiff." Boniface was also the pope who murdered Pope ("Saint") Celestine V.

Alexander VI (1492-1503) was a man who committed his first murder at the age of twelve, sired six bastard children, bought the papacy with bribes, and officially sanctioned the use of the rosary.

Leo X (1513-1521) was the pope who, at a banquet with seven intimates, raised a chalice of wine and made this toast: "How well we know what a profitable superstition this fable of Christ has been for us and our predecessors." (The event was recorded by Cardinal Bembo and Cardinal Jovius, who were present.)

Clement VII (1523-34) was the pope who issued a bull granting an "indulgence" to anyone venerating and viewing a peculiar relic, the alleged foreskin from the circumcised Jesus, in Charroux, France.

Julius III (1550-1555) was a homosexual and "a sodomite covered with shameful ulcers." He was so infatuated with a beautiful beggar boy, the fifteen-year-old Innocenzo Del Monte, that Julius ultimately appointed the teenager to the College of Cardinals.

Paul IV (1555-1559) was the pope who made this declaration: "If my own father were a heretic, I would personally gather the wood to burn him."

Gregory XVI (1831-1846), in his encyclical *Mirari Vos*, denounced freedom of conscience and freedom of the press.

Pius IX (1846-1878) was the pope who summoned the First Vatican Council, which declared the doctrine of papal infallibility. According to this extravagant notion, "When the pope speaks *ex cathedra* on matters of faith and morals, he is possessed of that infallibility with which the Divine Redeemer wishes his Church to be endowed."

Leo XIII (1878-1903), the first twentieth century pope, publicly made this declaration: "The death sentence is a necessary and efficacious means for the Church to attain its end when rebels act against it."

In the history of the papacy, eighty popes have been canonized as saints. The last was Saint (Pope) Pius X, who died 1914.

Historians estimate that seventeen popes have been assassinated, most by other popes.

PORNOCRACY

Pornocracy means the rule of filth. The term refers to the period between A.D. 928 and A.D. 932, an especially corrupt period of the papacy. In the period, profane men used the pontifical office to "feed, fatten, and fornicate."

PORNOGRAPHY

Pornography—printed or visual material intended to stimulate eroticism—has been called a crime, a kind of "blasphemy against love."

Pornography has also been called a great equalizer because it allows sexually underprivileged men and women to see perfectly shaped—and beautiful—naked human forms. Indeed, as one Frenchman pointed out, thanks to pornography, anyone can now "contemplate the most spectacular bodies."

In 1524, Pietro Aretino wrote sonnets to accompany the beautiful drawings of sixteen sexual positions by Giuliano Romano. The collaboration produced one of history's most notorious works of erotic art.

In 1747, John Cleland wrote *Fanny Hill (or Memoirs of a Lady of Pleasure)*, the first true work of pornographic literature. The British government gave Cleland a pension on condition that he write no more obscene books.

Perhaps the most depraved pornographic work is the *120 Days of Sodom*. Written by the Marquis de Sade, the book is an endless stream of filth and promiscuity. Every conceivable sexual perversion is described, including a reference to man who is sexually aroused by firing pregnant women from cannons.

Curiously, in the late 1960's, the Danish government legalized the production of *all* forms of pornography. As a result, child pornography was legally produced in Denmark between 1969 and 1979. Today, that old Danish pornography still circulates, but now possession is a serious felony.

"POTERE OCCULTO"

The phrase *potere occulto* means "occult power," and it refers to the hidden power that is rife in the world. According to this theory, kings, popes, and presidents are stooges and "front men." Real authority belongs to faceless individuals—the puppeteers behind the scenes—who pull the invisible strings that control the human race.

According to Woodrow Wilson, an American president, "There is a power somewhere so organized, so subtle, so watchful, so interlocked, so complete, so pervasive that they better not speak above their breath when they speak in condemnation of it."

Benjamin Disraeli, the British Prime Minister, noted "that the world is governed by very different personages from what is imagined by those who are not behind the scenes."

And, Colonel L. Fletcher Prouty, the author of *The Secret Team*, claimed that about thirty or so C.I.A. figures, drug lords, multinational capitalists, ideologues, and soldiers of fortune really control the American government.

POUND, EZRA (1885-1972)

An American poet and martyr, Ezra Pound made pro-Axis broadcasts on Italian radio during World War II. Because he dared to criticize the United States, Pound was captured and put into an iron cage.

Falsely accused of being mentally ill, Pound was forced to spend twelve years in a windowless cell in an American insane asylum.

Of course, if Pound had not been an artist, he probably would have been executed.

Released in 1958, Pound returned to Italy, and he eventually died in Venice.

While in detention, Pound wrote *Pisan Cantos*, his best poetry.

POWER

In naked terms, power is physical strength or force. With power, one can master and enjoy.

In the Slavic world, power is viewed as holy, whether it is the power of the tsar or the power of sex. Laws are not only incompatible with it—they are sinful and man-made and prevent the full development of the divine.

Others, however, have argued that power by nature is a source of contamination. Percy Bysshe Shelley, for example, declared that "power, like a desolating pestilence, pollutes whate'er it touches."

POWER, ABUSE OF

According to Charles de Montesquieu, the abuse of power is greatest when the laws do not anticipate it.

When framing any law, prudent people try to imagine how a "devil" in power could abuse that law.

POWER, PROGRESSIVE DISORIENTATION AND

According to Robert Anton Wilson, rulers tend to become progressively detached from reality.

These are his words:

Every ruling elite suffers from Progressive Disorientation: the longer they rule, the crazier they get. That is because everybody lies to the men in power—some to escape punishment, some to flatter and curry favor. The result is the elite get a very warped idea of the world indeed. This applies to all pyramidal organizations—armies, corporations, or governments.

PRANKS

A prank is a practical joke or a mischievous act.

In its most benign form, the prank is a harmless way to draw attention to an issue. As a non-violent protest against capitalism, for example, some

Marxists rented a safety-deposit box in a bank and filled it with frozen fish. When the fish ultimately thawed and aged, the point was made.

On a more inappropriate level, in Los Angeles in 1994 a man dressed as "The Grim Reaper"—complete with a scythe— amused himself at night by staring into the windows of retirement homes.

PRESIDENT

Called an "apprentice dictator," a president is a type of "pseudo-king." In the United States, the president lives in a 132-room mansion and has a staff of one hundred, including six butlers.

Although all successful attacks on American presidents have taken place away from the "White House," the presidential family residence (located in the rear of the building, on the second floor) has bulletproof windows and walls that are four feet thick.

Technically, in America's "sham democracy" the president is elected, but in reality certain elite families monopolize the office.

Historian Michael P. Merlie, in a 1975 article, noted that of the thirty-seven presidents before James Carter, twenty-one were close relatives.

Three presidents (Pierce, Garfield, and Cleveland) were cousins.

In the family trees of twenty-one presidents, genealogists have found thirteen Roosevelts, sixteen Coolidges, and fourteen Tylers.

Even an "outsider" like Richard Nixon was related to President Monroe.

PRIMITIVISM

Primitivism is the rejection of science, rationality, and technology, which are viewed as dangerous and pernicious. Primitivists hate civilization and technology because these things pervert humanity and defile the planet.

Primitivists glorify the archaic past—a time of fresh air, pure water, and abundant space. Primitivists note that in 10,000 B.C.—before the invention of agriculture—there were only ten million people on Earth. Today, in contrast, modern Manhattan is so crowded that Manhattanites have only thirty-eight square meters per person.

Primitivists also note that with civilization came institutionalized warfare, inequality, and slavery.

PRINCIP, GAVRILO (1894-1918)

The most influential assassin in history, Gavrilo Princip was nineteen years of age when he sparked World War I by firing two shots—with a pistol—and killed an heir to the Austrian throne.

Princep swallowed cyanide after the attack, but the poison was too old and it failed to kill him. Seized by military officers, their abuse caused Princep to lose an arm.

Too young for the death penalty (at that time reserved for people twenty-one years or older), Princip was sentenced to twenty years. He died in 1918 from tuberculosis.

Honored as a hero by the Serbs, the Gavrilo Princip Museum is dedicated to his memory. The museum preserves Princip's "Black Hand Oath" in his own handwriting:

> By the sun that warms me, by the Earth that feeds me, by God, by the blood of my ancestors, by my honor and life, I swear fidelity to the cause of Serbian nationalism, and to sacrifice my life for it.

The Black Hand was a secret society of Serb assassins, formed in 1911 as the Order of Death. Its purpose was to use assassination to liberate Serbian lands held by other nations.

Organized by Colonel Dragutin Dmitrievich, a Serbian army officer who used the code name "Apis," the Black Hand recruited young people who were dying from terminal diseases.

Initiation involved a dark, candlelit room and a table holding a skull, a pistol, a bomb, and a vial of poison. Initiates were told to place a hand on the skull and to repeat the oath of the Black Hand.

PRISCILLIAN (circa 340-385)

A religious rebel, in A.D. 386 Priscillian was executed with at least five followers. These were the first Christian heretics to be executed by other Christians.

A layman in Spain, Priscillian denied the trinity, honored Saturday as the Sabbath, and used some non-canonical books, such as the *Acts of Thomas*, as scripture.

After the executions, Priscillian's movement would persist another two hundred years.

PRISON

A place of confinement—typically with ugly, coercive discipline—the prison has many forms and many functions. In the modern world, the prison "embodies the largest power the state exercises over its citizens in time of peace."

In history, some celebrated prison inmates include Dante Alighieri, Thomas More, Miguel de Cervantes, Fyodor Dostoevsky, Oscar Wilde, O. Henry, Mahatma Gandhi, Eugene Debs, Bertrand Russell, Dashiell Hammett, Martin Luther King, Alexander Solzhenitsyn, and Nelson Mandela.

One infamous prison was "The Pit," a cell deep in the foundations of the Tower of London. Built below the high-water mark of the Thames, as the river rose periodically hundreds of rats were driven upward into the pit. Prisoners had to fight the rodents in the dark.

The Tower of London also had a cell called the "Little Ease." Extremely small—it was only four square feet in size—it was impossible for an inmate to sit or lie down in the cell. (Sitting requires six square feet.)

In France, some prisoners were confined in the infamous cell called the "Mouse Hole." Used until the nineteenth century, this maddening and claustrophobic cell was three feet square.

The largest prison in history was Australia. Between 1787 and 1868 Australia was used as a vast penal colony, and approximately 160,000 convicts were sent there in chains.

The oddest prison in history was located in the Aztec Empire. Called Coacalco, it was a special house in the Aztec capital. Literally a prison for gods, the patron deities of defeated cities were held captive there.

In the United States (where the typical prison cell is seven by eleven feet), the most notorious prison was Alcatraz. Used as a Federal penitentiary between 1934 and 1963, Alcatraz had one guard for every three inmates. Men were confined in their cells fourteen hours each day. Talking was prohibited in the mess hall and the cell block. One 1930's study suggested that 60 per cent of all Alcatraz inmates lost their sanity while confined in the hellish place.

The most liberal prisons in history may be the "Open Prisons" in Denmark. Ninety per cent of all Danish inmates are kept in "Open Prisons." Only inmates viewed as security threats are kept in more traditional "Closed Prisons."

The only punishment in the Open Prisons is deprivation of liberty. Inmates have their own rooms, they may bring items from home, they are paid for work and school, and they are allowed home visits.

The Open Prisons are surrounded by a low fence. Every escapee who is caught is simply returned to the Open Prison to complete his sentence. There is no extra punishment.

PRISON, ABOLITION OF

The prison abolition movement calls for the complete eradication of the prison system.

The movement is not interested in the amelioration of prison conditions or the reform of prison. The movement argues that we can no more reform prison—a basic violation of human rights—than we can reform slavery.

Does the idea of abolishing prison sound dangerously radical?

According to Angela Davis, slavery at one time seemed normal and ethical, and suggesting its abolition once seemed inflammatory.

PRISON AND JAILS, BEHAVIOR IN

Guilty or innocent, there are basic rules for the prudent inmate:

1. Do not write down anything about the crime. Do not talk about the crime on a telephone. Do not speak about the crime to anyone—even a co-defendant. Cells could contain listening devices.
2. Do not speak to fellow prisoners. Jails contain desperate men. If you provide personal details, they may contact prosecutors and falsely claim you confessed. Prosecutors reward informants.
3. As a prisoner, do not be conspicuous, and do not give the impression you have something others want.
4. Understand that other prisoners may be undercover police. According to the law, undercover operatives are under no obligation to truthfully identify themselves. When questioned directly, they may legally lie.
5. If you are physically assaulted, do not name the attacker. Claim you fell accidentally. Other inmates respect that.
6. In prison, develop fake traits, such as a limp or a stutter. When you escape, the limp or the stutter will be included in your description. Also, guards tend not to watch people with disabilities.
7. In prison, do not lend or borrow. If you lend to someone—and he does not pay you back—you will be seen as weak. If you borrow, a prison

convict may claim you broke his possession, and he will demand compensation in the form of money or sexual favors.

8. Remember the prison rule: "If it is not worth killing for, it is not worth fighting for."

In summary, in prison keep to yourself and "see no evil, speak no evil, and hear no evil."

PRISON, ENDURANCE OF

Jesse Pomeroy died in 1932, at the age of seventy-three, after a remarkable feat of endurance in the American penal system. Because he had murdered two children (a nine-year-old girl and a four-year-old boy) when he was fourteen years old, Pomeroy spent nearly sixty years in prison, of which forty of those years were in solitary confinement. He endured incarceration by reading books and writing.

How can living in a prison cell be described? According to one inmate, "imagine living for years in a public latrine with another man."

PRISON, ESCAPE FROM

"Escape from controlled custody," a phrase borrowed from a classic text on the subject, is the ultimate human achievement. Cunning, intelligence, strength, and swiftness are required.

Regarding escape, a masterful fictional work is Jacques Futrelle's *The Problem of Cell 13*. Professor Augustus Van Dusen–the character known as "The Thinking Machine"—declares that he could escape from any cell on death row in one week. Entering with only his shirt, trousers, freshly polished shoes, stockings, tooth polish, one five-dollar bill and two ten-dollar bills—and knowing that "anything is dangerous in the hands of a man who knows how to use it"—the "Thinking Machine" uses his ingenuity to complete the escape.

In the real world, of course, escape is difficult. At Leavenworth Penitentiary, the walls are thirty-five feet high and twelve feet wide. To prevent tunneling, the walls extend thirty-five feet into the ground.

Security is so tight in prison that when a female inmate gives birth, she is kept in handcuffs *throughout* the labor and delivery.

Even taking a hostage is ineffective in the real world. Since 1931 the Federal Bureau of Prisons has followed a rule that under no circumstances are guards to open a gate for a would-be escapee because he is holding a hostage. In other words, hostages are expendable.

Yet, in spite of the difficulties, a 1978 study shows that one out of every forty-three prisoners in the United States will escape at some point.

PRISON (ESCAPE), HAZARDS OF

When an inmate tries to escape from an American medium or maximum security prison, regulations allow guards to fire a warning shot.

If a prisoner fails to stop and is over the fence, a guard may shoot to injure.

If the guard's life is in danger, he may shoot to kill.

In contrast—in Nazi Germany—any inmate who stepped into the "neutral zone"—an area near the fence—was immediately murdered.

PRISON (ESCAPE), TECHNIQUES OF

When escaping from "controlled custody," never stage a mass escape. Mass escapes draw publicity and provoke the maximum effort by authorities.

Also, before making your escape, clean your bed and cell, leave another person's perspiration-soaked shirt on the floor, and rub the soles of your feet with turpentine or ammonia. These actions will help you evade the bloodhounds.

As for techniques, the following may be used:

1) Cutting the bars. To cut bars, you need an abrasive object harder than the steel. To reduce noise and preserve the cutting edge, always lubricate the blade with oil or soap.

   To disguise cuts in the bar, fill the gaps with a mixture of bread, dirt, and water. In some high-security prisons the guards touch the bars daily, so leave enough metal to keep it strong. When you are ultimately ready to escape, kick out the weakened bar.

   Remember that anything that can be used as a crowbar (like a bed frame) can save cutting time.

   To slip through an especially tight spot, apply oil to the naked body. In 1986, one svelte female inmate, using oil and nudity, was able to slip through the seven-inch space between the bars of her cell.

2) Make acid. With only a cooking pot, a heat source, and your own urine, it is possible to make phosphoric acid! A powerful agent, phosphoric acid will degrade steel bars if applied several times daily. As the bars corrode, cover the area that has been eaten away with a dirt-toothpaste mixture.

3) Make bombs. Explosives may be manufactured from common ingredients. In 1926, nine hundred rioting prisoners at Walla Walla prison in

Washington State used homemade explosives to blast open the main gates.

4) Tunnel or dig through the wall, the floor, or the ceiling. This method is especially useful for hostages who are locked in closets or rooms.

Many American prisons are built on granite or other rock, and tunneling is almost impossible. But in 1951 Joseph Holmes, using iron from the prison workshop, spent six months digging a tunnel (twenty-six feet long) under the main wall of the Maryland State Penitentiary. Holmes escaped into Baltimore and was never caught.

In 2003, eighty-four prisoners escaped a Brazilian prison by making a tunnel fifty meters long, one meter wide, and one meter high. The tunnel went under two buildings and beneath the wall.

5) Bribe the guards. The Knapp Commission of 1971, which studied police corruption in New York City, found that *half* of all street police accepted "payoffs." These corrupt police were either "meat-eaters" (police who aggressively misused power for personal gain) or the more common "grass-eaters" (police who accepted any "payoffs" that had been offered).

If corruption is widespread among police, it will be common among guards.

6) Place a confederate inside the prison staff. Since "jailer" pay is low, prisons will hire almost anyone who has no criminal record.

American outlaw gangs—such as the "Bloods"—routinely order members who are "arrest-free" to apply for such jobs.

7) Secure the keys through force or trickery. A guard can be disabled temporarily by throwing pepper or ammonia into his eyes. Ammonia can be made from old urine.

Basil Banghart escaped from an Illinois prison in 1932 by blowing pepper into a guard's face and seizing the guard's gun.

8) Use deception. A bogus gun can be made out of wood or soap. Shading with a lead pencil can give it a realistic metallic sheen.

John Dillinger reputedly escaped from Crown Point Jail (Indiana) in 1934 using a carved pistol made from a wooden washboard, which he had blackened with boot polish.

9) Stage a ghost escape. Create a diversion (cause an outbreak of diarrhea by using a kitchen job to mix rotten chicken into the inmates' food), and then hide in the prison during the chaos. Try to slip out later when the excitement dies down.

10) Make a rope and climb out.

A rope can be made out of anything. For example, a strand of dental floss holds twelve pounds. Twenty-seven strands—in a triple braid—will hold 324 pounds.

11) Use technology. In 1973, three Irish Republican Army men were rescued from a Dublin prison by helicopter.

This was the IRA plan: 1) an operative chartered a private helicopter and instructed the pilot to land at a certain spot. 2) When the pilot landed, armed and masked men emerged and forced the pilot to fly to the prison, pick up the three prisoners in the exercise yard, and fly them to a secure location. 3) At the secure location, getaway cars were waiting.

12) Use forgery. Willis Newton, one of the Newton gang of bank robbers, used a clever trick to escape from prison. Newton wrote letters to the sheriff who had arrested him and the judge who had sentenced him, and asked them to sign a petition favoring his parole. When they both wrote back to decline, he now had their signatures, and he used them to forge a petition to the governor. The forgery worked.

13) Use contraband smuggled into the prison by a confederate. In 1979, William Morales, a member of the "Armed Forces of National Liberation of Puerto Rico," escaped from the prison ward of Bellevue Hospital in New York, using smuggled wire cutters to cut open a metal widow grate.

14) Use pre-positioned contraband. Before committing any crimes, one French outlaw hid a weapon in the lavatory of a regional courthouse. He was careful to commit all his crimes in the district—so that he would be prosecuted in *that* courthouse. When he was eventually apprehended and put on trial, he was able to access the weapon and escape during his trial.

Finally—whatever method used—know what you will do when you are outside the walls. In the United States, 94 percent of escaped prisoners are recaptured because they plan the escape better than the evasion.

PRISON, IMPROVISED WEAPONS AND

Even in prison, clever humans can improvise weapons.

Perhaps the most ingenious improvised weapon ever made was the pipe bomb constructed by William Kogut, a death row inmate at San Quentin. Kogut constructed the bomb from an old-fashioned deck of cardboard playing cards and a length of metal from his cot.

Kogut knew that the spots on the red cards (diamonds and hearts) contained diazo dye, a material which acts with nitrogen. In effect, Kogut made a "poor man's" form of nitroglycerin. The prison was forced to consult chemists to determine how he had accomplished the feat!

PROFIT

Profit is a benefit, especially one that is financial in nature.

The profit motive was alien to the ancient Greeks. In Greek civilization, to gain in an exchange was taboo, and the abiding principle was equality and mutual benefit. To gain at the expense of another belonged to war and raiding, where it was achieved by acts or threats of prowess, not bargaining. Not surprisingly, the Greeks glorified piracy, disapproved of theft (the seizure of goods by stealth), and encouraged robbery (the seizure of goods by force).

America, in contrast, represents an entire civilization devoted to profit. In the United States, millions of Americans toil so that a few plutocrats in New York, Los Angeles, and Miami can enjoy more wealth.

PROPAGANDA

Propaganda is information—either false or true—intended to influence someone. When used as a weapon, it is a form of psychological warfare.

Propaganda has two functions: 1) create proselytes and militants and 2) neutralize opponents.

One type of propaganda is called "white" propaganda. Here the source, such as a politician's speech, is clearly identified.

During World War II, Japanese troops were told by their commanders that no man could become an American marine without killing one parent in front of the recruiter.

In "gray propaganda," the source is unidentified or concealed. To increase credibility, it is usually released through what appears to be an independent or foreign source.

During the *first* World War, the British released a fake news story, through the *New York Tribune*, describing the existence of a German factory which turned human corpses into soap.

Black propaganda is false information that purports to emanate from a source other than the true one. It is made to appear to come from a fake document, from fabricated enemy "defectors" that admit evil activities, from fake video or audio that are made to appear authentic, or from fake broadcasts that appear to come from the enemy.

A classic example of black propaganda was produced at the beginning of the "Cold War." Before the 1948 election in Italy, Americans "discovered" the "Zorin Plan," which was supposedly written by the Soviet foreign minister. It detailed an alleged plot to "Stalinize" Italy under Italian communists, a plan that included the execution of priests, the incarceration of shop owners in concentration camps, and the confiscation of all property.

"PROPAGANDA BY DEED"

"Propaganda by Deed" is the concept that action is more important than the spoken or written word. Real violence, in other words, is more effective than simple "verbal terrorism."

Or, as Peter Kropotkin declared: "A simple deed is better propaganda than a thousand pamphlets."

In recent history, several outlaw groups have effectively used the concept.

During the Algerian war for independence, the rebels used the knife to send messages. Throat-cutting, associated with sheep killing, was considered an insulting death, and the insurgents made these horrible mutilations to degrade and humiliate their enemies.

In 1947, after the British Empire sentenced to death three Jewish freedom fighters for "terrorism," the Stern Gang kidnapped two British sergeants. When the British executed the three Jewish fighters, the Stern Gang hanged the two British sergeants and placed booby traps on the corpses.

PROPAGANDA, THE TRUTH AND

Paul Joseph Goebbels, the Nazi propaganda wizard, understood that the most effective propaganda does not use lies.

Of course, Goebbels understood that there are many kinds of truth: half truths, limited truths, and truths out of context.

PROPHECY, FAILURE OF

One of the most notorious "false prophets" was Nongqawuse, a South African from the Xhosa nation. In April 1856, Nongqawuse, then a young girl, claimed that two male spirits appeared to her and gave her this message: if the Xhosa people slaughter all their cattle, plow no land, and abandon witchcraft, the dead would rise, the cattle would reappear in great numbers, grain pits would be filled, and all whites would be driven into the sea.

Filled with euphoria, the Xhosa slaughtered cattle and destroyed grain. The few who resisted were pressured by the majority. Days—then months—passed, and nothing occurred. Starvation soon stalked the land, and half the population perished.

Curiously, according to one study, *When Prophecy Fails*, "failed prophecy" can actually INCREASE faith, binding a remnant more closely to the movement.

It is interesting that Jesus appears to make an erroneous prophecy in Mark 13:30 ("this generation will not pass away before all these things take place"), yet Christianity was able to survive.

PROSTITUTION

A prostitute is a person who engages in sexual activity for payment. Called the "proletarians of love," prostitutes (along with priests and spies) belong to one of the oldest professions.

In ancient Corinth, the Greeks had a temple to "Aphrodite Porne" ("Aphrodite the Whore").

In medieval Europe, St. Thomas Aquinas argued that prostitutes are a necessary evil to protect the virtue of honest women. "Take away prostitutes from the world," wrote Aquinas, "and you will fill it with sodomy."

In the eighteenth century, Bernard Mandeville, the author of *A Modest Defence of Publick Stews: or an Essay upon Whoring*, had a similar opinion. Mandeville recommended a state-administered system of public "whores" to protect virgins.

In the nineteenth century, Gustav Flaubert made this declaration: "The idea of prostitution is a meeting place of so many elements—lust, bitterness, complete absence of human contact, muscular frenzy, the clink of gold—that to peer deeply into it makes one reel. One learns so many things in a brothel, and feels such sadness, and dreams so longingly of love."

In the modern world, some libertarians defend prostitution as a "capitalist act between consenting adults." Although illicit—prostitution is love bought and sold on the black market—they assert it is a venial offense.

Usually, however, moralists condemn prostitution as a vice that spreads potentially lethal diseases.

PROTECTION RACKET

The protection racket is a species of extortion. The victims are threatened with theft or violence unless money is paid.

The "protection racket" is used by various types of organized crime, from the Mafia to the government.

PSEUDOCIDE

When an individual fakes his own death, it is called a pseudocide. A pseudocide may be arranged to escape the law, rapacious creditors, or a spouse.

Or, a pseudocide may be staged by an artist to increase the value of his work.

PSEUDO-CONSPIRACY

A pseudo-conspiracy is a false group set up by the secret police. It can have many functions, from ferreting out local dissidents to embarrassing a foreign government.

A classic "pseudo-conspiracy" was the "Trust," a false insurgent organization established by Felix Dzerzhinsky, the Soviet spy chief and a master of counter-revolution and sabotage.

Ostensibly, the Trust appeared to be an anti-communist organization, and it received money and assistance from the United States, the British Empire, and the Russian exile community. In reality, it was designed to control, destroy, and identify the enemies of the communist state. The Trust enticed many Russian dissidents and some foreign agents to their deaths.

The Trust was in operation between 1918 and 1924.

PSEUDO-FORCES

The use of pseudo-forces—units of former insurgents who have been "turned"—has been a common feature of anti-guerrilla warfare since 1945.

The "Selous Scouts," who operated between 1973 and 1979 in the "Rhodesian" war, were a classic example of a pseudo-terror force. Composed of "turned" guerrillas, they operated as intelligence-gatherers for the Rhodesian state.

The Selous Scouts, who never had more than 420 men in active service, operated in eight-man units. Dressed and armed like guerrillas, their function was not to engage the enemy, but to report them to "fire force" teams or land units. For protection, all military activity was frozen in areas where the Selous Scouts were operating.

The Selous Scouts were also involved in waging a "dirty war." For example, they committed atrocities that were blamed on real guerrillas, such as burning black villages and murdering white missionaries.

To spread discord among the enemies of the Rhodesian state, the Selous Scouts also spread false rumors identifying real guerrillas as "informants."

PSEUDO-PROVOCATION

In military terms, a pseudo-provocation is a clandestine or "black operation" in which the perpetrators manufacture an offense to justify an overwhelming military response.

When states invent a provocation, the easiest method is to attack their own territory, their own installations, or their allies in a way that it appears to have been carried out by the enemy. States conduct these operations to fool their own citizens and allies. (The enemy, of course, knows he did not attack.)

At the start of World War II, Nazi Germany fabricated a Polish attack on a German radio station. Called Operation "Canned Ham," the Germans used the fake incident to justify their assault on Poland.

PSEUDO-TERRORISM

A type of "false-flag" operation, a pseudo-terrorist act is a state-orchestrated atrocity disguised as a real terrorist attack.

An alleged act of pseudo-terrorism was the "Reichstag Fire" in Germany on February 27, 1933. The Nazi government blamed a young Dutch communist Jew named Marinus van der Lubbe, who "confessed" while in police custody. Many believe, however, that the Nazis themselves ignited the fire. The incident allowed Hitler to invoke an "Enabling Act" that gave him dictatorial powers.

In American history, some individuals believe that the Oklahoma City bombing in 1995 was orchestrated by the federal government to justify draconian legislation. Soon after the attack, William Jefferson Davis Clinton signed the "Anti-Terrorism and Effective Death Penalty Act." The latter added sixty new capital crimes, including large-scale drug trafficking!

This technique of terrifying people into demanding the creation of a "police state" is called the "strategy of tension" by the Italians.

PSEUDO-THREAT

A pseudo-threat is a bogus menace created by the "ruling elite" to intimidate the gullible masses.

On the pseudo-threat, the authors of the *Report From Iron Mountain* made this observation: "The existence of an accepted external menace . . . is essential to social cohesiveness as well as to the acceptance of political authority. The menace must be believable, it must be of a magnitude consistent with the complexity of the society threatened, and it must appear, at least, to affect the entire society."

PSEUDO-WEAPONS

Pseudo-weapons are false weapons used to bluff the enemy.

In 1976, a Croatian terrorist hijacked an American airliner with a fake bomb made from a cooking pot, some ordinary wires, some common putty, and some other items. The terrorist assembled the fake bomb on board after he had passed through security.

PSYCHIATRY

Psychiatry is a form of social control disguised as therapy.

According to Thomas Szasz, a modern critic, psychiatry represents a new form of the "Inquisition" and psychiatrists are the new "witch hunters." Dedicating to protecting the *status quo,* psychiatry uses the insanity label to control dissidents, undesirables, and mavericks. Anyone who resists is drugged and institutionalized.

Interestingly, Jack Kerouac, Allen Ginsberg, and William S. Burroughs, Jr.—three rebel writers—had all experienced mental hospitals (and prisons) by the age of thirty.

PSYCHIATRY, TYRANTS AND

Tsar Nicholas I, who lived between 1796 and 1855, was the first ruler to use psychiatric wards to punish rebels, reformers, revolutionaries, and political dissidents. According to a perverse form of logic, anyone suggesting reform must be mad.

Totalitarian regimes often view unwelcome manifestations of individuality as *prima facie* evidence of insanity. Then, to camouflage their activities, they claim to treat or reeducate rather than punish. Of course, the "treatments" are indistinguishable from real punishment.

In the Soviet era of Russian history, people accused of "reformist delusions" could be sent to a psychiatric hospital by a court, a civil procedure, or on the word of a psychiatrist. Anyone was vulnerable because, as one psychiatrist pointed out, "The absence of symptoms of an illness cannot prove the absence of the illness itself."

One religious dissenter—Vasily Shipilov—was kept in a psychiatric hospital for thirty years.

PUNISHMENT

Punishment is a penalty imposed for an alleged offense. Often taking bizarre forms—in ancient Rome the poisoner Locusta was publicly raped by a specially trained giraffe and then torn apart by wild animals—its application seems to be an inherent part of human experience.

Punishing humans is an ancient practice. There is a Paleolithic-Age depiction of a man being punished in a Sicilian cave.

The reasons (or pretexts) for punishment are retribution, incapacitation, deterrence, and rehabilitation.

The Twelve Tables of the Romans, an early law code from *circa* 450 B.C., lists eight kinds of punishments: a fine, fetters, flogging, retaliation in kind, civil disgrace, banishment, slavery, and death.

For most of history, criminals were fined, branded, mutilated, enslaved, put into work gangs, exiled, or killed. Today, criminals are herded into prison complexes.

Interestingly, in Hinduism punishment itself is regarded as an evil institution (it is grouped with theft and lying), rather than a satisfactory answer to the problem of evil in man.

PUNISHMENT, COLLECTIVE

Collective punishment is the punishment of the group for the crime of one of its members.

In Roman law, if a slave killed his master, all the other slaves under the same roof were put to death.

In World War II, the Nazis issued an "Armed Forces High Command" in December 1941. According to this command, ten civilians were to be shot for every German soldier killed by the "Resistance."

The French used a policy of "collective responsibility" in their Algerian war—with disastrous results.

The British, on the other hand, were more clever. In Cyprus, the British fought the Cypriot insurgency with "collective fines." These "collective fines" were imposed on all the people in an area where a terrorist attack had occurred.

PUNISHMENT, FRIEDRICH NIETZSCHE ON

According to the philosopher Friedrich Nietzsche, punishment itself is born of weakness.

According to Nietzsche, "It is possible to imagine a society flushed with such a sense of power that it could afford to let its offenders go unpunished."

PUNISHMENT, THE MAFIA AND

The Mafia, which has its own rules, punishes transgressors with great ferocity. In its distinctive fashion, the Mafia tries to make the penalty fit the crime.

When the father of mobster Joe Columbo seduced another Mafiso's woman, the "lovers" were both shot in the head. Also, the man's penis was cut off and shoved into the woman's mouth.

In another case, when a Chicago mobster boss named Sam Giancana wanted to discipline one mafioso, Giancana forced the man's mother, father, wife, and children to urinate on his naked body.

PYGMIES

The pygmies of the African rain forest are free people. Known as the Twa, the pygmies have no leaders, no politics, no laws, no taxes, no social classes, and no priests.

Pygmies are small—but their heads are the same size as taller humans.

Curiously, although we tend to associate democracy, freedom. and gender equality with advanced civilizations, these things are actually characteristics of the most primitive societies.

QUICKLIME

A white caustic alkaline substance consisting of calcium oxide, quicklime is obtained by heating limestone.

A popular fallacy is that burying a murder victim in quicklime hastens decomposition. In reality, the quicklime combines with body fat to produce a hard soap that resists insects, rodents, and bacteria, thereby retarding decomposition.

The quicklime—unless treated with water— acts as a preservative by desiccating the victim.

In the 1980's Dorothy Puente murdered seven people and buried them in her backyard with dry quicklime. Her mistake led to her apprehension.

More intelligent murderers—such as dictators—have buried their victims with anaerobic bacteria, which is sold by hardware stores for septic-tank use.

Of course, forensic anthropologists can still determine a great deal from the teeth and bones that remain. From only a skeleton, there are clues that suggest age, gender, race, size, wounds, and identity.

RACE, MASTER

The concept of a "master race" is the idea that a certain ethnic group is superior to all others.

The Nazis made the concept their own, but their claim was ridiculed by Benito Mussolini. According to the Italian dictator, "We can look with contempt on the doctrine of a certain race which did not even know how to write when we had Caesar, Virgil, and Augustus."

RACISM

Racism is an antagonism based on the physical and cultural characteristics of others.

Racism comes in many forms. According to Eskimo legend, women copulating with dogs produced the first white people.

And Aristotle (in his *Politics,* Book VII) said that the northern races are brave and stupid, while the southern races are cowardly and intelligent. The Greeks, he asserted, are just right.

Some of the most dangerous racists are the anti-Semites, who are of three types: 1) those who hate Jews for their religion (Medieval anti-Semites), 2) those who hate Jews for their alleged ethnicity or "blood" (Nazis), and 3) those who hate Jews for their moral code, as defined in the Talmud (Neo-Nazis). Weirdly, Neo-Nazis believe that Jews belong to a crime syndicate—a "Mafia" disguised as a religion.

RAID

A raid is a sudden, unexpected, violent, and destructive assault. The raiders always withdraw immediately, whether the raid was successful or not.

Commonly used in asymmetric warfare, the guerrilla raid involves stealthy movement, surprise attack, and swift dispersal.

Native American warriors were masters of the raid. They attacked just before dawn, believing that sleeping men had the greatest difficulty arousing themselves at that time.

RANSOM

A ransom is the payment demanded or paid for the release of a captive.

The typical ransom involves currency, but some ransoms may be propaganda actions. A political leader or a plutocrat may be kidnapped, for example, and exchanged for food distributions to the poor.

RASPUTIN, GRIGORI (1871-1916)

The self-proclaimed holy man and miracle worker, Grigori Rasputin—the so-called "holy devil"—was an enigmatic Russian figure. He reached St. Petersburg—after walking one thousand miles—and quickly established himself as an advisor and confidant to the last tsarina and tsar of Russia.

Gerard Encausse, the French occultist, warned the tsar about the "holy devil" with these words: "Cabalistically speaking Rasputin is a vessel like Pandora's box. He contains all the vices, crimes, and filth of the Russian people. Should this vessel be broken its contents will spill across Russia."

Rasputin made this remarkable prophecy to the tsar in 1916: "If I am killed by common assassins, and especially if they are my brothers, the Russian peasants, you have nothing to fear. But if I am killed by the nobles, if they shed my blood their hands will remain soiled with my blood. Brothers will kill brothers. They will kill each other. There will be no nobles in the country."

Rasputin was murdered by the upper class—the conspirators were led by Prince Felix Yusupov—and the prophecy of the "holy devil" came to pass exactly.

REBEL

A nonconformist—untamed, ungelded, and undomesticated—a rebel is someone who resists authority, control, or convention. Like Prometheus, Satan, and Spartacus, he refuses to kneel and obey.

According to Mikhail Bakunin, what exalts us above the animals is "the power to think and the desire to rebel."

The consequences of rebellion are usually death, incarceration, impoverishment, infamy, or ridicule.

Sometimes, however, the consequences may be limitless power, endless wealth, and unrestrained devotion. Zeus, who ousted his father, became chief of the Olympians. George Washington, who betrayed his king, became the first president of the United States.

In general, there are three species of rebels: the rebels against nature (called deviants or perverts by their enemies), the rebels against knowledge (called heretics or blasphemers by their enemies), and the rebels against power (called terrorists or criminals by their enemies).

REBELLION, POLITICAL

According to Juvenal, the Roman writer, kings are killed not because of their tyranny but because of their weakness. The people erect scaffolds, not as the moral punishment for despotism, but as the biological penalty for powerlessness.

Curiously, if the people do rise up, blind and greedy stampedes for freedom usually end in slavery.

RECRUITMENT OF OPERATIVES

Innumerable techniques are used to identify and recruit operatives for an organization.

To identify potential guerrilla fighters, the Viet Minh held rallies. Trained observers monitored the crowd for individuals who reacted positively to the message.

The Soviet K.G.B., when recruiting "terrorists," searched for individuals hurt by fate or nature, people defeated by unfavorable circumstances, or the ugly.

Such people—according to the Russians—make effective terrorists. Their terrorism gives them a sense of importance and makes them feel empowered. For the first time in their lives, they can feel superior to the prosperous and the handsome.

When recruiting "assets," espionage organizations such as the C.I.A. use "night crawlers." A "night crawler" is a "talent spotter" who prowls night clubs, taverns, and so forth looking for government employees, military personnel, and other people in strategic positions who can be "compromised" (or blackmailed) using alcohol, drugs, or sex.

REED, MARY (died 1720)

Mary Reed was a celebrated female pirate.

Endowed with inviolate courage, Reed publicly declared that pirates *supported* the death penalty for piracy. She claimed that the penalty kept "some dastardly rogues honest." Without the gallows and the garrote, she argued, "the ocean would be crowded with rogues, like the land."

REPENTANCE

Repentance is the act of renouncing the past.

In the Aztec Empire a guilty person who had NOT been caught could escape punishment by confessing to the priests of Tlazolteotl, the goddess of filth. Only one such confession was allowed in a lifetime, but the guilty person could erase even a capital crime.

On the subject of repentance, the Marquis de Sade wrote: "Nothing simpler: one repents only what one is not in the habit of doing; frequently repeat what makes you remorseful and you will quickly have done with the business. "

RETREAT

According to the author of *Phantom Soldier*, the Occident is conditioned to think that victorious armies move only forward.

In contrast, Oriental strategists believe that to intentionally limit one's freedom of movement makes no sense, for retreat can lead to victory.

For example, under constant attack by Chiang Kai-shek's well-supplied army, Mao Tse-tung's forces retreated six thousand miles, from October 1934 to October 1935. The retreat cost thousands of lives, but Mao's movement survived. In January 1949, he won.

REVOLUTION

In a revolution, a new ruling class, using violence and crime, seizes power. The old ruling class is exterminated, imprisoned, or banished.

The first real revolution in the modern world was the French Revolution, which was a struggle between royal absolutism and popular absolutism. During the French Revolution, the king and more than three thousand aristocrats were guillotined.

Even more radical was the Russian Revolution. In this "proletarian" Revolution the private ownership of land was abolished, banks and industry were nationalized, the stock market was abolished, the right of inheritance was abolished, gold was declared a state monopoly, all government debts were declared void, old courts were replaced by revolutionary tribunals in which any citizen could act as a judge or a lawyer, marriage and divorce laws were liberalized, and Church lands were seized and the teaching of religion was prohibited in the schools.

Real revolution, according to Eric Hobsbawm, is always "puritan." The 1960's-era rebellion, according to Hobsbawm, was simply "play acting."

REVOLUTION, AMERICAN

Strictly speaking, the so-called American Revolution (1776-1783) was not in fact a revolution. Since 69 percent of the signers of the Declaration of Independence had held colonial office under Great Britain, historian Francis Jennings described the uprising as a "barons' revolt."

REVOLUTION, CRIMINALS AND

Criminals are conservative by nature. They have a vested interest in the preservation of the *status quo*, which guarantees their income.

If a revolution does occur, however, real criminals will exploit the situation. In the words of historian Eric Hobsbawm, "for the genuine underworld, revolutions are little more than unusually good occasions for crime."

REVOLUTION, EFFECTS OF

According to Albert Camus, "all modern revolutions have ended in a reinforcement of the power of the State: 1789 brings Napoleon; 1848, Napoleon III; 1917, Stalin; the Italian disturbances of the 1920's, Mussolini; the Weimar Republic, Hitler."

And, according to Jose Ortega y Gasset, the author of *The Revolt of the Masses*, a "revolution does not last more than fifteen years."

REVOLUTION, IRANIAN

The revolution in Iran in 1979 overturned the trend toward secularism that has characterized the modern world. It was led by an Islamic scholar, Ayatollah Ruhollah Khomeini.

Starting in the eighteenth century and continuing up to 1979, all Revolutions had been secular—even atheistic in nature. This includes the American "barons' revolt" of 1776, and the French, Russian, and Chinese revolutions.

The French revolutionaries, for example, installed a naked harlot on the high altar of Notre Dame Cathedral on November 10, 1793. To the revolutionaries who conducted the impious farce, the woman represented the "goddess of reason."

REVOLUTION, WORKERS AND

Mikhail Bakunin noticed the non-revolutionary nature of workers. Workers tend to have specific grievances—such as higher pay or fewer hours—and their demands can be satisfied within the existing social system. Workers seek reform, not revolution.

Also, by nature workers are conservative. The grievances of the people look backward, not forward. Rather than demanding new rights, they complain of being deprived of ancient rights, real or imagined.

According to Bakunin, authentic revolution can be made only by the politicized criminal class (bandits and brigands) in alliance with disaffected students, marginal intellectuals, and peasants.

REVOLUTION, YOUTH AND

Revolution belongs to the young.

Peter Tkachev, the nineteenth-century radical, proposed the elimination or suppression of all Russians older than twenty-five because they were incapable of assimilating new ideas.

RICIN

A deadly poison extracted from crushed castor beans, ricin has no known antidote. Because ricin works so quickly—and because a minuscule dose is fatal—toxicologists will not readily recognize it in the victim's body.

In the Soviet period, operatives used ricin to kill dissenters. One victim was Georgi Markov, a Bulgarian defector.

In 1995—in the United States—four members of a white supremacy group called the "Patriot's Council" were convicted of plotting to kill federal officials with ricin. The group planned to combine ricin with DMSO and place the mixture on doorknobs and steering wheels. DMSO, also called dimethyl sulfoxide, is a tissue solvent that can carry various substances through the skin into the bloodstream.

RIESEL, VICTOR (1914-1995)

A journalist and a martyr, Victor Riesel was permanently blinded in 1956 when a young man threw sulfuric acid into his face. After the attack, Riesel lived another thirty-nine years.

RIFKIN, STANLEY MARK (born 1946)

A non-violent bank robber, in 1978 Stanley Mark Rifkin implemented the first electronic bank "heist" in American history. Rifkin observed that tangible assets are guarded by armed men and steel vaults, but electronic assets are protected only by a code. Rifkin stole assets by stealing the code.

Curiously, Rifkin was apprehended only because he boasted to a friend. For stealing ten million dollars—more loot than Dillinger, the James Gang, and "Bonnie and Clyde" combined—Rifkin served only three and one-half years.

American law is notoriously lenient on non-violent crimes because the members of Congress—who make the laws—are normally capable of white-collar crimes only.

RIGHTS, HUMAN

The universe is a violent pageant of creation and destruction in which man has no special rights.

Even in modern democratic states, certain persons—namely, criminals, the mentally ill, the very young, and soldiers—are deprived of certain traditional rights.

A soldier who abruptly quits, for example, will be hunted down and punished. In the nineteenth century, runaway slaves received similar treatment.

RIOT

A bloody uprising of the poor, riots are urban affairs. Generally speaking, they quickly degenerate into poor-on-poor violence.

Riots are innumerable in history, but one infamous American outburst was the New York City Draft Riot, which began July 13, 1863 and lasted for three more days.

Fanned by racial hatred, the riot included the savage lynching of more than eighty-eight blacks, and the sight of mutilated corpses hanging from lampposts was common. Some were covered with oil and set ablaze, leaving charred skeletons.

The rioters, after totally burning large sections of New York (including three police stations and the so-called "Negro Orphanage"), were crushed by federal troops called back from Gettysburg.

According to some estimates, there were hundreds killed and thousands wounded. The New York City Draft Riot may have killed more Federal citizens than many Civil War battles.

ROBIN HOOD

A fabled medieval outlaw—skillful with the long-bow—the legendary Robin Hood was a Saxon who fled to Sherwood Forrest to escape the tyranny of the Normans. Robin Hood gathered a band of hardy followers—such as "Little John" and "Friar Tuck"—and they robbed rich Normans and gave the loot to poor Saxons.

The Sheriff of Nottingham made endless attempts to capture Robin and his "Band of Merry Men," but always in vain.

ROBOT

A robot is a mechanical slave. The term is derived from a Czech word which means "forced labor."

Although robots presently serve the human race, one Irish biologist has argued that machines may one day master the planet. Indeed, he has suggested that the purpose of man may be to develop the next higher form, which will be silicon-based.

On January 25, 1979, a one-ton robot at a Ford Motor Company plant killed Robert Williams. Williams is believed to be the first human killed by a robot.

ROME

A powerful state, Rome was established by the semi-mythical Romulus on April 21, 753 B.C. Originally a haven for outcasts and fugitives, murderers and runaway slaves, Rome would endure for twelve centuries.

According to the philosopher Allan Watts, "The principal error of academic historians is their belief that the Roman Empire *fell*. It never *fell*. It still controls the Western world through the Vatican and the Mafia."

RUBBISH, DANGER OF

Remember—even in a so-called free society—your refuse has no privacy rights. Any thing you discard may be used against you in a court of law.

RUMOR

Sun Tzu knew that rumor was a weapon of war.

While orchestrating a coup d'etat against Salvador Allende, the Marxist leader of a century-old democracy in Chile, the American C.I.A. used media assets to report shortages of sugar, gasoline, toilet paper, and other consumer goods. The rumor was false, but people, out of fear, began hoarding, and this created a real shortage!

Which rumors are believable?

According to the Russians, people readily believe that which they greatly fear or greatly desire.

RUSSIA

A vast Eurasian state, Russia is the largest country on the planet. It was calculated in 1914 that the Russian Empire had been expanding at an average daily rate of fifty-five square miles over four centuries, or an area of twenty thousand square miles per year (the area of modern Belgium).

Russia's history is soaked in blood. Since A.D. 901, Russia has been at war 46 out of every 100 years.

Russia is also the land of extremes. Russia gave the world modern tsarism, political terrorism, the pogrom, the gulag, the practical hydrogen bomb, and space travel.

Because of the Mongol influence on Russian character, the Russians have a special admiration for ferocity, tyrannical ways, and slyness.

RWANDA

Mountainous Rwanda, which is roughly the size of Vermont, is the most densely populated country in Africa. Blessed with an invigorating environment—one that is without malaria and the sleeping sickness—Rwanda is famous for its gorillas and its massacres.

The pygmies—known as the Twa—were the original inhabitants of Rwanda. They were hunters and gatherers. Today, the Twa represent 1 percent of the population of Rwanda.

Next, Bantu farmers, called the Hutu, arrived. Then, after 1500, fierce cattle-herders, the Tutsi, moved in and established themselves as rulers.

Originally, the Tutsi were tall and thin, with light brown skins, aquiline noses, and thin lips. The Hutu were short, dark, and had more classic "African" features. Intermarriage, however, has eroded the differences, and today both speak the same language.

In spite of assimilation, periodic massacres occur in Rwanda. In 1994, approximately 800,000 Tutsi were bludgeoned or hacked to death over a period of one hundred days.

An estimated one in fifty Hutus participated in the killings. Those who protested were themselves killed, so most remained silent.

As one observer noted, in 1994 the machete in Rwanda became a weapon of mass destruction.

SABOTAGE

To sabotage is to willfully destroy or obstruct, especially for political or military advantage.

The word "sabotage" came into general use after the French railway strike of 1912, when railwaymen promoted their cause by wrecking trains.

In 1940—in one spectacular example—four thousand people were killed when a German troop ship was destroyed through sabotage.

One especially effective form of sabotage is "cold sabotage." Also called "sabotage without means," cold sabotage is "malicious" interference with an enemy's equipment or communications, without using special equipment or weapons.

Examples of cold sabotage include disabling a vehicle by placing sugar in the gasoline tank, pouring instant rice into the radiator, or placing glue inside ignition locks.

Public utilities are especially vulnerable to cold sabotage. The system is heavily centralized, but the vulnerabilities are decentralized. The electrical grid, for example, has hundreds of thousands of miles of high-tension lines, and this grid may be compromised at any point. Terrorists may secretly remove bolts anchoring a power pole and escape. Days—even weeks later—the loosened bolts will cause the pole to topple in a storm.

Since it requires "twelve soldiers to guard one kilometer of infrastructure," protecting the entire grid from sabotage is impossible.

SACRIFICE

A sacrifice is a killing for a ritual purpose. Called a "festive act of sadism," the ultimate victim of a sacrifice is a human.

Traditionally, there are three reasons for sacrifice: consecration (to dedicate someone or something), expiation (to eliminate sin or guilt), and propitiation (to satisfy divine wrath).

Sacrifices are offered in the fire (burning), in the water (drowning), in the air (the gallows or crucifixion), or in the earth (burial alive).

Organized sacrifice emerged with the invention of farming and animal herding, and thousands—if not millions—of victims have been offered. At various times, as Georges Bataille noted, children have been offered to bronze idols, wicker figures crammed with humans have been set alight, and priests clad in the skins of flayed girls have danced to their gods.

In ancient Egypt, there is evidence the Egyptians sacrificed a red-headed man (red was associated with Set) on the tomb of Osiris.

In the case of classical Greece, when Pausanias visited Mount Lykaion in the second century after Christ, he heard rumors that a child was murdered, dismembered, and devoured every year at the mountaintop sanctuary of Zeus. Pausanias did not investigate, but wrote these cryptic words: "Let it be as it is and as it was from the beginning."

In Mexico, the Aztecs honored the rain-god named Tlaloc by sacrificing young children, who were either drowned or walled up in caves. The more the terrified children wept—it was believed—the more it was an omen of good rain.

In Europe, the Inquisition was (according to the author of *Crown Against Concubine*) "the guise under which Rome carried out one of its many programs of human sacrifice."

In the Ashanti kingdom (now in Ghana), humans were sacrificed in the city of Kumasi. After the British took Kumasi in 1874, a war correspondent estimated that he saw the skeletal remains of 120,000 people.

In India, in the Shiva temple of Tanjore, a male child was beheaded before the altar of Kali every Friday at the holy hour of twilight. Officially, this continued into the nineteenth century.

But—even today—newspapers in India still tell of human sacrifices or self-immolations.

SACRILEGE

Sacrilege is the violation of something considered sacred.

In one infamous example of sacrilege, Antiochus IV sacrificed a pig to Zeus on Jehovah's altar in Jerusalem. The priests of Antiochus ate pork and poured offal on the Torah, the scriptures of the Jewish people.

SADISM

Sadism is the tendency to derive sexual gratification or pleasure from inflicting pain, suffering, or humiliation on others. According to the moralists, sadism is the ultimate criminal depravity.

Among animals, the usual victim of sadism is male. The male bee, for example, does not survive intercourse with the queen. After intercourse, she calmly discards his corpse.

Among humans, the female is usually the victim of sadism.

The Marquis de Sade, the French writer after whom sadism was named, glorified the infliction of pain on others—especially women. He graphically described lewd enjoyments and erections caused by misery, tears, and the shedding of blood.

On the subject of pain, de Sade noted that "its impressions are certain and dependable," and these impressions "never deceive as may those of the pleasure women perpetually feign and almost never experience."

According to de Sade, to produce pleasure in a woman requires "self-confidence, youth, vigor, health," but to produce pain "requires no virtues at all: the more defects a man may have, the older he is, the less lovable, the more resounding his success." Thus, in the opinion of de Sade, the masterful sadist lover should be filthy, bald, and pox-ridden.

In his most extreme form, the sadist has a fascination with women dying. Weirdly, Edgar Allan Poe wrote these words: "The death of a beautiful woman is, unquestionably, the most poetical topic in the world."

SAINT-JUST, LOUIS DE (1767-1794)

A French revolutionary, Louis de Saint-Just was one of the architects of the "Reign of Terror."

Ironically, Saint-Just (like Robespierre) initially declared himself against the death penalty. Saint-Just demanded only that murderers be required to dress in black for the rest of their lives.

SALVATION

According to estimates, the total number of humans who have ever lived is about thirty to thirty-five billion individuals.

When people die, what happens to them?

According to Origen, an early Christian writer, everyone will eventually be saved–even Satan himself.

According to Berthold of Regensburg, a fourteenth-century Christian, only 100,000 people *in all history* will be "saved."

According to Encratism—an ancient Christian heresy—god will damn every man, woman, and child.

SANCTUARY

A protected enclave, a sanctuary is a place of refuge or safety. In a sanctuary a fugitive could not be arrested or taken to prison.

In ancient Greece, for example, a man who sat on a Greek altar—or next to it—could not be harmed.

In ancient Rome, to add to the manpower of the state, the Romans made Capitoline Hill a place of asylum for fugitives far and wide.

In Scotland, one sanctuary was the precinct of Holyrood Abbey known as Abbey Strand. Three symbols—three "S's" in the road—still mark the confines of this once safe-area, which included several taverns. Up to 1560, ANYONE could take refuge there without fear of capture. After the Protestant Reformation, however, Abbey Strand became a sanctuary only for debtors.

SATAN

To devotees of the monotheistic faiths, Satan is the symbol of wickedness. Called one of the "sons of God" in Job 1:6, he is the rebel who tried to dethrone a jealous Jehovah.

Cast into hell by Jehovah, Satan presides over a hellish army of demons amid eternal flames of punishment. With his demons, he tries to lure mankind into his foul embrace.

To anarchists, however, Satan is the spiritual head of revolutionaries. He is the supreme outlaw—the freedom fighter against the tyrant god. Mikhail Bakunin called Satan "the eternal rebel, the first freethinker, and emancipator of worlds."

Eliphas Levi, the occult author, said Satan is "brave enough to buy his independence at the price of eternal suffering and torture,""strong enough to reign in darkness amidst agony," and proud enough "to have built himself a throne on his inextinguishable pyre."

In the poem *Paradise Lost*, Satan makes this famous declaration: "Better to reign in Hell than serve in Heav'n."

SATANISM

An inverted religion—the mirror image of traditional Christianity—Satanism is a religion that execrates Jesus, curses Jehovah, and adores Satan.

Satanists believe that Satan is more powerful than the Judaic-Christian god and will ultimately triumph.

At various times, Satanism has been viewed as a sin, a crime, and (most recently) as a pathology. It has been fought by the priest, the police, and the psychiatrist.

SCAPEGOAT

A scapegoat is someone or something to blame. A designated expendable, a scapegoat is an immediate, tangible object of execration.

In ancient Ionia, when a calamity occurred, an ugly or deformed person was sacrificed as a scapegoat. He was laden with the community's ills, beaten on the genitals to the accompaniment of flutes, and then burned alive on a pyre.

In ancient Athens, the government fed, clothed, and sheltered several never-do-wells at its own expense. If disaster such as the plague hit Athens, two of the scapegoats were led around the city, and then were stoned to death outside the walls. The act, it was hoped, would expel the evil.

When Hannibal defeated the Romans at Cannae, the Romans blamed the "Vestial Virgins." Claiming that the Virgins had violated their vows of chastity, the Romans buried three of them alive.

In biblical Judaism, every year the high priest placed the sins of Israel on the head of a goat and drove the animal into the wilderness as an offering to Azazel, a desert demon. The practice is described in *Leviticus*, chapter sixteen.

In modern societies, scapegoating refers to a highly successful propaganda technique in which someone (or some group) is blamed as the source of all misery. The technique works as long as the "scapegoat" is not too powerful.

SCIENCE

Science is "priestcraft" for the modern world. Called a form of "nature worship" by Rene Guenon, science seeks "natural laws" in the place of gods.

Modern science is based on "scientific materialism" (the opinion that only matter exists) and "scientism" (the belief that the methods of science can eventually account for the whole of reality).

To its devotees, science is the fountain of knowledge and truth. Science, they believe, can penetrate all mysteries and ameliorate all problems. William Winwood Read, a disciple of the scientific method, made these predictions: "Finally, men will master the forces of Nature: they will become themselves architects of symptoms, manufacturers of worlds. Man will be perfect: he will be creator; he will therefore be what the vulgar worship as God."

To its critics, such as Martin Heidegger, science is a "degenerate philosophy." Rene Guenon claimed that modern science has not pushed back the boundaries of the known world, but has shrunk them by reducing the cosmos to "mere corporeal entities."

According to Albert Camus, Mikhail Bakunin—alone in his time—declared war against the idolatries of science.

SCIENCE, DESPOTS AND

Oddly, scientific scholarship often flourishes under despotic regimes.

Under tyrants, studying the humanities or the social sciences is danger-ous—such scholarship may undermine the ruling ideology—and dictators will defend their ideologies with firing squads and gulags.

In totalitarian states, however, it is safe to study the physical sciences. Indeed, dictators, seeking practical applications, will foster such fields.

SCIENCE, EVIL AND

When he was young, wrote Eric Hobsbawm, he thought that the only sci-entists who could cause evil were the chemists, the physicists, and the biologists. Later, however, he realized that the apparently innocuous social scientists held even more dangerous powers.

It was the "social scientists," for example, who convinced the Tutsi and the Hutu of Rwanda that they were separate races.

SECESSION

Secession is the act of seceding from a federation or an organization.

In a sixty-five-year period, the federal government of the United States of America supported the secession of Texas from Mexico, opposed the secession of the American southern states from the federal union, and then supported the secession of Panama from Columbia.

Abraham Lincoln, the American president who violently opposed the secession of the Confederacy, earlier supported the right of secession. These are the words of Lincoln (uttered on January 12, 1848):

> *Any people anywhere, being inclined and having the power, have the right to rise up and shake off the existing government, and form a new one that suits them better. This is a most valuable, a most sacred right—a right which we hope and believe is to liberate the world. Nor is this right confined to cases in which the whole people of an existing government may choose to exercise it. Any portion of such people, that can, may revolutionize and make their own of so much of the territory as they inhabit.*

Of course, Lincoln was not a consistent thinker. An opportunist, as president he opposed the secession of the South, but he supported the secession of West Virginia from Virginia.

SECESSION, EXAMPLES OF

From 1814 to 1905—a period of ninety-one years—Norway was united with Sweden. In 1905 the legislature of Norway declared that country's independence from Sweden. After some talk of war, Sweden peacefully acquiesced to the secession.

When the rebel states seceded from the U.S.A. in 1861, however, the independence of the Confederacy was destroyed in a war that killed 600,000 in a population of thirty million. The war was fought even though the American union had existed only eighty-four years.

Curiously, the term "perpetual union" never appears in the American Constitution, although it appears in the repudiated "Articles of Confederation."

SECESSION MOVEMENTS, SUCCESS OF

By definition, secession movements are weaker than their governments. If they were stronger, they would dominate and secession would be unnecessary.

When the American South seceded from the United States in 1861, the North had nine times the industrial capacity of the South and two and one-half times the population.

As a rule, the success of secession is determined by international factors. The rebels need foreign assistance to succeed.

SECRECY

A form of camouflage, secrecy is a form of defense.

Colonel Wendell Fetig, an American commander in World War II, made this observation about secrecy: "It is almost impossible to maintain but often can be better achieved through the use of misleading rumors than through tight security."

SECRETS

As the poet Ibn Qutayba lamented, not only does a man disappear after death; his secrets are spread abroad.

While alive, however, never reveal your secrets to anyone.

In particular, tell your spouse or romantic consort nothing. In many cases in history, outlaws have been destroyed by ex-wives and former girlfriends.

In America, a wife cannot be *forced* to testify against her husband. She may, however, *volunteer*.

SEMINOLES

The Seminoles of Florida were some of the most effective guerrilla fighters in history.

Not a tribe, the Seminoles were mainly Lower Creek refugees and runaway slaves from the United States who moved into Spanish Florida. The name "Seminole" is derived from the Spanish word for runaway or separatist.

Protected by their ferocity and the swamp lands to which they had fled, the Seminoles of Florida were never completely conquered by the armed forces of the United States.

The thee Seminole Wars (1816-1818, 1835-42, and 1855-58) caused more American military deaths than all other nineteenth-century Indian wars combined.

In World War II the Seminoles claimed exemption from the draft because they belonged to a sovereign and undefeated nation. Their claim—although true—was rejected by the federal government.

SEXUAL INTERCOURSE

In the Western world, sexual intercourse is a biological act, the most tangible of all pleasures. The meeting of genitals, the goal is to unite all the senses.

In the Orient, in contrast, sexual intercourse is a sacred ritual. Thus, the *Kama Sutra*, the Hindu manual on sex, is a religious text in India. It is not considered pornography.

Because Hindus believe that the parents' mental state at conception influences the character of the child, pious Hindus perform a special rite during coition.

If the copulating parents focus on pleasure, the Hindus believe, their child will be passionate. If the parents' minds are loving and clear, however, the child they conceive will be spiritually advanced.

SEXUAL INTERCOURSE, CHASTITY AND

Chastity is a phobic distaste for sex. According to Remy de Gourmont, "Of all the sexual aberrations, perhaps the most peculiar is chastity."

In America, the Cheyenne Indians prized both male and female chastity. Cheyenne girls had no hope of a respectable marriage if a boy had merely touched her breasts or genitalia.

At puberty, Cheyenne girls had to wear a special chastity belt made of rope and rawhide.

If any man attempted to remove it, her male relatives would kill him and her female relatives would destroy his family property.

In the European world, a famous lifelong virgin was Lewis Carroll (the pen name of Charles L. Dodgson), a mathematician and a logic professor at Oxford University who conceived *Alice's Adventures in Wonderland* in 1862 for Alice Liddell, a ten-year-old girl.

Although Carroll thought that boys were "not an attractive race of beings," he adored nymphets, and he lost his stutter only in the presence of little girls. He liked them to be upper class, pretty, lithely built, intelligent, and energetic. Although he had Platonic (non-sexual) relationships with more than one hundred girls, he lost interest in them when they turned sixteen, and he died a virgin.

Immanuel Kant, the philosopher, and Sir Isaac Newton, the scientist, were also lifelong virgins.

SEXUAL INTERCOURSE, CRIME AND

A sexual crime is a sexual activity that is repugnant to society. In its worst form, it has been described as "stuffing hardened genitals into an unwilling young virgin."

Legally, sexual battery is the intentional physical contact with the intimate parts of another without consent. Aggravated sexual battery is the penetration of another person's intimate parts with a foreign object. If the penetration occurs with flesh, the act is an act of rape.

Weirdly, St. Thomas Aquinas, the medieval Catholic theologian, argued that since rape could produce children, it was less sinful than masturbation.

SEXUAL INTERCOURSE, CRIMINAL USE OF DRUGS AND

Ketamine hydrochloride, used in the American-Vietnamese war as an as anesthetic, has been described as the "chemical weapon" of sexual crime.

Rapists use it on victims to render them unconscious and vulnerable to attack. Since the drug conveniently impairs memory, the victims may not remember the sexual assault when consciousness returns.

Ketamine hydrochloride is also used by prostitutes who rob their customers.

SHOCK, SYMPTOMS OF

The signs of shock are low blood pressure, rapid heartbeat, confusion, decreased urine output, and cool, "clammy" skin.

"SHOOTING IN ARCADE"

An arrow (or other projectile) should be launched at a 45-degree angle for maximum distance. The arrow will land on the target almost vertically.

SHOW TRIALS

A "show trial" is a corrupt legal procedure. In a show trial the verdict is predetermined in spite of the appearance of legal process.

Perhaps the most famous "show trial" in history was the "trial" of Jesus the Nazarene in Roman Palestine. If the gospel accounts are accurate, the murder of Jesus was carried out quickly, and "false witnesses" were induced to testify against him.

According to the Bible, there were only twelve hours between the arrest of Jesus and his execution. In those twelve hours he appeared before the Sanhedrin, he was examined by Pontius Pilate, he appeared before Herod Antipas, he was sentenced by Pilate, he was scourged by soldiers (in a Roman crucifixion, the condemned was given exactly 720 lashes), and finally he was crucified.

Another noted "show trial" involved Marie Antoinette, the deposed queen who was executed during the French Revolutionary "Reign of Terror." She was accused of endless crimes, from smuggling a fortune out of France to teaching her eleven-year-old son how to masturbate. Her child, languishing in solitary confinement, was forced to sign a declaration that his mother and his aunt had taught him the vice.

Curiously, in the long history of the Inquisition, there is *no* record of an Inquisition acquittal.

SIGNATURES

The term "signatures," used in law enforcement, refers to the unique ways a person commits his crimes.

Criminals leave signatures to torment or taunt the police. This increases the criminal's sense of power and control over the law-enforcement operatives.

The infamous "Jack the Ripper," the first modern serial killer, left signatures, including a letter written in his victim's blood.

The signature of William Heirens, a 1940's serial killer, was a desperate, lipstick-scrawled plea on a mirror: "For heaven's sake, catch me before I kill more. I cannot control myself."

SIN

Sin—a kind of moral transgression—is an act of disobedience. In effect, the sinner is someone who refuses to be a slave.

The priestly caste defines sins and also creates purification rituals to eradicate the stain.

Hinduism, for example, teaches that reciting the Sivasahasranaman prayer—the 1008 names of Siva, the destroyer god—will eradicate all sin, if the recitation is made with concentration and a pure heart.

And Roman Catholicism has developed the "plenary indulgence." This guarantees salvation, declared one observer, even if the sinner had "raped the Virgin Mary."

SKEPTICISM

According to a Jewish tradition, the grandfather believes, the father doubts, and the son denies.

Of course, at a real level all knowledge is uncertain. Jorge Luis Borges, in his masterful *Tlon, Uqbar, Orbis Tertius,* refers to a Bertrand Russell conjecture that (in Borges's words) "our planet was created a few moments ago, and provided with a humanity which 'remembers' an illusionary past."

SKULL AND BONES, ORDER OF

"The Order," which is also called Chapter 322, and was once known as the "Brotherhood of Death," is called "Skull and Bones" by those who make light of it. A mysterious secret society, it was founded in 1833 at Yale University by Huntington Russell (an opium trader) and Alphonso Taft (an ancestor of the president).

The emblem of the Order is the Death's Head, or two crossed bones and a skull. Its headquarters, called the "tomb," is a dark, windowless building. There are claims that the Order possesses the skulls of Geronimo, Pancho Villa, and Martin Van Buren—all stolen.

According to Anthony C. Sutton, the author of *America's Secret Establishment*, no one can ask to join Skull and Bones, which admits only fifteen new members each year. Membership is by invitation only.

Allegedly, the Order does not want loners, iconoclasts, or individualists in the organization. They want amoral team players—people who will sacrifice themselves for the group.

According to Sutton, the initiation of new members involves some nudity. The initiate is placed in a coffin—he is carried to the center of the building—he is chanted over—and his name is inscribed in a bone.

Other sources—some of them quite dubious—claim that initiates must lie naked in a coffin and masturbate.

New members are called knights. After one year, they are called patriarchs, and they will remain patriarchs for the rest of their lives. The Order refers to all outsiders as vandals.

The patriarchs of the Order meet annually, on the oddly spelled "Deer Iland," in the St. Lawrence River, in New York.

Members may not discuss the organization, its procedures, or its objectives. Words spoken within the Order may not be written–even in letters to fellow members.

Members must always deny membership to outsiders. If the Order is under discussion, members may not remain in the room.

The function of the Order is to bring about certain mysterious objectives. Honors and financial awards are guaranteed, and initiates are assured career advancement–success-even wealth.

SKYJACKING

Skyjacking—or the seizing of an aircraft—was first attempted in 1931. By the end of the twentieth century, another nine hundred skyjackings had been attempted.

The Israelis, who have experience with skyjackers, identify five types:
1. Naive Skyjacker. He carries a bomb, but is unaware of the fact. He may think he is carrying a gift.
2. Partly Naive. He thinks that he is carrying contraband—like drugs or cash—but not a bomb.
3. Framed Terrorist. He thinks he is carrying a disassembled bomb– not a live one.
4. Terrorist Skyjacker. He wants to seize a plane.
5. Suicide Terrorist. He is prepared to die with the aircraft.

Someone popularly called D.B. Cooper—who skyjacked a commercial airliner on the day before Thanksgiving Day in 1971 (an especially busy travel time)—is America's most celebrated example. He demanded and received $200,000 and four parachutes.

He bailed out of the skyjacked airplane—with the ransom money—somewhere over the state of Washington. A massive manhunt failed to find him.

In the seven months following Cooper's "parajacking," five other Americans tried his technique. All were caught.

SLAVE, REVOLT OF

Although the Bible, in Colossians 3:22 and Ephesians 6:5, orders slaves to obey their masters, Alonso de Castrillo said that eventually people grow "weary of obedience."

The Haitian slave revolt, the only *successful* slave revolt in history, began on a stormy, lightning-filled night on August 14, 1791. In a wooded clearing near an alligator swamp on the outskirts of Cap Haitian, a Voodoo priest and runaway slave named Boukman performed a grim and powerful ceremony.

To the sound of drums and chanting, Boukman invoked the Petro *loa*—the gods of Voodoo. He slit the throat of a black pig—caught the blood in a bowl—and wrote the words "liberty or death" in the blood. Boukman consumed some of the hot liquid—called upon all who sought freedom to do the same—and then asked all the men present to swear an oath to kill slaveholders. Every man complied.

The actual violence broke out on August 22. Within two months, two thousand plantations had been burned and one thousand whites had been massacred.

Boukman himself would be caught by the French and decapitated. But the rebellion he unleashed—which lasted twelve years—would succeed.

SLAVERY

Slavery is utter, sub-human abjection.

In general, there are three kinds of slavery: chattel slavery (a traditional bondsman), serf slavery (a type of slave who pays taxes), and wage slavery (a slave who may chose his own master).

Pre-colonial Africa had chattel slavery. Property in land was not recognized in custom or law in Africa, but ownership of people was.

Post-classical Europe had serf slavery. Serfdom was an attempt to control labor when there was an abundance of land and a labor shortage. Curiously, Macedonia and Bosnia had legal serfdom until 1919!

Wage slavery—the glorification of the "virtuous toiler"—is a modern development. According to Baron Giulio Evola, "If there ever was a civilization of slaves on a grand scale, the one in which we are living is it. No traditional civilization ever saw such great masses of people condemned to perform shallow, impersonal, automatic jobs."

According to Friedrich Nietzsche, anyone who cannot spend two-thirds of the day as they please is a slave.

Oddly, Aristotle claimed that there are those who are "by nature slaves, for whom to be governed by this kind of authority is beneficial."

SLAVERY, MODERN FORMS OF

One can abolish the name of slavery, wrote one nineteenth-century observer, but not the thing. Under euphemistic titles, it continues to survive.

In dictatorships, the political leader is the master and the citizens are neo-slaves. Citizens in such states experience a form of socialized slavery—the state literally owns them.

In democracies, prisoners are temporary slaves. Prisoners sentenced to death—or prisoners serving life sentences—are permanent slaves.

SLAVES, FAMOUS EXAMPLES OF

Sevius Tullius, who was born a slave, became the king of Rome. He reigned between 578 B.C. and 535 B.C.

In the late second century after Christ, a slave named Callistus became the pope, the bishop of Rome.

Diocletian, who was born a slave in Dalmatia, became the Emperor of the Roman Empire in A.D. 284.

Jean-Jacques Dessalines, who was born a slave in the French colony of Saint-Domingue, became emperor of Haiti. Ultimately, he was deified as a god, or *loa*, in the Voodoo pantheon.

SLEEPER

A sleeper is an undercover operative who waits until a predetermined time or a given signal before going into action. Most commonly, he is activated for assassination or sabotage.

Before activation, the sleeper may work under "deep cover" for years. He will marry, hold a job, and raise a family.

The ideal sleeper is a bland or nondescript man (or woman). His behavior and views should be typical of the community. His family is probably ignorant of his double life. He avoids contact with the police or anything that will instigate an investigation into his life.

Before German reunification, the East German state had an estimated 20,000 sleepers in Western countries.

In some cases, sleepers will infiltrate a region in groups or cells. These cells will remain dormant until activated for a mission.

SMITH ACT

Promulgated in 1940, the Smith Act imposes a prison sentence on anyone who "knowingly or willingly advocates, abets, advises, or teaches the duty, necessity, desirability, or propriety of violently overthrowing" the government of the United States.

In 1948 the Supreme Court ruled that people could be prosecuted even if they had never acted on that advocacy, had never bought guns, and had never committed criminal acts.

Had Americans forgotten their history?

Starting with Bacon's Rebellion in Virginia, by 1760 there had been eighteen uprisings aimed at overthrowing colonial governments. Moreover, there also had been six major black rebellions.

And, one of America's fundamental documents, the Declaration of Independence, declares that citizens have an "inalienable" right to overthrow their government by armed force.

SMUGGLING

Smuggling is the act of moving goods secretly and "illicitly" across political frontiers. Only governments consider smuggling a crime.

The techniques used by smugglers are often quite creative. Carrier pigeons, for example, have been used to smuggle diamonds.

During the American-Vietnamese War, the Viet Cong used the "ant method" to smuggle explosives into "Saigon": they concealed small amounts in bicycle frames, shopping baskets, baby carriages—even women's brassieres. From these small amounts, huge bombs were constructed.

And, during the same war, heroin dealers used the bodies of dead American soldiers to smuggle their drug into the United States. (One corpse— with the internal organs removed—could hold thirty kilograms of heroin.) The smugglers knew that border officials would not inspect the cadavers of combat troops.

SMUGGLERS, PROFITS AND

For smugglers, illegal drugs, illegal weapons, and stolen artifacts produce the greatest profits.

SNIPER

A sniper is someone who kills from a hiding place at long range. Used by modern armies, a sniper is an invisible hunter, a kind of stealthy murderer.

To make a sniper, certain attributes are necessary. In particular, a sniper needs the patience of a mountain cat.

Because killing an individual is psychologically difficult—even in war—snipers operate in groups of two. The presence of the second soldier—called the spotter—reinforces the killing ability of the shooter.

SOCIALISM

Socialism is a political and economic theory of social organization which advocates that the economy—the means of production, distribution, and exchange—should be owned or controlled by the community as a whole. In effect, this means the control of the economy by the state.

According to John Steinbeck, socialism never thrived in America because the poor see themselves not as an exploited proletariat but as temporarily embarrassed millionaires.

Anarchists—extremists in the cause of freedom—are opposed to socialism. They believe that state ownership and management of the means of production leads to bureaucratic despotism.

Stalinism has been called socialism, but some claim Stalinism is simply a particularly vicious form of "state capitalism."

SODOMY

Traditionally viewed as a rebellion against nature—an unnatural sexual act—permissive societies view sodomy as a lifestyle choice.

Medieval canon law defined two types of sodomy: 1) "imperfect sodomy," or sexual intercourse with a girl in the "unlawful vessel" (the mouth or the anus) and 2) "perfect sodomy," or any sexual intercourse with a boy.

In the later medieval period, the laws against male homosexuals (who were guilty of "perfect sodomy) were especially fierce. In 1260 the French ordered the amputation of the testicles for the first offense, the amputation of the penis for the second offense, and burning at the stake for the third offense.

By the nineteenth century, the idea developed the idea that homosexuality is a disease, the result of defective upbringing, or an inherited flaw.

At the time of writing, same-sex intercourse is illegal in seventy countries. In nine countries, the penalty is death.

SODOMY, FAMOUS EXAMPLES OF

Historically the most notorious of sodomites, the ancient Greeks even constructed a special temple, *Aphrodite Kallipygeia*, to "the beautiful buttocks" of the goddess of loveliness and sexual desire.

And—although the Greeks scorned any adult male who allowed himself to be penetrated by a penis—the penetration of a boy by a man was considered acceptable—even commendable. Zeus, Apollo, Poseidon, and Heracles all had pederast experiences, as did Solon, Pythagoras, Socrates, and Plato.

Plato, in his *Symposium*, said that pederasty, philosophy, and nude sports were the three things that set the Greeks apart from the "barbarians."

SOFT FILES

"Soft Files" are the unofficial and unregistered files of an intelligence agency. They contain scandalous details on the drinking habits, sexual habits, money problems, and odd interests on anyone considered important, such as political activists or journalists.

SOLANAS, VALERIE (1936-1988)

A radical feminist, Valerie Solanas wrote the *Scum Manifesto*, which she self-published in 1967. "Scum" is an abbreviation for the "Society for Cutting Up Men."

Solanas urged women to overthrow the government, eliminate the money system, institute complete automation, and destroy the male sex.

In 1968 Solanas was arrested for trying to murder an artist named Andy Warhol (at trial, he refused to testify against her).

After spending some time in prison and a mental hospital—and becoming involved in drugs and prostitution—Solanas died poor and alone in 1988 in a welfare hotel.

SOLAR TEMPLE, ORDER OF

A suicide cult, originally led by Joseph Di Mambro and Luc Jouret, the Order of the Solar Temple was founded in 1977.

Members believe that if they die through fire, they will be reborn as perfect beings—gods— around a planet that orbits Sirius.

In October 1994, at two locations in Canada and Switzerland, the two leaders and fifty-one other members of the Order of the Solar Temple burned themselves to death.

Before committing collective suicide, the members hammered a stake through the heart of a three-month-old baby named Emanuelle Dutoit. According to the Solar Temple, the child was the Anti-Christ, and his murder would help humanity.

SOLDIERS

In contrast to a warrior, who seeks his own glory and enrichment, a soldier suffers hardship, wounds, and death for the aggrandizement of another. When the soldier makes the supreme sacrifice—and dies bravely in war— it is the most altruistic of human activities because the dead soldier gains absolutely nothing.

Historically, the status of the soldier was often low. In traditional China, the soldier's status was especially base, on the level of prostitutes and criminals.

The soldier's life is more honored today, but when a soldier enlists, he loses many of the legal rights other citizens possess. In the United States, for example, the Bill of Rights applies only to civilians: military personnel do not enjoy freedom of speech, and they do not have a constitutional right to a "speedy and public trial" with an "impartial jury."

SOLDIERS, CONDITIONING OF

According to a conspiracy theorist named David Icke, military training is a form of mental conditioning.

Heavy exercise and little sleep cause the body to overproduce endorphins in the brain. This makes a person robotically obey commands.

SOLDIERS (OFFICER CLASS)

In modern armies, rather curiously, killing is considered "plebeian" or lower class.

Beginning in the eighteenth century, the Western world developed the tradition of officers entering the battlefield with symbolic weapons, such as pistols and swagger sticks. Oddly, for the modern officer, as one Israeli historian has pointed out, "war can consist only of being killed."

During officer training, the trainees are taught that if they are firing their weapons, they are not doing their jobs correctly. As officers, they should be ordering enlisted men to kill.

SOLDIERS (OFFICER CLASS), EXPENDABILITY OF

As Edward N. Luttwak pointed out, "Officers are amazingly expendable. In both France and Russia many officers left their units following their respective revolutions, and yet their armies seemed to experience a sudden increase in their efficiency."

By the late 1930's, Stalin had executed 75 percent of his officer corps, yet the Red army would win World War II. Before his death, Hitler regretted that he had not also purged his officer class.

SOLDIERS, POVERTY AND

Napoleon Bonaparte said that poverty makes the best soldier. Courage, said Napoleon, was less important than the ability to endure fatigue and hardship.

Armies from rich countries—such as the United States—have huge logistical needs. American soldiers come from a pampered and pasteurized society, and the troops can function only four to five days without supply.

Indeed, the U.S.A. helicoptered "iced beer" to units operating in the field in the American-Vietnamese War. In Afghanistan, heavily muscled American soldiers from "special forces" were unable to drink the water that was routinely consumed by eight-year-old Afghan girls.

SOLDIERS, SLAVES AS

The best warriors—men fighting as individuals—are free men. The best soldiers—men fighting in disciplined masses—are slaves.

Regarding trained soldiers—men conditioned like Ivan Pavlov's dogs and B. F. Skinner's rats—perhaps the best were the Mamelukes (the name means slave or "owned men"). The Mameluks, white slaves imported from Europe and south Eurasia, were formidable fighters. By the end of the thirteenth century, the Mamelukes had taken over Egypt and had defeated the crusaders and the Mongols.

Another group of elite slave soldiers were the Janissaries of the Ottoman Empire.

First organized in the fourteenth century, the Janissaries were known for their bravery, ferocity, and discipline.

To form the Janissaries, the Muslim Turks exacted a regular levy of male children from their southeastern European dominions. The people were required to provide tribute of three thousand boys every four years. (Before the practice died out, perhaps 200,000 boys had been taken.) Led away as slaves, the boys were taught Turkish and Islam. Eventually, the best ones would become Janissaries.

SPECIAL SUPPORT GROUP

An F.B.I. term, the "Special Support Group" refers to the ordinary people—students, housewives, and retirees—who "tail" and spy on people for the Bureau. These amateur spies receive one-third of the pay of a "Special Agent."

In a similar way, the Mossad, Israel's intelligence service, has the *Sayanim* or "volunteers." These "volunteers," who receive only "expenses," number in the tens of thousands, with an estimated 15,000 in the U.S.A. alone. Their services are invaluable to the 1,500 professional agents in the Mossad.

SPECIALIZATION

By the end of the nineteenth century, according to Jose Ortega y Gasset, Western civilization had developed the "specialist," a type of academic unparalleled in history. The master of his little "corner" of knowledge, the specialist knows nothing else.

Ultimately, according to Jose Ortega y Gasset, the specialist strangles scholarship. In earlier times, people were either "learned or ignorant," but the specialist is neither.

In a famous statement, Robert Heinlein said that "specialization is for insects."

SPIES

The spy–like the priest and the prostitute–is one of the oldest professions. Interestingly, spying is one of few occupations that has always provided equal opportunities for women.

Sun Tzu, the Chinese military theorist, said that there are five types of spies: local spies (spies hired among people in the target area), inside spies (enemy officials who are recruited), reverse spies (double agents), doomed spies (expendable pawns who will be caught by the enemy, and who will provide false information that the enemy thinks is true), and "surviving"spies (those who come back to report).

In the modern era, the Union of Soviet Socialist Republics developed the system that was copied by others.

In the Russian model, undercover operatives are recruited in the target country. These operatives—agents called "illegals"—are recruited to spy on or sabotage their own country. They are supported by money and equipment.

The "illegals" may be given immediate tasks, they may be given a long-term career in target organization, or they may be left to live a normal life as part of a "sleeper" network. If caught, the illegal will be disowned. No effort will be made to save them from prison or death.

Once their usefulness is exhausted, "illegals" may be discarded or compromised.

In the Russian model, the "legals" are another type of spy. "Legals" are Russian citizens who carry diplomatic passports and who pose as government officials. Their "cover" gives them *prima facie* reason to be in the target country. And, if caught, they can claim diplomatic immunity.

Of all spies, the "double agent" is the most effective. A double agent is a spy disguised as a defector who is planted in the enemy apparatus.

SPIES, CHARACTER OF

According to British Intelligence, the best spies are "gray men and women"—nondescript people who are not noticed in crowds.

Also, the best spy is everyone's friend, not a shadowy figure in a corner.

Because spies may never discuss their jobs—even with their parents or spouses—people NOT interested in fame or celebrity are recruited.

Curiously, Britain's most famous spy, the fictional James Bond character, is totally unrealistic. If James Bond had lived, one scholar estimates that Bond would have averaged seventy women each year, would have smoked more than seventy unfiltered Russian cigarettes per day, and would have consumed enough martinis ("shaken, not stirred") to have destroyed his liver.

SPIES, COVER FOR

To camouflage themselves, spies frequently pose as diplomats, journalists, university professors, or dealers in rare books.

The diplomat is the safest disguise (they have diplomatic immunity), but the journalist is the most productive disguise. It does not appear suspicious when a journalist travels, asks questions, or uses a camera.

Typically, spies will enter the target country via a neutral country.

SPIES, VATICAN AND

The spy is ubiquitous, and even the Vatican has a spy service. It is euphemistically called the Vatican Information Service.

One noted Vatican spy was Walter M. Ciszek, a priest, who used the name Vladimir Lipinski. Arrested by the Soviet Union for espionage, he received a twenty-three-year prison sentence.

Giovanni Montini, the father of the modern Vatican spy service, went on to become Pope Paul VI, who reigned between 1963 and 1978. There is talk of making this spy a saint!

STALIN, JOSEPH (1879-1953)

A sullen and paranoid tyrant, Stalin ruled the Union of Soviet Socialist Republics between 1929 and 1953. He gave his name to Stalinism, which is defined as a personal dictatorship, resting upon the use of terror as an instrument of rule.

Under Stalin's iron hand, Soviet Russia featured secret police forces, "show trials," labor camps, torture chambers, and firing squads.

To his credit, however, Stalin did stay in Moscow during the Nazi military assault in 1941. Ultimately, his Red Army triumphed over the Nazi war machine.

On the subject of World War II, General Albert C. Wedemeyer wrote: "Stalin emerged as the only victor of the war. The Allies insured the emergence of a more hostile, menacing predatory power than Nazi Germany, one which enslaved more people than we liberated."

STATE

The state, an artificial collective of human beings, is a "pragmatic fiction." Like other "pragmatic fictions," such as "Divine Right" or "absolute rule," the state is a workable fiction treated as a "reality."

Robert Anton Wilson, in an excellent analysis of *God and the State* by Mikhail Bakunin, made these observations:

> *Bakunin argued in "God and the State" that nobody has ever seen 'God' or the 'State.' This, although startling, is true. Human beings, called priests, claim to represent 'God,' and other human beings, called civil servants, claim to represent the 'state,' and this metaphysical sleight-of-hand is alleged to justify acts which would be regarded as not only criminal but barbarous if it were not remembered that mere human beings were doing these things. Similar verbal magic—meaningless words like 'heresy' and 'treason'—are used to*

convince victims that resistance is evil, and even thinking that you are being victimized is somehow sinful.

Oddly, Georg Hegel thought that the state constituted the supreme human achievement.

STATE, POWER OF

In modern states, the citizen is politically impotent. A citizen, it is true, may complain, make suggestions, or cause disruptions, but in the ancient world these were privileges that belonged to any slave.

In a sense, the modern citizen is a demented slave who thinks that he is free. In America, for example, no one has ever or will ever consult the citizens about deploying nuclear weapons.

Internally, the power of the modern state is symbolized by the sheriff, the judge, and the hangman.

STATUTE OF LIMITATIONS

A statute of limitations is a statute setting forth the maximum period of time that legal proceedings may begin for a crime. The length of this period varies from country to country, and province to province, and it depends on the seriousness of the crime. Some offenses, such as murder or war crimes, have no time limitation on prosecution.

If the statute of limitations applies, it must be pleaded (or asserted) by the suspect before the court. Failure to do so is a waiver. (If the accused does not raise the issue, the court will not apply it.)

STING OPERATION

A weapon of the police, a sting operation is a "legal" entrapment scheme.

In a traditional sting operation, undercover agents try to purchase drugs, weapons, stolen goods, illegal pornography, or political influence. When the victim agrees to a sale, he is arrested.

In a "Reverse Sting," undercover agents pose as smugglers or dealers and try to sell something that is illegal. Here, the goods do not have to actually change hands. Any target who agrees to the transaction can be prosecuted for "conspiring" to commit a crime.

STRIKE

A strike is an organized protest, a refusal to work by employees. It is a pacifist weapon.

The earliest recorded strike—that of workmen constructing the tomb of pharaoh Ramses III in the twelfth century before Christ—was caused by a delay in wages.

Governments, however, have often tried to criminalize this proletarian weapon. The Combination Acts of 1799-1800 in Great Britain, for example, outlawed trade unionism.

Interestingly, Honore Mirabeau issued this warning: "Take care, do not despise these people who produce everything, this people who, to be formidable, have only to stand motionless."

STRIKE, GENERAL

A general strike is an attempt to bring national life to a halt by a cessation of work in all industries. A non-violent form of civil disobedience, the general strike is the most powerful of all pacifist weapons.

According to Georges Sorel (the syndicalist leader), the "general strike" can bring down the existing order. Barricades in the streets and urban insurrections by the workers are no longer effective, Sorel argued, but an organized and non-violent general strike can triumph.

According to H.G. Wells, the plebeians of ancient Rome invented the general strike. Although technically free, these commoners were excluded from political power and lived under some economic injustices.

The plebes peacefully left Rome in 494 B.C. to establish an independent community on Mons Sacre. They said that they would not return until they were granted a share of the government. The plebeians repeated this tactic more than once, and ultimately the ruling patricians were forced to concede political and economic rights to the plebes.

In the modern world, general strikes have been called in several nations:

* Italy, 1904

* Russia, 1905 (This strike helped to force the tsar to grant a Constitution.)

* Sweden, 1909

* Argentina, 1917 (The working-class movement in Argentina, by means of a general strike, forced the government to abandon a plan to enter World War I against Germany.)

* Germany, 1920 (This strike brought about the failure of a right-wing coup d'etat.)

* Britain, 1926

* France, 1938 and 1968

Although the general strike has been virtually unknown in North America, W.E.B. DuBois claimed that slaves in the Civil War helped to defeat the Confederacy by engaging in a "general strike." Certainly, from mid-1863 the slaves were refusing to work and were running to the union lines.

SUBHUMAN

A subhuman is defined as "a lower order of being than the human." Throughout history, marginal and outcast people have often been classified as "subhuman."

In nineteenth century Australia, for example, shooting aboriginal people, called ("shooting abos") became a sport among British settlers. Typically practiced on Saturdays, the local police took part in the hunts. In Tasmania alone, nearly three hundred aboriginal people were hunted down and killed as if they were rabbits or stags.

In the United States—as recently as 1906—the Bronx Zoo displayed an African Pygmy named Ota Benga alongside an orangutan.

SUBMISSION MARKERS AND GESTURES

All tyrants enjoy abject behavior. They want to see fear and compliance.

In ancient Sparta the warrior master class wore their hair long and uncovered. The helots—the servile people—were forced to wear dog-skin caps.

Under the Manchu dynasty in China, the pigtail was the compulsory symbol of peasant servitude. In 1911 some army officers openly rebelled by cutting pigtails.

More traditional submission gestures include kneeling, prostration, and the *kotow*.

SUBPROLETARIAT

The subproletariat—the people below the proletariat itself—are the prisoners and criminals in a society. In revolutionary terms, the subproletariat is far more dangerous to the ruling elite than the proletariat.

Whereas the masses have specific grievances—and can be satisfied within the existing social system—members of the subproletariat have "universal grievances" and know that nothing can change unless everything changes.

Mikhail Bakunin argued that robbers and brigands are the only true revolutionary element in society. If they would unite with the terrorists, they would become an invincible power.

SUICIDE

Suicide, which is the act of self-destruction, has been called "the perfect crime."

SUICIDE (AS AN ACT OF PROTEST)

Suicide attackers use suicide as a weapon. People who practice self-immolation, in contrast, use suicide as a protest.

In Saigon, on June 11, 1963, a Buddhist monk named Thich Quang Duc, sitting in a lotus position at a crossroads, saturated with petrol, burned himself to death. Dying "bravely and peacefully, enveloped in flames," he was protesting the regime of Ngo Dinh Diem.

On November 11, 1965, a young Quaker named Norman Morrison protested against the American-Vietnamese War by burning himself to death outside the Pentagon, under the windows of the Secretary of Defense. In Morrison's honor, the Hanoi regime issued a stamp bearing his likeness.

SUICIDE ATTACKS

A suicide attacker is someone who wants to martyr himself and murder others. In other words, he wants to die and kill.

Of all terrorist operations, the suicide mission is the easiest to plan—because no escape is necessary.

The biblical Samson, a fabled mass murderer, is the most celebrated suicide attacker. Blinded, shackled, and humiliated by his enemies, the Bible (Judges 16:23-31) says that Samson killed three thousand children, women, and men when he destroyed himself and a temple of Dagon.

Modern suicide attackers, who are often viewed as "burnt offerings to God," are told to recite prayers during the entire operation. (Constant prayer blocks thought.) Also, suicide attackers are told to remain awake all night. (This induces self-hypnosis.)

Today, the favorite disguises of most suicide attackers are policemen, soldiers, and ambulance workers.

SUICIDE ATTACKS, STATE USE OF

The "Samson Option" is a plan of the modern Israeli state. Rather than submit to Arab conquest, the Israeli state will detonate its nuclear arsenal, thereby killing itself and its Arab enemies.

In a sense, the Samson Option would create a state-sized suicide bomber.

SUICIDE, UNUSUAL METHODS OF

The most unusual suicide method is the Japanese Buddhist technique of self-mummification.

A monk, surrounded by candles, eats less and less, and slowly starves to death. The candles help to dry him, and, after his death, other monks further dry him until he is mummified.

Self-mummification is practiced by monks who want to stay on Earth to help a new Buddha when he comes.

The technique was common in the eleventh and twelfth centuries. It was last done in 1903.

SUPERMAN

The superman or overman is a "higher" or "superior man."

As envisioned by Friedrich Nietzsche, the superman is a self-confident predator. With effortless superiority, he molds history like wax, and he impresses his will on the ages.

In contrast to a human or a subhuman, the superman acknowledges no authority but his own will and no morality but his own advantage.

Nietzsche, who wrote about "toppling boundary markers" and "violating pieties," believed that society should be dedicated not to the common good, but to promoting the highest type of man.

SURPRISE ATTACKS

Surprise is a means to gain temporary superiority. According to Carl von Clausewitz, "The two factors that surprise are secrecy and speed."

Effective surprise attacks on the U.S.A. include Pearl Harbor, Kasserine Pass, the Battle of the Bulge, the Chinese intervention along the Yalu River, the Tet Offensive, and the suicide attacks on the World Trade Towers.

The ultimate surprise attack would involve atomic or nuclear weapons. According to a report issued by the Manhattan Project on eve of first atomic bomb test, "In no other type of warfare does the advantage lie so heavily with the aggressor."

In a missile attack from a submerged submarine, the target would have a thirteen-minute warning. If the weapon were pre-positioned (in a 1958 study the American government assumed the U.S.S.R. would pre-position bombs), there would be no warning.

SURRENDER

According to the Chinese way of war, three options remain to a warrior who is losing: surrender (complete defeat), compromise (half defeat), and escape (no defeat). The Chinese always choose escape. As long as one is not defeated, one has a chance.

When someone surrenders, EXPECT his betrayal. After he surrendered to the French, the rebel Jean-Jacques Dessalines betrayed the French.

Dessalines made this declaration to his followers: "Listen well! If Dessalines surrenders to them a hundred times, he will betray them a thousand times."

SURVEILLANCE

Surveillance is observation by the state.

In the Russian autocracy, a surveillance operative was told to watch a person twenty-four hours per day. The operative was not told the name of the person he was watching or the reason for the espionage.

In important cases, two agents (unbeknownst to each other) would spy on the same person. Their reports were later cross-checked by the secret police.

SURVIVALISM

Survivalism is literally the art of staying alive.

In case of a disaster, every individual should keep an emergency knapsack. This should contain a miniature flashlight (with extra batteries), a small compass, a map, waterproof matches, dry lint (to use as tinder), a large knife, large plastic trash bags (for emergency shelter and camouflage), a "space blanket" made of aluminum or mylar, a metallic container (to cook, collect water, and signal), women's nylon stockings (nylons can be used to catch fish, filter water, scrub surfaces, and store things), two quarts of water (note that water weighs about sixty pounds per square foot), some (dried) high-energy food, money, and soft earplugs (to sleep in a battle zone).

Remember, the basics of survival are a fire, water, and food.

SURVIVALISM (DANGERS OF)

Being a survivalist—using foresight to protect oneself from anticipated disasters—can itself be perilous.

In 1499, a noted German astrologer named Johannes Stoeffler claimed that a conjunction of the planets would cause a great flood on February 20, 1524.

Count von Iggleheim, to prepare for the disaster, built a three-story ark for his family. His foresight made him an early survivalist.

Oddly, heavy rains actually struck Europe on February 20, 1524. A terrified mob tried to enter the ark, and hundreds were killed in the riot, including the count himself.

The moral of this true story: all refuges must be defended.

SURVIVALISM (FIRE AND)

Humans are tropical animals by nature: humans need technology (fire, clothing, shelter) to live in cold areas.

To make a fire, align regular "C" batteries in a row. A strand of steel wool—connected to terminals–will start a fire.

To start a fire "from scratch," using flint and steel is the only reliable method. If flint cannot be located, any rock that looks glassy will serve. The tinder receiving the spark must be absolutely dry. Mix some gunpowder into the tinder.

A friction fire is difficult to start. The Cheyenne Indian technique was to rotate between the hands a pointed stick of hard wood (they used grease wood) in a hole in a flat piece of soft wood (they used cottonwood). In the hole they put a little sand quartz and dry leaves or powdered buffalo dung (use gunpowder instead). Press hard, and blow the breath at the contact point.

A third method involves the sun. A magnifying glass, a pair of magnifying eyeglasses (reading spectacles), or a camera lens will work. The more light gathering the better, so the bigger the lens, the higher the sun, and the brighter the day, the better are the results.

Regarding the lens method, it is technically possible to start a fire with ice, but this is impractical. It is also possible to start a fire with water! Make a hole in bark or in paper— place a droplet of water on the hole— and use this makeshift lens to start a fire in dry tinder. If this method sounds dubious, note that arsonists have started forest fires by leaving half-filled jars of water on their sides in grassy areas.

SURVIVALISM (FOOD AND)

Although leather gloves can be eaten after a little cooking, in the long term the survivalist must survive on what he can gather, kill, or grow.

If foraging for wild plant food, avoid anything with a milky sap (dandelions, which are nutritious, are the exception). Avoid red plants, fruit divided into five segments, anything that smells like bitter almonds or peaches, grass and other plants with tiny barbs on the stems or leaves, and all plants that produce a dry, stinging, or burning sensation when applied to the skin or tongue. Also, avoid all old and withered leaves. The leaves of some trees and plants develop deadly hydrocyanic acid when they wilt.

Do not eat mushrooms. For the few nutrients mushrooms contain, mushrooms are not worth the risk.

If farming in a post-apocalyptic world, remember that five bushels of rice can feed one person for one year.

If raising pulses—such as peas, lentils, and beans—know that some species contain a toxic factor. When pulses make up a large part of an individual's diet, the toxins may cause health to deteriorate. The condition is called Lathyrism.

If hunting the meat of wild animals, be resourceful. Remember, sugar-fed rats from the cane fields were considered a delicacy in eighteenth-century Jamaica. In Aztec Mexico, the people ate ants, water-flies, white worms, and tadpoles.

When hunting game, beware of animals that are caught too easily. They may be diseased.

If raising livestock, remember that rabbits and chickens are the most efficient in terms of producing food. Cattle, in contrast, are highly inefficient, unless they are used creatively. The Masai of Africa, for example, live exclusively on the blood of their cows, mixed with milk and some urine.

Regarding meat, there is a limit to the amount of meat humans can eat and remain healthy. Liver function is strained when meat protein constitutes more than 50 percent of daily calories over a prolonged period, especially if the meat is low in fat. According to one authority, "a diet consisting solely of lean meat would kill a human in a matter of weeks."

In a famous experiment, however, V. Stefansson demonstrated that a human can live healthfully on just meat AND fat for an entire year, if 25 percent of calories are from protein and 75 percent of calories are from fat!

Oddly, fat is needed for good health. Fat is a critical source of vitamins and fatty acids and is a highly concentrated source of energy. Women in particular have a critical fatness threshold, and they need fat reserves in their bodies to ovulate.

SURVIVALISM (WATER AND)

Water is especially essential for human survival. A man may live without food for three weeks, but he can live only three days without water.

The symptoms of dehydration are dark urine, nausea, and a nagging headache. The survivalist should always watch for these three signs.

The safest water is rainwater. There is no need to purify rainwater that has just fallen. (Do not collect the water off toxic vegetation, however.)

The water from a fast-flowing stream with a stone and sand bed is normally safe. As a precaution, boil the water for thirty minutes.

Note that drinking sea water will cause the kidneys to stop functioning, so it should never be done. On the beach, however, the survivalist can dig a hole into the sand just above the high-water mark. When the water seeps into the hole, fairly fresh water will gather on top, and saltier water will be at the bottom. The water collected should be boiled for safety.

Boiling all water for thirty minutes is always prudent. No water filter can stop viruses—they are too small—but heat kills them.

Another method of purifying water is to place two or three drops of iodine in every quart of water. Let the mixture stand for thirty minutes. (Remember that iodine fumes can be toxic in an enclosed space.)

Still another method to disinfect water is to add sixteen drops of liquid chlorine bleach (4-6 percent sodium hypochlorite) to each gallon of water. That is one teaspoon per five gallons.

As a general rule, human waste should be kept at least one hundred yards from a water supply.

SURVIVOR

In terror actions, the "survivor" is someone left alive to tell the tale of the massacre.

The Mongols—the masters of calculated terror— used wholesale slaughter together with the selective sparing of small numbers. The latter were induced to flee to spread panic.

When the Kutchin, a sub-arctic tribe, annihilated an enemy camp, they always left one man alive. This man, the survivor, would spread the word of the deed.

On April 9, 1948, when Israeli "freedom fighters" attacked an Arab village named Deir Yassin, they killed all its inhabitants, except two old women and one child. These survivors spread news of the massacre, causing many Arabs to flee their homes when the Arab-Israeli war broke out in the following month.

Sometimes, however, leaving a survivor may backfire.

In A.D. 680, the Sunni (the orthodox Muslims) almost succeeded in wiping out their rivals (the Shi'a) when the Sunni surprised and massacred virtually all the Shi'a, including the prophet's daughter Fatima. But the killers overlooked one sick boy—the son of Fatima—and from that one survivor the Shi'a tradition grew.

SWINDLE

To swindle is to use deception to obtain money or possessions.

One noted swindler was William H. Johnson, of Middlesboro, Kentucky. Beginning in 1946, Johnson sent letters to people—mostly reactionaries of German extraction in the United States and Canada. Johnson claimed that he was Adolf Hitler—that he had escaped and was living in Kentucky—that he was planning a comeback–and that he needed money to succeed. Over a period of ten years, Johnson collected more than fifteen thousand dollars from his "dupes."

Victor Lustig, a master swindler from the 1920's and 1930's (among other things, he sold the Eiffel Tower twice to "scrap metal" merchants), had the ten "Commandments of the Confidence Man":

1. Be a patient listener.
2. Never look bored.
3. Pretend to have the same political views as the victim.
4. Pretend to have the same religious views of the victim.
5. Talk about sexual matters.
6. Avoid the subject of illness.
7. Never pry into the victim's private affairs.
8. Never boast.
9. Never be "untidy."
10. Never become drunk.

P.T. Barnum knew that the public does not mind being lied to, as long as the lies are more sensational and entertaining than the dull, everyday truth.

SYNARCHIST MOVEMENT

The Synarchist Movement was founded in the 1870's by Alexandre Saint-Yves d'Alveydre. It became especially important in the era after World War I.

According to Synarchist teachings, a government should be run by a secret society or cabal—an elite of enlightened initiates who rule from behind the scenes.

Saint-Yves considered the Templars—a select and powerful order medieval knights—to be the ultimate synarchists of their time.

SYNDICALISM

Syndicalism, a form of radical trade unionism, is a working-class movement dedicated to extirpating every vestige of capitalism.

Syndicalists act outside the political arena. Parliaments, courts, and civil institutions, they believe, are snares and illusions.

Syndicalists want worker insurrections—the proletarian fury of the "general strike"—to reconstruct society on socialist lines. The state would be supplanted by autonomous and self-governing units called "syndicates."

Georges Sorel wrote the textbook of syndicalism, *Reflections on Violence*, in 1908. Sorel argued that violence, which is cathartic, is a useful tool against capitalism.

Interestingly, Syndicalists believe that the state would not wither away (as Marx predicted), but it must be brought to its knees by direct and frontal assaults.

TABUN

A chemical weapon invented by German science, one breath causes temporary blindness, two lungfuls incapacitate, and three will cause death in a few hours.

The Nazis manufactured and stockpiled enough tabun to kill twelve *trillion* people. Fortunately, they surrendered without ever deploying the weapon.

TANTRIC HINDUISM

A radical form of religion, the underlying principle of Tantric Hinduism is that only a god can worship a god.

The most extreme form of Tantric Hinduism—the so-called "left-handed" form—makes use of forbidden items such as wine, meat, fish, aphrodisiacs, and sexual union as sacraments. Tantrics attempt to gain power by breaking orthodox taboos.

The Tantrics thrive on paradox. Thus, in the words of one Hindu Tantric: "By the same acts that cause some men to burn in hell for thousands of years, the yogin gains his eternal salvation."

TAXES

Taxes, which critics have called a "tithe for the beast," are a form of legalized plunder. Although modern governments can print paper money at will, they insist on paying debts with "taxes" collected from other citizens.

At the present time—in the United States—a pair of shoes is burdened with 156 taxes!

Interestingly, in ancient Rome, throughout the greater part of the second and first centuries B.C., the Romans paid no taxes. Taxes, however, were reintroduced by Augustus, the first emperor.

TAZ (TEMPORARY AUTONOMOUS ZONE)

TAZ refers to "temporary autonomous zone," a concept developed by Hakim Bey, the pseudonym of Peter Lamborn Wilson.

According to Bey, the ruling tyrants will never give the people rest or freedom, and the servile masses are too "robotized" to demand it.

The best an individual can do is to find a temporary zone of freedom, keep it secret as long as possible, and move elsewhere when the "authorities" discover him.

TAZ—the nomadic anonymity of the fugitive slave—is probably the most realistic form of freedom in all ages.

According to Bey, "the TAZ is like an uprising which does not engage directly with the state." TAZ is "a guerrilla operation which liberates an area (of land, of time, of imagination) and then dissolves itself to reform elsewhere/elsewhen, before the state can crush it."

Bey said that he would "rather be a rat in the wall than a rat in the cage."

TERRORISM

Terrorism is the weapon of the outlaw against the oppressor. A form of asymmetric warfare, terrorism opposes the state-sponsored violence of soldiers and policemen.

In technologically advanced states which have a rich and developed infrastructure, terrorism is more likely than traditional guerrilla warfare.

The citizens of rich states—softened by luxury and wealth—cannot endure the privations, sacrifices, and burdens of a traditional insurgency—so they are incapable of waging a guerrilla campaign in the countryside. They are suitable only for terrorism in the cities.

Curiously, the word "terrorism" was originally coined by Maximilien Robespierre during the French Revolution. Originally, a practitioner of terrorism was someone who used violence to foster democracy and equality.

TERRORISM, COMPUTERS AND

The Internet is an interconnected web of computers. Intentionally decentralized, it was developed in the 1960's because the Americans—during the "Cold War"—believed that their communications were vulnerable.

Today, terrorists may use the Internet as a weapon. From anywhere on the planet—and at virtually no cost—a "cyberterrorist" may electronically break into a computer system and cause havoc. During the entire attack, the cyberterrorist can remain anonymous and escape capture, injury, or death.

Nuclear weapons, sensitive military systems, and the computer systems of institutions such as the C.I.A. and the F.B.I. are "air-gapped" (they are not connected to the Internet), and they are actually inaccessible to outside "hackers." But critical infrastructure in the financial and service sectors of advanced economies are networked through computers and are vulnerable.

Islamic cyberterrorists—specifically, the Abu Hafs el-Masri Brigades, an al-Qaeda satellite—claimed that they caused the "Great Blackout" in the United States and Canada on August 14, 2003. A massive electric-utility failure, fifty million people were affected when "the soldiers of God" "darkened the lives of Americans." During the episode, sixteen nuclear power plants automatically shut down.

TERRORISM, DEFENSE AGAINST

The most civilized defense against terrorism is the so-called "Sanctuary Doctrine" pursued by France. To protect the country from transnational terrorism, the government maintains strict neutrality and promotes the idea that terrorists in France have "nothing to achieve and nothing to fear."

TERRORISM, EFFECTIVENESS OF

Guerrilla warfare succeeded in Yugoslavia, China, Vietnam, and Cuba in the last fifty years of the twentieth century. Terrorism has had fewer successes.

Both the Irish and the Israelis, however, used terrorism to establish their modern states. The operative groups were the Irish Republican Army and the Irgun Zvai Leumi.

TERRORISM, ENTREPRENEURIAL

Entrepreneurial terrorism is terrorism for profit. Entrepreneurial terrorists use extortion, robbery, or kidnapping to raise money. Or, they sell their terrorist abilities to a buyer.

The Macedonian Revolutionary Organization was an entrepreneurial terrorist group. They began as a nationalist society in 1900, but became a "criminal-for-hire" murder squad by World War II.

TERRORISM, FIGHTING AGAINST

In South America, when traditional police methods failed to stop terror, the state applied massive violence. The offensive, called the "Dirty War," crushed dissent and committed atrocities against activists. In effect, the state fought terror with terror.

The classic "Dirty War" occurred in Argentina in 1976-77. After a coup d'etat had ousted Eva Peron in 1976, the Argentine army, assisted by death squads such as the Argentine Anticommunist Alliance, kidnapped, tortured, and executed without trial urban guerrillas, their sympathizers, and others considered dangerous. Perhaps fifteen thousand men, women, and children disappeared.

One technique was to throw living people into the ocean from airplanes. According to Captain Adolfo Scilingo—who made a public confession in 1995—the Argentine military threw more than 1,500 leftists, radicals, and "undesirables" to the sharks.

General Iberico Saint-Jean, a provincial governor in the Argentine military state, made this declaration: "First we kill all the subversives; then, their collaborators; later, those who sympathize with them; afterward, those who remain indifferent; and finally, the undecided."

Once terrorism endangers the state—there is no mercy from the state. Legal restraints and moral scruples are ignored.

TERRORISM, HISTORY OF

The Sicarii of first-century Palestine and the Assassins from the eleventh-century Muslim world were early terrorists.

Modern terrorism, however, was forged in nineteenth-century Russia. In 1878, a pamphlet entitled *Death for Death* articulated the principles of terror.

In 1879 thirty Russian radicals formed a political conspiracy to bring down the tsar. Their organization was the first political terrorist organization in history—the model of all others.

The terror in Russia came in two waves: the late 1870's and the early twentieth century. Early Russian terrorists were selfless young people who wanted to sacrifice themselves so that Russia would have a better future.

Albert Camus, writing on Russian terrorism, made this memorable statement: "The entire history of Russian terrorism can be summed up in the struggle of a handful of intellectuals to abolish tyranny, against a background of a silent populace."

Camus noted that "entirely on their own" and "in defiance of the most integrated absolutism of the time," the terrorists helped to liberate millions of people. "Almost all" of the terrorists "paid for this liberation by suicide, execution, prison, or madness."

Although their victory was finally betrayed, Camus noted that their actions were "exemplary, if not efficacious."

Thanks to the writings of men such as Sergi Nachaev and Mikhail Bakunin, the ideas of terrorism would spread though Europe, the United States, and elsewhere.

In the twentieth century, terrorism would trigger World War I. Terrorism, moreover, would help win the freedom of Ireland, Israel, and Algeria.

TERRORISM, LITERARY

Robert W. Chambers, in *The King in Yellow*, has a story of a book so evil that its perusal caused dire consequences. H.P. Lovecraft also used the idea. He called his wicked text the *Necronomicon*.

Literary terrorism, to apply the words of the notorious Marquis de Sade, is the act of writing a "monstrous" or "accursed" book that causes "a chaos of such proportions" that it inspires others to commit crimes.

Because the evils caused by a dangerous book can be perpetual—a book or pamphlet can continue to cause havoc and "moral crimes" long after the author has decomposed in the grave—literary terrorism may be the ultimate weapon of terrorism, more dangerous than bombs or daggers.

A number of written texts can be classified as forms of literary terrorism. In addition to the Marquis de Sade's own *The Hundred and Twenty Days of Sodom* (a catalog or list of every possible form of sexual depravity), one may include *The Science of Revolutionary Warfare* (a bomb-making manual for terrorists) by Johann Most, and *The Protocols of the Elders of Zion,* (an anonymous anti-Semitic text that first surfaced in tsarist Russia).

TERRORISM, MADNESS AND

In a haunting passage, the novelist Joseph Conrad wrote—in *The Secret Agent*—that "madness alone is truly terrifying, inasmuch as you cannot placate it either by threats, persuasion, or bribes."

Conrad added that to qualify as an insane terror incident "the attack must have all the shocking senselessness of gratuitous blasphemy."

In twentieth-century Germany, Dr. Wolfgang Huber and his wife started the "Socialist Patients' Collective." In the insane asylum where Dr. Huber worked, he trained psychiatric patients to be terrorists to fight the society that had made them sick. Their slogans were "Therapy through Violence," "Bomb for Mental Health," and "Kill for Inner Peace."

TERRORISM (PERFECT SPOKESMAN FOR)

When a terror organization needs to disseminate battle instructions, disinformation, or propaganda, the perfect spokesman is a dead man that the world thinks is alive.

By using computers and modern technology, terrorists can fabricate the dead man's image and voice. The message can then be delivered through videos, audio recordings, and Internet sites.

Since a dead spokesman cannot be captured or killed, he can also be used as the perfect "figurehead."

TERRORISM, SELECTIVE

To target certain groups, terrorists target the group's peculiar habits.

For example, intentionally spreading the so-called "mad cow disease"—a disease found in tainted beef—would be an ideal weapon for Hindu terrorists (who do not eat beef) to use against non-Hindus (who do eat beef).

In like manner, radical Muslim or Jewish terrorists could target pork-eaters, and radical vegetarian terrorists (who support the rights of animals) could target meat eaters.

On a different level, bigoted Christians could foster lethal venereal infections—such as "Acquired Immune Deficiency Syndrome" (A.I.D.S.)—to eliminate people who indulge in immoral sexual activities. If such infections were endemic, virgins who marry virgins would be safe, as long as they remain faithful to their spouses.

TERRORISM, SEXUALITY OF

According to Robin Morgan, the author of *The Demon Lover: The Sexuality of Terrorism*, the real cause of terrorism is not the so-called sponsors, such as communists or radical Muslims.

Instead, terrorism springs from the male psyche. Terrorism occurs, according to Morgan, because violence is sexually exciting for males.

The terrorist, according to Morgan, is the "ultimate sexual idol of a male-centered cultural tradition." Apparently, firing automatic weapons is sexually exciting, and explosively spewing bullets is similar to explosively spewing streams of semen.

Interestingly, the Weather Underground, a leftist terror group in the U.S.A., used the slogan "wargasm."

TERRORISM (STATE-SPONSORED)

Organized states can secretly use terror groups as "guns for hire" to attack other states. A kind of "warfare by proxy," surrogate warfare is cheaper than ordinary war. The sponsoring state simply has to provide weapons, documents, information, and money to their favored terrorists.

And, if secrecy is maintained, surrogate warfare is a relatively risk-free method of attacking another country.

There is some evidence that the Japanese Red Army was hired by Libya in the 1980's for terror actions. By using the diplomatic pouch to supply the Japanese terror group, the Libyans could move anything into a target country free of inspection under the cover of diplomatic immunity. The "pouch—which could contain a bomb—could be the size of a briefcase or could be a freighter labeled "spare parts."

The 1991 Gulf War increased interest in surrogate warriors. The overt invasion of Kuwait was punished, but if Iraq had used surrogates to attack Kuwait—or even America—it could have escaped identification and retaliation.

Was the destruction of the World Trade Center in 2001 an Iraqi-sponsored attack? Perhaps. Or, it could have been sponsored by the intelligence services of Serbia. By secretly hiring Muslim extremists, the Serbs *could* have avenged America's aggression in the Kosovo War, discredited Serbia's Muslim enemy, and avoided all reprisals. All this for a cost of approximately five hundred thousand dollars.

TERRORISM (STATE-SPONSORED), ATROCITIES AND

Horrifically, since state-sponsored terrorists do not need the support of the local population, state-sponsored terrorists are indifferent to public opinion. They can therefore carry out more destructive attacks. Indeed, they are free to commit atrocities.

TERRORISM (TECHNIQUES OF)

According to Sergius Stepniak, the Russian terrorist, terror attacks are not employed to overthrow a government, but to compel it to neglect everything else.

Like the guerrilla, the terrorist attacks weakness. The terrorist engages in 1) material terror (sabotage and disruption), 2) personal terror (acts against enemy soldiers and government officials), and 3) total terror (acts against the general public). Total terror is supposed to create pure anxiety, so that the people clamor for any settlement.

According to the *Turner Diaries*, "One of the major purposes of political terror, always and everywhere, is to force the authorities to take reprisals and become more repressive, thus alienating a portion of the population. . . . And the other purpose is to create unrest by destroying the population's sense of security and their belief in the invincibility of the government."

The strategy is as follows:

1. Terrorist attacks begin with bombing, hostage-taking, and assassination. All targets have high visibility and symbolic importance.

2. The attacks make the government appear inept and incapable of protecting the public. This fosters anxiety among the people.

3. As the terrorist assaults continue, their attacks—seemingly at will—make the terrorists appear omnipotent and invincible.

4. Since humans are drawn to strength, the striking contrast between the power of the terrorists and the impotence of the government increases the popular support for the terrorists.

5. As the government becomes more beleaguered, the attacks promote government overreaction such as martial law, mass arrests, trials without due process, and censorship.

6. Finally, the repression of the government and the terror of the terrorists creates the climate for revolution.

TERRORISM, WEAPONS AND

Although the dagger—and later the pistol—were the original tools of the terrorist, in later years a wide variety of weapons have been used.

The terror bomb was first used in the Napoleonic Age. By the late nineteenth century, it had become the weapon of choice for anarchists.

The standard bomb is the pre-positioned bomb. Such weapons are usually deployed in pairs. The first device drives the frightened crowds into the path of a secondary explosion.

To destroy a home, terrorists sometimes target the natural gas utility. A gas leak has a built-in timer (the gas must first saturate the air)—and a built-in ignition system is the pilot light of any gas appliance.

The letter bomb—or, more commonly, the parcel bomb—was first proposed in the late nineteenth century. The typical parcel bomb is a hollowed-out book filled with explosives. A common trigger is a mousetrap attached to incendiaries.

The vehicle bomb was first deployed in 1920. Invented by Mario Buda, an Italian anarchist, he parked a horse-drawn wagon loaded with stolen dynamite and scrap iron on Wall Street in New York City. More than thirty people were killed by the explosion.

In 1970, four American college students revolutionized the car bomb by building one from cheap and commercially available ingredients (ammonium nitrate and fuel oil).

Today, trucks and vans can carry the explosive equivalent of a B-24 heavy bomber from World War Two. If the vehicle is semi-trailer size, it can carry the equivalent of sixty tons of TNT.

A variation on the vehicle bomb uses a boat or a ship. On October 12, 2000 a small boat laden with explosives inflicted lethal damage on an American naval vessel.

Yet another variation involves using an airplane as a weapon. Aircraft can be lethal (if the speed is doubled, the energy is quadrupled—if the speed is tripled, the energy increases nine times), and they were used with great effect on September 11, 2001. Samuel Byck, who tried to crash a commercial airliner into the Richard Nixon White House in 1974, was the first person who tried to use aircraft in such a fashion.

TERRORISM (WEAPONS OF MASS DESTRUCTION)

Terrorists—especially those interested in megaterrorism—may use weapons of mass destruction.

One terrorist scenario (described by Ken Alibek) involves a "Human Biological Weapon." A terrorist inoculated against a specific form of infection (such as smallpox) carries a sample of the agent on to an airplane headed for New York, Paris, or Moscow. In flight, the crew and the passengers would become infected. The infected would then disperse throughout the city—or even depart for other cities—before anyone noticed symptoms. Since the smallpox virus has an incubation period of two weeks, millions could become infected before the world realized it had been attacked.

In another version of the "Human Biological Weapon," a suicide operative deliberately infects himself with a lethal disease, such as the Ebola virus. He spreads the illness far and wide before succumbing.

In terms of naked destructiveness, however, the ultimate terrorism weapon of mass destruction is an atomic or thermonuclear bomb.

According to one estimate, exploding a one-kiloton bomb at "Times Square" in New York City would immediately reduce the American Gross National Product by 3 percent. And, since half a million people crowd the area within a half-mile radius of Times Square during a normal business day, the casualties would be horrific.

The one-kiloton device would produce blast, heat, radiation, and fallout. The fireball would be three hundred feet across, and the crater would be 120 feet deep. Buildings within six hundred feet would collapse. People one-quarter of a mile away would be killed or maimed by the heat. Radiation would quickly kill those one-half of a mile away. The mushroom cloud would be ten thousand feet high, and the radioactive fallout would start arriving in twenty-four hours. The victims of the fallout would die within two weeks. Hundreds of miles away, cancer rates would rise.

If such a weapon were pre-positioned, there would be no warning. In the middle of a speech—or during an elegant state dinner—the most powerful man on Earth could be reduced to a shadow on a concrete slab.

And, if deployed anonymously—especially by domestic terrorists—there would be no identifiable "return address." In other words, the terrorists staging the attack could do so without fear of reprisal.

Although biological and nuclear weapons are terrifying, the future may hold additional horrors, such as weapons not yet developed.

Some day, an "anti-matter bomb" may be perfected. A quantity of matter meeting an equal quantity of anti-matter would result in the annihilation of both, and the energy released would be far greater than that released by a thermonuclear bomb.

TERRORIST GROUPS, FINANCE OF

To pay for their campaign, terrorists use crime. Having already abandoned traditional morality—viewing themselves as "beyond good and evil"—terrorists finance their agendas by robbing, kidnapping, extorting, hijacking, smuggling, and selling illegal drugs.

The Irish terrorists have used everything from video piracy to armed robbery to raise money, and in 1995 they teamed up with Irish gangsters to steal three million pounds sterling.

TERRORIST GROUPS, ORGANIZATION OF

Traditionally, terror groups tactically divide into sections: 1) an overt propaganda arm that always stays within the law, and 2) attack units, who sabotage, bomb, and assassinate.

The attack units may be underground phantom cells—or lone wolves who may have no links to a central command.

The typical operative—who stages the assaults—is an activist dabbling in weekend terrorism. He will have a normal occupation and a regular identity.

The Provisional IRA (PIRA) deploys cells consisting of four or five individuals who arm and finance themselves, select their own targets, and carry out their own missions. The commander of a cell, through an assumed name, may have contact with a PIRA command quartermaster for explosives or weapons.

TERRORIST GROUPS, SIZE OF

By definition, terror groups are small in size. If too many terrorists are involved in an operation, it is difficult for them to escape after an attack.

Also, if a terrorist group becomes too large overall, its stealthiness is compromised and penetration by informants becomes easier.

Lehi (also called the Stern Gang, after its leader Abraham Stern), the classic Israeli terror group, had about two hundred to three hundred active members. The Japanese Red Army, the Baader-Meinhof Gang, the Red Brigades, and the Symbionese Liberation Army were all diminutive. The largest of these, the Red Brigades, had fifty active members. The smallest, the Symbionese Liberation Army, had eight members.

TERRORIST, MIND OF

According to one observer, "the terrorist is fundamentally a violent intellectual." Fighting for a cause, the terrorist is altruistic—not selfish.

Generally speaking, in terms of motivation, there are two kinds of terrorists: 1) the terrorist who wants to punish his father and 2) the terrorist who wants to avenge his father.

The first rejects everything that his father represents: the establishment, the law, and traditional morality.

The second, in contrast, has seen his father unjustly treated by society—exploited, tortured, murdered—and he wants revenge for the horrors.

In terms of final goals, there are three types of terrorists.

The most ferocious type believes that the "system" is a monster that must be pulverized. Committed to regeneration through violence, he wants to destroy civilization and live off its corpse.

The second type—rather less dangerous—believes that disrupting the "system" will purify it.

And the third type of terrorist—the least destructive of all—simply wants to see something in flames, such as the White House, the Kremlin, or the Vatican.

TERRORIST, PUBLIC FACE OF

Regarding the public face of the terrorist, the classic manual is by the Red Brigades, a pamphlet entitled *Security Rules and Work Methods.*

The manual suggests that terrorists should be inconspicuous, they should appear to be regularly employed, they should rent apartments which do not have resident landlords, and they should avoid streets with public buildings that could be used by police spies.

Terrorists should also retain as little compromising material as possible. They should keep weapons and essential equipment in bags ready for a quick escape.

TERRORISTS, PUBLIC CLAIMS OF

Taking credit invites retaliation. So extreme terror groups, such as the Supreme Truth cult, do not take credit for their operations.

In contrast, more moderate groups, such as the Irish Republican Army—will claim credit for propaganda purposes.

And, to minimize casualties, the Irish Republican army will even warn the police *before* a specific attack.

THEFT

A crime against property, theft is the act of stealing.

Traditional thieves are worse than capitalist ones. Traditional thieves do not produce or create wealth—they just steal.

Regarding types of theft, robbery is theft with a weapon. Larceny is theft with no weapon. Burglary is breaking and entering, with or without a weapon.

Burglary and larceny, which involve no personal contact, are safer than robbery, so why do some people rob? According to Colin Wilson, robbery involves personal contact, a weapon, giving orders, and being obeyed–and these things appeal to some personality types.

THEFT (PUNISHMENT OF)

Under the *Sharia,* the traditional law of Islam, the hand of the thief is amputated. For the penalty to be applied, however, the theft must be intentional, the thief must be an adult, and his theft must be by stealth. Also, the stolen item must be a legal item. Thus, there is no punishment for stealing wine.

Interestingly, under the *Sharia,* taking a book is not considered theft. Under *Sharia*, it is assumed that the thief took the book for the contents, and in Islam no one owns knowledge.

THELEMA, ABBEY OF

Created by Francois Rabelais, a French writer, the fictional abbey of Thelema is a place of seclusion, dedicated to the pleasures of the flesh.

Only the brightest, the most beautiful, and the best are permitted within its walls. The fabled motto of the abbey is "Do What You Will."

THIRTEEN SOCIETY

The Thirteen Society, founded in France in 1857, was a rebellion against "superstition." Members swore great oaths to disregard and flout all superstitions.

Membership in the society was limited to thirteen, the street address of their organization premises was number thirteen, and meetings were on the thirteenth of the month. At meetings the members dined with thirteen persons at the table.

Members promised to walk under ladders, spill salt at meals, and wear green at the weddings they attended.

THOUGHT CRIMES

The worst tyrants try to control human thought itself.

In medieval Christendom, "heretics" could be tortured and executed for their theological notions. In Mussolini's Italy, anti-fascists could be sentenced to death for "crimes of opinion." In twenty-first century America, "hate crime" legislation has outlawed the emotion of hate.

In the words of Robert Anton Wilson, "anybody who questions the reality-tunnel gets the hemlock (Socrates, fourth century B.C.), burning at the stake (Giordano Bruno, seventeenth century), the bottom cell in the basement at Folsom (Timothy Leary, twentieth century), or some similar discouragement."

THOUGHT POLICE

An infamous invention, "thought police" try to control the minds of men. Committing crimes against ideas, the thought police force rebels to die as martyrs or live as apostates.

The most notorious "thought police" in modern times were the "Special Higher Police" in the Japanese Empire. Called the TOKKO, their function was to monitor "dangerous thoughts."

More than 59,000 people were arrested by the Japanese thought police. More than 2,500 of these received prison sentences.

THUGGEE, CULT OF

The Thuggee—an ancient cult of murder and terror—have been called "the most successful terror organization in history" and "the most remarkable example of organized crime on record." Allegedly extinct, there are reports that they still exist today.

The Thuggee are devotees of Kali, the Hindu goddess of death. Kali is depicted as black-skinned, with four arms. In her first hand she carries a sword, in her second hand she carries a severed head, her third hand is raised in a gesture of peace, and her remaining hand is grasping for power. The city of Calcutta is named in her honor.

According to legend, the first Thuggee were created (from the brow of the goddess) to help Kali destroy a horde of demons. The demons had to be strangled, for their blood—once shed—turned into more demons. So Kali gave the Thuggee the noose to kill demons.

In return for helping Kali, the Thuggee believe that they received the right to kill in perpetuity and to keep the loot from their victims. They are obliged to strangle at least one person per year. The victim must never be a woman or a wandering holy man.

The Thuggee believe that their victims go straight to paradise. By serving Kali, the Thuggee also go to paradise.

The word Thug (pronounced t'ug) is derived from the Sanskrit word which means deceiver or swindler. Members of this secret cult lead double lives. For most of the year, the Thuggee have regular employment and live openly in the community as respected and orderly citizens.

In autumn, however, when the roads are crowded with pilgrims, the Thuggee hunt humans. They attack in November and December—always at least one hundred miles from their homes. When the killing season ends, they melt back into ordinary life.

The Thuggee work in units of ten to fifty men. Divided into small groups, some serve as scouts, some as killers, and some as grave diggers.

The Thuggee strangle their selected victims, using garrotes fashioned from white or yellow silk. (White and yellow are sacred to Kali.) The agony of the victim is prolonged because Kali enjoys terror.

Usually, there are three Thuggee killers per victim. While one strangles, one holds the dying man's feet, and one holds the arms or sits on the chest of the victim.

After the killings, the victims are buried in small, deep graves, with their backs and thigh bones broken. To hide the activity, the graves are dug inside tents.

The graves are dug with shovels and at least one symbolic strike from a silver pick axe. The site is strewn with pungent herbs to mislead dogs.

The Thuggee always conduct an ancient ceremony on the graves. They place "goor," a kind of coarse sugar, on a cloth. After pouring some sugar and "holy water," those that had killed that day (in order of seniority) eat the "sugar of Kali" as a sacrament. It is said that once a man tastes goor, he will always serve the goddess of death.

To perpetuate the movement, men recruit their sons and nephews. The training of the boys begins in childhood, but only at the age of eighteen are the boys allowed to kill and taste the sacred sugar for the first time.

TIMING, SIGNIFICANCE OF

Choosing a significant time has useful propaganda value. The attacks on the Pentagon and the World Trade Towers on September 11, 2001, for example, occurred on a Tuesday, the day Allah created darkness.

Interestingly, the Warsaw Pact was dissolved by the Russians on April 1, 1991. Note that the day chosen was "April Fools' Day."

TORTURE

Torture, a forcible means of persuasion, involves the infliction of extreme pain. The victims of torture claim it is a shameful crime. The torturers claim it is a grim necessity.

The techniques of torture are many and varied. According to Octave Mirbeau, the torturer takes "the same care over human flesh as a sculptor does over his clay or piece of ivory."

In the Roman Empire, Caligula had a man flogged with chains daily. Caligula had his victim killed only when the stench of the man's brain seeping out of his fractured skull became intolerable.

In the medieval Inquisition, the favorite torture was the rack. The victim's feet were tied down—his arms were pulled—and this broke the spine apart.

During the Renaissance, Marsilius of Bologna invented the torture of "sleep deprivation" in 1529. This torment, which leaves no scars on the body, maddens the mind and potentially is lethal.

During World War II, the torture techniques of the Japanese secret police included flogging, the water torture (lungs), burning, scalding, electric shocks, knee joint separation, suspension (hanging from the middle fingers or from the wrists tied behind back), kneeling on sharp edges, finger and toenail removal, and finger crushing.

In the Korean War, the North Koreans used a hammer to crush finger joints. Reportedly, no American soldier could endure more than three crushed joints.

In Paraguay under Alfredo Stroessner, the secret police immersed their victims in tubs of human excrement until the victims complied.

In America's wars, the United States has used "stress positions," hooding, twenty-hour interrogations, nakedness, exploiting phobias (such as fear of dogs, feces, and so forth), prolonged isolation, and sensory deprivation.

Technically, torture remained a legal option in the Roman Catholic church until 1917, when the new *Codex Juris Canonici* was put into effect.

TOTAL WAR

Total war is the direction of a nation's resources—demographic, economic, and military—toward a war effort.

With his call for a "nation in arms," total war was invented during the French Revolution by Lazare Carnot.

TOTALITARIANISM

Jacobins, after killing the French king in January 1793, created the first totalitarian government in history when they instituted decrees requiring every citizen to subject himself to the service of the state. Thus began a "reign of terror and virtue."

It has been said that the ubiquity of authority is the essence of totalitarianism. Hence Benito Mussolini, who actually coined the term, defined totalitarianism as "everything within the state; nothing against the state; nothing outside the state."

Curiously, Teilhard de Chardin, said that "monstrous as it is, is not totalitarianism really the distortion of something magnificent, and thus quite near the truth?"

According to George Orwell, "totalitarianism, if not fought against, could triumph anywhere."

TRAINING OF OPERATIVES

To train terrorists and guerrillas, the Renamo of Mozambique used a savage and effective ritual.

First, automatic weapons were discharged close to the ears of the recruits. Then, a group of recruits were forced to kill an animal. Next, each recruit—acting alone—was forced to kill an animal. Then, a group of recruits were forced to kill a human. Finally—each recruit—acting alone—was forced to kill a man, a woman, or a child.

The training stripped the recruits of natural human sensitivities and bound them tightly to Renamo, an outlaw organization that was "beyond the pale." The recruits became perfect killing machines.

TRAITORS

Traitors are individuals who betray a country or a cause. Some traitors are motivated by money—others are motivated by ideology.

Traitors are an effective force in history. On August 24, 410, for example, an unknown hand unbarred the Salarian gate in Rome and admitted Alaric and his destructive Teutonic horde.

Sometimes, a traitor may encounter a shocking end. In the Vietnam War against America, the Viet Cong cut open traitors and let wild pigs eat them. In northern Ireland, the IRA stabbed informants in the ear with a hat pin. The wound, which would probably not be noticed during an autopsy, caused almost certain death.

Other traitors, however, reap fame and fortune. One outstanding example of a successful traitor was Jean Baptiste Jules Bernadotte. Fighting against France, his native country, this opportunist finished life as the King of Sweden.

Initially a sergeant in the king's army, Bernadotte became a brigadier general in the army of the Revolutionary republic in 1793. Later, he became a marshal under Napoleon Bonaparte.

In 1810, when Sweden's royal line became extinct, Bernadotte—with Napoleon's concurrence—was elected crown prince and regent. After Napoleon's disastrous Russian campaign, Bernadotte turned on Bonaparte and led the Swedish army against France at the Battle of Leipzig in 1813. Bernadotte was crowned king of Sweden in 1818.

His family still reigns in Sweden to this day.

TRAVEL (CLANDESTINE)

For the outlaw, travel is always dangerous. Remember, most fugitives are caught when they are trying to move.

If you must travel, wear unobtrusive clothing. Never carry two sets of identification at the same time. If possible, keep clean.

If you ride in a taxi, give the driver an address, but always stop the cab and exit a few blocks before you reach it. If you arrive at a destination and see the police, it looks suspicious if you order the driver to keep going.

If you are traveling a great distance, do not hitchhike. Instead, ride a bus. Bus lines do not require identification papers and they do not make passenger lists.

If you are crossing international frontiers, use desolate areas. According to Abbie Hoffman, the leftist radical, a good place to enter Canada is at Kingsgate, just north of Montana. The site is especially good on weekdays, especially after ten o'clock at night.

TREATIES

In international law, a treaty is a formally concluded and ratified agreement between states.

In the real world of Machiavellian politics, however, treaties are cunning swindles used by unscrupulous men to deceive naive dupes.

In the process of stealing land from the aboriginal inhabitants of what would become the United States, for example, the whites made more than eight hundred treaties!

TRIAD SOCIETY

The Triad, a secret society originally dedicated to overthrowing the foreign dynasty that then controlled China, eventually moved into organized crime.

In 1911, Sun Yat-sen, an influential member of the Hong Kong Triad called the Chung Wo Tong Society, led the revolution that overthrew the imperial dynasty in Beijing and established a republic. Demanding compensation for their role in the revolution, for the next forty years the members of the Triad Society were ensconced in the Chinese government. Corruption was rife, and membership in the Triad was necessary for a position in the civil service or the government.

In 1949 Mao Tse-tung and the communists seized power, and the old government fled with its Triad supporters to Taiwan. Today, the Triad Society is strong in the Taiwanese secret service.

TRIAD SOCIETY, SIZE OF

Note that the United States has approximately two thousand people in the Mafia. In contrast, Hong Kong alone has 300,000 Triad members.

TRUTH

In India, the value of a statement is the amount of good rendered to people by one's words. Thus, a false statement—if beneficial to all beings—is preferable to a truthful statement that is harmful.

According to the occultist named Aleister Crowley, "The Master (in technical language, the Magus) does not concern himself with facts; he does not care whether a thing is true or not: he uses truth and falsehood indiscriminately to serve his ends."

TRUTH, OPPOSITE OF

The opposite of a truth is not always a falsehood. As one sage pointed out, the opposite of a profound truth may be another profound truth.

TRUTH SERUM

A "truth serum" is a substance that allegedly compels a victim to speak the truth. The term was coined in the 1920's, after scopolamine was used in an Alabama murder trial.

Scopolamine is derived from burundanga, a Columbian tree. The effect of the drug is immediate and spectacular. The subject is unaware of what he is doing, and he retains no memory of what he says or does under the influence of the substance.

Scopolamine was used by Nazi interrogators and Central Intelligence Agency "interlocutors," but it is now discredited. Scopolamine does not bring out the truth. Instead, it heightens suggestibility, and it places the subject under the influence of others. Subjects confess to anything and tell interrogators whatever the interrogators want to hear.

Interrogators now use sodium amytal or sodium pentothal. In reality, these drugs are no more effective than alcohol in bringing out the truth.

TUCKER, BENJAMIN (1854-1939)

A theorist on civil disobedience, Benjamin Tucker argued that a powerful weapon against a government is the simple refusal to pay taxes.

According to Tucker, "Power feeds on its spoils, and dies when its victims refuse to be despoiled."

Regarding people and government, Tucker wrote that people "cannot persuade it to death; they cannot vote it to death; they cannot shoot it to death; but they can always starve it to death."

Tucker believed that "if one-fifth of the people were to resist taxation, it would cost more to collect their taxes, or try to collect them, than the other four-fifths would consent to pay into the treasury."

TURNER DIARIES

A reviled novel, Andrew MacDonald (the pseudonym of Dr. William Pierce) wrote the *Turner Diaries*. The book, which features racist and anti-government themes, was published in 1985.

The apocalyptic novel describes the activities of a character named Earl Turner, the leader of a secret conspiracy called the "Order," which fights a terrorist race war against a fictional Jewish-controlled federal government.

In the novel, Turner and his confederates overthrow the government through counterfeit currency, armed robbery, murder, and assassination—and they even stage an attack on a Federal building with a fertilizer bomb. At the end the novel, terrorists capture American nuclear weapons and use them against Israel and other nations.

The book inspired real terrorists, including Robert Jay Matthews and Timothy McVeigh.

In the *Turner Diaries*, the "hero" makes this statement: "Six months ago I could not imagine myself calmly butchering a teenaged white girl, no matter what she had done. But I have become much more realistic about life lately."

TYRANNICAL GOVERNMENTS, VULNERABILITY OF

For tyrannical governments, according to Alexis de Tocqueville, their moment of greatest danger is the moment they begin to reform.

TYRANNY, CIVILIZATION AND

According to Sir James Fraser, the celebrated author of *The Golden Bough*, despots made civilization possible.

These are his words: "For the rise of monarchy appears to be an essential condition of the emergence of mankind from savagery. No human being is so hidebound by custom and tradition as your democratic savage; in no state of society consequently is progress so slow and difficult. The old notion that the savage is the freest of mankind is the reverse of truth. He is a slave, not indeed to a visible master, but to the past, to the spirits of his dead forefathers, who haunt his steps from birth to death, and rule him with a rod of iron."

According to Fraser, when one man rose to supreme power—a king or a tyrant—he could carry through changes in one lifetime that previously several lifetimes could not accomplish.

"At this early epoch despotism is the best friend of humanity and, as paradoxical as it may sound, of liberty. For after all there is more liberty in the best sense—liberty to think our own thoughts and to fashion our own destinies—under the most absolute despotism, the most grinding tyranny, than under the apparent freedom of savage life, where the individual's lot is cast from cradle to grave in the iron mold of hereditary custom."

TYRANNY, FOUR TYPES OF

Tyranny comes in many forms. The Hindu sages—perceptive in all matters—refer to the "four tyrannies."

Equally pernicious, the four tyrannies are 1) the unchecked rule of priests (scholars belong to this caste), 2) the unchecked rule of warriors (kings belong to this caste), 3) the unchecked rule of merchants (plutocrats), and 4) the unchecked rule of workers.

Western Civilization has seen tyranny in every form. The West has endured pontifical Rome, Napoleonic Paris, grubby, bourgeois New York, and Bolshevik Moscow.

TYRANTS (POLITICAL)

"Tyrant" is derived from the Greek word for "single ruler." Classical Greek tyrants were demagogues who exploited the dissatisfaction of the poor for political power. From the eighth through the sixth centuries before Christ, they flourished in Greece.

Usually, tyrants enter like foxes, rule like wolves, and die like dogs.

Good citizens—people who obey the law, pay their taxes, and render military service—make tyrants possible.

TYRANTS (POLITICAL), LOVE OF

Common people are strangely drawn to tyrants.

Giovanni Botero, an Italian political philosopher, said that people will always prefer a strong, irascible, triumphant ruler to a wise and prudent one, just as they "prefer a tumbling torrent to a calm river."

At the funeral of Joseph Stalin, millions of mourners crowded into Red Square in Moscow, and hundreds were trampled or crushed to death.

TYRANTS (POLITICAL), MORAL INCONSISTENCIES OF

No human seems to be purely evil (or purely good). And even the worst tyrants have morally acceptable traits.

Herod "the Great," for example, who killed three sons, one wife, two brothers-in-law and a mother-in-law, piously kept kosher and zealously expanded the Jerusalem temple.

And Heinrich Himmler, a moving force behind the Nazi concentration camps, could be oddly scrupulous. When his parents used an official car, he paid for the gasoline from his salary!

UGLINESS

To be ugly is to be repulsive in appearance.

According to Herbert Spencer, the three principal sources of ugliness are recession of the forehead, jaw protuberances, and large cheekbones. Beauty, in contrast, is an "idealization away from the ape."

Alesister Crowley said that ugliness—not beauty—is the source of the ultimate ecstasy in lovemaking. "For what is pleasant is assimilated easily and without ecstasy," but "the self is shaken to the root" by "the transfiguration of the loathsome and abhorred."

According to Georges Bataille, however, "Beauty has a cardinal importance, for ugliness cannot be spoiled, and to despoil is the essence of eroticism."

Indeed, added Bataille, "the greater the beauty, the more it is befouled."

UNDERCOVER OPERATIVES

Undercover operatives are police disguised as terrorists, outlaws, or other enemies of the state. They are planted as spies or agent provocateurs among subversives or criminals.

On the eve of the Russian Revolution, the tsarist secret police had throughly penetrated the Bolshevik party with agents. The chief spokesman for the party in the Duma (parliament) worked for the Imperial security police, for example, and so did the editor of *Pravda*, Vladimir Lenin's principal propaganda organ.

In the United States, J. Edgar Hoover, the legendary head of the F.B.I., never allowed his agents to personally infiltrate suspected subversive organizations. (Hoover believed that if a subversive organization could "turn" one of his agents, the damage to the bureau would be incalculable.) Instead, Hoover recruited state and local police as operatives.

In 1965, there were fourteen Ku Klux Klan groups in the U.S.A., and the F.B.I. penetrated *all* of them with undercover operatives. In seven of the Klan groups, the F.B.I. had undercover operatives in leadership positions. Oddly, the F.B.I. at the time may have been largest single source of Klan funds through dues-paying informants!

UNABOMBER

Theodore Kaczynski was active as the "Unabomber" between 1978 and 1995. An enemy of modern technology—and a proponent of primitivism—Kaczynski wrote a manifesto entitled *Industrial Society and Its Future.*

During his terror campaign against technology, Theodore Kaczynski lived on a few hundred dollars a year. A vegetarian, he occupied a ten-by-twelve-foot shack situated on 1.4 acres of forest. Kaczynski lived without electricity, plumbing, a telephone, or an automobile.

During his twenty-year campaign as a lone terrorist, Kaczynski made his own explosives out of commonly available chemicals. He was careful to scrape the labels off batteries, he used postal stamps long after their issue dates, and he left no fingerprints.

In spite of his precautions, however, Kaczynski was subdued because he was betrayed by his brother.

UNDERCOVER OPERATIVES (RECOGNITION OF)

David Lane, a convicted white supremacist and an original member of the Silent Brotherhood, said that undercover operatives can be identified.

According to Lane, these precautions are necessary: 1) be suspicious of someone whose education and background are different from the people with whom he is trying to associate (ordinarily, people seek their own kind) and 2) be suspicious of a stranger or a new acquaintance who suggests illegal activities.

Be aware that undercover operatives are under no obligation to truthfully identify themselves as police. When questioned directly, they may legally lie.

UNHAPPINESS

Why are men unhappy? According to Friedrich Nietzsche, Marxists blame others and Christians blame themselves.

UNINTENDED CONSEQUENCES, THE LAW OF

According to Karl Popper, historians should contemplate the unintended consequences of deliberate acts.

For example, when the Atlantic slave trade was abolished in the nineteenth century, slavery actually *increased* in Africa. And—when the first fascist party in history was established in Italy in 1919—the "half a dozen Jews" who were "among the fifty founders of the fascist movement" did not realize the significance of their actions.

Always remember that Victor Frankenstein did not set out to create a monster. . . .

UNION OF SOVIET SOCIALIST REPUBLICS

A vast empire in Eurasia–larger in size than the continent of South America–the Union of Soviet Socialist Republics defeated Nazi Germany, built the first practical hydrogen bomb, launched the first satellite and the first man into space, built the first operational nuclear-power reactor, built the largest nuclear force in history, and detonated the most powerful weapon ever built, the 58-megaton *Tsar Bomba*.

Yet, in August 1991, the U.S.S.R., the most powerful state in history, ceased to exist.

The change was not triggered by social unrest. There were no waves of strikes, no massive demonstrations, and no widespread violence. The U.S.S.R. disintegrated because of political decisions made at the top.

Oddly, the formal decision to dissolve the U.S.S.R. was made by the "presidents" of Russia, the Ukraine, and Belarus–without the participation of the other republics or of Mikhail Gorbachev, the Soviet leader.

In other words, the Soviet Union did not collapse. Hitler's Reich collapsed, the British Empire (exhausted and bankrupted by two world wars) also collapsed, but the U.S.S.R. did not. It underwent a metamorphosis.

Leon Trotsky in exile had predicted that Soviet bureaucrats would one day sell all the socialized property they had expropriated, and they would go into business on their own account.

Trotsky's prediction was correct. Ultimately, the Union of Soviet Socialist Republics became a robber-baron and Mafia-dominated capitalist state.

UNITED STATES OF AMERICA

The United States of America—populated by "honest reprobates"—has been called the land of high ideals and no morals.

Admired—and hated—by the world, the United States is noted for its wealth, its technology, and the infamous promiscuity of its people.

To its admirers, the United States represents the pinnacle of human achievement. It is a beautiful country, with justice, happiness, and prosperity.

To its detractors, however, the United States is a civilization on the edge of the abyss, rotting from the inside out. A shallow culture, its most admired personalities are actors, musicians, and athletes.

Horst Mahler, a German radical, said that there is no such thing as an American people, but a crude, immoral, violent mass which produces corruption, pseudo-democracy, spurious egalitarianism, imperialism, censorship, robbery, stupidity, and smut.

UNITED STATES OF AMERICA, GOLDEN AGE OF

The golden age of American freedom was clearly the nineteenth century. George Orwell thought that the civilization of nineteenth-century America was "capitalist civilization at its best."

In 1874, the standing army of the United States had only sixteen thousand men. Americans needed no passport to travel abroad. Immigrants did not have to report to anyone and did not require special papers. No drugs were prohibited. There was no income tax. Best of all, the government had no secret documents.

On the dark side, however, "secondhand-food markets" existed in the larger cities of late nineteenth-century America. In those markets, the poor could purchase the cast-off scraps of food discarded by butcher shops, markets, and restaurants.

VAILLANT, AUGUSTE (1861-1894)

A failed assassin, Auguste Vaillant was guillotined for *attempting* to assassinate the prime minister of France. Supporters placed fresh flowers and a crown of thorns on his grave.

VENDETTA

A vendetta is a blood feud. The word vendetta means vengeance.

According to the Sicilian Mafia, "Vendetta is firstly a duty and secondly, a pleasure and a right."

VERTICAL ENVELOPMENT

The deployment of troops by air behind enemy lines is called vertical envelopment.

When a nation has air superiority, it can use air power to go anywhere, establish base, and then withdraw at will.

This creates the illusion of control. Such an illusion beguiled the Americans during the American-Vietnamese War.

VICTIMS

A victim is a person harmed or killed as a result of a crime.

In a haunting passage in the novel *1984*, a character notes that the Inquisition failed because it made victims into martyrs. The totalitarian leadership described in the book, however, does not make that mistake:

> *You must stop imagining that posterity will vindicate you, Winston. Posterity will never hear of you. You will be lifted clean out from the stream of history. We shall turn you into gas and pour you into the stratosphere. Nothing will remain of you: not a name in a register, not a memory in a living brain. You will be annihilated in the past as in the future. You will never have existed.*

The passage reminds us of the cold-blooded words of Max Stirner: "Kill them, do not martyr them."

VICTIMS, CROWDS AND

According to Elias Canetti, "Once a . . . crowd has attained its victim it disintegrates rapidly. Rulers in danger are well aware of this fact and throw a victim to a crowd in order to impede its growth. Many political executions are arranged solely for this purpose."

VICTORY

Some victories are spectacularly quick and decisive. The Battle of Hastings, on October 14, 1066, lasted eight hours, and England was conquered in one day by the Normans.

Afterwards, twenty thousand French-speaking Normans controlled two million Anglo-Saxons.

But other victories bring exhaustion and ruin—even to the winner.

Pyrrhus, king of Epirus, invaded Italy in 280 B.C. and inflicted two crushing defeats on the Romans. The victories were so costly, however, that he was unable to master the Romans.

VICTORY, HAZARDS OF

Winning a war can be dangerous, for the victor may become fossilized and unimaginative.

In 1904, the Japanese started the Russian-Japanese war with a surprise attack on the Russian fleet at Port Arthur. The war ended the following year when Russia agreed to a humiliating peace.

In 1941, the Japanese started the American-Japanese War with a surprise attack on the American fleet at Pearl Harbor. This time, however, the same strategy led to a catastrophic Japanese defeat.

VIOLENCE

Violence is a force that hurts, damages, or kills.

Childbirth is the most common violence on Earth. It is estimated that at any given moment 300,000 women on Earth are in labor.

Gorges Sorel said that violence must cease being an archaic reflex and must have a purpose.

VIOLENCE, GOVERNMENT MONOPOLY OF

States arrogate to themselves the power of coercive violence. There are exceptions—Swiss law requires each able-bodied man to keep an automatic weapon in his home to defend against invasion—but most modern governments monopolize violence.

When John Brown, an unsuccessful rebel, tried to use violence to end human slavery in 1859, he was executed by the government. (John Wilkes Booth watched the hanging). A few years later, Abraham Lincoln and the federal government would use violence to end slavery.

When Donald Black tried to invade the Caribbean nation of Dominica and overthrow its government, he was sentenced to three years in prison. Of course, Ronald Reagan would invade and overthrow the government of Grenada—another Caribbean nation— with impunity.

VIOLENCE, ORIGINS OF

Regarding the origins of violence, the classic statement was made by Mahatma Gandhi: "Seven blunders of the world that lead to violence: wealth without work, pleasure without conscience, knowledge without character, commerce without morality, science without humanity, worship without sacrifice, politics without principle."

VIOLENCE, PURIFICATION RITES AND

Many societies link violence and purification rituals.

Among the Zulu of Africa, a warrior who killed was polluted. Before he could return to ordinary life, he had to pass the pollution to a stranger by having sexual intercourse with a woman he did not know.

If no woman could be found, he copulated between the thighs of a boy he did not know.

VIRTUE, PLEASURE OF

According to the Chinese, virtue is its own reward.

The Maquis de Sade, however, claimed that "moral" pleasures exist only in the imagination. In other words, virtue is "pleasurable" only if one believes that it is. Thinking makes it so.

VIRTUE, RELATIVITY OF

What is good? It depends on the time and the place.

"Are you unaware," asked the Marquis de Sade, "that murder was honored in China, rape in New Zealand, theft in Sparta? That man you watch being drawn and quartered in the market place, what has he done? He ventured to acquit himself in Paris of some Japanese virtue."

It is significant that the Mongols, who forged the largest contiguous land empire in history, despised the "work ethic," thought that loyalty was the *highest* virtue, and believed that it was acceptable to indulge in cannabis and alcohol.

VIRTUE, THE MARQUIS DE SADE ON

On virtue, the Marquis de Sade made this declaration:

> *I love to hear these rich ones, these titled ones, these magistrates and these priests, I love to see them preach virtue to us. It is not very difficult to forswear theft when one has three or four times what one needs to live; it is not very necessary to plot murder when one is surrounded by nothing but adulators and thralls unto whom one's will is law; nor is it very hard to be temperate and sober when one has the most succulent dainties constantly within one's reach; they can contrive to be sincere when there is never any apparent advantage in falsehood.*

VITUPERATION

Vituperation is bitter and abusive language. According to the Marquis de

Sade, "The true libertine loves even the reproaches he receives for the unspeakable deeds he has done."

Filippo Tommaso Marinetti, the futurist leader, referred to "the voluptuousness of being booed."

WALKER, WILLIAM (1824-1860)

William Walker was an American physician, journalist, adventurer, and soldier of fortune. A cultural imperialist, Walker conceived the idea (called filibustering) of privately conquering areas of Latin America and creating states ruled by English speakers.

A native of Nashville, Tennessee, Walker raised small armies of Americans and led them against Mexico, Nicaragua, and Honduras. His most spectacular achievement was an invasion of Nicaragua with 57 men. With his small force—and the assistance of 170 locals and another 100 Americans in Nicaragua—Walker defeated the Nicaraguan national army at La Virgen and, a month later, occupied the capital and took control of the country.

After Walker declared himself president of Nicaragua in 1856, he made English the national language and legalized slavery!

Walker's position soon became precarious, however. His army was thinned by cholera and massive defections, and he fled.

After additional adventures, Walker was executed by a firing squad in Honduras on September 12, 1860.

WAR

Like social insects, humans engage in something called war. It is a carnival of sadism and death—an endless series of atrocities and counter-atrocities.

To modern humans, war is systematic terrorism between the armed forces of governments. Everything else is regarded as rebellion and crime and has a different set of rules.

For all of recorded human history, estimates of those killed in war range from 150 million to one billion.

In the past 3,400 years, humans have been entirely at peace only 268 years. (Eight percent of the 3,400 years.)

In the twentieth century alone, forty-three wars have ravaged the Earth, including two world wars. The conflicts caused an estimated eighty-five million direct deaths. (Indirect deaths, from concentration camps to disease and famine caused by war, added an additional half a billion deaths.)

WAR, ATROCITIES AND

All war produces atrocities.

In Liberia's civil war, in which two-thirds of the rebel fighters were aged twelve to seventeen years, there were reports of rape, blood drinking and cannibalism. Young soldiers placed wagers on the genders of the fetuses inside pregnant women, and then ripped open the women to see who won.

WAR, CONDUCT OF

The conduct of war is determined by two factors: the nature of the weapons available and the modes of transportation.

WAR, COST OF

When the ancient Roman army was not fighting, it was building. In the modern era, however, many armies are unproductive. According to historian Lewis Mumford, "an army is a body of pure consumers."

In one period, the years between 1948 and 2003, the U.S.A. spent fifteen trillion dollars on the military. That was more than the *cumulative* manmade wealth in the United States at that time (the value of all factories, homes, schools, hospitals, bridges, roads, and so forth *combined*).

Military weapons are the ultimate capitalist products: they destroy other products, they can typically be used only once, and their high cost yields large profits.

WAR, CRIMES AND

When the "Black Prince" of England captured King John of France at the Battle of Poitiers in 1356, he treated the king honorably, and housed John in Windsor Castle.

After World War II, however, when the Japanese lost what they called "The Holy War for the Liberation of a Billion Asians," many of their leaders were given "a mock-trial followed by a hanging."

Today, the war criminals who win a war inflict harsh punishments on those who lose.

WAR, LETHALITY OF

The population of the Earth was 200 million during the time of Christ. During the twentieth century alone, wars have killed 100 million men, women, and children.

Modern wars, extreme examples of strategic crime, are exceptionally deadly. Nearly 80 percent of all males born in the U.S.S.R. in 1923 did not survive World War II.

WAR, MADNESS OF

In 1968, after annihilating a hamlet called Ben Tre, an American military officer commented: "It was necessary to destroy the village in order to save it."

Curiously, in World War II, the United States, in order to save democracy, ended up taking measures that ruined democracy, such as the introduction of spying, "official secrets," conscription, exorbitant taxation, and censorship.

WAR, MODERN

Whatever its lethality, modern war brings glory, power, and wealth to a small elite.

Of the 164 men in the West Point Academy class of 1915, sixty-one of these would end up as generals (two with five stars, two with four stars, seven with three stars, fifty with two stars, and one with one star).

After Douglas MacArthur had lost the Philippines and had fled to Australia, he was given the "Medal of Honor"! Appropriately, he was given the coveted award on "April Fools' Day."

Even more bizarre was the career of Dwight Eisenhower, who began World War II as a lieutenant colonel. By June 1942, Eisenhower was the commander of the Allied European theater, even though he had never experienced hostile gunfire. By 1953, Eisenhower was president of the United States.

WAR, OPPOSITION TO

While a war is being fought, opposition can be perilous. During both world wars—in all the countries involved—those who openly questioned the legitimacy of the conflicts were ignored, scorned, ostracized, hounded, interned, and sometimes executed.

In the United States, no one has ever been punished for war-mongering, but anti-war protesters are routinely sanctioned.

Interestingly, an anti-war or peace movement has worked only once in American history: it stopped the war against Vietnam.

WAR, PROFITS AND

Waging war—like establishing colonies—impoverishes a nation, but it fantastically enriches a small elite.

According to historian Lewis Mumford, "usurious oligarchies" finance a ruler's "mischievous policies of war," and then live "sumptuously on the profits and loot." The masses, meanwhile, pay the taxes and sacrifice their lives.

In World War I, for example, common soldiers were paid thirty dollars a month, and from that small amount they had to pay six dollars a month for an "insurance policy." Meanwhile, according to Smedly Butler, the same war produced at least 21,000 new American millionaires and billionaires, and that number does not include the profiteers who falsified their tax returns.

WAR (PSYCHOLOGICAL)

Psychological warfare (the term was coined by the Nazis in 1941) is war against the mind.

In the Algerian War (1954-1962), the French used psychological weapons, divided into two types: 1) psychological war (directed against the enemy to undermine his will to resist) and 2) psychological action (directed against the population and the French security forces, to strengthen morale and allegiance and fighting will).

The French called their two techniques "destruction and construction."

WAR, RULES OF

A series of international agreements, most dating from 1859 to 1907, distinguishes war from mere crime.

According to these rules, only official violence on behalf of the state is allowed. Soldiers must fight only in uniform, they must carry their arms openly, and they must obey a commander responsible for them.

Also, soldiers must not violate truces or take up arms again if captured. Civilians must be left alone and, in return, civilians are not supposed to meddle with war.

The rules of war—although meritorious—are often irrational, however. Thus, "dum-dum bullets" are forbidden by the rules of war, but thermonuclear bombs are not!

WAR, STUPIDITY OF

War is imbecilic at many levels. In the Battle of the Somme—a manic bloodbath in World War I—1,200,000 men were killed on both sides and nothing was achieved.

In the American Civil War—a destructive and ruinous conflict— one economic historian has calculated that the money squandered (by both sides) would have been sufficient to purchase the freedom of all the slaves, to provide them with free land, and to pay them a hundred years of back wages.

In Vietnam, the U.S.A. intervened militarily even though no Vietnamese soldier (or guerrilla) had destroyed American property or injured an American. The U.S.A. thought that the war was important to its security, even though Washington, D.C. is closer to the south pole than to Hanoi.

In 1969 the world witnessed the so-called Soccer War. A border dispute turned into a war when El Salvador's soccer team scored a last-minute winning goal against neighboring Honduras in the World Cup. A war began within hours. The struggle would claim three thousand dead and six thousand injured.

On rare occasions, however, rationality can prevail. In 1078, in the Siege of Seville, King Alfonso VI prepared for a siege to expel the Moors. When the Moorish ruler, Al-Mutamid, heard that Alfonso was a chess enthusiast, he sent his chess champion, Ibn-Ammar, to play the king for possession of the city. Ibn-Ammar won the contest and the Castilians—true to their word—withdrew.

WAR, SUPPLY AND

According to Major H. von Dach, the author of *Total Resistance*, regular armies are supplied by factories, warehouses, and depots. Guerrilla units, however, "live on the war" and must steal everything they need.

By World War II, an armored division consumed 100,000 gallons of gasoline daily.

And, as the Nazis discovered in the U.S.S.R., the further an attacker advances, his supply problems grow greater, his forces become weaker, and the environment becomes more hostile.

WAR, TECHNOLOGY AND

When technology is developed, "weaponizing" that technology is the easy part. Building an atomic bomb requires less expertise than building a nuclear power plant.

Historically, advanced technology has sometimes been applied to war with deadly results.

At the Battle of Omdurman in 1898, for example, the British under General Horatio Kitchener used machine guns against the Sudanese. The British lost only forty-three men while destroying an army of 52,000 Sudanese. The British fired 500,000 rounds of ammunition.

Against a clever foe, however, technology is less effective. In the case of the American-Vietnamese War, light infantry, without air power, usually with no artillery support larger than mortars, defeated the United States, the most technologically advanced empire in history.

Regarding military technology, this general rule applies: the simpler the environment, the more effective the technology.

Thus, high-technology weapons are most effective in featureless environments, such as in the air, or at sea, or in desert landscapes. They are least effective in complex environments, such as built-up urban areas.

WAR, TRUTH AND

All belligerents lie during war.

These are the words of John Laurence, a journalist, on the military reports from the Pentagon during the American-Vietnamese War:

> At times, lies were deliberate. Body counts were exaggerated. Civilian dead, wounded, and captured became enemy dead wounded or captured. . . . Details of combat were adjusted to look more favorable to the U.S.A. side. Successful enemy ambushes were not reported. . . . Mistakes of all kinds were unreported. Cover-ups were commonplace.

WAR, TYPES OF

According to Hans Delbruck, there are two types of war: 1) war involving a strategy of annihilation and 2) war involving a strategy of exhaustion.

The first tries to force a decisive battle, and the second uses battle, maneuver, and economic attack to wear down an enemy.

WAR, VICTORY AND

To win in war, innovate in a revolutionary—not evolutionary—manner. And remember that no measure, no matter how original, is effective for long.

That is, of course, if winning a war is really possible. As one observer noted, one can no more win a war than one can win an earthquake.

WARRIOR

A warrior is a belligerent who fights for revenge, for prestige, and for loot. Unlike a soldier, the warrior does not fight for religion or for country.

Always, the warrior's fight is personal. No one fights for him and no one can force him to fight.

Ideally, the warrior indulges in the spirit of fighting without hatred. He knows that men of honor, before proceeding to murder, first exchange greetings.

Warriors, like hunters, never insult or mock the prey that they have killed.

Interestingly, Ludwig von Mises noted that much of the pseudo-Homeric prattle about the virtues of war comes from the pens of physically weak men like Friedrich Nietzsche.

WARSAW GHETTO UPRISING (1943)

A desperate rebellion by Nazi-tormented Jews, the Warsaw Ghetto Uprising began on April 19, 1943 and lasted thirty-seven days.

Under the Nazis, the walled Warsaw ghetto had once held 450,000 Jews. By the spring of 1943, deportations had reduced the number to forty thousand.

Finally, squeezed into an area which measured one thousand yards by three hundred yards, 600 of the Jews revolted. They had only a small number of arms and molotov cocktails.

Jurgen Stroop, a German SS General, counterattacked with 2,090 well-armed men. Stroop bombarded the rebels with artillery, and then sent soldiers and tanks into the enclave.

After the rising had been crushed, the Nazis ordered that there should be no large concentration of Jews anywhere.

WEAPONS

A weapon is a thing designed to harm or damage. Since an "an unarmed man is less well endowed then some herbivores," weapons originated with the first humans.

The first weapon may have been a rock, a club, or a sharpened human bone.

In the modern world, the staple weapon is a massed-produced assault rifle. The rifle costs one one-millionth of the price of a jet fighter.

WEAPONS (AIR POWER)

On Nov 1, 1911—near Tripoli in North Africa—the Italians dropped the first bomb ever unleashed from an airplane. In 1913, Giulio Douhet and Gianni Caproni constructed the first heavy bomber, a three-engine monster. By 1946, the U.S.A. had developed the B-36, the first intercontinental bomber. And by 1957, the Union of Soviet Socialist Republics had constructed the first intercontinental ballistic missile.

Air power has transformed war, making conflict three dimensional. Airplanes have also ended the immunity of civilians, and they have obliterated the distinction between front and rear lines.

Air power is weirdly terrifying to the victims and strangely intoxicating to the pilots. Regarding the pilots, philosopher Bertrand Russell noted that humans experience godlike feelings of power when they can easily and playfully destroy others from an unreachable position on high.

Modern warfare often uses aircraft excessively. During World War II, the Axis powers bombed Malta (122 square miles in size) fourteen thousand times. Meanwhile, Allied bombing destroyed seventy-nine square miles of Germany and 178 square miles of Japan. In the American-Vietnamese War, the U.S.A. dropped 250 pounds of high explosive for every man, woman, and child in that part of southeast Asia.

Paradoxically, as a high-technology weapon, air power is most effective against highly developed countries. In the words of Alexander de Seversky, writing in 1942, "Total war from the air upon an undeveloped country or region is well-nigh futile; it is one of the curious features of the most modern weapon that it is especially effective against the most modern type of civilization."

WEAPONS (AIR POWER), CITIES AND

Avoid cities during air wars. Not only do towns draw attacks, the bombs cause more danger in an urban setting. The collapsing structures and flying debris increase the hazard.

If you must remain in an urban area during an air war, a crowbar is an essential item. If buried alive in the rubble, use the crowbar to tap messages to rescuers. Also, the crowbar can be used to dig through walls to adjoining rooms or even adjoining buildings.

The urban dweller must also keep water, rags, and sand around the house. During bombings, moisten the rags and breath through them. When running through fires, first wrap yourself in wet rags. Use the water and sand to control flames.

WEAPONS (AIR POWER), COUNTER-MEASURES USED BY THE VIETNAMESE

During the American-Vietnamese War, the United States dropped thirty-six tons of bombs for *every* square mile of both North and South Vietnamese territory.

The Vietnamese, however, developed ingenious methods to counter air-power. When America attacked their petroleum reserves, for example, the Vietnamese put the oil in barrels and scattered the barrels around the country.

And when America bombed her villages, the villagers waded into the South China Sea up to their necks for safety.

When facing air power, the Vietnamese applied these rules: 1) they dispersed their forces and assets, 2) they placed their forces and assets in tunnels and foxholes, 3) whenever possible, they intermingled their forces with the civilian population, and 4) they mastered the Soviet technique of the "close embrace."

Regarding the "close embrace," at the Battle of Stalingrad the Red Army was never more than fifty yards from the German soldiers. The idea is that "hugging"—or "close embrace"—makes it difficult for the enemy to employ his air power (and artillery) without killing his own troops.

To neutralize American air assets, the Vietnamese would move extremely close before firing, and they would move even closer when the Americans called in air strikes.

WEAPONS (AIR POWER), DEFENSE AGAINST

To remain invisible to modern aircraft, avoid all targets (such as buildings, vehicles, and tanks) and remain motionless. To neutralize infrared-detection devices, cover yourself in mud, or wrap yourself in space blankets made of aluminum or mylar (space blankets reflect body heat back toward the body).

If caught in the open during an aircraft bomb attack, take refuge in the lowest depression available (this minimizes injury from shrapnel). Also, cover your ears and open your mouth to avoid the effects of concussion.

Remember, low-flying aircraft are vulnerable to small-arms fire. In Rhodesia, guerrillas fired their automatic weapons ahead of an attacking aircraft— making it fly into a stream of lead. The guerrillas fired two hundred yards ahead of jet aircraft and fifty yards ahead of helicopters and propeller-driven airplanes.

WEAPONS (ATOMIC AND THERMONUCLEAR)

A gruesome invention, atomic and thermonuclear weapons involve the human manipulation of the atom. An inversion of genesis, with these weapons man turns matter back into energy.

An atomic bomb is a fission device. A thermonuclear bomb—also called a hydrogen bomb— is a fusion weapon. The yield of the latter is potentially unlimited.

A single thermonuclear weapon can have an explosive yield greater than the total of all explosives ever used in war since gunpowder was invented. And one study suggested that a twenty-megaton weapon could spread heat over five thousand square miles, or an area the size of Connecticut.

In effect, it is now possible to annihilate a small country with a single bomb.

Nikita Khrushchev, the late Soviet leader, predicted that nuclear weapons would make ground forces archaic, expensive, and unnecessary. For him, a nuclear device was "the weapon of the future."

WEAPONS (ATOMIC AND THERMONUCLEAR), CONSTRUCTION OF

If fissile material (highly enriched uranium or plutonium) is available, constructing a bomb is elementary. Indeed, it is theoretically possible to produce a nuclear explosion by dropping two pieces of plutonium on to each other from a suitable height.

The Hiroshima bomb of 1945 was a simple and reliable gun-type weapon. It used an anti-aircraft gun barrel that was 6.5 inches wide, 6 feet long, and weighed 1,000 pounds. A smokeless powder, called cordite (used in conventional artillery), fired a fifty-six -pound highly enriched uranium bullet into a target composed of eight-five pounds of highly enriched uranium.

In 1977, a Princeton undergraduate named John Phillips showed in his senior thesis that he could design a nuclear weapon with publicly available material. He designed a ten-kiloton weapon, an implosion bomb that would use plutonium available from the nuclear power industry. The size of a beach ball, its cost would be 2,000 dollars in 1977 moneys.

To fashion a bomb of mass destruction, one needs only 2.2 pounds of plutonium or 5.5 pounds of enriched uranium.

Although John Phillips' senior thesis was disturbing, he was eclipsed in 1995 by David Hahn, an adolescent boy from Clinton Township, Michigan.

Using radium (from old junkyard radium clocks), americium-241 (a radioactive isotope found in smoke detectors), beryllium, aluminum, and some other ingredients, Hahn formed a makeshift reactor core. He held it together with duct tape!

On June 26, 1995 Hahn—then aged seventeen years—contacted authorities. His makeshift core was really heating up and was producing large amounts of radiation.

A dangerous boy, Hahn had made his first nitroglycerin by the age of fourteen.

WEAPONS (ATOMIC AND THERMONUCLEAR), DEFENSE AGAINST

Atomic and thermonuclear bombs can produce four lethal effects: the blast, the heat, the radiation, and the radioactive fallout.

In addition, the weapon can produce an "electro-magnetic pulse" which will disable cars, cellular telephones, computers, and so forth.

If caught out in the open, take cover behind a hill or lie in a ditch, with your head away from the blast. Cover all exposed skin (if possible, place a wet towel over your nose and mouth), and do not look at the detonation.

Remember, that during tests soldiers in trenches 2,500 yards from ground zero survived.

Tragically, if a person happens to be looking in the direction of a nuclear flash, there is no time to blink. The blast burns away the retina, and the victim will be blinded forever. Over thousands of square miles, pilots will be blinded.

The prudent survivalist will wear an eye patch. If a blast occurs—and he is caught by surprise—at least he will not be totally blind. (In the early days of the cold war, American B-47 bomber pilots were instructed to wear an eye patch in case of a nuclear attack.)

Stay down until the blast wave passes. Remember, after the detonation, it could take thirty seconds or more for the blast wave to arrive.

If you are close enough to see the blast, fallout will arrive in about twenty minutes. Eighty per cent of the fallout will arrive in the first twenty-four hours.

If possible, leave the area. Discard your clothes and shower.

If you cannot leave the area—and no fallout shelter is available—place as much distance as possible between you and the radioactive dust. In a building, go to the corner of the basement. In a large building, take refuge in the center of the middle floors, equidistant from the dust on the roof and the dust on the ground.

WEAPONS (ATOMIC AND THERMONUCLEAR), FALLOUT SHELTERS AND

Fallout refers to the dangerous radioactive particles dispersed over a wide area after a nuclear explosion.

A fallout shelter—a structure which is part foxhole and part bunker—is essential in a thermonuclear age.

In Switzerland, the law requires the structures in private homes. In Marxist Albania, the dictator Enver Hoxha built 700,000 concrete bunkers, or one for every four people.

In the Union of Soviet Socialist Republics, under Ramenki, a suburb of Moscow, the U.S.S.R. built the most elaborate shelter ever constructed. It could protect thirty thousand members of the elite for several months. Completed in the 1970's—and maintained by the secret police—the refuge had an underground railroad to transport people into the shelter.

Elsewhere in the world, individuals will have to build their own shelters. This includes people in the United States.

With a fallout shelter, the three principles are shielding, distance, and time.

Regarding shielding, bricks, concrete, books, or earth may be used, and the more used the better. At least two feet of concrete or three feet of earth will stop gamma rays (the most lethal form of radiation).

Regarding distance, the farther you are from the fallout, the better. In a house, use the corner of a basement. In a high rise structure, the center of a middle floor is best, halfway between the fallout on the roof and the fallout on the ground.

Regarding time, fallout is most dangerous within the first two weeks. After 48 hours, radioactive fallout diminishes to one one-hundredth of its original strength. After two weeks, radioactive fallout diminishes to one ten-thousandth of its original level.

If someone is close enough to see an atomic or nuclear blast, the radioactive fallout will start arriving in twenty minutes. In other words, he has twenty minutes to reach a shelter.

The amount of fallout that eventually arrives will depend on the location of the blast. An air burst—a detonation at eight hundred to sixteen hundred feet—will produce almost no radioactive fallout.

A ground-burst, however, will produce a great deal. The wind will carry the fallout in an elliptical pattern about two hundred miles long and fifty miles wide.

An underwater blast of an atomic or nuclear weapon is especially "dirty." The detonation will produce a massive plume of water followed by a radioactive mist. (In a 1946 test, an underwater nuclear blast destroyed only a few test ships, but the radioactivity contaminated more than a hundred. Despite vigorous washing, the ships could not be decontaminated.)

WEAPONS (ATOMIC AND THERMONUCLEAR), FALLOUT SHELTERS AND SUPPLIES

To be effective, a fallout shelter needs to be stocked with water, food, and weapons.

The shelter needs at *least* a two-week supply of water. At a *minimum* level, an adult requires two and one-half quarts of water per day.

For food, the shelter should contain four airtight plastic containers filled with wheat, sugar (honey), powdered milk, and salt respectively. A year's supply of these items can be purchased for one-half ounce of gold.

Properly stored, the powdered milk will last a long time, the wheat has almost unlimited shelf life, and the sugar and salt will last forever.

The shelter should also include canned foods (such as meats, vegetables, soups, and fruits), a supply of multi-vitamins, and (as a last resort) bags of dried dog food. (Dry dog food is cheap, it does not spoil, and a hundred-pound sack contains as many calories as a ton of potatoes.)

For defense, the shelter should contain a shotgun and a small .22-caliber handgun. Note that five hundred rounds of .22 ammunition weighs 3.5 pounds and fits inside a pocket. Five hundred rounds of .357-magnum ammunition, in contrast, weighs thirty-five pounds and requires a briefcase.

Why are weapons required? Remember, as one survivalist noted, "The homeless, the starving, the nuclear sick, and the mobs of survivors will be roaming the countryside, looking for two things, food and loot, and someone to blame."

WEAPONS (ATOMIC AND THERMONUCLEAR), RADIATION SICKNESS AND

Radiation sickness—caused by receiving a high dose of radioactivity in a short time—is a stealth weapon. Radiation cannot be seen, smelled, felt, or tasted by humans, but exposure may cause sickness and death.

If a person receives a *lethal* dose of radiation, there is no known cure and no way to reverse its course. Children—because of their small size and rapid metabolism— are more at risk than adults.

The symptoms of radiation sickness (in order of frequency) are nausea, vomiting, diarrhea, loss of appetite, malaise, loss of hair, a tendency to bleed, and susceptibility to infections.

If the victim remains symptom-free for more than twenty-four hours he probably received a low dose and will require little or no immediate medical attention.

At Hiroshima in 1945, Japanese doctors observed radiation sickness directly. They noticed that some people who seemed uninjured died days later. Symptoms resembled an overdose of X-rays.

The physicians also noticed that those who remained quiet after the bomb detonated were less likely to become sick than those who were active. They also observed that radiation sickness was not communicable.

WEAPONS (ATOMIC AND THERMONUCLEAR), STATE AND

According to Martin van Creveld, the invention of nuclear weapons will ultimately undermine the state.

With nuclear weapons, two orthodox states cannot survive at war, and a "community which cannot safeguard the lives of members . . . is unlikely either to command their loyalty or survive for long."

Indeed, according to Martin Van Creveld, "Nuclear weapons work against geographical distinctions of any kind." If armed units and the political units that field them are to survive and fight, they will have to become intermingled with each other and the civilian population. Once intermingled, battles will be replaced by skirmishes, bombings, and massacres. Military bases will be replaced by hideouts and caches. Geographical sovereignty will be replaced by a kind of population control achieved by a mixture of propaganda and terror.

WEAPONS (BIOLOGICAL)

Biological weapons are weapons using viruses, bacteria, and fungi to kill or injure. A "mass-casualty weapon," they cause death and injury without harming property.

The ultimate stealth weapon, biological weapons can be released silently and invisibly. Since the agents are odorless and colorless, the attack would not be noticed until people fall ill.

"Indeed," to use the words of one authority, "it is doubtful that most biological attacks would even be recognized for what they are. Even if it could be proven with certainty that the outbreak of a particular disease was not a natural occurrence and instead was deliberately instigated, it would be almost impossible to pinpoint the exact source."

In some respects, biological weapons are the most horrible weapons of mass destruction. The Ebola virus, for example, has a kill rate up to 90 percent. Every orifice bleeds—even the eyes fill with blood that runs down the cheeks–and the skin becomes like soft bread that can be spread apart with the fingers.

With some agents, the lethal dose is shockingly small. In the case of parrot fever, only one-tenth of a microgram is required to infect the victim. Theoretically, distributing a lethal dose to each square meter of the earth's surface would require merely fifty tons of material (a cube thirteen feet on each side).

Often viewed as modern weapons, biological weapons are quite old. Jehovah, for example, sent a plague against the Egyptians which appears to be anthrax (see Exodus 9:16).

In the 14th century—at the siege of Kaffa—the Tartars catapulted plague cadavers into the city to spread the "Black Death" to their enemies.

During the so-called "Age of Reason," the British distributed small-pox-infected blankets to native Americans.

During the era World War II, the Japanese Empire disseminated millions of fleas, infected with plague, over Chinese cities. The Japanese also contaminated Chinese water and food supplies with several agents.

And Detachment 731—the secret unit of the Japanese Empire—even considered high-altitude balloons to carry plague-infected rats to North America.

During the Korean War, China and North Korea accused the United States of using biological weapons. The American government denied the charges.

WEAPONS (BIOLOGICAL), DEFENSE AGAINST

To defend against biological weapons, understand there are four ways to dispense bio-weapons: 1) through the air, 2) contamination of food or water, 3) contact with infected persons or animals (such as rats, birds, or insects), and 4) touching objects that have been contaminated.

The best defense against biological weapons is isolation. Against small-pox and plague, for example, lock your doors and remain alone. The death rate from smallpox is 30 percent, and smallpox can be passed through the air to another person.

Surgical masks and goggles are useful, and good hygiene is important. The body—as well as anything touching the body—should be thoroughly washed. To decontaminate, it is important to have a supply of soap, water, chlorine bleach, and pure alcohol.

For protection, avoid the bodily secretions of others, including their blood, saliva, sexual fluids, and bodily wastes. Most viruses cannot survive outside the host, but some, like the cold virus, live long enough to be dangerous.

Note that sunlight kills most—but not all—biological agents. Alcohol kills living organisms, but not spores. Chlorine bleach is also a useful disinfectant.

To decontaminate a landscape, use sodium hydroxide (soda lye).

During a serious attack, all food must be cooked and all water must be boiled. Nearly all microorganisms are killed by heat.

Beware of disease-carrying vectors, such as insects, rodents, other humans, dead bodies, and contaminated material.

Parrot fever, for example, can be spread from human to human. There is no known vaccine against it.

Be especially prudent around cadavers. The bodies of all anthrax victims must be destroyed because corpses can generate new spores. Oddly, although you cannot contract anthrax from a sick person, you can contract it from the decaying corpse of an anthrax victim.

WEAPONS (BIOLOGICAL), MANUFACTURE OF

Called the "poor man's bomb," biological weapons yield more death per dollar, franc, or ruble than chemical or nuclear weapons. Indeed, biological weapons can be built for the equivalent of one ounce of gold.

And—since small amounts of bio-agent seed culture can multiply into large quantities in two weeks—this weapon is especially economical.

Of all the biological weapons, the ones involving bacteria are the simplest to produce. Viruses, which must be grown on living tissue, are difficult to cultivate and are more perishable than bacterial agents.

Bacteria, however, can be grown in an artificial medium using a method similar to that of the brewing industry. With a beer fermenter, a gas mask, a protein-based culture, and a plastic over-garment, a person can cultivate trillions of lethal bacteria at little risk to himself.

Indeed, during World War II, the British made anthrax cakes and the protective procedures they used were no more sophisticated than rubber gloves, aprons with detachable sleeves, and vigorous washing.

And, since anthrax is carried by plant-eating animals, the bacterium causing anthrax is easily found in soil worldwide.

WEAPONS (CHEMICAL)

Chemical weapons use non-living chemicals to kill or injure. Effective against humans and animals, they do not harm property.

Chemical weapons are cheap, easy to manufacture, and are effective in the confined, built-up areas of a modern city. Chemical agents may be solid, liquid, or gas, but most are delivered as aerosolized liquids.

Chemical agents have limitations: they do not work when it is freezing, they do not last when it is hot, and high winds weaken their effectiveness by spreading them too thinly and too quickly. Flat areas become decontaminated more rapidly than rough areas.

A chemical attack is most effective in an enclosed space (such as a subway, a shopping mall, or a building). If the weapon is used outdoors, it is most lethal during a "temperature inversion." (A temperature inversion occurs when the weather suddenly warms up after a cold period.)

The first real chemical attack in combat occurred on April 22, 1915. The Germans attacked with chlorine gas, killing five thousand and wounding ten thousand. Two days later, another gas attack was stopped by soldiers breathing through cloths dipped in urine or bicarbonate of soda.

In 1917 mustard gas (sulfur mustard), a yellowish, oily liquid, was introduced. Typically sprayed at night, it evaporates the next morning in the sun, producing a vapor that attacks the lungs. In a sheltered location, mustard gas may persist for weeks.

All together, about twenty-five "poison gases" were used in World War I. After the war, the British used chemical weapons against the Russians and the Afghans in 1919, and the Italians used "mustard gas" against the Ethiopians in 1935 and 1936.

The Germans invented nerve gas in 1936. Odorless, colorless, and tasteless, nerve agents disrupt the nervous system that makes the body function. Harmful on the skin, nerve agents are deadliest in the lungs.

Symptoms of a nerve agent include a sudden headache, dimness of vision, runny nose, drooling, difficulty breathing, tightness in the chest, nausea, stomach cramps, and a twitching of the skin where the liquid is.

WEAPONS (CHEMICAL), DEFENSE AGAINST

Although chemical weapons are classified as "weapons of mass destruction," they are actually "area denial" weapons. Leave the area (be careful to go upwind) and you leave the risk.

If you cannot evacuate, however, there are measures that can be taken.

First, understand that chemical weapons are not gases. They are vapors and airborne particles. To be effective they must contaminate you—or your lungs—in sufficient quantities.

Since chemical agents are heavier than air, the safest place is above street level. The higher the location, the better it is. Chemical agents will gather in low places, like basements, underground garages, or ditches.

If you are inside a house or an apartment, take refuge inside a windowless inner room. Seal off the room with plastic sheeting, aluminum foil, and duct tape. Turn off the furnace or the air conditioner.

To detect the presence of chemical weapons, the best method is the oldest. Miners have traditionally used birds to detect poisons in mines, and in 1995—when the Japanese police raided the Aum Shinrikyo compound— the police carried canaries to detect chemical agents.

Technology has created devices which register the presence of choking, blister, and blood agents, but they are susceptible to "false positives," and they react to antifreeze, body lotion, and perfume.

WEAPONS (CHEMICAL), MANUFACTURE OF

Of all weapons of mass destruction, the materials and equipment used to produce chemical weapons are the easiest to acquire.

To make chlorine gas, a World War I chemical weapon, one needs to mix only two ingredients sold by any supermarket.

WEAPONS (EXPLOSIVE)

Gunpowder, invented in eighth-century China, is the most ancient explosive. When fire is added to unconfined "black powder," the gunpowder burns with a blue flame. If fire is added to "black powder" that is confined in a container, the latter will rupture violently, producing a blast.

Later explosives include nitroglycerin, invented in 1846, and dynamite (which is safer to handle), invented in 1867. Trinitrotoluene (TNT) was developed in 1904, and ammonium nitrate-fuel oil explosive, a favorite of terrorists, was developed in 1955.

More recently, TATP (triacertone triperoxide), which can be made from hydrogen peroxide (from a pharmacy), acetone (from a hardware store), and a small amount of hydrochloric acid (or sulfuric acid), was developed. Often used by insurgents, it is dangerous to make. At least forty Palestinian "freedom fighters" have killed themselves trying to manufacture it.

WEAPONS (EXPLOSIVE), DEFENSE AGAINST

Note that even small explosive weapons—such as grenades—can kill at one hundred feet.

If you cannot find a hole or a trench, fall on your belly, your head away from the blast. Open your mouth and cover your ears to protect against concussion.

WEAPONS (EXPLOSIVE), MANUFACTURE OF

Conventional explosives can be manufactured from ordinary agricultural and industrial chemicals.

To attack the World Trade Towers in 1993, for example, operatives constructed a bomb from commercially available materials, including lawn fertilizer (urea nitrate) and diesel fuel. The bomb cost only four hundred dollars to build, but it created a crater 180 feet across and six stories deep.

The most basic explosive, gunpowder, consists of seven parts potassium nitrate (saltpeter), one part sulfur, and two parts charcoal. Grind each into fine powder and mix together.

WEAPONS (EXPLOSIVE), SHRAPNEL AND

An important aspect of modern explosive weapons is shrapnel. First used by the Chinese (who loaded bombs with pieces of porcelain and scrap iron), the technique was rediscovered in 1784 by Lieutenant Henry Shrapnel, who loaded bombs with gunpowder and scrap iron.

By the time of the American-Vietnamese War, the United States had designed the fiendish "plastic fragmentation bombs." These anti-personnel weapons cause hideous injuries with plastic shrapnel. Virtually untreatable—the fragments in the body cannot be detected by X-rays—they cause medical complications and excruciating pain.

WEAPONS (FIREARMS)

A medieval invention, firearms are omnipresent in the modern world.

The best commandos—hired killers trained and employed by the state—can, with their backs to the target, draw, turn, fire, and hit a target in one second.

When hunting humans, these commandos fire three shots per kill. They will make one head shot and two torso shots.

With any firearm, prudent people always leave the first chamber empty. This precaution reduces accidents, and if someone seizes your gun and tries to use it against you, his first shot will abort.

WEAPONS (FIREARMS), MAFIA SILENCERS AND

The Mafia has used great ingenuity to silence weapons. They discovered, for example, that the rubber nipple of a baby bottle—when fastened to the muzzle of a 22-caliber automatic pistol—provides fair suppression. Also, by wrapping the nozzle of an automatic pistol in a pillow, a gunman has a cheap silencer.

Even more unusual, Joe "the Animal" Barboza, a Mafia killer, managed to silence an M1 Garand rifle. Although experts believed that the noise of such a weapon could not be suppressed, Barboza used a truck muffler!

WEAPONS (FIREARMS), SILENCERS AND

Silencers for guns are more accurately called "suppressors." They have been restricted by American federal law since 1934.

It is impossible to silence a revolver (sound and flash escape through the open space around the cylinder), but a silencer will suppress *some* of the noise of an automatic pistol, if the pistol fires subsonic ammunition (supersonic bullets will produce a secondary noise).

Although the Americans believed that it was impossible, the Soviet K.G.B. developed a gun that was *completely* silent. The weapon used compressed air.

WEAPONS, HIDDEN

Hiding a weapon requires imagination. During the "Cold War," the Soviet K.G.B. invented a single-shot pistol that could be hidden in the rectum!

In Japan, a seductive female assassin kept a poisoned hairpin in her elaborate coiffure. When a man let down his guard, the assassin struck.

In India, the Thuggee, who killed by throttling, openly displayed their weapon of choice, a scarf made from silk. Innocuous in the hands of most people, the scarf was deadly in the skillful hands of the Thuggee.

In prison, where the mere possession of weapons is a crime, inmates make improvised blackjacks by putting two batteries in a sock. When kept apart, the batteries and the sock are perfectly legal. When the batteries are put inside a sock—an action which requires a few seconds—a lethal weapon is created.

WEAPONS (HIGH-TECHNOLOGY)

High-technology weapons—the products of depraved science—are also called weapons of mass destruction. Now deployed against humans, Baron Giulio Evola noted that "such systems could once have been devised only to exterminate germs and insects."

High-technology weapons are produced by perverted biology (biological weapons), perverted chemistry (chemical weapons), and perverted physics (nuclear weapons). Some day perverted geological weapons of mass destruction (causing earthquakes, volcanoes, hurricanes, and other Earth changes) may be available.

WEAPONS (HIGH-TECHNOLOGY), DEFENSE AGAINST

During World War II, the U.S.A. could carry out global missions free from enemy reprisal. But modern high-technology weapons are so precise and so powerful they have changed the nature of war.

Because such weapons allow an enemy to kill anyone, at any time, in any place, it is madness to fight traditional "battles," establish bases, and defend territorial units.

To survive against high-technology weapons, according to Martin Van Creveld, "armed units" must resort to "low-intensity" conflict. They must use extreme dispersion of forces, they must mix with the civilian population to become indistinguishable from the civilian environment, and they must intermingle with enemy forces.

Possibly, a future world war could resemble a worldwide Maoist guerrilla movement.

WEAPONS (IMPROVISED)

Humans can turn virtually anything into a weapon. Not only does every ordinary home have something to cut or stab or bludgeon with, but more ingenious devices can be fabricated. The *Improvised Munitions Handbook* (1969) of the United States army, for example, describes an "animal blood bomb" made out of a mixture of animal blood, gasoline, and common household items such as Epson salts and sugar.

During the Algerian war, insurgents placed a thousand match heads in a can or tin. Screws were taped to the exterior of the can for extra shrapnel. A wick was added, and the activist had an instant bomb.

To create an improvised wick, the Algerians drew a glue-soaked string through granulated match heads (or black powder) until the string was completely covered. They wrapped the treated string with cellophane tape.

Against the French and the Americans, the Vietnamese guerrillas used sharpened "punji" sticks smeared with feces. When hidden at the bottom of a concealed pit, such stakes inflict horrible wounds—even death.

If the victim survived the impaling, the excrement could cause infection and death.

WEAPONS, NON-LETHAL

The most effective non-lethal weapon is violence against property, especially if the violence is used with imagination.

During the 1871 Paris Commune rebellion, for example, when the defeat of the radical workers became inevitable, the workers burned the city's records. By this final act of defiance, the workers erased mountains of debt and the criminal records of fellow citizens.

Sometimes, however, a simple protest may convey a message. This may range for hurling butyric acid (a "stink bomb"), to imitating Jean-Paul Sartre, who declined to accept a Nobel Prize for literature in 1964.

WEAPONS (NON-LETHAL) HANDS AND FEET AS

To incapacitate without killing, direct a blow against your opponent's groin, solar plexus, or knee cap.

WEAPONS, NON-VIOLENT

According to Sun Tzu, "to subdue the enemy without violence is the supreme excellence."

Non-violent weapons include various forms of civil disobedience, such as the general strike or the boycott.

WEAPONS (POISON)

Poison is a substance that causes "non-violent" death or injury to a living organism. A stealth weapon, the best poisons produce symptoms that suggest another (less suspicious) cause of death.

Traditionally the weapon of the weak against the strong, poison has been used against oppressive masters (by slaves) and burdensome husbands (by wives).

Poison is typically administered through food and drink. Since cooking degrades poison, it is placed in salads or cold drinks, but not always. Julia Agrippina, the sister and lover of Caligula, and the mother of Nero, murdered her husband (and uncle), the Emperor Claudius, by putting deadly mushrooms in his stew. After Claudius was dead, Agrippina had him proclaimed a god.

Poison has also been conveyed through clothing, tobacco products, holy water, communion wine, and other imaginative ways.

Murderers have placed poison on the nipples of prostitutes (to kill a customer) or a mother (to kill a baby).

Poison has been added to aftershave lotion, so that it would enter through the broken skin caused by shaving.

Poison has been placed in toothpaste (the United States tried to put radioactive isotopes in the toothpaste of an African leader) and in enemas (cardinals tried to place poison in the enema of Pope Leo X).

WEAPONS (POISON), DEFENSE AGAINST

Although some poisons are absolutely lethal, sometimes the effects can be neutralized.

The best first aid for any swallowed poison is to administer one or two tablespoons of activated charcoal dissolved in water or juice. Activated charcoal is very porous and can absorb poisons and render them harmless. The poison—absorbed by the charcoal—can then pass safely through the intestines.

A convenient form of activated charcoal, available in virtually any household, is "burnt toast."

WEAPONS (POISON), MANUFACTURE OF

Many poisons are easily manufactured.

In the "Old South," disgruntled slaves made nicotine poison, which is as deadly as cyanide or curare, by soaking dried tobacco in water overnight. They boiled the liquid until a sticky syrup formed–then dried the syrup in the open air.

The final product—a brown mass—contained concentrated nicotine. A few drops—placed in the food of the master—were deadly.

Slaves used a similar process to extract poison from the oleander plant or the water hemlock.

WEAPONS (POISON), UNIVERSALITY OF

According to Paracelsus, the legendary physician, "All substances are poison. There is none which is not a poison. The right dose differentiates a poison from a remedy."

In the twentieth century, one Brazilian bandit (named Virgulino Ferreira da Silva) killed a man by forcing him to eat a liter of salt. Salt, harmless in small quantities, is lethal in such a dose.

WEAPONS (QUANTITIES NEEDED)

According to American estimates, to produce same harvest of death in a square mile of territory, it would require the following quantities of material: 705,000 pounds of fragmentation cluster-bomb material, 7,000 pounds of mustard gas, 1,700 pounds of nerve gas, 11 pounds of material from a fission weapon, 3 ounces of "botulinal toxin type A," or half an ounce of anthrax spores.

WEAPONS (RADIOLOGICAL)

A radiological weapon—also called a "dirty weapon"—is a conventional weapon packaged with radioactive materials.

A radiological weapon is an economic weapon and a fear weapon. It would kill few people when detonated, but the cancer-causing dust it produces would contaminate the target area for years.

Unlike the fallout from a nuclear explosion, the radioactive materials in a "dirty weapon" do NOT decay rapidly.

Plutonium, for example, has a half-life of 24,000 years. Once in the environment, it stays.

Almost immediately, business activity in the targeted area would come to a halt, real estate values would plummet, and segments of the city would have to be abandoned or demolished.

Although a true "dirty bomb" has never been used in war, Iraq tested a one-ton radiological device in 1987.

And other countries, such as the United States, Russia, and Israel, have deployed "dirty munitions" which contain "depleted uranium." Known as uranium-238, "depleted uranium" is a waste product from power-generating nuclear reactors.

Used in armor-piercing shells, the depleted uranium breaks up and vaporizes on contact. Each shell has three to ten pounds of nuclear waste, making a little "dirty weapon" which contaminates the environment indefinitely.

In the first "Gulf War" alone, the United States fired 944,000 "depleted uranium" rounds. This littered the "theater of operations" with at least 320 metric tons of "nuclear waste." Even more "dirty munitions" were fired in the Second Gulf War.

WEAPONS (RADIOLOGICAL), CONSTRUCTION OF

The simplest nuclear device to make, construction of a radiological device is elementary. A truck bomb detonated at a nuclear facility, for example, could create a "dirty bomb."

And, detonating a few sticks of dynamite in a trash can of powdered nuclear waste also makes a "dirty bomb."

A measuring cup of plutonium attached to a conventional bomb could make a city uninhabitable. Plutonium is one of most toxic substances known.

The bomber could also use cobalt-60, cesium-137, or strontium-90.

WEAPONS (RADIOLOGICAL) DEFENSE AGAINST

If a radiological bomb is detonated, leave the contaminated area immediately. After an attack, remember to avoid all government "officials." They will try to quarantine you.

When you reach a place of safety, abandon your vehicle, shower with warm water, and change your clothing. For safety, bury the clothes and shoes you were wearing.

Remember, you must never return to the targeted area. To decontaminate a city, washing would not be sufficient. Indeed, washing would create massive amounts of toxic, contaminated water.

Also, some substances used in a radiological weapon—such as radio-active cesium chloride powder —chemically bind to asphalt, concrete and glass. Decontamination would require abrasives and chemical solvents.

WEAPONS TECHNOLOGY, POLITICAL FORMS AND

According to historian Carroll Quigley, political forms are a product of the prevailing technology of violence. In other words, easy-to-use weapons—like the handgun— lead to individualism and democracy, while difficult-to-use weapons that require professional expertise—such as armor, swords, and modern technological weapons—lead to a tightly knit professional soldiery surrounding despots.

WEAPONS (TOXIN)

A toxin is a poison created by a living organism. Toxins themselves are non-living chemicals. More than four hundred toxins are known.

In the 1930's, the Japanese researched toxin weapons. During World War II, the British allegedly used a toxin to kill Reinhard Heydrich, a Nazi leader.

As weapons, toxins are usually deployed as aerosols. They should be thought of as chemical weapons, since toxins are poisons—they do not infect.

Botulinum—gram for gram—is most the poisonous toxin known. Only eight ounces of this substance—properly distributed—could eradicate the entire human race.

Since the botulinum toxin has no odor or taste, a Botulinum aerosol attack would be invisible.

WEAPONS (TOXIN), DEFENSE AGAINST

Toxin weapons are different from microbial bio-weapons because toxin weapons are non-living. They will poison anyone directly exposed, but they will not reproduce themselves in the victim.

Surgical masks, gloves, and goggles are effective defenses, but the best defense is to flee the contaminated area.

WEAPONS (TOXIN), MANUFACTURE OF

The organism that produces the botulinum toxin is founds in soils world-wide. A shovel of earth from any backyard probably contains enough bacteria to start the production of toxic weapons.

WHITE ROSE

The White Rose movement, which began in 1942, was an anti-Nazi group at the University of Munich. Composed of Hans Scholl, his sister Sophie Scholl, their friend Christopher Probst, and Professor Kurt Hub, they circulated anti-Hitler pamphlets, claiming that "our present 'state' is the dictatorship of evil." All four were arrested and beheaded.

Curiously, the philosopher Martin Heidegger and two Nobel prize winners in physics supported the Nazis.

WILDE, OSCAR (1854-1900)

An amoral literary rebel, celebrated for his one novel, *The Portrait of Dorian Gray*, Oscar Wilde believed that beauty has the "divine right of sovereignty."

Beauty, according to Wilde, "makes princes of those who have it," and it has a perfect right to be cruel.

In 1895 a British court sentenced Wilde to two years hard labor for "committing acts of gross indecency with other male persons."

WILDNESS

According to Henry David Thoreau, what is wildest is most alive.

A Scythian named Anacharsis—described by Herodotus—said that "the wildest animals" are the bravest of all living beings, "for they alone died willingly for their freedom."

WOMEN, AS TERRORISTS

Voluptuous and savage—with a beatific smile—the ultimate terrorist is a woman.

In the nineteenth century, about one-fourth of all Russian political terrorists were women. In the twentieth century, the German terror group, the Red Army Faction (also called the Baader-Meinoff Gang), had more women than men. (Thirteen of its twenty-two core members were female.)

Perhaps the ultimate female terror group was Red Zora, an ultra-feminist organization that recruited only women. Red Zora was dedicated to ending patriarchy, sexism, and racism.

Red Zora carried out hundreds of attacks between 1974 and 1995—bombing courthouses, the cars of landlords, pornography shops, corporate buildings, and other targets. While conducting their attacks, Red Zora carefully avoided inflicting injuries.

WOMEN, EQUALITY OF

Mary Wollstonecraft was the first person to declare the equality of women in a complete form. In *A Vindication of the Rights of Women*, published in 1792, Wollstonecraft asserted the equality of the sexes intellectually and morally, and demanded equal access to education and employment.

In 1974—in the Family Code of Communist Cuba—sex roles were equalized by law. The code ordered the husband and the wife to share housework.

WOMEN, FERTILITY OF

As De Sade pointed out in *Philosophy in the Bedroom*, "out of a hundred years of life the sex destined to produce cannot do so more than seven years."

Since a woman can conceive children only a few days each month—and ovulation ceases about thirty years after puberty—De Sade's estimate is correct.

In traditional societies, it is interesting to note, post-menstrual women are often allowed to indulge in promiscuity.

WOMEN, INFERIORITY OF

Several misogynists have proclaimed the inferiority of women.

According to St. Paul (see 1 Corinthians, chapter 11), "Neither was the man created for the woman; but the woman for the man."

According to St Augustine, "man was made to rule, woman to obey."

The Marquis de Sade declared: "Why! Were it not Nature's intention that one of the sexes tyrannize over the other, would she not have created them equally strong?"

Charles Darwin, the noted biologist, believed that the female brain is less highly evolved than the male. Oddly, even when accounting for the difference in body size, a woman's brain is 10 percent smaller than a man's.

And, according to Lord Chesterfield, women "are only children of large growth." "A man of sense," argued Chesterfield, "only trifles with them, plays with them, humors and flatters them, as he does an engaging child; but he neither consults them, nor trusts them in serious matters."

WOMEN, REPRESSION OF

According to Theodore Besterman, the author of the 1934 work *Men Against Women*, the "primitive's" fear of the female is due to the belief that human qualities can be transmitted through contact.

Since female inferiority is assumed, primitive societies keep women subordinate and marginalized and separate so that female "weakness" will not contaminate the men.

WOMEN, SEDUCTION OF

According to Theophrastus, a pupil of Aristotle, a beautiful woman attracts lovers, but an ugly woman is easily seduced.

Curiously, in ancient Athens seduction was considered a worse crime than rape. Seduction, the Athenians reasoned, corrupts the mind, whereas rape corrupts only the body.

WOMEN, SUPERIORITY OF

According to the Hindus, man is the master of woman—except during sexual intercourse—when he becomes her slave.

Cato, a Roman writer, issued this warning to men about women: "The moment they begin to be your equals, they will be your superiors."

And Tacitus, a Roman historian, said that obeying a woman is worse than slavery.

WORK

According to Ragnar Redbeard, the author of *Might is Right or the Survival of the Fittest*, "Hard, continuous, methodical labor destroys courage, saps vitality, and demoralizes character. It tames and subdues men, just as it tames and subdues the wild steer or the young colt."

To the ancient Greeks, manual labor was intrinsically bad. The Greek word for work was *ponos*. Meaning "toil," *ponos* meant or implied "pain, punishment, and sorrow."

At entrance of Auschwitz, the notorious concentration camp, was this slogan: "Work Shall Make You Free."

Friedrich Nietzsche issued this recommendation: "You I advise not to work but to fight."

WORLD, END OF

Commenting on the annihilation at the end, Jean Baudrillard made this observation:

Imagine the amazing good fortune of the generation that gets to see the end of the world. This is as marvelous as being there at the beginning. How could one not wish for that with all one's heart? How could one not lend one's feeble resources to bringing it about?

"WORSE-THAN-LETHAL" INJURIES

A "worse-than-lethal" injury leaves the victim permanently disabled and dependent on others. In its most horrific form, a worse-than-lethal injury leaves the victim permanently disfigured.

In 1014, Basil II, the Byzantine emperor, blinded fifteen thousand Bulgarian prisoners. He left every hundredth man with one eye to lead the others home to Bulgaria.

In World War II, the Nazis deployed special anti-personnel mines that were designed to castrate rather than kill.

WOUNDS, IMMEDIATE CARE OF

Have you been stabbed or shot?

Remain calm. Movement and panic cause your heart to beat faster, making you bleed faster.

If stabbed, leave the knife in the wound. This plugs the hole and helps staunch blood flow. Keep pressure on the wound. It hurts, but pain never killed anyone. Loss of blood kills.

If possible, use ice. Ice helps stop the flow of blood.

WRATH OF GOD

A "counter-terror" organization, the "Wrath of God" was created by Israel after the massacre of Israeli Olympic athletes in Munich in 1972.

A form of "dirty war," the "Wrath of God" dispatched ultra-secret killers around the world to track and kill terrorists.

Initially successful, the unit was "formally dissolved" in 1973 after the 'Wrath of God" mistakenly murdered Achmed Bouchiki, a Moroccan waiter working in a restaurant in Norway.

The Norwegian government prosecuted six members of the unit.

WU HOU (625-705)

A former concubine who became a tyrant, the Empress Wu Hou ruled China during the T'ang dynasty.

As empress, Wu Hou ordered government officials and visiting dignitaries to pay homage by performing cunnilingus on her. Euphemistically, the ritual was called the "licking of the lotus stamen."

YAKUZA

A violent conspiratorial group, the Yakuza of Japan are one of the most powerful organized crime groups on the planet.

Originally folk heroes fighting evil landlords in the seventeenth century, the Yakuza evolved into traditional gangsters in the nineteenth century, when they took control of the standard vices, such as prostitution, gambling, liquor distribution, and entertainment.

In the modern period, the Yakuza have become a force in Japanese politics (they played a role in the assassination of two prime ministers and two finance ministers.) They have also become a major force in legitimate Japanese business, such as construction.

Much larger than the Sicilian Mafia, there were already 180,000 Yakuza by 1963, making them larger than the Japanese army.

In the 1960's—under the influence of American films—the Yakuza began the custom of wearing dark glasses, expensive dark suits, white shirts, black shoes, and short hair.

YEZIDISM

The followers of Yezidism, who call themselves the Dasni or the Dasin, live in Kurdistan and elsewhere. Unlike the rest of mankind, they believe that they are descended from Adam alone.

Viewing themselves as unique, no one is allowed to join the Yezidis. A person must be born into the movement.

The Yezidis have their own scriptures, which consist of a *Book of Revelation* and a *Black Book*. The latter contains the Yezidi version of Genesis.

The Yezidis teach that Satan—whose name must never be pronounced—rules our world. God, they believe, is passive.

They believe that a good god will forgive no matter how they regard him. It is the evil one—euphemistically called the Peacock Angel— whose favor they must secure.

Scholars assert that this religion dates back at least to Sheikh Adi, who died in 1161.

YOUTH

Young people—individuals between the time of puberty and marriage—make the most effective rebels, revolutionaries, guerrillas, terrorists, and suicide attackers.

Filled with fanaticism, the young doubt everything but desperately want to believe in something. If the young can be inflamed by a cause or an ideology, they are ideal operatives.

Muslim extremists often use boys aged fourteen or fifteen years for dangerous missions. Boys are less likely to ask questions and are less likely to attract attention.

YOUTH, FEAR AND

According to Carl Jung, while the old fear death, the young fear life.

YUSUPOV, PRINCE FELIX (1887-1967)

A resourceful survivor, Prince Felix Yusupov (Youssoupov) was a notorious dandy. Twenty-nine-years old in 1916, Yusupov was the heir to Russia's largest fortune—and married to the niece of the tsar—when he supervised the murder of Grigori Rasputin.

For his crime, Yusupov was exiled for a few months.

Later, Prince Yusupov fled Russia during the Revolution with the clothes on his back, two paintings by Rembrandt, a string of black pearls once owned by Catherine the Great, and hundreds of gemstones.

Yusupov lived to an advanced age.

ZIP GUNS

Improvised firearms are called "zip guns." Easily built, they are used by prisoners and fugitives.

To make a zip gun, the fabricator must create a controlled explosion in a tube. Gases will escape in the direction of least resistance, carrying a projectile.

Prisoners manufacture zip guns from a length metal pipe (or a plastic pipe, reinforced with duct tape). The pipe is open at only one end, with a small hole bored in the closed end for a fuse. Prisoners insert granulated match heads (the propellant), then some wadding (to keep the powder in place), then the bullet (nuts and bolts, small stones, or pieces of tin can be used), and finally more wadding (to keep the bullet in place).

When using a zip gun, prisoners wear thick gloves and protective glasses—they hold the device far from their bodies—they place a barrier between themselves and the gun—and they hold the weapon as close to the target as possible. Prudent people always have a back-up weapon—just in case the zip gun misfires.

ZOMBI

A zombi is a soulless husk deprived of freedom.

Postscript

The human race has a savage past and will have a violent future. Some day, when visitors arrive on our little planet, may they find more than bones, pottery shards, and nuclear waste.

BIBLIOGRAPHY

The following works, written by rebels, outlaws, heretics, blasphemers, tyrants, psychopaths, and academics, belong in every maverick's library.

The dates provided indicate the publication year of the edition used.

Abaygo, Kenn. *Advanced Fugitive: Running, Hiding, Surviving, and Thriving Forever.* 1997.

Abaygo, Kenn. *Fugitive How to Run, Hide, and Survive.* 1994.

Abaygo, Kenn. *International Fugitive: Secrets of Clandestine Travel Overseas.* 1999.

Abbott, Elizabeth. *A History of Celibacy.* 2005.

Abbott, Geoffrey. *Execution: The Guillotine, the Pendulum, the Thousand Cuts, the Spanish Donkey, and 66 Other Ways of Putting Someone to Death.* 2006.

Abbott, Peter. *Modern African Wars : Angola and Mozambique, 1961-1974.* 1988.

Abbott, P. E. and Botham, Philip. *Modern African Wars: Rhodesia, 1965-1980.* 1986.

Abbott, Jack Henry. *In the Belly of the Beast: Letters from Prison.* 1991.

Acharya S. *The Christ Conspiracy: The Greatest Story Ever Told.* 1999.

Acquista, Angelo. *The Survival Guide: What to Do in a Biological, Chemical, or Nuclear Emergency.* 2003.

Ahmad, Eqbal, Barasamian, David, and Ruggiero, Greg. *Terrorism: Theirs and Ours.* 2001.

Airaksinen, Timo. *The Philosophy of Marquis de Sade.* 1995.

Akerley, Ben Edward. *The X-Rated Bible. An Irreverent Survey of Sex in the Scriptures.* 1985.

Alao, Charles Abiodun. *Mau-Mau Warrior.* 2006.

Aldrich, Robert. *Greater France: A History of French Overseas Expansion.* 1996.

Alexander, David. *How You Can Manipulate the Media: Guerrilla Methods to Get Your Story Covered by TV, Radio, and Newspapers.* 1993.

Alexander, John B. *Future War: Non-Lethal Weapons in Modern Warfare.* 1999.

Ali, Tariq and Barsamian, David. *Speaking of Empire and Resistance. Conversations with Tariq Ali.* 2005.

Allegro, John Marco. *The Sacred Mushroom and the Cross: A Study of the Nature and Origins of Christianity within the Fertility Cults of the Ancient Near East.* 1970.

Allison, Graham. *Nuclear Terrorism: The Ultimate Preventable Catastrophe.* 2005.

Alpern, Stanley B. *Amazons of Black Sparta: The Women Warriors of Dahomey.* 1998.

Almond, M. *Uprising Political Upheavals that Have Shaped the World.* 2002.

Alpine Enterprises (Author). *The Occult Technology of Power.* 1974.

Anonymous. *How to Create a New Identity.* 1983.

Anderson, Benedict. *Imagined Communities.* 2006.

Anderson, Kindon Peter. *Undercover Operations: A Manual for the Private Investigator.* 1990.

Anderson, Sean K. And Sloan, Stephen. *Historical Dictionary of Terrorism.* 2002.

Anthony, Edward. *Thy Rod and Staff: New Light on the Flagellatory Impulse.* 1996.

Arendt, Hannah. *Origins of Totalitarianism.* 1951.

Arendt, Hannah. *On Revolution.* 1963.

Arnold, James. *Tet Offensive 1968: Turning Point in Vietnam.* 1990.

Aristotle. *Politics.* 20000.

Arreguin-Toft, Ivan. *How the Weak Win Wars: A Theory of Asymmetric Conflict.* 2006.

Ashley, Leonard R. N. *The Complete Book of Devils and Demons.* 1996.

Assistance in Hunger Strikes: A Manual for Physicians and Other Health Personnel Dealing *with Hunger Strikers.* 1995.

Auguet, Roland. *Cruelty and Civilization: The Roman Games.* 1994.

Awerbuck, Louis. *The Defensive Shotgun.* 1989.

Axell, Albert and Kase, Hideaki. *Kamikaze: Japan's Suicide Gods.* 2002.

Bahmanyar, Mir. *Afghanistan Cave Complexes 1979-2004: Mountain Strongholds of the Mujahideen, Taliban, and Al Qaeda.* 2004.

Baigent, Michael. *The Dead Sea Scrolls Deception.* 1993.

Baigent, Michael and Leigh, Richard. *Holy Blood, Holy Grail.* 1983.

Bakunin, Mikhail. *God and the State.* 1970.

Baldick, Robert. *The Duel: A History.* 1996.

Ballou, James. *Long-Term Survival in the Coming Dark Age.* 2007.

Bamford, James. *The Puzzle Palace: Inside the National Security Agency, America's Most Secret Intelligence Organization.* 2001.

Barker, Jonathan. *The No-Nonsense Guide to Terrorism.* 2003.

Barnaby, Frank. *How to Build a Nuclear Bomb.* 2004.

Barnstone, Willis. *The Other Bible.* 2005.

Barrett, David V. *Secret Societies: From the Ancient and Arcane to the Modern and Clandestine.* 1999.

Barton, Blanche. *The Church of Satan: A History of the World's Most Notorious Religion.* 1990.

Barton, Blanche. *The Secret Life of a Satanist: The Authorized Biography of Anton LaVey.* 1992.

Barty-King, Hugh. *The Worst Poverty: A History of Debt and Debtors.* 1991.

Barzini, Luigi. *The Italians.* 1996.

Barzini, Luigi. *The Europeans.* 1984.

Bastiat, Frederic. *The Law.* 2007.

Bataille, Georges. *Erotism: Death and Sensuality.* 1986.

Bataille, Georges. *Literature and Evil.* 2001.

Baudelaire, Charles. *The Flowers of Evil.* 2006.

Baudrillard, Jean. *Fragments: Cool Memories III, 1990-1995.* 2007.

Baudrillard, Jean. *The Gulf War Did Not Take Place.* 2004.

Baudrillard, Jean. *The Spirit of Terrorism.* 2003.

Baudrillard, Jean. *The Transparency of Evil: Essays on Extreme Phenomena.* 1993.

Bayo, Alberto. *150 Questions For A Guerrilla.* 1996.

Beatty, Kenneth J. *Human Leopards.* 1915.

Beaumont, Ned. *The Policeman is Your Friend and Other Lies.* 2002.

Beccaria, Cesar. *An Essay on Crimes and Punishments.* 1986.

Becker, Carl B. *Paranormal Experience and Survival of Death.* 1993.

Beckett, Ian. *Modern Insurgencies and Counter-Insurgencies: Guerrillas and Their Opponents Since 1750.* 2005.

Begin, Menachem. *The Revolt: Story of the Irgun.* 1951.

Belfield, Richard. *The Assassination Business: A History of State-Sponsored Murder.* 2005.

Bell-Fialkoff, Andrew. *Ethnic Cleansing.* 1999.

Belloc, Hilaire. *Servile State.* 1977.

Benson, Ragnar. *David's Tool Kit: A Citizen's Guide to Taking Out Big Brother's Heavy Weapons.* 1996.

Benson, Ragnar. *Mantrapping.* 1981.

Benson, Ragnar. *Ragnar's Action Encyclopedia of Practical Knowledge and Proven Techniques.* 1999.

Benson, Ragnar. *Ragnar's Urban Survival: A Hard-Times Guide to Stying Alive in the City.* 2000.

Benson, Ragnar. *Survival Retreat: A Total Plan for Retreat Defense.* 1983.

Bergman, Paul and Berman-Barrett, Sara J. *Criminal Law Handbook: Know Your Rights, Survive the System.* 2006.

Bettmann, Otto L. *The Good Old Days—They Were Terrible.* 1974.

Biddiscombe, Perry. *The Last Nazis: SS Werewolf Guerrilla Resistance in Europe 1944-1947.* 2006.

Bierce, Ambrose and Bufe, Chaz. *The Devil's Dictionaries, Second Edition: The Best of "The Devil's Dictionary" and "The American Heretic's Dictionary."* 2004.

Bintliff, Russell. *Police Procedural: A Writer's Guide to the Police and How They Work.* 1993.

Bischoff, Erich. *Kabbala: An Introduction to Jewish Mysticism and Its Secret Doctrine.* 1985.

Black, Jason S. and Hyatt, Christopher S. *Pacts With the Devil: A Chronicle of Sex, Blasphemy, and Liberation*. 1993.

Blackledge, Catherine. *The Story of V: A Natural History of Female Sexuality*. 2004.

Blaut, J. M. *The Colonizer's Manual of the World: Geographical Diffusionism and Eurocentric History*. 1993.

Bloch, Robert. *Psycho*. 2003.

Block, Walter. *Defending the Undefendable: The Pimp, Prostitute, Scab, Slumlord, Libeler, Moneylender, and Other Scapegoats in the Rogue's Gallery of American Society*. 1991.

Boire, Richard Glen and McKenna, Terence. *Sacred Mushrooms and the Law*. 2002.

Bold, Bat-Ochir. *Mongolian Nomadic Society: A Reconstruction of the Medieval History of Mongolia*. 2001.

Bolinger, Matt. *Recognizing and Treating Exposure to Anthrax, Smallpox, Nerve Gas, Radiation, and other Likely Agents of Terrorist Attack*. 2004.

Boozhie, E. X. *The Outlaw's Bible*. 1988.

Borges, Jorge Luis. *Borges: Collected Fictions*. 1999.

Bourke, John G. *Scatalogic Rites of All Nations*. 1891.

Bova, Ben. *Immortality: How Science is Extending Your Life Span–And Changing the World*. 2000.

Bovard, James. *Freedom in Chains: The Rise of the State and the Demise of the Citizen*. 1999.

Bovard, James. *Lost Rights: The Destruction of American Liberty*. 1995.

Bovard, James. *Terrorism and Tyranny: Trampling Freedom, Justice, and Peace to Rid the World of Evil*. 2004.

Bowman, A.R. *Be Your Own Undertaker: How to Dispose of a Dead Body*. 1992.

Blum, William. *Killing Hope: US Military and C.I.A. Interventions since World War 2*. 1996.

Bracken, Len. *The Arch Conspirator*. 1999.

Bracken, Len. *The Shadow Government: 9-11 and State Terror*. 2002.

Bradley, Michael. *Secrets of the Freemasons.* 2006.

Bradley, Michael. *Secret Societies Handbook.* 2005.

Brandt, R. P. *Survival at Sea.* 1994.

Branscomb, Anne Wells. *Who Owns Information?* 1995.

Bridgman, Jon. *The End of the Holocaust: The Liberation of the Camps.* 1990.

Brinton, Crane. *The Anatomy of Revolution.* 1965.

Brodie, Thomas G. *Bombs and Bombings: A Handbook to Detection, Disposal, and Investigation for Police and Fire Departments.* 1973.

Brooks, M. Evan. *Military History's Most Wanted: The Top 10 Book of Improbable Victories, Unlikely Heroes, and Other Martial Oddities.* 2002.

Brothwell, Don R. *Food in Antiquity: A Survey of the Diet of Early Peoples.* 1997.

Brown, Ronald B. *Homemade Guns and Homemade Ammo.* 1999.

Bruges, James. *The Little Earth Book.* 2004.

Budiansky, Stephen. *Air Power: The Men, Machines, and Ideas that Revolutionized War, from Kitty Hawk to Iraq.* 2005.

Bufe, Charles, ed. *The Heretic's Handbook of Quotations.* 2001.

Bufe, Chaz. *Anarchism; What It Is and What It Isn't.* 2003.

Bullough, Vern L. *Sexual Variance in Society and History.* 1980.

Burkert, Walter. *Ancient Mystery Cults.* 2005.

Burkert, Walter. *Greek Religion.* 2006.

Burkert, Walter. *Homo Necans: The Anthropology of Ancient Greek Sacrificial Ritual.* 1986.

Burnett, C., trans. *Night Movements.* 1988.

Burnett, Thom. *Conspiracy Encyclopedia: The Encyclopedia of Conspiracy Theories.* 2005.

Bush, M. L. *Servitude in Modern Times.* 2000.

Bushby, Tony. *The Crucifixion of Truth.* 2005.

Butler, Smedley D. *War is a Racket: The Anti-War Classic by America's Most Decorate General.* 2003.

Butler, William S. and Keeney, L. Douglas. *Secret Messages: Concealment Codes and Other Types of Ingenious Communication.* 2001.

Cabot, John. *Strike Back at Terror.* 1987.

Campbell, Joseph. *The Hero with a Thousand Faces.* 1972.

Camus, Albert. *The Rebel: An Essay on Man in Revolt.* 1992.

Campbell, Mavis. *The Maroons of Jamaica.* 1988.

Cann, John P. *Counterinsurgency in Africa: The Portuguese Way of War, 1961-1974.* 2005.

Cannetti, Elias. *Crowds and Power.* 1984.

Capaldi, Nicholas. *The Art of Deception: An Introduction to Critical Thinking: How to Win an Argument, Defend a Case, Recognize a Fallacy, See Through a Deception.* 1987.

Carr, Matthew. *The Infernal Machine: A History of Terrorism from the Assassination of Tsar Alexander II to Al-Qaeda.* 2007.

Carrasco, David. *City of Sacrifice: Violence from the Aztec Empire to the Modern Americas.* 2000.

Carss, Bob. *The SAS Guide to Tracking.* 2000.

Carter, John. *Sex and Rockets: The Occult World of Jack Parsons.* 2005.

Cartledge, Paul. *Spartan Reflections.* 2003.

Cartledge, Paul. *The World of the Warrior-Heroes of Ancient Greece.* 2004

Cash, Adam. *Guerrilla Capitalism: How to Practice Free Enterprise in an Unfree Economy.* 1984.

Celsus. *On the True Doctrine: A Discourse Against the Christians.* Edited by R. Joseph Hoffman. 1987.

Chamberlin, Russell Eric. *The Bad Popes.* 2003.

Chesbro, Michael. *Wilderness Evasion: A Guide to Hiding Out and Eluding Pursuit in Remote Areas.* 2002.

Chittum, Thomas W. *Civil War Two: The Coming Breakup of America.* 1996.

Chomsky, Noam and Barsamian, David. *Secrets, Lies, and Democracy.* 1994.

Christianson, Scott. *Notorious Prisons: An Inside Look at the World's Most Feared Institutions.* 2004.

Christie, Stuart. *Stefano Della Chaie: Portrait of a Black Terrorist.* 2002.

Chubb, Judith. *The Mafia and Politics: The Italian State Under Siege.* 1989.

C.I.A. *Interrogation: The C.I.A.'s Secret Manual on Coercive Questioning.* 1997.

C.I.A. *A Study of Assassination.* 1954.

C.I.A. *Psychological Operations in Guerrilla Warfare.* 2004.

C.I.A. *Sabotage Manual: The Tips and Tricks Recommended and Endorsed by the United States Central Intelligence Agency for Bringing Down a Government or Political System.* 1999.

Cilliers, J. K. *Counter-Insurgency in Rhodesia.* 1985.

Cirincione, Joseph, Wolfsthal, Jon B., and Rajkumar, Miriam. *Deadly Arsenals: Nuclear, Biological, and Chemical Threats.* 2005.

Clarke, M. L. *Noblest Roman: Marcus Brutus and His Reputation.* 1981.

Clausewitz, Carl von. *Principles of War.* 2003.

Clayton, Anthony. *Counterinsurgency in Kenya: A Study of Military Operations Against the Mau Mau, 1952-1960.* 1984.

Clayton, Bruce D. *Life After Doomsday.* 1992.

Clayton, Bruce D. *Life After Terrorism.* 2002.

Cleckley, Hervey M. *The Mask of Sanity: An Attempt to Clarify Some Issues About the So-Called Psychopathic Personality.* 1988.

Clendinnen, Inga. *Aztecs: An Interpretation.* 1995.

Coats, C. David. *Old MacDonald's Factory Farm: The Myth of the Traditional Farm and the Shocking Truth about Animal Suffering in Today's Agribusiness.* 1991.

Cockburn, Patrick. *The Occupation: War and Resistance in Iraq.* 2007.

Coleman, Kim. *A History of Chemical Warfare.* 2005.

Condon, Richard. *The Manchurian Candidate.* 2004.

Connell, Richard. *The Most Dangerous Game.* 2007.

Connor, Michael. *How to Hide Anything.* 1984

Connor, Michael. *Sneak it Through: Smuggling Made Easier.* 1983.

Conor, Ken. *How to Stage a Military Coup: Planning to Execution.* 2006

Conquest, Robert. *The Great Terror: A Reassessment.* 1991.

Conrad, Joseph. *Heart of Darkness*. 1990.

Conrad, Joseph. *The Secret Agent*. 1907.

Constantine, Alex. *Psychic Dictatorship in the U.S.A.* 1995.

Cordingly, David. *Under the Black Flag: The Romance and the Reality of Life Among the Pirates*. 2006.

Cornog, Martha. *The Big Book of Masturbation: From Angst to Zeal*. 2003.

Coronado, Rod and Western Wildlife Unit of the Animal Liberation Front. *Memories of Freedom*. 2006.

Couch, Dick and Boswell, John. *U.S. Armed Forces Nuclear, Biological, and Chemical Survival Manual*. 2003.

Cross, James Eliot. *Conflict in the Shadows: The Nature and Politics of Guerrilla War*. 1963.

Crowley, Aleister. *Book of Lies*. 1986.

Crowley, Aleister. *Book of the Law*. 1987.

Crowley, Aleister. *Portable Darkness: An Aleister Crowley Reader*. Edited by Scott Michaelsen. 2007.

Corvasce, Mauro V. And Paglino, Joseph R. *Modus Operandi: A Writer's Guide to How Criminals Work*. 2001.

Corvasce, Mauro V. And Paglino, Joseph R. *Murder One: A Writer's Guide to Homicide*. 1997.

Corvasce, Mauro V. and Paglino, Joseph. *Police Procedural: A Writer's Guide to the Police and How They Work*. 2001.

Couplan, Francois. *The Encyclopedia of Edible Plants of North America*. 1998.

Croddy, Eric. *Chemical and Biological Warfare*. 1997.

Cumings, Bruce. *North Korea: Another Country*. 2004.

Curtin, Philip D. *The Rise and Fall of the Plantation Complex: Essays in Atlantic History*. 1998.

Cuthbert, S. J. *We Shall Fight in the Streets: A Guide to Street Fighting*. 1985.

Dach, H. von. *Total Resistance*. 1992.

Danielou, Alain. *The Myths and Gods of India*. 1991.

Danielou, Alain. *The Phallus: Sacred Symbol of Male Creative Power.* 1995.

Danielou, Alain. *While the Gods Play: Shiva Oracles and Predictions on the Cycles of History and the Destiny of Mankind.* 1987.

Daraul, Arkon. *A History of Secret Societies.* 2000.

Davenport, Gregory J. *Wilderness Living.* 2001.

Davenport, Guy. *Herakleitos and Diogenes.* 1981.

Davies, Barry. *The SAS Escape, Evasion, and Survival Manual.* 1996.

Davies, Nigel. *Human Sacrifice–In History and Today.* 1981.

Davis, Angela. *Are Prisons Obsolete?* 2003.

Davis, David Brion. *Inhuman Bondage: The Rise and Fall of Slavery in the New World.* 2006.

Davis, David Brion. *The Problem of Slavery in Western Culture.* 2003.

Davis, David Brion. *Slavery and Human Progress.* 2001.

Davis, F. James. *Who is Black? One Nation's Definition.* 1991.

Davis, Mike. *Buda's Wagon: A Brief History of the Car Bomb.* 2007.

Dearn, Alan and Sharp, Elizabeth. *The Hitler Youth 1933-1945.* 2006.

DeGrazia, David. *Animal Rights: A Very Short Introduction.* 2002.

Degrelle, Leon. *Epic: The Story of the Waffen SS.* 1983.

De Ligt, Bart. *The Conquest of Violence: An Essay on War and Revolution.* 1989.

Denson, John, ed. *The Costs of War: America's Pyrrhic Victories.* 1999.

Department of the Army. *The Illustrated Guide to Edible Wild Plants.* 2003.

Department of the Army. *Improvised Munitions Handbook* . 1969

Department of the Army. *U.S. Army Survival Handbook.* 2002.

Depugh, Robert B. *Can You Survive?* 1973.

De Quincey, Thomas. *Confessions of an English Opium Eater.* 2006.

De Quincey. Thomas. *On Murder Considered as One of the Fine Arts and Other Related Texts.* 2004.

De Rosa, Peter. *Vicars of Christ: The Dark Side of the Papacy.* 2000.

Derrer, Douglas S. *We Are All the Target: A Handbook of Terrorism Avoidance and Hostage Survival.* 1992.

Desert Publications. *Lock Out: Techniques of Forced Entry.* 1975.

Dewald, Jonathan. *The European Nobility-1400-1800.* 2005.

Dewar, Michael. *The Art of Deception in Warfare.* 1989.

Dewar, Michael. *War in the Streets: The Story of Urban Combat from Calais to Khafji.* 1992.

Diamond, Jared. *Collapse: How Societies Choose to Fail or Succeed.* 2005.

Diaz-Cobo, Oscar. *Silencing Sentries.* 1988.

Diaz-Cobo, Oscar. *Unarmed Against the Knife.* 1987.

Dick, Philip K. *The Man in the High Castle.* 2001.

Dick, Philip K. *Selected Stories of Philip K. Dick.* 2002.

Diehl, Daniel and Donnelly, Mark. *Eat Thy Neighbor: A History of Cannibalism.* 2006.

Dilorenzo, Thomas. *The Real Lincoln: A New Look at Abraham Lincoln, His Agenda, and an Unnecessary War.* 2002.

Diop, Cheikh Anta. *The African Origin of Civilization: Myth or Reality?* 1974.

Dobson, Christopher and Payne, Ronald. *Terrorists: Their Weapons, Leaders, and Tactics.* 1982.

Dollison, John. *Pope-Pourri: What You Don't Remember from Catholic School.* 1994.

Dolmatov, A. I. *The KBG Alpha Team Manual: How the Soviets Trained for Personal Combat, Assassination, and Subversion.* 1993.

Dorsch, Glenn E. and Schweitzer, Carol C. *Superterrorism: Assassins, Mobsters, and Weapons of Mass Destruction.* 1998.

Dough, Jon. *Guns for Hire: How the C.I.A. and the U.S. Army Recruit Mercenaries for White Rhodesia.* 2005.

Dough, Jon. *The Urban Guerrilla Concept.* 2005.

Douglas, Mary. *Purity and Danger: An Analysis of the Concepts of Pollution and Taboo.* 2002.

Dower, John W. *War Without Mercy: Race and Power in the Pacific War.* 1987.

Drake, Lincoln. *The Revolutionary Mystique and Terrorism in Contemporary Italy.* 1989.

Duclos, Denis. *Werewolf Complex: America's Fascination with Violence.* 1998.

Duff, Charles. *A Handbook on Hanging.* 1999.

Duggan, Christopher. *Fascism and the Mafia.* 1989

Duffy, James P. *Target: America: Hitler's Plan to Attack the United States.* 2004.

Dulaure, Jacques Antoine. *Gods of Generation: History of Phallic Cults among Ancients and Moderns.* 2003.

Dunn, C. J. And Broderick, Laurence. *Everyday Life in Imperial Japan.* 1990.

Dunn, John S. *The City of the Gods: A Study in Myth and Mortality.* 1978.

Dunnigan, James F. *Dirty Little Secrets of the Twentieth Century.* 1999.

Dunnigan, James F. *How to Make War.* 2003

Dunnigan, James F. *The Perfect Soldier: Special Operations, Commandos, and the Future of U.S. Warfare.* 2004.

Durschmied, Erik. *Blood of Revolution: From the Reign of Terror to the Rise of Khomeini.* 2003.

Eccardt, Thomas M. *Secrets of the Seven Smallest States in Europe: Andorra, Liechtenstein, Luxembourg, Malta, Monaco, San Marino, and Vatican City.* 2005.

Eccarius, J. G. *The Last Days of Christ the Vampire.* 1990.

Eddie the Wire. *The Complete Guide to Lock Picking.* 1981.

Eddie the Wire. *How to Bury Your Goods: The Complete Manual of Long-Term Underground Storage.* 1999.

Edgerton, Robert B. *Africa's Armies: From Honor to Infamy.* 2004.

Edwards, Aton. *Preparedness Now An Emergency Survival Guide for Civilians and Their Families.* 2006.

Edwards, Bryan. *Observations on the Disposition, Character, Manners, and Habits of Life, of the Maroon Negroes of the Island of Jamaica.* 1796.

Edwards, Sean. *Mars Unmasked: The Changing Face of Urban Operations.* 2000.

Ehrman, Bart D. *The Orthodox Corruption of Scripture: The Effect of Early Christological Controversies on the Text of the New Testament.* 1996.

Ellerbe, Helen. *The Dark Side of Christian History.* 1998.

Eisler, Robert. *Man into Wolf: An Anthropological Interpretation of Sadism, Masochism, and Lycanthropy; a Lecture Delivered at a Meeting of the Royal Society of Medicine.* 1969.

Ellam, John E. *Buddhism and Lamaism: A Study of the Religion of Tibet.* 1924.

Elliot, Paul. *Assassin The Bloody History of Political Murder.* 1999.

Elliot, Paul. *Brotherhoods of Fear: A History of Violent Organizations.* 1998.

Elliot, Paul. *Warrior Cults: A History of Magical, Mystical, and Murderous Organizations.* 1998.

Ellis, John W. *Police Analysis and Planning for Vehicular Bombings: Prevention, Defense, and Response.* 1999.

Ellul, Jacques. *Propaganda.* 1973.

Elsom, John R. *Lightning Over the Treasury Building: Or an Expose of Our Banking and Currency Monstrosity–America's Most Reprehensible and Un-American Racket.* 1976.

Eltzbacher, Paul. *The Great Anarchists: Ideas and Teachings of Seven Major Thinkers.* 2004.

Emmons, Nuel and Manson, Charles. *Manson in His Own Words.* 1988.

Emsley, John. *The 13th Element: The Sordid Tale of Murder, Fire, and Phosphorus.* 2002.

Epperson, A. Ralph. *The Unseen Hand.* 1985.

Eriksen, Ronald G. II. *Getaway: Driving Techniques for Evasion and Escape.* 1983.

Evans, E. P. *The Criminal Prosecution and Capital Punishment of Animals.* 1998.

Evans, Hilary. *Gods, Spirits, Cosmic Guardians: A Comparative Study of the Encounter Experience.* 1988.

Evans, Rudolf C. *The Resurrection of Aristocracy.* 1988.

Evola, Julius. *Eros and the Mysteries of Love: The Metaphysics of Sex.* 1991.

Evola, Julius. *Men Among the Ruins: Post-War Reflections of a Radical Traditionalist.* 2002.

Evola, Julius. *Revolt Against the Modern World: Politics, Religion, and Social Order in the Kali Yuga.* 1995.

Evola, Julius. *Ride the Tiger: A Survival Manual for the Aristocrats of the Soul.* 2003.

Fagin, James A. *When Terrorism Strikes Home: Defending the United States.* 2005.

Fagnon, Michael. *SS Werewolf Combat Instruction Manual.* 1982.

Fairbairn, W. E. *Get Tough: How to Win in Hand-to-Hand Fighting.* 1996.

Falconbridge, Alexander. *An Account of the Slave Trade on the Coast of Africa.* 1788.

Fall, Richard B. *Street Without Joy: The Bloody Road to Dien Bien Phu.* 1994.

Fanon, Fratz. *The Wretched of the Earth.* 2005

Faron, Fay. *Rip-Off: A Writer's Guide to Crimes of Deception.* 1998.

Farrell, Joseph P. *Reich of the Black Sun: Nazi Secret Weapons and the Cold War Allied Legend.* 2005.

Farwell, Byron. *The Great War in Africa, 1914-1918.* 1989.

Fast, Julius. *Body Language.* 1988.

F.B.I. *They Write their Own Sentences: The F.B.I. Handwriting Analysis Manual.* 1987.

Felix, Christopher. *A Short Course in the Secret War.* 2000.

Ferguson, Gregor. *Coup D'Etat: A Practical Manual.* 1987.

Ferguson, Niall. *The Cash Nexus: Money and Power in the Modern World, 1700-2000.* 2002.

Fetherling, George. *The Book of Assassins: A Biographical Dictionary from Ancient Times to the Present.* 2006.

Fiery, Dennis. *How to Hide Things in Public Places.* 1996.

Finlan, Alastair. *The Collapse of Yugoslavia.* 2004.

Finnegan, William. *Complicated War: The Harrowing of Mozambique.* 1992.

Firenzuola, Agnolo. *On the Beauty of Women.* 2000.

Fisher, John. *Last Frontiers on Earth.* 1985.

Fisher, John. *Uninhabited Ocean Islands.* 1999.

Flynn, Kevin and Gerhardt, Gary. *The Silent Brotherhood.* 1990.

Foote, G. W., and Ball, W. P., *The Bible Handbook.* 1992.

Dave Foreman, Dave and Haywood, Bill. *Ecodefense: A Field Guide to Monkeywrenching.* 1987.

Fort, Charles. *The Book of the Damned.* 2006.

Foucault, Michel. *Discipline and Punish: The Birth of the Prison.* 1995.

Foucault, Michel. *History of Madness.* 2007.

Fraser, James. *The Golden Bough: A Study in Magic and Religion.* 1998.

Fredrickson, George M. *White Supremacy: A Comparative study of American and South African History.* 1982.

Freedman, Lawrence. *Superterrorism: Policy Responses.* 2002.

Fremion, Ives. *Orgasms of History: 3000 Years of Spontaneous Insurrection.* 2002.

French, Scott and Van Houten, Paul. *Never Say Lie: How to Beat the Machines, the Interviews, the Chemical Tests.* 1987.

Friedman, David M. *A Mind of Its Own: A Cultural History of the Penis.* 2001.

Friedman, George. *The Future of War: Power, Technology, and American World Dominance in the Twenty-first century.* 1998.

Friedrich, Otto. *The Kingdom of Auschwitz.* 1994.

Froude, James Anthony. *The Knights Templars.* 2003.

Futrelle, Jacques. *The Problem of Cell 13.* 2004.

Galula, David. *Counterinsurgency Warfare: Theory and Practice.* 1964.

Galula, David. *Pacification in Algeria, 1956-1958.* 2006.

Gambetta, Diego, ed. *Making Sense of Suicide Missions.* 2006.

Gardner, Gerald B. *Witchcraft Today.* 1954.

Garnsey, Peter. *Ideas of Slavery from Aristotle to Augustine.* 1997.

Garrigus, John D. *Before Haiti: Race and Citizenship in French Saint-Domingue.* 2006.

Gaskin, Carol and Hawkins, Vince. *The Ways of the Samurai: From Ronins to Ninjas to the Fiercest Warriors in Japanese History*. 2005.

Gelderloos, Peter. *How Nonviolence Protects the State*. 2007.

George, John and Wilcox, Laird M. *American Extremists: Militias, Supremacists, Klansmen, Communists, and Others*. 1996.

Gentile, Giovanni. *Origins and Doctrine of Fascism: With Selections from Other Works*. 2002.

Gibson, James William. *Warrior Dreams: Violence and Manhood in Post-Vietnam America*. 1994.

Gimlette, John. *At the Tomb of the Inflatable Pig: Travels through Paraguay*. 2005.

Girard, Rene. *The Scapegoat*. 1989.

Girard, Rene. *Violence and the Sacred*. 1979.

Glenny, Misha. *The Fall of Yugoslavia*. 1996.

Glick, Brian. *War at Home: Covert Action against U.S. Activists and What We Can Do About It*. 1989.

Goad, Jim. *The Redneck Manifesto: How Hillbillies, Hicks, and White Trash Became America's Scapegoats*. 1998.

Godwin, Joscelyn. *Arktos: The Polar Myth in Science, Symbolism, and Nazi Survival*. 1996.

Goff, Stan. *Full Spectrum Disorder: The Military in the New American Century*. 2004.

Goldstein, Joshua. *The Real Price of War: How You Pay for the War on Terror*. 2005.

Golitsyn, Anatoliy. *The Perestroika Deception: Memoranda to the Central Intelligence Agency*. 1998.

Goodrick-Clarke, Nicholas. *Black Sun: Aryan Cults, Esoteric Nazism, and the Politics of Identity*. 2003.

Goodrick-Clarke, Nicholas. *Hitler's Priestess: Savitri Devi, the Hindu-Aryan Myth, and Neo-Nazism*. 2000.

Goodrick-Clarke, Nicholas. *The Occult Roots of Nazism*. 2003.

Gordon, Stuart. *The Encyclopedia of Myths and Legends*. 1994.

Gottschalk, Jack A., Flanagan, Brian P., Kahn, Lawrence J., and Larochelle, Dennis M. *Jolly Roger with an Uzi: The Rise and Threat of Modern Piracy*. 2000.

Graves, Kersey. *The World's Sixteen Crucified Saviors: Christianity Before Christ*. 2001.

Graham, Lloyd M. *Deceptions and Myths of the Bible*. 2000.

Gray, Jim, Monday, Mark, and Gary Stublefield. *Maritime Terror: Protecting Your Vessel and Your Crew Against Piracy*. 1999.

Greeley, Roger E., ed. *Best of Robert Ingersoll*. 1983.

Green, Miranda J. *Dying for the Gods: Human Sacrifice in Iron Age and Roman Europe*. 2002.

Griffith, Paddy. *The Viking Art of War*. 1995.

Gross, Jan T. *Revolution from Abroad: The Soviet Conquest of Poland's Western Ukraine and Western Belorussia*. 2002.

Grosser, Philip. *Alcatraz–Uncle Sam's Devil's Island: Experiences of a Conscientious Objector in America During the First World War*. 2006.

Grossman, Dave. *On Killing: The Psychological Cost of Learning to Kill in War and Society*. 1996.

Grosso, Michael. *The Millennium Myth: Love and Death at the End of Time*. 1994.

Guevara, Ernesto "Che." *Guerrilla Warfare*. 1998.

Guicciardini, Francesco. *Maxims and Reflections: Ricordi*. 1972.

Gunaratna, Rohan. *Inside Al Qaeda: Global Network of Terror*. 2003.

Gur, Nadine and Cole, Benjamin. *The New Face of Terrorism*. 2002.

Gutman, Roy and Rieff, David, eds. *Crimes of War: What the Public Should Know* . 1999.

Gutzman, Kevin R. C. *The Politically Incorrect Guide to the Constitution*. 2007.

Hagger, Nicholas. *The Secret History of the West: The Influence of Secret Organizations on Western History from the Renaissance to the Twentieth Century*. 2005.

Hall, Marshall. *The Earth is Not Moving*. 1991.

Hamilton, Joseph. *The Duelling Handbook*, 1829. 2007.

Hammer, Carl. *Techniques of Secret Warfare*. 1996.

Hammerstein, Trent. *Stealth Juror: The Ultimate Defense Against Bad Laws and Government Tyranny*. 2002.

Hammes, Thomas X. *The Sling and the Stone: On War in the 21st Century*. 2004.

Hamud, Randal B., ed. *Osama bin Laden: America's Enemy in His Own Words*. 2005.

Handbook for Volunteers of the Irish Republican Army: Notes on Guerrilla Warfare. 1996.

Harber, David. *Assorted Nasties*. 1993.

Harold, Thomas, ed. *The World Power Foundation: Its Goals and Platform*. 1980.

Harris, David. *Our War: What We Did in Vietnam and What It Did to Us*. 1996.

Harris, Robert and Paxman, Jeremy. *A Higher Form of Killing: The Secret History of Chemical and Biological Warfare*. 1990.

Harrison, John M. *C.I.A. Flaps and Seals Manual*. 1975.

Hart, Dick and Santoro, Victor. *Screw the Bitch: Divorce Tactics for Men*. 1991.

Hartshorne, Charles. *Omnipotence and Other Theological Mistakes*. 1983.

Heckethorn, Charles William. *Secret Societies of All Ages and Countries*. 1997.

Hedges, Chris. *What Every Person Should Know About War*. 2003.

Heggoy, Alf Andrew. *Insurgency and Counterinsurgency in Algeria*. 1972

Heitman, Helmoed-Romer. *Modern African Wars: South-West Africa*. 1991.

Helms, Harry. *Inside the Shadow Government: National Emergencies and the Cult of Secrecy*. 2003.

Helms, Harry. *Top Secret Tourism: Your Travel Guide to Germ Warfare Laboratories, Clandestine Aircraft Bases, and Other Places in The United States You're Not Supposed to Know About*. 2007.

Herodotus. *The Histories*. 2003.

Hersey, John. *Hiroshima*. 2002.

Hess, Henner. *Mafia and Mafiosi: Origin, Power, and Myth*. 1998

Hibbert, Christopher. *The Roots of Evil: A Social History of Crime and Punishment.* 2003.

Hidell, Al. *The Conspiracy Reader: From the Deaths of JFK and John Lennon to Government-Sponsored Alien Cover-ups.* 2000.

Hidell, Al and d'Arc, Joan. *The New Conspiracy Reader: From Planet X to the War on Terrorism–What You Really Don't Know.* 2004.

Hill, Peter B. E., *The Japanese Mafia: Yakuza, Law, and the State.* 2006.

Hitler, Adolf. *Mein Kampf.* 1998.

Hively, John. *The Rigged Game: Corporate America and a People Betrayed.* 2006.

Hobbes, Nicholas. *Essential Militaria: Facts, Legends, and Curiosities about Warfare Through the Ages.* 2004.

Hobbes, Thomas. *Leviathan.* 1997.

Hobsbawm, Eric J. *Bandits.* 2001.

Hoffer, Eric. *The True Believer: Thoughts on the Nature of Mass Movements.* 2002.

Hoffman, Abbie. *Steal This Book.* 2002.

Hoffman, Bruce. *Inside Terrorism.* 2006.

Hoffman, Bruce, Taw, Jennifer M., and Arnold, David. *Lessons for Contemporary Counterinsurgencies: The Rhodesian Experience.* 1991.

Hoffman, Michael A. *Judaism's Strange Gods.* 2000.

Hoffman, Michael A. *Secret Societies and Psychological Warfare.* 2001.

Hoffman, Michael A. *They Were White and They Were Slaves: The Untold History of the Enslavement of Whites in Early America.* 1993.

Hogg, Garry. *Cannibalism and Human Sacrifice.* 1958.

Hogshire, Jim. *Opium for the Masses: A Practical Guide for Growing Poppies and Making Opium.* 1994.

Hogshire, Jim. *Sell Yourself to Science: The Complete Guide to Selling Your Organs, Body Fluids, Bodily Functions and Being a Human Guinea Pig.* 1992.

Hogshire, Jim. *You Are Going to Prison.* 1994.

Hollander, Lee M., trans. *The Saga of the Jomsvikings.* 1988.

Holmes, Richard. *Acts of War.* 2004.

Homer. *The Iliad.* 2004.

Horne, Gerald. *Race War White Supremacy and the Japanese Attack on the British Empire.* 2005.

Hoskins, Richard Kelly. *Vigilantes of Christendom: The Story of the Phineas Priesthood.* 1990.

Hoss, Rudolf. *Death Dealer: The Memoirs of the SS Kommandant at Auschwitz.* 1996.

Hough, Harold. *Freedom Road.* 1991.

Hoffman, Michael A. II. *Secret Societies and Psychological Warfare.* 2001.

Houellebecq, Michel. *H. P. Lovecraft Against the World, Against Life.* 2006.

Howard, David A. *The Survival Chemist: Vital Information for Anyone Who Wished to Survive and Resist Any Threat to Their Freedom.* 2006.

Howard, Michael. *The Occult Conspiracy: Secret Societies–Their Influence and Power in World History.* 1989.

Howard, Roger. *Great Escapes and Rescues: An Encyclopedia.* 2001.

Hoy, Michael, ed. *Loompanics' Golden Records: Articles and Features from the Best Book Catalog in the World.* 1993.

Hoy, Michael, ed. *Loompanics' Greatest Hits: Articles and Features from the Best Book Catalog in the World.* 1990.

Hoy, Michael, ed. *Loompanics Unlimited Conquers the Universe.* 1998.

Hoy, Michael, ed. *Loompanics Unlimited Live In Las Vegas: Articles and Features from the Best Book Catalog in the World.* 1996.

Hubert, Henri and Mauss, Marcel. *Sacrifice: Its Nature and Functions.* 1981.

Huff, Darrell. *How to Lie with Statistics.* 1982.

Hume, David. *Dialogues Concerning Natural Religion.* 2007.

Humphreys, Richard and Apollonio, Umbro, eds. *Futurist Manifestos.* 2001.

Humphry, Derek. *Final Exit: The Practicalities of Self-Deliverance and Assisted Suicide for the Dying.* 2002.

Huntington, Samuel P. *The Clash of Civilizations and the Remaking of the World Order.* 1998.

Hutchinson, Maxwell. *The Poisoner's Handbook*. 1988.

Hutchkinson, Maxwell. *The Get Out of Jail Free Book*. 1992.

Huxley, Aldous. *The Doors of Perception and Heaven and Hell*. 2004.

Huysmans, Joris-Karl. *The Damned (La-Bas)*. 2002.

Hyde, H. Montgomery. *A History of Pornography*. 1965.

Icke, David. *The Biggest Secret: The Book that Will Change the World*. 1999.

Ide, Arthur Frederick. *Unzipped: The Popes Bare All: A Frank Study of Sex and Corruption in the Vatican*. 1987.

Ingersoll, Robert G. *Some Mistakes of Moses*. 1986.

Innes, Brian. *The History of Torture*. 1998.

Irwin, John. *The Felon*. 1987.

Irwin, John. *The Jail: Managing the Underclass in American Society*. 1992.

Iserson, Kenneth V. *Death to Dust: What Happens to Dead Bodies*. 1994.

Ives, Geoerge. *History of Penal Methods: Criminals, Witches, Lunatics*. 1914.

Jackson, Devon. *Conspiranoia: The Mother of All Conspiracy Theories*. 2000.

Jacob, Alexander. *Nobilitas*. 2000.

James, C. L. R. James. *Every Cook Can Govern: A Study of Democracy in Ancient Greece: Its Meaning Today*. 1956.

Jekel, Pamela. *The Perfect Crime and How to Commit It*. 1982.

Joes, Anthony James. *America and Guerrilla Warfare*. 2000.

Joes, Anthony James. *The History and Politics of Counterinsurgency*. 2004.

Joes, Anthony James. *Urban Guerrilla Warfare*. 2007.

Johnson, Chalmers. *Blowback: The Costs and Consequences of American Empire*. 2004.

Johnson, Chalmers. *The Sorrows of Empire: Military, Secrecy, and the End of the Republic*. 2004.

Johnson, Captain Charles. *A General History of the Robberies and Murders of the Most Notorious Pirates*. 2002.

Jones, Bernard E. *Freemasons' Guide and Compendium*. 2006.

Jones, Tony L. *Booby Trap Identification and Response Guide for Law Enforcement Personnel.* 1998.

Joseph, Isya. *Devil Worship: The Scared Books and Traditions of the Yezidiz.* 2007.

Josephus, Falvius. *Against Apion.* 2004.

Jung, Carl . G. Edited by Aniela Jaffe. *Memories, Dreams, Reflections.* 1989.

Kaczynski, Theodore. *The Unabomber Manifesto: Industrial Society and its Future.* 2005.

Kafton-Minkel, Walter. *Subterranean Worlds: 100,000 Years of Dragons, Dwarfs, the Dead, Lost Races, and UFOs from Inside the Earth.* 1989.

Kahane, Meir. *Never Again A Program for Survival.* 1972.

Kahane, Meir. *They Must Go.* 1981.

Kains, M. G. *Five Acres and Independence: A Handbook of Small Farm Management.* 1973.

Kaplan, David E. And Dubro, Alec. *Yakuza: Japan's Criminal Underworld.* 2003.

Kaplan, Jeffrey. *Encyclopedia of White Power: A Source Book of the Radical Racist Right.* 2000.

Kaplan, Robert D. *The Coming Anarchy: Shattering the Dreams of the Post Cold War.* 2001.

Kaplan, Stephen. *Vampires Are.* 1984.

Karagiozis, Michael Fitting and Sgaglio, Richard. *Forensic Investigation Handbook: An Introduction to the Collection, Preservation, Analysis, and Preservation of Evidence.* 2005.

Kasmar, Gene. *All the Obscenities of the Bible.* 1995.

Katz, Eric. *Death by Design: Science, Technology, and Engineering in Nazi Germany.* 2005.

Kaysing, Bill and Reid, Randy. *We Never Went to the Moon: America's Thirty Billion Dollar Swindle.* 1976.

Kearny, Cresson H. *Nuclear War Survival Skills. 2001.*

Keegan, John. *The Battle for History: Re-fighting World War II.* 1996.

Keegan, John. *The Face of Battle*. 2001.

Keegan, John. *A History of Warfare*. 1994.

Keeley, Lawrence H. *War Before Civilization: The Myth of the Peaceful Savage*. 1997.

Keen, Maurice. *The Outlaws of Medieval Legend*. 2001.

Keeney, Douglas. *The Doomsday Scenario: How America Ends*. 2002.

Keightley, Thomas. *Secret Societies of the Middle Ages: The Assassins, Templars, and the Secret Tribunals of Westphalia*. 2005.

Keith, Jim. *Biowarfare in America*. 1999.

Keith, Jim. *Casebook on Alternative 3: Ufo's, Secret Societies, and World Control*. 1993.

Keith, Jim. *Mind Control, World Control*. 1998.

Keith, Jim. *Okbomb : Conspiracy and Cover-up*. 1996.

Keith, Jim. *Secret and Suppressed: Banned Ideas and Hidden History*. 1993.

Kelling, Brian D., Rapp, Burt, and Lesce, Tony. *Bodyguarding: A Complete Manual*. 1999.

Kennedy, James Ronald and Kennedy, Walter Donald. *The South Was Right* 1994.

Kennedy, Paul. *The Rise and Fall of the Great Powers*. 1989.

Kennedy, Robert M. *Hold the Balkans : German Antiguerrilla Operations in the Balkans 1941-1945*. 2001.

Kennedy, Walter Donald. *Myths of American Slavery*. 2002.

Kerrigan, Michael. *The Instruments of Torture*. 2001.

Kersten, Holger. *Jesus Lived in India*. 1994.

Keuls, Eva. C. *The Reign of the Phallus: Sexual Politics in Ancient Athens*. 1993.

K.G.B.. K.G.B. *Alpha Team Training Manual: How the Soviets Trained for Personal Combat, Assassination, and Subversion*. 1993.

Kiernan, Victor G. *Duel in European History: Honour and the Reign of Aristocracy*. 1988.

Kick, Russ. *Abuse Your Illusions: The Disinformation Guide to Media Mirages and Establishment Lies.* 2003.

Kick, Russ. *The Disinformation Book of Lists.* 2004.

Kick, Russ, ed. *50 Things You're Not Supposed to Know.* 2003.

Kick, Russ, ed. *50 Things You're Not Supposed to Know, Volume 2.* 2004.

Kick, Russ. *Outposts: A Catalog of Rare and Disturbing Alternative Information.* 1995.

Kick, Russ. *Psychotropedia: A Guide to Publications on the Periphery.* 2002.

King, Francis. *Sexuality, Magic, and Perversion.* 2002.

King, Gilbert. *Dirty Bomb: Weapons of Mass Destruction.* 2004.

King, John L. *Chaos in America: Surviving the Depression.* 2002.

King, Namida, ed. *Straight to Hell: Great Suicides of the Twentieth Century.* 2004.

Kinzer, Stephen. *Overthrow: America's Century of Regime Change from Hawaii to Iraq.* 2007.

Kitson, Frank. *Low Intensity Operations: Subversion, Insurgency, Peace-Keeping.* 1971.

Klein, Shelley. *The Most Evil Secret Societies in History.* 2005.

Kline-Graber, Georgia and Graber, Benjamin. *Woman's Orgasm.* 1988.

Klostermaier, Klaus K. *A Survey of Hinduism.* 1994.

Koehler, John O. *Stasi: The Untold Story of The East German Secret Police.* 2000.

Kogon, Eugen. *The Theory and Practice of Hell: The German Concentration Camps and the System Behind Them.* 2006.

Komisaruk, Katya. *Beat the Heat: How to Handle Encounters with Law Enforcement.* 2004.

Konstam, Angus. *The History of Pirates.* 2002.

Konstam, Angus and McBride, Angus. *Pirates: Terror on the High Seas.* 2001.

Koon, Tracy H. *Believe, Obey, Fight: Political Socialization of Youth in Fascist Italy, 1922-1943.* 2001.

Kossy, Donna. *Kooks: A Guide to the Outer Limits of Human Belief.* 2001.

Kossy, Donna. *Strange Creations: Aberrant Ideas of Human Origins from Ancient Astronauts to Aquatic Apes.* 2001.

Koten, David C. *When Corporations Rule the World.* 2001.

Kreyenbroek, Philp G. *Yezidism: Its Background, Observances, and Textual Tradition.* 1995.

Krousher, Richard. *Physical Interrogation Techniques.* 1985.

Kurland, Michael. *How to Solve a Murder: The Forensic Handbook.* 2001.

Kurland, Michael. *How to Try a Murder: The Handbook for Armchair Lawyers.* 1997.

Laband, John, ed. *Daily Lives of Civilians in Wartime Africa: From Slavery days to Rwandan Genocide.* 2006.

Laband, John. *The Rise and Fall of the Zulu Nation.* 1997.

La Boetie, Etienne de. *The Discourse on Voluntary Servitude.* 1576.

Lachman, Gary. *Turn Off Your Mind: The Mystic Sixties and the Dark Side of the Age of Aquarius.* 2003.

Laffin, John. *Jackboot: The Story of the German Soldier.* 2004.

Lamb, Christina. *House of Stone: The True Story of a Family Divided in a War Zone.* 2006.

Lambeth, Benjamin S. *Air Power Against Terror: America's Conduct of Operation Enduring Freedom.* 2005.

Lamont-Brown, Raymond. *Kamikaze: Japan's Suicide Samurai.* 2004.

Lamont-Brown, Raymond. *Kempeitai: Japan's Dreaded Military Police.* 1998.

Lane, David. *Deceived, Damned, and Defiant: The Revolutionary Writings of David Lane.* 1999.

Lao Tzu. *Tao Te Ching.* 1964.

Lane, Fred H. *Concerned Citizen's Guide to Surviving Nuclear, Biological, and Chemical Terrorist Attack.* 2004.

Laquer, Walter. *Guerrilla Warfare: A Historical and Critical Study.* 1997.

Laquer, Walter. *A History of Terrorism.* 2001.

Laqueur, Walter. *The New Terrorism: Fanaticism and the Arms of Mass Destruction.* 2007.

Laquer, Walter, ed. *Voices of Terror: Manifestos, Writings, and Manuals of Al Qaeda, Hamas, and Other Terrorists from Around the World and Throughout the Ages.* 2004.

Latimer, Jon. *Deception in War.* 2001.

Laucella, Linda. *Assassination: The Politics of Murder.* 1999.

Laurence, John. *The History of Capital Punishment.* 1983.

Law, Larry. *A True Historie & Account of Pyrate Captain Mission, his Crew and their Colony of Libertatia founded on People's Rights and Liberty.* 2001.

Lawrence, Ken. *The New State Repression.* 2006.

Le Bon, Gustav. *The Crowd.* 2002.

Lee, Martin. *The Beast Reawakens: Fascism's Resurgence from Hitler's Spymasters to Today's Neo-Nazi Groups.* 1999.

Leedom, Tim C, ed. *The Book Your Church Doesn't Want You to Read.* 2003.

Lesce, Tony. *Escape from Controlled Custody.* 1990.

Lesce, Tony. *Modern Frauds and Con Games.* 2002.

Lesce, Tony. *They're Watching You: The Age of Surveillance.* 1998.

Lesce, Tony. *Wide Open to Terrorism.* 1996.

Lesser, Ian O., Lesser, Ian, Hoffman, Bruce, Arguilla, John, Ronfeldt, David, and Zanini, Michele. *Countering the New Terrorism.* 1999.

Leuchars, Chris. *To the Bitter End: Paraguay and the War of the Triple Alliance.* 2002.

Lewin, Leonard C. *Report from Iron Mountain: On the Possibility and Desirability of Peace.* 1967.

Lewis, Bernard. *The Assassins: A Radical Sect in Islam.* 2002.

Lewis, Brenda. *Ritual Sacrifice: A Concise History.* 2001.

Lewis, Norman. *The Honored Society: The Sicilian Mafia Observed.* 1964.

Lewis, Paul H. *Guerrillas and Generals: The Dirty War in Argentina.* 2001.

Licklider, Roy, ed. *Stopping the Killing: How Civil Wars End.* 1993.

Lincoln, Bruce. *Death, War, and Sacrifice: Studies in Ideology and Practice*. 1991.

Lindqvist, Sven. *Exterminate All the Brutes*. 2002.

Lindqvist, Sven. *A History of Bombing*. 2003.

Lloyd, Mark. *The Guiness Book of Espionage*. 1994.

London, Jack. *The Iron Heel*. 2006.

Long, David E. *Anatomy of Terrorism*. 1990.

Long, Duncan. *Apocalypse Tomorrow*. 1994.

Long, Duncan. *Bioterrorism: Secrets for Survival*. 2000.

Long, Duncan. *How to Survive a Nuclear Accident*. 1987.

Long, Duncan. *Modern Camouflage*. 1992.

Long, Duncan. *To Break a Tyrant's Chains: Neo Guerrilla Techniques for Combat*. 1991.

Love, Brenda. *Encyclopedia of Unusual Sex Practices*. 2002.

Long, Duncan. *Surviving Major Chemical Accidents and Chemical-Biological Warfare*. 1986.

Long, Harold S. *Making Crime Pay*. 1988.

Lovecraft, H.P. *The Call of Cthulhu*. 2002.

Lowes, John Livingston. *The Road to Xanadu: A Study in the Ways of the Imagination*. 1959.

Lowie, Robert. *Indians of the Plains*. 1954.

Luger, Jack. *Ask Me No Questions, I'll Tell You No Lies: How to Survive Being Interviewed, Interrogated, Questioned, Quizzed, Sweated, Grilled*. 1998.

Luger, Jack. *The Big Book of Secret Hiding Places*. 1987.

Luger, Jack. *How to Use Mail Drops for Profit, Privacy, and Self-Protection*. 1996.

Luger, Jack. *Snitch: A Handbook for Informers*. 1991.

Luggar, J. *Improvised Weapons in American Prisons*. 1985.

Luna, J.J. *How to Be Invisible: The Essential Guide to Protecting Your Personal Privacy, Your Assets, and Your Life*. 2004.

Lung, Haha. *Ancient Art of Strangulation*. 1985.

Lung, Haha. *Theatre of Hell: Dr. Lung''s Complete Guide to Torture.* 2003.

Lunev, Stanislav. *Through the Eyes of the Enemy. The Autobiography of Stanislav Lunev.* 1998.

Luttwak, Edward N. *Coup d'Etat: A Practical Handbook.* 2006.

McArdle, Phil and McArdle, Karen. *Fatal Fascination: Where Fact Meets Fiction in Police Work.* 1988.

McCabe, Joseph. *The Forgery of the Old Testament and Other Essays.* 1993.

McCabe, Joseph. *The Myth of the Resurrection and Other Essays.* 1993.

MacDonald, Andrew. *Turner Diaries.* 1999.

McGowan, David. *Derailing Democracy: The America the Media Don't Want You to See.* 2000.

Machiavelli, Niccolo. *Discourses.*1984.

Machiavelli, Niccolo. *The Prince.* 1984.

MacInaugh, Edmond A. *Disguise Techniques.* 1988.

Mack, Jefferson. *Invisible Resistance to Tyranny: How to Lead a Secret Life of Insurgency in an Increasingly Unfree World.* 2002.

Mack, Jefferson. *The Safe House.* 1998.

Mack, Jefferson. *Underground Railroad: Practical Advice for Finding Passengers, Getting them to Safety, and Staying One Step Ahead of the Tyrants.* 2000.

McKenna, Terence. *Food of the Gods: The Search for the Original Tree of Knowledge.* 1993.

Mackenzie, Angus. *Secrets: The C.I.A.'s War at Home.* 1999.

McKinsey, C. Dennis. *Encyclopedia of Biblical Errancy.* 1995.

McLean, Don. *Do-It-Yourself Gunpowder Cookbook.* 1992

McNab, Chris. *How to Survive Anything, Anywhere.* 2004.

McNab, Chris. *The SAS Mental Endurance Handbook.* 2002.

MacTire, Sean. *Malicious Intent: A Writer's Guide to How Murderers, Robbers, Rapists, and Other Criminals Think.* 1995.

McWilliams, Peter. *Ain't Nobody's Business if You Do: The Absurdity of Consensual Crimes in a Free Society.* 1996.

Madden, James W. *The Art of Throwing Weapons.* 1992.

Mahl, Tom E. *Espionage's Most Wanted: The Top 10 Book of Malicious Moles, Blown Covers, and Intelligence Oddities.* 2006.

Malaclypse. *Principia Discordia: Or How I found the Goddess and What I Did to Her When I Found Her.* 1980.

Malaparte, Curzio. *Technique of the Coup d'etat.* 1931.

Mallon, Thomas. *Stolen Words.* 2001.

Maloba, Wunyabari O. *Mau Mau and Kenya: An Analysis of a Peasant Revolt.* 1998.

Mamdani, Mahmood. *When Victims Become Killers: Colonialism, Nativism, and the Genocide in Rwanda.* 2002.

Manhattan, Avro. *The Vatican Billions.* 1983.

Manning, Patrick. *Slavery and African Life: Occidental, Oriental, and African Slave Trades.* 1990.

Mannix, Daniel P. *Freaks: We Who Are Not As Others.* 2000.

Mannix, Daniel P. *History of Torture.* 2003.

Mao Tse-tung. *On Guerrilla Warfare.* 2000.

Marighella, Carlos. *Minimanual of the Urban Guerrilla.* 1969.

Marinetti, Filippo Tommaso. *Manifesto of Futurism: Published in Le Figaro, February 20, 1909.* 1983.

Marlowe, Christopher. *Doctor Faustus.* 2001.

Marotta, Michael E. *The Code Book: All About Unbreakable Codes and How to Use Them.* 1983.

Martin, David. *The Use of Poison and Biological Weapons in the Rhodesian War: Lecture for the University of Zimbabwe War and Strategic Studies Seminar Series, University of Zimbabwe on July 1993.* 1993.

Martin, James S. *SCRAM: Relocating Under a New Identity.* 1999.

Martin, Malachi. *The Decline and Fall of the Roman Church.* 1983.

Marx, Gary T. *Undercover: Police Surveillance in America.* 1989.

Marx, Karl and Engels, Friedrich. *The Communist Manifesto.* 1998.

Martin, Roy A. *Inside Nuremberg: Military Justice for Nazi War Criminals.* 2000.

Mashiro, N. *Black Medicine I: The Dark Art of Death.* 1979.

Mashiro, N. *Black Medicine II: Weapons at Hand.* 1979.

Maternus, Julius Firmicus. *The Error of the Pagan Religions.* 1970.

May, Timothy. *The Mongol Art of War.* 2007.

Meltzer, Milton. *Slavery: A World History.* 2005.

Menchen, H. L. *A Menken Chrestomathy.* 1982.

Mencken, H. L. *The Vintage Mencken.* 1990.

Meredith, Martin. *Mugabe: Power, Plunder, and the Struggle for Zimbabwe's Future.* 2007.

Merritt, Nathaniel. *Jehovah Unmasked* 2005.

Merton, N. H. *Crown Against Concubine: The Untold Story of the Recent Struggle Between the House of Windsor and the Vatican.* 1994.

Metraux, Alfred. *Voodoo in Haiti.* 1989.

Mettler, John J. *Basic Butchering of Livestock and Game.* 1986.

Metzger, Richard. *The Book of Lies: The Disinformation Guide to Magick and the Occult.* 2003.

Michel, Lou and Herbeck, Dan. *American Terrorist: Timothy McVeigh and the Oklahoma City Bombing.* 2001.

Middleton, Richard. *The Practical Guide to Man-Powered Weapons and Ammunition: Experiemnts with Catapults, Musketballs, Stonebows, Blowpipes, Big Airguns, and Bulletbows.* 2007.

Migana, Alphonse. *The Yezidis: The Devil Worshipers of the Middle East.* 1993.

Miles, Alexander. *Devil's Island: Colony of the Damned.* 1988.

Mill, John Stuart. *The Subjection of Women.* 1997.

Millot, B. *Divine Thunder. The Life and Death of the Kamikaze.* 1971.

Mills, C. Wright. *The Power Elite.* 1956.

Minnery, John. *Kill Without Joy The Complete How to Kill Book.* 1992.

Minns, Michael, Minns, Michael Louis, Feray, C Michel, Adams, David. *The Underground Lawyer.* 2001.

Minor, Charles L. C. *The Real Lincoln*. 1927.

Mirabello, Mark. *The Cannibal Within*. 2002.

Mirabello, Mark. *The Crimes of Jehovah*. 1997.

Mirabello, Mark. *The Odin Brotherhood*. 2003.

Mirbeau, Octave. *The Torture Garden*. 2004.

Mishima, Yukio. *Patriotism*. 1995

Montesquieu, Charles de. *The Spirit of the Laws*. 1989.

Moore, Marilyn. *Survival Medicine*. 1982.

Moran, Richard. *Doomsday: End of the World Scenarios*. 2002.

Moreno, Jonathan. *Undue Risk: Secret State Experiments in Humans*. 2000.

Morgan, Robin. *The Demon Lover: The Sexuality of Terrorism*. 1989.

Morgan, William. *Illustrations of Masonry*. 2000.

Morris, I. *The Nobility of Failure: Tragic Heroes in the History of Japan*. 1988.

Morris, Norval and Rothman, David J., eds. *The Oxford History of Prison: The Practice of Punishment in Western Society*. 1997.

Most, Johann. *The Science of Revolutionary Warfare*. 1884.

Mumford, Lewis. *The City in History: Its Origins, Transformations, and Its Prospects*. 1968.

Murphey, Dewight D., *Lynching: History and Analysis*. 1996.

Murray, Margaret Alice. *The God of the Witches*. 2005.

Nabokov, Vladimir. *Lolita*. 1992.

Naimark, Norman M. *Fires of Hatred: Ethnic Cleansing in Twentieth-Century Europe*. 2002.

Nathan, John. *Mishima: A Biography*. 2000.

Naylor, Thomas. *Secession*. 2008.

Nelson, Brent A. *America Balkanized: Immigration's Challenge to Government*. 1994.

Neumeyer, Ken. *Sailing the Farm: A Survival Guide to Homesteading in the Ocean*. 1981.

Newkey-Burden, Chas. *Nuclear Paranoia.* 2003.

Newman, Bob. *Guerrillas in the Mist: A Battlefield Guide to Clandestine Warfare.* 1997.

Newman, John Q. *Be Your Own Dick: Private Investigating Made Easy.* 1999.

Newman, John Q. *The Heavy Duty New Identity.* 1998.

Newman, John Q. *Identity Theft: The Cybercrime of the Millenium.* 1999.

Newton, Michael. *Armed and Dangerous: A Writer's Guide to Weapons.* 1990.

Newton, Michael. *Bad Girls Do It An Encyclopedia of Female Murderers.* 1993.

Newton, Michael. *The Encyclopedia of Robberies, Heists, and Capers.* 2002.

Newton, Michael. *The Encyclopedia of Serial Killers.* 2006.

Newton, Michael. *Holy Homicide: An Encyclopedia of Those Who Go With Their God and Kill.* 1998.

Newton, Michael. *Hunting Humans: An Encyclopedia of Modern Serial Killers.* 1990.

Newton, Michael. *Killer Cops: An Encyclopedia of Lawless Lawmen.* 1997.

Nicholls, C. S. *Red Strangers: The White Tribe of Kenya.* 2007.

Nietzsche, Friedrich. *The Anti-Christ.* 2002.

Nietzsche, Friedrich. *Beyond Good and Evil.* 2003.

Nietzsche, Friedrich. *Ecce Homo.* 2004.

Nietzsche, Friedrich. *Genealogy of Morals* . 1998.

Nietzsche, Friedrich. *Thus Spake Zarathustra.* 2006.

Nietzsche, Friedrich. *The Twilight of the Idols: or How to Philosophize with a Hammer.* 1998.

Nietzsche, Friedrich. *The Will to Power.* 1968.

Nitobe, Ihazo. *Bushido: The Warrior's Code.* 1975.

Nkrumah, Kwame. *Handbook of Revolutionary Warfare.* 1968.

Norman, Bruce. *Secret Warfare: The Battle of Codes and Cyphers.* 1989.

Norman, F. J. *The Fighting Man of Japan: The Training and Exercises of the Samurai.* 2006.

Nutter, John Jacob. *The C.I.A.'s Black Ops: Covert Action, Foreign Policy, and Democracy.* 2000.

Nyquist, Jeffrey R. *Origins of the Fourth World War and the Coming Wars of Mass Destruction.* 1999.

O'Flaherty, Wendy Doniger. *The Origin of Evil in Hindu Mythology.* 1980.

Oliker, Olga. *Russia's Chechen Wars 1994-2000: Lessons from the Urban Combat.* 2001.

Oliver, Douglas L. *Polynesia: In Early Historic Times.* 2002.

Omar, Ralf Dean. *Prison Killing Techniques: Blade, Bludgeon, and Bomb.* 2001.

O'Neill, Richard. *Suicide Squads of World War II.* 1989.

Ono, Sokyo. *Shinto: The Kami Way.* 2004.

Ortega y Gasset, Jose. *The Revolt of the Masses.* 1994.

Orwell, George. *1984.* 1977.

O'Toole, Laurence. *Pornocopia: Porn, Sex, Technology, and Desire.* 2000.

Owen, Mark, ed. *Encyclopedia of Human Cruelty* (CD-ROM, Felicity Press in Australia). No date.

Page, David W. *Body Trauma: A Writer's Guide to Wounds and Injuries.* 2007.

Paget, Julian. *Counter-Insurgency Operations: Techniques of Guerrilla Warfare.* 1967.

Paglia, Camille. *Sexual Personae: Art and Decadence from Nefertiti to Emily Dickinson.* 2001.

Paine, Thomas. *The Age of Reason.* 2004.

Paladin Press, ed. *Interrogation: Techniques and Tricks to Secure Evidence.* 1991.

Panati, Charles. *Extraordinary Origins of Everyday Things.* 1989.

Panati, Charles. *Panati's Extraordinary Endings of Practically Everything and Everybody.* 1989.

Panati, Charles. *Sacred Origins of Profound Things: The Stories Behind the Rites and Rituals of the World's Religions.* 1996.

Panati, Charles. *Sexy Origins and Intimate Things.* 1998.

Pape, Robert. *Dying to Win: The Strategic Logic of Suicide Terrorism.* 2005.

Parenti, Christian. *The Soft Cage: Surveillance in America from Slavery to the War on Terror.* 2004.

Parenti, Michael. *Against Empire.* 1995.

Parenti, Michael. *The Assassination of Julius Caesar: A People's History of Ancient Rome.* 2003.

Parenti, Michael. *Dirty Truths: Reflections on Politics, Media, Ideology, Conspiracy, Ethnic Life, and Class Power.* 1996.

Parfrey, Adam, ed. *Apocalypse Culture.* 1991.

Parfrey, Adam, ed. *Apocalypse Culture II.* 2000.

Parfrey, Adam, ed. *Cult Rapture: Revelations of the Apocalyptic Mind.* 1995.

Parfrey, Adam, ed. *Extreme Islam: Anti-American Propaganda of Muslim Fundamentalism.* 2001.

Parrinder, Geoffrey. *Jesus in the Qur'an.* 1995.

Parry, Albert. *Terrorism: From Robespierre to the Weather Underground.* 2006.

Parsons, John Whiteside. *Freedom is a Two-Edged Sword.* 1989.

Partridge, Burgo. *A History of Orgies.* 2002.

Party, Boston T. *Bulletproof Privacy: How to Live Hidden, Happy, and Free.* 1997.

Party, Boston T. And Royce, Kenneth W. *You and the Police.* 2005.

Patterson, Orlando. *Slavery and Social Death: A Comparative Study.* 2005.

Pausanias. *Guide to Greece.* 1984.

Payson, Seth. *Proof of the Illuminati.* 1802.

Pelton, Robert Young. *Come Back Alive.* 1999.

Pelton, Robert Young. *Licensed to Kill: Hired Guns in the War on Terror.* 2006.

Pelton, Robert Young. *World's Most Dangerous Places: Professional Strength.* 2007.

Percy, William Armstrong III. *Pederasty and Pedagogy in Ancient Greece.* 1998.

Perkins, Rodney. *Cosmic Suicide: The Tragedy and Transcendence of Heaven's Gate.* 1997.

Perlmutter, Dawn. *Investigating Religious Terrorism and Ritualistic Crimes.* 2003.

Perrett, Bryan. *Against All Odds : More Dramatic 'Last Stand' Actions.* 1998.

Perrett, Bryan. *Last Stand : Famous Battles Against All Odds.* 1994.

Perin, Noel. *Giving Up the Gun: Japan's Reversion to the Sword, 1543-1879.* 1995.

Pipes, Richard. *Three "Whys" of the Russian Revolution.* 1997.

Piven, Joshua and Borgenicht, David. *The Worst-Case Scenario Survival Handbook.* 1999.

Plato. *Gorgias.* 2004.

Plato. *The Laws.* 2005.

Plato. *The Republic.* 2003.

Plato. *Symposium.* 1989.

Plutarch. *On Sparta.* 2005.

Poe, Edgar Allan. *Complete Tales and Poems.* 2003.

Poe, Marshall T. *The Russian Moment in World History.* 2006.

Poliakov, Leon. *The Aryan Myth: A History of Racists and Nationalistic Ideas in Europe.* 1996.

Polmar, Norman. *Encyclopedia of Espionage.* 1998.

Poole, H. John. *Militant Tricks: Battlefield Ruses of the Islamic Insurgent.* 2005.

Poole, H. John. *Phantom Soldier: The Enemy's Answer to U.S. Firepower.* 2001.

Poole, H. John. *Tactics of the Crescent Moon: Militant Muslim Combat Methods.* 2004.

Porphyry. *Against the Christians.* 1994.

Porphyry. *On Abstinence from Killing Animals.* 2000.

Porphyry. *On the Life of Plotinus.* 1969.

Powell, William. *The Anarchist Cookbook.* 2002.

Pranaitis, I. B. *The Talmud Unmasked: The Secret Rabbinical Teachings Concerning Christians.* 2006.

Pratap, Anita. *Island of Blood: Frontline Reports from Sri Lanka, Afghanistan, and Other European Flashpoints.* 2003.

Puzyr, A. *Dirty Fighting.* 1982

Pyne, Stephen J. *The Ice: A Journey to Antarctica.* 2004.

Quigley, Carroll. *Evolution of Civilizations.* 1979.

Ranke-Heinemann, Uta. *Putting Away Childish Things: The Virgin Birth, the Empty Tomb, and Other Fairy Tales You Don't Need to Believe to Have a Living Faith.* 1994.

Rapoport, David C. *Assassination and Terrorism.* 1971.

Rapoport, David C., ed. *Inside Terrorist Organizations.* 2001.

Rapp, Burt. *Deep Cover: Police Intelligence Operations.* 1989.

Rapp, Burt. *Interrogation: A Complete Manual.* 1987.

Rapp, Burt. *Professional Killers: An Inside Look.* 1990.

Rapp, Burt. *Shadowing and Surveillance.* 1985.

Randall, J. *Personal Defense Weapons.* 1992.

Rauschning, Hermann. *The Voice of Destruction: Conversations with Hitler 1940.* 2004.

Rayo, Jon. *Vonu: The Search for Personal Freedom.* 1983.

Red Army Faction. *The Urban Guerrilla Concept.* 2004.

Redbeard, Ragnar. *Might is Right or the Survival of the Fittest.* 2005.

Redden, Jim. *Snitch Culture: How Citizens are Turned into the Eyes and Ears of the State.* 2000.

Rediker, Marcus. *Villains of All Nations: Atlantic Pirates in the Golden Age of Piracy.* 2005.

Reiter, Dan and Stam, Allan C. *Democracies at War.* 2002.

Regan, Geoffrey. *Brassey's Book of Military Blunders.* 2000.

Regan, Geoffrey. *Brassey's Book of Naval Blunders.* 2000.

John Reeves. *Pirates.* 2006.

Reuchlin, Abelard. *The True Authorship of the New Testament.* 1998.

Reynolds, John Lawrence. *Secret Societies: Inside the World's Most Notorious Organizations.* 2006.

Rhodes, Anthony. *D'Annunzio: The Poet as Superman.* 1960.

Rhodes, Henry T. F. *Satanic Mass.* 1905.

Rice, Edward E. *Wars of the Third Kind: Conflict in Underdeveloped Countries.* 1990.

Richmond, Doug. *How to Disappear Completely and Never Be Found.* 1986.

Ridgeway, James. *Blood in the Face: The Ku Klux Klan, Aryan Nations, Nazi Skinheads, and the Rise of a New White Culture.* 1995.

Rigaud, Milo. *Secrets of Voodoo.* 1985.

Rimmer, Gary. *Number Freaking: How to Change the World with Delightfully Surreal Statistics.* 2006.

Ripley, Tim. *Mercenaries: Soldiers of Fortune.* 2000.

Robertson, Wilmot. *Dispossessed Majority.* 1986

Robinson, Charles. *The Construction of Secret Hiding Places.* 1981.

Rogo, D. Scott. *Life after Death: The Case for the Survival of Bodily Death.* 1986.

Rommel, Bart. *Execution Tools and Techniques.* 1990.

Rooney, David. *Guerrilla: Insurgents, Rebels, and Terrorists from Sun Tzu to Bin Laden.* 2004.

Roper, A. G. *Ancient Eugenics: The Arnold Prize Essay for 1913.* 1992.

Rosenberg, Alfred. *The Myth of the Twentieth Century.* 1982.

Rottman, Gordon. *Viet Cong and NVA Tunnels and Fortifications of the Vietnam War.* 2006.

Rottman, Gordon. *Vietnam Airmobile Tactics.* 2007.

Rousseau, Jean-Jacques. *The Government of Poland.* 1985.

Rose, Kenneth. *One Nation Underground: The Fallout Shelter in American Culture.* 2004.

Ross, Jeffrey Ian and Richards, Stephen C. *Behind Bars: Surviving Prison.* 2002.

Rossi, Melissa. *What Every American Should Know About Who's Really Running America.* 2007.

Rossi, Melissa. *What Every American Should Know About Who's Really Running the World.* 2005.

Rothbard, Murray N. *The Case Against the Fed.* 1994.

Roy, James Charles Roy. *The Vanished Kingdom: Travels through the History of Prussia.* 2000.

Rowland, Desmond and Bailey, James. *The Law Enforcement Handbook.* 1994.

Rudwin. Maximilian Josef. *The Devil in Legend and Literature.* 1931.

Rummel, R. J. *Death by Government.* 1997.

Russell, Sharman Apt. *Hunger: An Unnatural History.* 2006.

Ryan, John, Dunford, George, and Sellars, Simon. *Lonely Planet Micronations.* 2006.

Sacher-Masoch, Leopold von. *Venus in Furs.* 2007.

Sade, Marquis de. *Dialogue Between a Priest and a Dying Atheist.* 1997.

Sade, Marquis de. *Juliette.* 1994.

Sade, Marquis de. *Justine, Philosophy in the Bedroom, and Other Writings.* 1990.

Sade, Marquis de. *The 120 Days of Sodom and Other Writings.* 1987.

Salinger, Lawrence M. *Encyclopedia of White-Collar and Corporate Crime.* 2004.

Sallust. *Conspiracy of Catiline.* 2004.

Salvucci, Angelo A. *Biological Terrorism, Responding to the Threat: A Personal Safety Manual.* 2001.

Sample, John. *Methods of Disguise.* 1993

Sands, Trent. *Personal Privacy Through Foreign Investing.* 1993.

Santoro, Victor. *Vigilante Handbook.* 1981.

Sargeant, Jack. *Death Cults: Murder, Mayhem, and Mind Control.* 2002.

Sartre, Jean-Paul. *Baudelaire.* 1988.

Sauder, Richard. *Underground Bases and Tunnels: What is the Government Trying to Hide?* 1996.

Savage, Cliff. *The Sling for Sport and Survival.* 1999.

Saxon, Kurt. *The Poor Man's James Bond.* 2007.

Scales, Robert. *Firepower in Limited War.* 1997.

Schaefer, G. J. And London, Sondra. *Killer Fiction: The Sordid Confessional Stories that Convicted Serial Killer G. J. Schaefer.* 1997.

Schafer, Peter. *Jesus in the Talmud.* 2007.

Schechter, Harold. *The Serial Killer Files: The Who, What, Where, How, and Why of the World's Most Terrifying Murderers.* 2003.

Scheuer, Michael. *Imperial Hubris: Why the West is Losing the War on Terrorism.* 2004.

Scheuer, Michael. *Through Our Enemies' Eyes: Osama bin Laden, Radical Islam, and the Future of America.* 2006.

Schmaltz, William H. *Hate: George Lincoln Rockwell and the American Nazi Party.* 2000.

Schopenhauer, Arthur. *Essays and Aphorisms.* 1973.

Schwartau, Winn. *Information Warfare.* 1996.

Scott, George Ryley. *History of Capital Punishment.* 2007.

Scott, George Ryley. *The History of Corporal Punishment. A Survey of Flagellation in Its Historical, Anthropological, and Sociological Aspects.* 2006.

Scott, George Ryley. *A History of Prostitution: From Antiquity to the Present Day.* 2005.

Scott, George Ryley. *The History of Torture Throughout the Ages.* 1954.

Scott, George Ryley. *Phallic Worship: A History of Sex and Sex Rights in Relation to the Religions of All Races from Antiquity to the Present Day.* 1970

Scott, Wimberley. *Special Forces Guerrilla Warfare Manual.* 2000.

Seabrook, Jeremy. *The No- Nonsense Guide to Class, Caste, and Hierarchies.* 2005.

Seale, Bobby. *The Black Panther Party.* 1999.

Serge, Victor and Hashad, Dalia. *What Every Radical Should Know About State Repression: A Guide for Activists.* 2005.

Shahak, Israel. *Jewish History, Jewish Religion: The Weight of Three Thousand Years.* 1994.

Shannon, Lawrence. *The Predatory Female: A Field Guide to Dating and the Marriage- Divorce Industry.* 1992.

Shea, Robert and Wilson, Robert Anton. *The Illuminatus Trilogy: The Eye in the Pyramid, The Golden Apple, Leviathan.* 1983.

Shklovskii, I. S. and Carl Sagan. *Intelligent Life in the Universe.* 1998.

Shoats, Russell "Maroon." *The Real Resistance to Slavery in North America.* 2006.

Sifakis, Carl. *Encyclopedia of Assassinations.* 2001.

Sifakis, Carl. *The Encyclopedia of American Crime.* 1982.

Sifakis, Carl. *The Encyclopedia of American Prisons.* 2003.

Sifakis, Carl. *Frauds, Deceptions, and Swindles.* 2001.

Sifakis, Carl. *The Mafia Encyclopedia.* 2005.

Sifakis, Carl. *Strange Crimes and Criminals.* 2001.

Sibley, Bruce. *Surviving Doomsday.* 1977.

Simon. *Papal Magic: Occult Practices within the Catholic Church.* 2007.

Sinclair, Andrew. *An Anatomy of Terror: A History of Terrorism.* 2004.

Singer, Peter. *Animal Liberation.* 2001.

Smith, Dennis Mack. *Mussolini: A Biography.* 1983.

Smith, Ken. *Ken's Guide to the Bible.* 1996.

Smith, Morton. *Jesus the Magician.* 1981.

Smith, Morton and Hoffman, R. Joseph. *What the Bible Really Says.* 1989.

Smith, Warren Allen. *Who's Who in Hell: A Handbook and International Directory for Humanists, Freethinkers, Naturalists, Rationalists, and Non-Theists.* 2000.

Sockut, Eugene. *Secrets of Street Survival–Israeli Style: Staying Alive in a Civilian War Zone.* 1995.

SOE Secret Operations Manual. 1993.

Solanas, Valerie. *S.C.U.M., Society for Cutting Up Men, Manifesto.* 1968.

Sora, Steven. *Secret Societies of America's Elite: From the Knights Templar to Skull and Bones.* 2003.

Sorel, Georges. *Reflections on Violence.* 2004.

Soustell, Jacques. *Daily Life of the Aztecs.* 2002.

Southwell, David and Twist, Sean. *Conspiracy Files: Real-Life Stories of Paranoia, Secrecy, and Intrigue.* 2004.

Spaulding Athletic Company. *Boxing: Complete Illustrated Instructions in the Art of Self-Defense.* 2006.

Spear, Robert K. *Surviving Global Slavery.* 1992.

Speidel, Michael P. *Ancient Germanic Warriors: Warrior Styles from Trajan's Column to Icelandic Sagas.* 2004.

Spencer, Colin. *Vegetarianism: A History.* 2004.

Spengler, Oswald. *The Decline of the West.* 2006.

Spigarelli, Jack A. *Crisis Preparedness Handbook: A Complete Guide to Home Storage and Physical Survival.* 2002.

Spignesi, Stephen J. *In the Crosshairs: Famous Assassination and Attempts from Julius Caesar to John Lennon.* 2003.

Spillane, Mickey. *I, the Jury.* 2006.

Spooner, Lysander. *No Treason.* 1973.

Springhall, John. *Decolonization Since 1945.: The Collapse of European Overseas Empires.* 2003.

Stahlberg, Rainer. *The Complete Book of Survival: How to Protect Yourself Against Revolution, Riots, Hurricanes, Famines, and Other Natural and Man-Made Disasters.* 1998.

Stannard, David E. *American Holocaust: The Conquest of the New World.* 1993.

Starchild, Adam. *Portable Wealth: The Complete Guide to Precious Metals.* 1998.

Starchild, Adam. *Swiss Money Secrets: How You Can Legally Hide Your Money in Switzerland.* 1996.

Stark, John T. *Selective Assassination as an Instrument of National Policy.* 2002.

Staten, Clifford L. *The History of Cuba.* 2005.

Stevens, Serita Deborah and Klarner, Ann. *Deadly Doses: A Writer's Guide to Poisons.* 1990.

Stillwell, Alexander. *The Encyclopedia of Survival Techniques.* 2000.

Stirner, Max. *The Ego and Its Own.* 2005.

Stokes, Henry Scott. *The Life and Death of Yukio Mishima.* 2000.

Stone, Geo. *Suicide and Attempted Suicide.* 2001.

Storl, Wolf-Dieter. *Shiva: The Wild God of Power and Ecstasy.* 2004.

Straus, Scott. *The Order of Genocide: Race, Power, and War in Rwanda.* 2006.

Strauss, Edwin S. *Basement Nukes and the Consequences of Cheap Weapons of Mass Destruction.* 1984.

Strauss, Erwin S. *How To Start Your Own Country.* 1999.

Sutton, Anthony C. *America's Secret Establishment: An Introduction to the Order of Skull and Bones.* 2004.

Sun Tzu. *The Art of War.* 2002.

Swierczynski, Duane. *This Here's a Stick-Up: The Big Bad Book of American Bank Robbery.* 2002.

Swift, Jonathan. *Abolishing Christianity and Other Essays.* 2006.

Sykes, Gresham M. *The Society of Captives: A Studt of a Maximum Security Prison.* 2007.

Szasz, Thomas S. *The Manufacture of Madness: A Comparative Study of the Inquisition and the Mental Health Movement.* 1997.

Szasz, Thomas S. *The Myth of Mental Illness.* 1984.

Taber, Robert. *War of the Flea.* 2002.

Takada, Shiguro. *Contingency Cannibalism: Superhardcore Survivalism's Dirty Little Secret.* 1999.

Tarpley, Webster Griffin. *9/11 Synthetic Terror: Made in the U.S.A.* 2006.

Taw, J. *The Urbanization of Insurgency: The Potential Challenge to U.S. Army Operations.* 1994.

Taylor, Philip M. *Munitions of the Mind: A History of Propaganda.* 2003.

Tenzer, Lawrence R. *The Forgotten Cause of the Civil War: A New Look at The Slavery Issue.* 1997.

Thomas, Harold. *The World Power Foundation: Its Goals and Platform.* 1980.

Thomas, Kenn. *Popular Alienation: A Steamshovel Press Reader.* 1995.

Thomas, Kenn. *Popular Paranoia: A Steamshovel Press Anthology.* 2002.

Thomas, William. *All Fall Down: The Politics of Terror and Mass Persuasion.* 2002.

Thompson, C. J. S. *Poisons and Poisoners: With Historical Accounts of Some Famous Mysteries in Ancient and Modern Times.* 2007.

Thompson, Hunter S. *Hell's Angel's: A Strange and Terrible Saga.* 1999.

Thompson, Leroy. *The Counter-Insurgency Manual.* 2006.

Thompson, Leroy. *Hostage Rescue Manual.* 2006.

Thomson, Oliver. *A History of Sin.* 1994.

Thompson, Thomas L. *The Mythic Past: Biblical Archaelogy and the Myth of Israel.* 2005.

Thoreau, Henry David. *Civil Disobedience and Other Essays.* 2005.

Thornton, Allen. *Laws of the Jungle.* 1987.

Thornton, John. *Africa and the Africans in the Making of the Atlantic World, 1400-1800.* 1998.

Torgovnick, Marianna. *Gone Primitive: Savage Intellects, Modern Lives.* 1991.

Townsend, Richard F. *The Aztecs.* 2000.

Tracy, James, ed. *The Civil Disobedience Handbook: A Brief History and Practical Advice for the Politically Disenfranchised.* 2002.

Tracy, James, ed. *The Military Draft Handbook: A Brief History and Practical Advice for the Curious and Concerned.* 2005.

Trestrail, John H. *Criminal Poisoning: Investigational Guide for Law Enforcement, Toxicologists, Forensic Scientists, and Attorneys.* 2000.

Trinquier, Roger. *Modern Warfare: A French View of Counterinsurgency.* 2006.

Truby, J. David. *Zips, Pipes, and Pens: Arsenal of Improvised Weapons.* 1993

Tucker, Jonathan B. *Toxic Terror: Assessing Terrorist Use of Chemical and Biological Weapons.* 2000.

Turlington, Shannon R. *The Complete Idiot's Guide to Voodoo.* 2001.

Turnbull, Stephen and McBride, Angus. *Mongols.* 1980.

Turner, Stephen. *Terrorist Explosives Source Book: Countering Terrorist Use of Improvised Explosive Devices.* 2005.

21st Century Complete Guide to Bioterrorism, Biological and Chemical Weapons, Germs and Germ Warfare, Nuclear and Radiation Terrorism. CD-ROM. 2001.

Twitchell, James B. *Carnival Culture: The Trashing of Taste in America.* 1992.

Uncle Fester. *Home Workshop Explosives.* 1989.

Uncle Fester. *Silent Death.* 1997.

Urbano. *Fighting in the Streets: A Manual of Urban Guerrilla Warfare.* 1992.

U.S. Army. *Guide to Viet Cong Boobytraps and Devices.* 1966.

U.S. Government. *Cold Weather Survival.* 1981.

U.S. Marine Corps. *Close Combat and Hand-to-Hand Fighting.* 2006.

U.S.S.R. Communist Party. Translated by Paul J. Schmitt. *Partisan's Companion: Deadly Techniques of Soviet Freedom fighters During World War II.* 2005.

Valentino, Benjamin. *Final Solutions: Mass Killing and Genocide in the 20th Century.* 2005.

Van Creveld, Martin. *The Art of War: War and Military Thought.* 2000.

Van Creveld, Martin. *The Encyclopedia of Revolutions and Revolutionaries: From Anarchism to Zhou Enlai.* 1996.

Van Creveld, Martin. *The Rise and Decline of the State.* 1999.

Van Creveld, Martin. *Supplying War: Logistics from Wallenstein to Patton.* 2004.

Van Creveld, Martin. *Technology and War: From 2000 B.C. to the Present.* 1991.

Van Creveld. Martin. *Transformation of War.* 1991.

Vandereycken, Walter and Van Deth, Ron. *From Fasting Saints to Anorexic Girls: The History of Self-Starvation.* 1994.

Vankin, Jonathan. *Conspiracies, Cover-ups, and Crimes.* 1996.

Vankin, Jonathan and Whalen, John. *The 80 Greatest Conspiracies of All Time.* 2004.

Van Rooyen, Johann. *Hard Right: The New White Power in South Africa.* 1994.

Verbitsky, Horacio. *Confessions of an Argentine Dirty Warrior: A Firsthand Account of Atrocity.* 2005.

Verstappen, Stefan H. *The Thirty-Six Strategies of Ancient China.* 1999.

Verton, Dan. *Black Ice: The Invisible Threat of Cyber-Terrorism.* 2003.

Vico, Giambattista. *New Science.* 2000.

Vidal, Gore. *Perpetual War for Perpetual Peace.* 2002.

Viswanathan, Neeraja. *The Street Law Handbook: Surviving Sex, Drugs, and Petty Crime*. 2004.

Voegtlin, Walter L. *The Stone Age Diet: Based on in-depth Studies of Human Ecology and the Diet of Man*. 1975.

Voltaire, Francois. *Candide*. 1991.

Voltaire, Francois. *Philosophical Dictionary*. 1984.

Vo Nguyen Giap. *How We Won the War*. 1976.

Voorhees, Don. *Quickies: Fascinating Facts about the Facts of Life*. 2004.

Wade, Wyn Craig. *The Fiery Cross: The Ku Klux Klan in America*. 1998.

Wait, Robert G. L. *The Psychopathic God: Adolf Hitler*. 1993.

Walter, Ingo. *Secret Money: The World of International Financial Secrecy*. 1986.

Warraq, Ibn. *Why I am Not a Muslim*. 2003.

Watson, Lyall. *The Nature of Things: The Secret Life of Inanimate Objects*. 1992.

Watson, Tom. *How to Think Like a Survivor*. 2006.

Wearne, Phillip. And Kelly, John. *Tainting Evidence: Inside the Scandals at the F.B.I. Crime Lab*. 2002.

Weatherford, Jack. *The History of Money*. 1998.

Webster, Nesta H. *Secret Societies and Subversive Movements*. 1924.

Wells, Patrick and Rushkoff, Douglas. *Stoned Free: How to Get High Without Drugs*. 1995.

Wells-Barnett, Ida B. *On Lynchings*. 2002.

Wescott, David, ed. *Primitive Technology. A Book of Earth Skills*. 2001.

Wescott, David. *Primitive Technology II: Ancestral Skill*. 2001.

Westermarck, Edward. *Short History of Marriage*. 2003.

Whittaker, David J. *The Terrorism Reader*. 2007.

Whittaker, David J. *Terrorists and Terrorism in the Contemporary World*. 2004.

White, P. C. *Crime Scene to Court: The Essentials of Forensic Science*. 2004.

Whitney, Lyle. *The Black Book of Boobytraps*. 1996.

Wickham-Crowley. Timothy P. *Guerrillas and Revolution in Latin America.* 1993.

Wilde, Oscar. *The Picture of Dorian Gray.* 2003.

Wilkinson, Anthony R. *Insurgency in Rhodesia, 1957-1973.* 1973.

Wilcox, Laird M. *Crying Wolf: Hate Crime Hoaxes in America.* 1994.

Wilde, Oscar. *The Picture of Dorian Gray.* 2003.

Williams, Eric. *Capitalism and Slavery.* 1994.

Williams, Jack. *The Complete Idiot's Guide to the Arctic and the Antarctic.* 2003.

Williams, Jessica. *50 Facts That Should Change The World.* 2004.

Williams, Judy. *The Modern Sherlock Holmes: An Introduction to Forensic Science Today.* 1991.

Williams, Paul L. *Al Qaeda: Brotherhood of Terror.* 2002.

Williams, Paul L.. *Dunces of Doomsday: 10 Blunders that Gave Rise to Radical Islam, Terrorist Regimes, and the Threat of an American Hiroshima.* 2006.

Williamson, Benedict J. *The Rosicrucian Manuscripts.* 2002.

Wilson, Bill. *Under the Table and Into Your Pocket: The How and Why of the Underground Economy.* 2005.

Wilson, Carol. *Freedom at Risk: The Kidnapping of Free Blacks in America, 1780-1865.* 1994.

Wilson, Colin. *The Mammoth Book of the History of Murder.* 2000.

Wilson, Colin. *The Mammoth Book of True Crime.* 1998.

Wilson, Colin. *Written in Blood: A History of Forensic Detection.* 2003.

Wilson, Ian. *Jesus: The Evidence.* 2000.

Wilson, Keith D. *Cause of Death: A Writer's Guide to Death, Murder, and Forensic Medicine.* 1992.

Wilson, Peter Lamborn. *Pirate Utopias.* 2003.

Wilson, Robert Anton. *Cosmic Trigger I: Final Secret of the Illuminati.* 1991.

Wilson, Robert Anton. *Cosmic Trigger II: Down to Earth.* 1996.

Wilson, Robert Anton. *Cosmic Trigger III: My Life After Death.* 2004.

Wilson, Robert Anton. *Everything is Under Control: Conspiracies, Cults, and Cover-ups.* 1998.

Wilson, Robert Anton. *The New Inquisition.* 1988.

Wingate, Anne. *Scene of the Crime: A Writer's Guide to Crime-Scene Investigations.* 1992.

Winn, Denise. *The Manipulated Mind: Brainwashing, Conditioning, and Indoctrination.* 2000.

Wiseman, Jon. *SAS Survival Handbook: How to Survive in the Wild, in Any Climate, on Land or at Sea.* 2004.

Wiseman, John. *SAS Urban Survival Handbook.* 1997.

Wolfe, Claire. *Freedom Outlaw's Handbook: 179 Things to Do 'Til the Revolution.* 2004.

Wolfe, Clair. *Think Free to Live Free.* 2001.

Wollstonecraft, Nary. *Vindication of the Rights of Women.* 2001.

Wright, Ronald. *A Short History of Progress.* 2005.

Wright, Thomas and Knight, Richard Payne. *Sexual Symbolism: A History of Phallic Worship.* 2006.

Wrixon, Fred B. *Codes, Ciphers, Secrets, and Cryptic Communication: Making and Breaking Secret Messages from Hieroglyphics to the Internet.* 2005.

Wynn, Douglas. *The Crime Writer's Handbook: 65 Way to Kill Your Victim–in Print.* 2004.

Yalom, Marilyn. *History of the Breast.* 1998.

Yates, Frances A. *The Rosicrucian Enlightenment.* 2001.

Yount, Johnny. *Vanish: Disappearance Through I.D. Acquisition.* 1986.

Yousaf, Mohammad and Adkin, Mark. *The Bear Trap: Afghanistan's Untold Story.* 1992.

Yurchak, Alexei. *Everything Was Forever, Until It Was No More: The Last Soviet Generation.* 2005.

Zacks, Richard. *An Underground Education.* 1999.

Zadka, Saul. *Blood in Zion: How the Jewish Guerrillas Drove the British Out of Palestine.* 2003.

Zamyatin, Yevgeny. *We.* 1993.

Zepezauer, Mark. *The C.I.A.'s Greatest Hits.* 1996.

Zepazauer, Mark. *Take the Rich Off Welfare.* 2004.

Zerzan, John. *Future Primitive: And Other Essays.* 1994.

Zezima, Michael. *Saving Private Power: The Hidden History of the "Good War."* 2000.

Zindler, Frank R. *The Jesus the Jews Never Knew: Sepher Toldoth Yeshu and the Quest for the Historical Jesus in Jewish Sources.* 2003.

Zinn, Howard. *A People's History of the United States.* 1995.

Zips, Werner. *Black Rebels: African-Caribbean Freedom Fighters in Jamaica.* 2000.

Mandrake

'Books you don't see everyday'

The Odin Brotherhood by Mark Mirabello

£10.99, ISBN 978-1869928-711, 128pp.

'When the world is pregnant with lies, a secret long hidden will be revealed.'

An Odinist Prophecy

Called an "occult religion" for adepts, a "creed of iron" for warriors, and a "secret society" for higher men and women who value "knowledge, freedom and power," the Odin Brotherhood honors the gods and goddesses of the Norse pantheon. This non-fiction book details the legends, the rituals, and the mysteries of an ancient and enigmatic movement.

The Cannibal Within by Mark Mirabello

£7.99, ISBN 978-1869928-278.paperback

'They raped me and ate my friend alive.' Thus starts this work of erotic horror fiction filled with "sacrilege, blasphemy, and crime"—written in a style that is part H. P. Lovecraft, part Marquis de Sade, and part Octave Mirbeau—*The Cannibal Within* is literally "wet with sin, slippery with blood, and slimy with fornication."

The novel's central character is part Lara Croft part Sarah Connor. She/We has a choice: the evil may be patiently borne or savagely resisted.

We may think we are special--holy, honored, valued--god's chosen primates--but that is a fraud. The dupes of superhuman forces, we are misfits and abominations. We have no higher purpose --no savior god died for our sins--we exist, only because our masters are infatuated with our meat.

The Apophenion: A Chaos Magic Paradigm by Peter J Carroll.

£10.99, 978-1869928-421,

My final Magnum Opus if its ideas remain unfalsified within my lifetime, otherwise its back to the drawing board. Yet I've tried to keep it as short and simple as possible, it consists of eight fairly brief and terse chapters and five appendices.

It attacks most of the great questions of being, free will, consciousness, meaning, the nature of mind, and humanity's place in the cosmos, from a magical perspective. Some of the conclusions seem to challenge many of the deeply held assumptions that our culture has taught us, so brace yourself for the paradigm crash and look for the jewels revealed in the wreckage.

This book contains something to offend everyone; enough science to upset the magicians, enough magic to upset the scientists, and enough blasphemy to upset most trancendentalists.

"The most original, and probably the most important, writer on Magick since Aleister Crowley.
-Robert Anton Wilson, author of the *Cosmic Trigger* trilogy.

Magick Works: Pleasure, Freedom and Power
by Julian Vayne

978-1869928-469

Enter the world of the occultist: where the spirits of the dead dwell amongst us, where the politics of ecstasy are played out, and where magick spills into every aspect of life.

It's all right here; sex, drugs, witchcraft and gardening. From academic papers, through to first person accounts of high-octaine rituals. In Magick Works you will find cutting edge essays from the path of Pleasure, Freedom and Power.

In this seminal collection Julian Vayne explores;
*   The Tantric use of Ketamine.
*   Social Justice, Green Politics and Druidry.
*   English Witchcraft and Macumba
*   The Magickal use of Space.
*   Cognitive Liberty and the Occult.
*   Psychogeography & Chaos Magick.
*   Tai Chi and Apocalyptic Paranoia.
*   Self-identity, Extropianism and the Abyss.
*   Parenthood as Spiritual Practice.
*   Aleister Crowley as Shaman

...and much more!

Order direct from
Mandrake of Oxford
PO Box 250, Oxford, OX1 1AP (UK)
Phone: 01865 243671
(for credit card sales)
Prices include economy postage
Visit our web site www.mandrake.uk.net

Lightning Source UK Ltd.
Milton Keynes UK
22 November 2010

163248UK00002B/83/P